Amílcar Cabral's
Revolutionary
Theory and Practice

Amílcar Cabral's
Revolutionary
Theory and Practice

A Critical Guide

Ronald H. Chilcote

Lynne Rienner Publishers · Boulder & London

All photos courtesy of the Commissary of Information and Culture of Guinea-Bissau unless otherwise indicated.

Published in the United States of America in 1991 by
Lynne Rienner Publishers, Inc.
1800 30th Street, Boulder, Colorado 80301

and in the United Kingdom by
Lynne Rienner Publishers, Inc.
3 Henrietta Street, Covent Garden, London WC2E 8LU

Library of Congress Cataloging-in-Publication Data
Chilcote, Ronald H.
  Amílcar Cabral's revolutionary theory and practice : a critical
guide / by Ronald H. Chilcote.
  Includes bibliographical references and index.
  ISBN 1-55587-058-9
  1. Cabral, Amílcar, 1924–1973—Contributions in revolutionary
theory. 2. Revolutions—Philosophy. I. Title.
DT613.76.C3C54 1991
322.4'2'092—dc20   91-11829
                                                            CIP

British Cataloguing in Publication Data
A Cataloguing in Publication record for this book
is available from the British Library.

Printed and bound in the United States of America

The paper used in this publication meets the requirements
of the American National Standard for Permanence of
Paper for Printed Library Materials Z39.48-1984.

For Amílcar Lopes Cabral
September 12, 1924–January 20, 1973

May his example guide people everywhere in unity and struggle

Contents

Photographs

Preface

This guide is the product of effort related to my interest in the life and thought of Amílcar Cabral. In the early 1960s I began to collect materials on the emerging national liberation movements in Lusophone Africa, including ephemeral documents issued by the movements and their leaders. My purpose was to build an archive that could serve as a foundation for understanding the African struggle for independence (see Chilcote, 1972).

During 1960 and 1961 I studied at the University of Lisbon, where I first met African students from the colonies. At the time the Salazar dictatorship faced a multidimensional crisis, conspicuously marked by the visibility of the opposition at home and in exile; the dramatic seizure of the luxury liner, *Santa Maria*, by Henrique Galvão, a former colonial official and writer; and African uprisings in Angola (and later in Guinea-Bissau and Mozambique). During the summer of 1965 I traveled to Conakry and first met Cabral and his brother, Luís, and Aristides Pereira, who later became presidents of independent Guinea-Bissau and Cape Verde, respectively. (See Luís Cabral [1978A] and Pereira [1976A] for memoirs of these developments.) This association with them helped me in my initial effort to write about the struggle for independence from an African perspective (Chilcote, 1967). It also led to the founding of the Research Group for the Liberation of Portuguese Africa (perhaps the first solidarity movement in the United States concerned with the liberation of Portugal's African colonies), established by myself and students at the University of California, Riverside. Cabral formally endorsed this group, which worked to raise consciousness about the liberation struggle through research, publications, films, and lectures.

My early assessment of Cabral focused on his political thought and writings (Chilcote, 1968, 1974); later work included a reappraisal and a retrospective view (Chilcote, 1983, 1984) stimulated by a conference in commemoration of Cabral on the tenth anniversary of his assassination, held in Praia in January 1983 (see Simpósio Internacional Amílcar Cabral, 1984). Just before Amílcar's death, and with his encouragement, I had seriously considered writing his biography, but his passing and other pressing commitments at that time distracted me from that possibility.

The present contribution represents a culmination of all my work and a fulfillment of my desire to contribute to a further understanding of Cabral, his life, and his work. I feel strongly that Cabral ranks high among African and Third World revolutionaries and that his example as theorist and practitioner is firmly embedded in the historical record.

This guide is also a product of field research in Cape Verde and Guinea-Bissau during the summer 1975. I wish to acknowledge the support of the Social Science Research Council, which provided me a postdoctoral grant to travel and carry out research in Cape Verde and Guinea-Bissau. An intramural grant from the Senate Research Committee and typing assistance from the office of the Dean of Humanities and Social Science of the University of California, Riverside, are also gratefully acknowledged. Claudia Moura Pompan, a doctoral recipient in political science at the University of California, Riverside, translated the interviews from Portuguese to English. I am also thankful to Luís Moita and Elena and Luisa Pereira for assistance in examining the archives and library of the Centro de Informação e Documentação Amílcar Cabral (CIDAC) in Lisbon.

Rosemary Galli, Carlos Lopes, and Lars Rudebeck accompanied my attempts to bring this guide to a closure, and although I was unable to contribute to their important research, in spite of my promises to collaborate with them, I hope my own modest effort will prove useful to them and other scholars who are interested in Cabral. Thanks also to Lynne Rienner for her confidence in my work and patience in seeing it through to completion. Steve Barr, the project editor, and Alice Colwell, who copyedited parts of the manuscript, were instrumental in the final phase, as was Jennifer Dugan-Abassi, who prepared the index.

The present work has evolved over many years and thus differs substantially from its original conception. I hope that Gerald Bender, Allen Isaacman, and John Marcum will not be surprised at its appearance fifteen years after their endorsement of my applications for research support. Now they can rest assured that I never deterred from my objective of synthesizing and analyzing the available information on Cabral.

Ronald H. Chilcote

Introduction

This is a guide to the life and thought of Amílcar Lopes Cabral (1924–1973), one of the important thinkers of the Third World, who fought and died for the independence of Guinea-Bissau and Cape Verde. This volume is organized to facilitate its use by both layman and specialist. Beyond the preface, which describes my personal experience and investigation of Amílcar Cabral and Guinea-Bissau and Cape Verde, and the photographs, which give a glimpse into the revolutionary struggle that led to independence, this guide is organized into three principal parts.

The main text is divided into five chapters and a conclusion. The first chapter identifies Cabral's life, and the ensuing four chapters focus on particular themes in his thinking. These themes necessarily deal with the ideas that emanate from his revolutionary experience, but they also are themes found in most twentieth-century revolutions. Although Cabral was aware of other revolutionary experiences and their theoretical contributions, he rarely drew upon them formally, tending instead to build around the unique revolutionary conditions in his own movement's struggle for liberation and independence. In his writings and speeches, a theory of colonialism and imperialism thus emerges, based on the colonial system in which he evolved, the mystique of the Portuguese empire, and penetration of outside influence in the form of capital and investment, as well as foreign cultural influences that impacted on the colonies in Africa. A theory of revolutionary nationalism and national liberation evolved from the leadership and contributions Cabral provided to the liberation movement, its armed struggle, and the drive for independence around a theme of unity of the diverse ethnic and other groupings that historically had divided African peoples in the Portuguese colonies. Cabral also emphasized a theory of class and class struggle, noting especially the role of the petty bourgeoisie and the peasantry. At the same time he was sensitive to the fact that Guinea-Bissau and Cape Verde were relatively undeveloped and lacking an industrial base and a salaried working class, both in urban areas and the countryside. Finally, he offered perspectives on the state and development, in particular with the construction of state institutions in liberated areas and the provision of human needs though schools, health clinics, food distribution centers, and so on; these, in turn, were to provide the foundation for the new state after independence and Cabral's own untimely death by assassination.

The second part of this volume comprises the perspectives of important members of the revolutionary vanguard, based on my interviews with them in 1975, shortly after independence, when Cabral's movement had come to power. The purpose of the interviews was to delve into the respondents' understanding of Cabral through a series of questions that related to the major themes in his thinking. The results are synthesized into two tables and a brief discussion, followed by the verbatim interviews. These interviews have never been published, and they constitute part of the historical and documentary record. They were obtained under very difficult conditions in the wake of independence and the confusion of organization under the new states of Guinea-Bissau and Cape Verde. Some of the revolutionary leaders provided insightful and significant analysis, whereas others appeared to be somewhat superficial and lacking comprehension of the complexity of ideas and concepts in the theories of Cabral. Yet this diversity in comprehension and interpretation reveals some of the underlying tension and differences that were to impact the revolutionary movement in later years.

The final part of this work consists of a full annotated bibliography of writings by and about Cabral. It is based on a quarter century of gathering and reading documents, the organization of a large personal archive, and the delving into several other important archives. Each entry has been examined carefully and annotated to guide the reader to the source, suggest its usefulness, and reveal its content. I have attempted to identify where many of these items can be found. The entries are organized into several sections: first, books, collections of writings, pamphlets, and ephemera under Cabral's authorship; second, articles by Cabral that appeared in periodicals, ranging from an early poem in 1946 to articles written just before his death, as well as reprints of his work until the present; and third, interpretations and reviews of books and articles by journalists, historians, social scientists, and others interested in Cabral and his thinking.

The bibliography reveals the writings not only of Cabral but of the hundreds of biographers, scholars, and journalists who have focused on him and his movement. Although some very important work has appeared, the study of Cabral has not been exhausted. It is my hope that this guide will stimulate scholars to delve more deeply into his thinking, but even more important it is also my desire that this guide will serve to perpetuate interest in Cabral and ensure that future generations be aware of his substantial contributions to the theory and practice of revolution in the Third World.

1

Cabral and His Historical Context

Amílcar Cabral's lifetime, from birth in Bafatá, Guinea-Bissau, on September 12, 1924, until his death by assassination on January 20, 1973, spanned the period prior to independence of Guinea-Bissau and Cape Verde. In the tradition of intellectuals of Cape Verde, where he lived and studied for many years, Cabral wrote poetry, reflecting on the harsh insular conditions and learning to interpret culture as a weapon in the struggle for independence (Moser, 1978). Later, as an agronomist, his agricultural surveys and analyses provided a basis for planning the future economy of his homeland (see Cabral, *Unity and Struggle*, 1979: 4–16; 1988; and McCulloch, 1983: 36–58). As a revolutionary and political organizer, Cabral confronted Portuguese colonialism by guiding a vanguard party through a decade of war while constructing an infrastructure of social, economic, and political institutions among his people in the liberated areas. Finally, his independent Marxist analysis and original thought assessed the possibilities and limitations of struggle for independence.

As poet, agronomist, fighter, theorist, and diplomat, Cabral approached life dialectically. On the one hand, he was an intellectual and theoretician; on the other, he was an organizer and unifier. Throughout his life he struggled to eliminate the Portuguese presence in the colonies and strove to undermine imperialism in the broader international context.

A comprehensive but inexhaustible view of Amílcar Cabral now exists. Patrick Chabal (1983A), the Cambridge historian, gave us what he called "the first full biography" of Cabral. Chabal drew from primary and secondary sources as well as personal interviews with those who associated with Cabral, but he did not personally know Cabral nor did he observe the independence movement first hand as had French political writer Gérard Chaliand (1964) and English historian Basil Davidson (1964), who wrote the early journalistic portraits of Cabral; or Angolan expatriate Mário de Andrade (1980), the cultural writer whose biography of Cabral includes useful insights, analysis, and documents; or Russian journalist Oleg Ignatiev (1975A), who also provided impressionistic but detailed accounts based on personal contact and experience with Cabral.

Of all these and other writers Davidson did well in capturing the character and spirit of Cabral. In the introduction to Cabral's (1979) *Unity and Action*, Davidson wrote of Cabral's

> spirituality and sympathy, his directness, his love for life, his enduring interest in everyone and everything that came his way . . . the depth and complexity of his thought and meditation . . . large hearted, entirely committed, devoted to his people's insistence on the study of reality . . . the intellectual groundwork of an overall theory of society . . . always riveted to the reality of time and place. [His texts] deal repeatedly with the necessary bases of revolutionary democracy, whether in the liberation of women, in anti-elitist education, in a decentralized system of public health . . . in the building of participatory political structure at and from the grassroots. (pp. x–xii)

It is essential to deal briefly with recent scholarly accounts that tend to misrepresent Cabral's thinking with hindsight analysis or to attribute many of the problems and policies of the Luís Cabral and Nino Vieira regimes to the legacy of Amílcar's theory and practice. Serious criticisms are leveled by these writers in an effort to expose some of the mythology that emanated from the liberation struggle and those who observed and wrote about it. Either consciously or unconsciously these criticisms serve to discredit Cabral and the significant role he played in the struggle and the ideas he contributed to it.

Chabal (1978: 4) correctly identified some of the ambiguity and contradiction in the experience of Cabral: he was an African born in a Portuguese colony; he was an African of mixed origins; he held Portuguese citizenship under an oppressive colonial system; he was highly educated in a land of illiteracy; and as a pacifist he resorted to one of the longest liberation struggles in Africa. Chabal, however, arrived at some controversial assertions: he suggests that what emerges from Cabral's university thesis and agricultural writings is attention to a scientific approach mixed with "loose Marxist notions" (Chabal, 1983A: 39). In my view, Cabral's (1988) work as an agronomist and the writing of many scientific papers imbued him with a disciplined approach to problems and emphasis on detail leading to resolution of problems; his use of Marxism was intended not to mimic approaches of others but to set his own political thinking and teachings within a coherent framework and to provide a means and a method for analyzing the difficult problems encountered in the liberation wars. Chabal (1983A: 51) believed that the writings on agriculture made use of Marxist concepts in a manner that "was crude, simplistic, uncertain and somewhat naive . . . an indication of the sort of Marxist theory to which he had been exposed in Portugal." But in all fairness, it is important to recognize that awareness of Marxism under a repressive dictatorship was possible in only clandestine circles, and, further, scientific practice as well as political reality within Portugal limited the application of Marxist concepts, not to mention that Cabral was working out his ideas in an early formative stage of his career.

Chabal (1983A: 34) also affirmed that culturally and intellectually Cabral "was seen by many, and he probably viewed himself, as Portuguese despite the fact that he looked very much like an African." Undoubtedly, as Chabal demonstrated, Cabral fully comprehended Portuguese life and culture; as a bright and intellectually curious African, he impressed peers and teachers, but there is no doubt that he was profoundly African in his thinking, as the historical record abundantly confirms. Mário de Andrade (1973B) recalled Cabral's clandestine activity in Angola: "Today many young Angolan youth were his students of revolution because the revolutionary always is a teacher" (p. 21) and, as Andrade stated, despite his work as an agronomist "Cabral was a revolutionary messenger, always available for all fronts of common struggle in the Portuguese colonies" (p. 27). Chabal's observations thus distort an otherwise solid treatment of the man and his thought and account for the strong criticism emanating from some specialists such as Andrade and others who expose some of its limitations. (See the reference to their reviews in my annotation under Chabal [1983A].)

Two other recent studies deserve mention because they are also critical of Cabral. Rosemary Galli and Jocelyn Jones (1987: 4) described Cabral as a Leninist and hardliner: "Cabral and other leaders of the PAIGC shared Lenin's and the Bolsheviks' conception of socialism and combination of political control and technological development." Although they correctly identified the locus of power during the liberation struggle as being in the hands of Amílcar Cabral, Luís Cabral, and Aristides Pereira, they played down the seemingly insurmountable obstacles facing the movement. They attributed the problems of the postindependence period to the tendency in the past to consolidate power in a small circle of leaders and to ignore the demands and needs of the peasantry, precluding the possibility of open democratic politics. Further, Galli (1986) argued that the contemporary leadership has confused politics with control, the consequence of a misunderstanding based on Cabral's idealistic conception of the state's role in economic development and the power relationship of the state to the Guinean peasantry. Elsewhere, Galli (1987) asserted that the new state has appropriated as much surplus as possible from the peasants for purposes other than rural development and that this also is an outcome of contradictions in Cabral's thinking and PAIGC (Partido Africano da Independência da Guiné e Cabo Verde) policies and practices.

Such views overlook the firsthand accounts by observers such as Davidson (1974C) and Rudebeck (1974), who noted both democratic trends and the provision of people's needs in the preindependence period; and they contradict the analysis of another observer, Paulo Freire (1978: 18), who saw Cabral as pragmatic and progressive:

> His political clarity, the coherence between his choices and his practice, is at the root both of his refusal to be drawn into making undisciplined responses and of his rejection of manipulation. He dismissed any idea of the masses divided, following their own inclinations, marching in response to whatever happened, without a revolutionary party or leaders who could mobilize, organize and orient. In the same way he also rejected a leadership which felt it "owned" the masses. Unlimited freedom and bureaucratic authoritarianism were equally abhorrent.

But in fact the serious contemporary problems of Guinea-Bissau do not stem from the thought and practice of Amílcar Cabral, and it is unreasonable to distort the historical record and blame him for current practices. Clearly, there have been problems in the postindependence period, and Cabral's absence during these times has lessened the prospects for balancing direct and indirect democratic practices with efficient and egalitarian economic policies.

Joshua B. Forrest (1987A) abruptly dismissed the majority of foreign observers, journalists, and academicians who interpreted Cabral and the liberation movement as representing a popularly supported, peasant-oriented, and nationally integrated political system. Although initially caught up on these interpretations, Forrest (1987A) took issue with Cabral's argument that political and economic divisions are the result of class conflicts or ideological disputes and argued that at the heart of politics in the postcolonial period are struggles for power among competing institutions, ethnic groups, and individuals: "I finally came to the conclusion that neither class nor ideology are important in explaining political conflict in the centralized political arena" (pp. xxi–xxii). Forrest's (1987B: 116) observation that "Amílcar Cabral's goals of national integration and revolutionary democracy have receded onto a distant plane of historical thought, as the country remains mired in conflicts" simply overlooked that those goals serve as measures against which the historical experience since Cabral's death can be judged. One can only speculate on how Cabral, had he lived, might have implemented those goals in the postcolonial period, but his success in guiding the reconstruction of liberated areas under PAIGC control prior to 1973 was one positive indicator.

The remainder of this chapter briefly examines and highlights some important aspects of Cabral's life. Chabal divided his biography into three periods: the formative influences (1924–1959); nationalist agitation (1956–1964); and consolidation of power and creation of the new state (1964–1973). However, the discussion here does not follow this chronological pattern. Instead I concentrate on Cabral as student, agronomist, political organizer, theorist, and diplomat.

Formative Years as Student and Poet

There is no need to do more than sketch some of the details of the early years of Cabral, for the accounts in Andrade (1980) and Chabal (1983A) are quite complete. Amílcar Lopes Cabral was born on September 12, 1924, in Bafatá, in the Portuguese colony of Guinea. He spent his early youth in Bafatá with his mother, Iva Pinhel Evora, and father, Juvenal Cabral. Both parents were originally from the Cape Verdean island of São Tiago. Juvenal was from a prosperous family and had studied in Portugal to become a priest but eventually taught elementary school. He seems to have influenced his son with his intellectual curiosity and knowledge of politics and social and economic conditions, as reflected in his memoirs (Juvenal Cabral, 1947), which Amílcar carried with him during his student years (Chaliand, 1977–1978: 4). Iva Evora, a seamstress of humble origins with no formal education, apparently imbued Amílcar with a sense of commitment and determination. Amílcar's parents separated in 1929, and they both eventually moved to Cape Verde. Amílcar joined his father in Praia, where he studied in elementary school, and at the age of 12 he moved with his mother to Mindelo on São Vicente island in order to attend the only secondary school. He finished these studies with exceptionally high marks at age 20, worked a year in the National Printing Office, and in 1945 received a scholarship to study agronomy in Lisbon.

During this period Cabral lived both on the mainland and the archipelago, and although Chabal made a convincing case that he was very much a Cape Verdean, his roots tied him to both places and eventually to the vision not only of independence for but of unity between the two colonies. In Cape Verde the drought and famine and his own family's difficulties impressed him with the need to rid the poverty brought by both natural conditions and exploitative colonialism. At the Liceu Infante Dom Henrique (later called Gil Eanes), Cabral was familiar with the movement around the literary journal, *Claridade*, which reflected a cultural renaissance and consciousness of writers and poets who wished to focus on the realities of the archipelago and seek a break with classical European formulations (Andrade, 1986; Cabral, 1951). Early poems of love (Cabral, 1942–1943) under the pseudonym of Larbac evolved into poems of his youth (Cabral, 1944–1949), some of which focused on concerns about the living conditions and isolation of the islands. (See "A Ilha," written about 1944 but published two years later [Cabral, 1946].) Two essays reflected his outlook: "Fidemar," written in 1942, the story of a young Cape Verdean who seeks to liberate his country and resolve its problems; and "Hoje e amanhã," written in 1944 and published in 1949 as a romantic statement on war, hate, injustice, misery, and optimism for a better world.

Although there may be doubts that Cabral had been politicized in a serious way by his years in the colonies, his biographers agree that the years as a student in Lisbon were decisive. His university training prepared him for a professional career, but contacts with other African students made him aware of the need to rediscover their African heritage, and involvement with the Portuguese political opposition allowed for maturation of his political ideas. At the Instituto Superior de Agronomia he received high marks in his courses and distinction for a thesis (Cabral, 1951) on the Cuba region of the Alentejo, a province of large landed estates and a mass of landless rural workers dependent on seasonal employment where agriculture was affected by soil erosion. Cabral attributed soil erosion to patterns of land tenure and the maximization of crop production by both large and small landowners without attention to the consequences of soil erosion. Soil erosion, of course, was also a major problem in his homeland, and he addressed this problem in a series of articles (Cabral, 1949, 1950, 1952).

Cabral married twice. His first wife, Maria Helena Ataíde Vilhena Rodrigues, was Portuguese and a fellow agronomy student in Lisbon. His second wife, Ana Maria Filomena de Sá Cabral, a Cape Verdean, was with him when he was assassinated and later became Cape Verde's ambassador to the German Federal Republic and head of the Fundação Amílcar Cabral. Maria Helena recounted their experience together, beginning in the late 1940s and during their marriage from December 1952 to 1966—in the agronomy school and the years in Lisbon, Bissau, Luanda, and Conakry—in an interview (António Duarte, 1983). Their first child, Iva Maria, was born in Lisbon. Maria Helena described Amílcar as modest, having a sense of humor, friendly with everybody, and especially sympathetic to her problems. She revealed the circle of African friends that formed in the Ajuda district of Lisbon, including Alda Espírito Santo, Mário de Andrade, Agostinho Neto, Marcelino dos Santos, and Eduardo dos Santos. Amílcar left Portugal in December 1959 for Paris and later for Conakry, where he worked for a while as an agronomist; Maria Helena joined him and taught high school in Conarky, but left for Rabat about 1963 for the birth of their second child, Ana Luisa. They separated in 1966, and Amílcar married Ana Maria a year later. Maria Helena married Henrique Cerqueira, once an aide to the assassinated General Humberto Delgado, who in 1958 had mobilized the opposition around his candidacy for the Portuguese presidency.

During this period Cabral was active politically and supportive of the Portuguese political opposition in campaigns for peace and opposition to nuclear power and in support of presidential candidate Norton de Matos in 1949. He associated with the Movimento de Unidade Democrático (MUD) and its youth affiliate, the MUD Juvenil. The MUD was a front of liberal and progressive intellectuals, including Communists. Some Africans, such as Guinean Vasco Cabral (no relation), actually joined and became leaders of the MUD Juvenil and, according to Ignatiev (1975A: 13), affiliated with the Partido Comunista Português (PCP). However, Cabral never formally joined any Portuguese political party, probably because at that time these parties, including the PCP, did not seriously question the Portuguese empire in Africa and elsewhere.

One of the Africans in Lisbon at this time, Francisco José Teneiro, a São Tomé geographer and poet, was older than the generation around Cabral and was influential with affirmation of his blackness. This was a time for reading and reflection on European theory, including Marxism-Leninism, despite the repressive conditions, which did not tolerate the open distribution of such literature. Among the early reading was that of progressive Brazilians (Jorge Amado), revolutionary poets (Nicolás Guillén and Pablo Neruda); and U.S. blacks (Langsdon Hughes). It was an opportunity for Cabral to reflect on his African origins through the "negritude" movements sponsored by Léopold Senghor and French-speaking Africans who sought to distinguish their African culture from that of Europe. These Africans were eventually joined by Andrade, Cabral, and others from Lusophone Africa in expressing their views in the journal, *Présence Africaine* (Cabral, 1953). Finally, Cabral was active in the Casa dos Estudantes do Império and its journal *Mensagem*, where he published poems (1949) and an essay "Hoje e amanhã" (1949). He also helped in organizing the Centro de Estudos Africanos (CEA) in 1951, where African students organized informal weekly seminars (see Vasco Cabral and Andrade, 1978).

Agronomist and Researcher

The decision to seek a career as agronomist may have related to Cabral's father's interests in the agricultural problems of Cape Verde and Guinea-Bissau. Cabral's student thesis (1951) and early studies on soil erosion (1949, 1950, 1952) were but a departure point for a series of useful studies he conducted as an agronomist in Angola and Guinea-Bissau. (See Cabral [1988], as well as Azevedo [1983], who reminisces on Cabral as an agronomist.)

In 1952 Cabral returned to Guinea-Bissau to head investigations at the Pessubé experimental station near Bissau. At first, his research focused on the cultivation of existing and new crops. A year later he conducted an agricultural census of the colony, involving a team of some thirty researchers, including his Portuguese wife, Maria Helena Rodriques, who also was an agronomist and had studied with Amílcar in Lisbon. Five months of field research, visits to 356 population centers and forty-one administrative districts, and nearly a year of data analysis and writing produced the final report (Cabral, 1956) and the most exhaustive survey ever conducted in Guinea. The project had given Cabral an opportunity to visit village chiefs and district leaders everywhere—an invaluable experience for his later political work.

During his stay in Guinea, Cabral also established contacts with Cape

Verdeans active in the colonial service or in business. An effort to establish a sports and cultural club in Bissau was rejected by colonial officials, but Cabral was permitted to set up a club for young people. He had begun to form a network of contacts among Cape Verdean and Guinean civil servants and others in the city and countryside, and apparently he was asked to leave for political reasons. Cabral returned to Portugal in 1955, after the founding of the unsuccessful Movimento da Independência Nacional da Guiné Portuguesa (MING). During a brief authorized visit with his family in Bissau, Cabral and five others, including his half brother Luís and Aristides Pereira, founded on September 19, 1956, the Partido Africano da Independência e da União dos Povos da Guiné, known initially as the PAI. The PAI operated clandestinely until about 1960, when it located in Conakry and was known as the Partido Africano da Independência da Guiné e Cape Verde (PAIGC).

After returning to Portugal, Cabral worked as a soils consultant for various private firms, including the Angolan Sociedade Agrícola de Cassequel. Andrade (1973B) explained how, during research visits to Angola, Cabral contributed to the formation of the Partido da Luta Unida dos Povos Africanos de Angola (PLUA) as well as the Movimento Popular de Liberatação de Angola (MPLA). During a brief stop in Paris in November 1957 he was involved in the formation of the Movimento Anti-Colonialista (MAC—see Cabral, *O Militante* No. 11, January–February 1979). He also was able to visit and become familiar with conditions on São Tomé, known for a massacre of workers during February 1953.

Cabral's research and writing as an agronomist were productive. The Guinea census report yielded data systematically organized by region, crop, cultivated area, ethnic group, and other categories. The conclusions emphasized the impact on groundnut monoculture, the reliance on a fluctuating international market, and the need for diversification of crop production. In addition, he published a series of other reports, based on data from the census. One on soil erosion in Guinea (1954) was drawn from his university thesis; five other articles (1954) and three articles published later (1958 and 1959) were drawn from the Guinea survey. The research in Angola also yielded publications on entomological infestation and phyto-sanitary control in relation to his work as head of a section related to the storage of agricultural products (see Cabral's monographs published in 1958 and 1959 together with two journal articles in 1956 and another in 1960).

The scientific and research publications of Cabral have been collected in an anthology (Cabral, 1988) published jointly by Guinean and Portuguese research centers. The collection includes a good share of the fifty-nine scientific studies produced by Cabral and is a magnificent testament to his role and contribution as agronomist. Brief summary analyses of different aspects of these writings are found in Barreto (1988), David Francisco Vera

Cruz (1988), Ferrão (1988), Gouveia (1988), Ricardo (1988A, 1988B), Schwarz (1988), and José Avito da Silva (1988).

Political Organizer and Mobilizer

All evidence emphasizes Cabral as political organizer and a mobilizer of people around him. During his student days, he participated in the MUD Juvenil and student movements in Lisbon. During a vacation visit to Praia during the summer 1949, he convinced the governor to allow him to broadcast on the Radio Clube de Cabo Verde; the ensuing program ("A Nossa Cultura"), dedicated to Cape Verdean culture with emphasis on its African ties, was quickly suspended despite its popularity, especially among students. He associated with other Africans in Lisbon, first in the Casa dos Estudantes do Império and the Casa da Africa Portuguesa and later in the founding of the Centro de Estudos Africanos. In November 1949, Cabral organized opposition to the administrator of the Casa, and during a meeting when it appeared that the government would prevail and manipulate the situation in its favor, Cabral called upon and convinced all the African students to vacate the premises. The incident taught them that united they could defend their own interests.

As an agronomist, Cabral found time for political activity, including involvement in the MING; an attempt to set up a sports and recreation club in Bissau; encouragement of his Angolan comrades to establish national liberation movements; founding of the PAIGC on September 19, 1956; and formation of the MAC in November 1957 and later the Conferência das Organizações Nacionais das Colónias Portuguesas (CONCP) on April 18, 1961. At the same time he carried out an extensive agricultural survey in Guinea, and in ensuing years he headed a research team in Angola.

Cabral was instrumental in organizing the armed struggle. During his last visit to Bissau, in September 1959, he was influential in shifting strategy away from urban areas and toward the organization of the peasant masses, and he transferred party operations to Conakry. On October 8, 1960, the party name was changed to the PAIGC, and on August 3, 1961, he proclaimed that his movement would shift from political opposition to national insurrection. Two months later, on October 13, in an open letter, he called upon the Portuguese government to resolve the colonial crisis peacefully. On January 23, 1963, the PAIGC launched its first attack, on the Portuguese barracks at Tite. Within six months 15 percent of the area to the south of the Geba and Corubal rivers was under rebel control. On February 13–17, 1964, the First Congress of the PAIGC was held in liberated territory, at Cassacá. A year later, Cabral (1965) provided eight directives on theoretical and practical guidance for party militants. And on January 1, 1973, he delivered his last message and called for the formation of an independent state within the year.

Cabral died in Conakry on January 20, 1973, the victim of a plot apparently intended to kidnap and deliver him to Portuguese naval ships waiting in nearby international waters, although Bragança (1973C: 5) suggested the conspirators' intention was to shoot Cabral and other PAIGC leaders the next morning. Cabral was surprised late at night near the party headquarters and his home, and when he protested the tying of his hands, Inocêncio Kani, a former PAIGC commander who had been expelled for abuse of power, panicked and shot him. The conspirators comprised three groups: The first was made up of former militants of the PAIGC, led by Rafael Barbosa, who had collaborated with the Portuguese after being imprisoned by them, and Mamadou Touré, a former member of the PAIGC Central Committee before the armed struggle, who had infiltrated the PAIGC in 1971 and was exposed a year later. A second group was made up of corrupt PAIGC elements living in Conakry who had been recruited by the Portuguese secret police and were led by Kani and others. A third group was made up of Portuguese agents who had joined the PAIGC as deserters from the colonial army. Most of the conspirators had been involved in an abortive 1972 plot but had been amnestied on Cabral's orders. Although the Portuguese alleged that Guinean President Sekou Touré was responsible for the assassination, claiming he intended to annex Guinea-Bissau after the war, later investigation showed the plot was the result of an operation initiated by the Portuguese secret police. Following the death of Cabral, an inquiry of 465 persons found 43 of them guilty. (For further details and interpretations, see Bragança [1976], Chabal [1983A: 132–143], Crimi [1975], and Ignatiev [1975B].)

Chabal was laudatory of Cabral as a leader, affirming that his party was the most successful in black Africa and the first to achieve independence through armed struggle. Further, the organization of a social and political order in liberated areas was due largely to his leadership:

> Perhaps more than most revolutionary leaders, he was in a position to shape and mold the party he created according to his vision and ambitions. Because he was the original architect and the undisputed leader of the PAIGC, he had great freedom in developing its organization, training its leaders, and defining the policies which he considered were most suited to the struggle." (Chabal, 1983A: 8)

A series of crises affected the PAIGC, and three of them were efficiently and capably resolved under Amílcar's leadership. The first was the massacre at a dockworkers' strike at the Pidjiguiti wharf on August 3, 1959. The demonstration had been organized by Luís Cabral (1984: 65–73), who had been elected head of the union of industrial and commercial workers, and its suppression constituted a defeat for a tactic of urban agitation. The incident convinced Amílcar and others to shift attention to the mobilization of the peasant masses and to the organization of the party outside as well as within Guinea.

A second crisis was evident in the tension and dissent among the national liberation groups in Dakar and Conakry where Cabral in the early 1960s began a process of coalescing diverse elements and isolating rival movements so that the PAIGC would emerge as the dominant force in the armed struggle. Short-lived coalitions of groups under PAIGC control—the Frente de Libertação da Guiné e Cabo Verde (FLGGC) during 1959, the Movimento de Libertação da Guiné e Cabo Verde (MLGCV) in 1960, and the Frente Unida da Libertação da Guiné e Cabo Verde (FUL) in 1961—were unable to prevail.

The third crisis evolved as the armed struggle progressed under the PAIGC, when problems appeared between field commanders (most of whom came from urban areas) and their fighters (mostly peasants recruited from local areas) and the rural population. The problem was defined by Cabral as excessive militarism because field commanders were carrying out their battles independently of the Conakry leadership; political and military policies were not effectively integrated, and there were abuses of power. (See Chabal [1983A: 77–81] for an analysis of three basic problems: militarism, localism, and cultural constraints.)

Under Cabral's direction the Cassacá Congress resulted in a reorganization of the military and political structures. Although problems of internal dissension were mitigated at this time, they reappeared well before and were manifested more openly after the assassination of Cabral and ultimately were played out in the November 1980 coup that deposed Luís Cabral as president of Guinea-Bissau.

Revolutionary Theorist

Cabral emerged as a thinker in the tradition of Marx, Lenin, Trotsky, and others who left us a legacy of revolutionary experience, but although he certainly read from their works and indeed was influenced by them, he rarely referred to them and never cited them in his major writings. (In 1970 during a visit to Moscow and Alma Ata, however, he spoke on Lenin and his own national liberation struggle—see *Nô Pintcha*, No. 247 [November 6, 1976] and *O Militante* No. 1 [July 1979].) McCulloch (1983: 57), in his biography of Cabral, compared his work to that of Lenin:

> Revolutionary theorists of the Third World and African Socialists in particular pay little if any attention to the role of material production when building theories about revolutionary change. The kind of massively detailed and intricate study of political economy found in

Lenin's *The Development of Capitalism in Russia* is, with the exception of Cabral's agronomic writings, a solitary work.

Cabral was a contemporary of renowned revolutionaries Ernesto Ché Guevara, Ho Chi Ming, and Mao Zedong. Although undoubtedly influenced by their ideas and experience, his own ideas were based largely on his own experiences. In the decades following World War II and the breakup of the empire in Africa, Cabral was perhaps overshadowed by other revolutionaries such as Lumumba and Nkrumah, but history already has shown that Cabral was one of the significant African thinkers of our times. Kofi (1981: 856) commented:

> It was Cabral more than Nkrumah or Touré or any other African leader who concretized African realities into the framework of Marxist-Leninism. Cabral developed not only the theory and tactics of wars of liberation from colonial rule but also was the one who looked beyond the seizure of power.

Cabral was a contemporary of Frantz Fanon, who was from Martinique, educated in Paris, and wrote about the Algerian revolution. Both were born within a year of each other, both were members of a petty bourgeoisie, both were educated in a European setting and influenced by the cultural renaissance movements after World War II, and both were committed to the destruction of colonialism. Professionally, they pursued different vocations (as agronomist and psychiatrist, respectively), and although their writing stemmed from their revolutionary experiences, Cabral's role in the revolutionary party was major and Fanon's was insignificant. (See McCulloch [1983: 8–9] for a comparison of the two personalities.)

Scholars close to Cabral have passed positive judgment on his stature. Mário de Andrade compared him to other outstanding Africans: "Kwame Nkrumah, the visionary; Patrice Lumumba, the martyr; Amílcar Cabral, the unifier—As a unifier and mobilizer, he was both a theoretician and a man of action indefatigably in pursuit of reality, by revealing the deep roots, fundamental causes, so often blurred in the tumult of revolutionary action" (Andrade, in Cabral, 1979: xviii). Gérard Chaliand (1977–1978: 3) also identified three examples of revolutionary African leaders: "the martyr Patrice Lumumba, the visionary Kwame Nkrumah, and the revolutionary par excellence, Amílcar Cabral. Both his thought and his stature place Cabral beyond the struggle against Portuguese colonialism, and he must be regarded as one of the major figures of the Third World." Basil Davidson (1979: 35) wrote: "A supreme educator in the wisest sense . . . among the great figures of our times." Paulo Freire (1978: 18) affirmed: "As with every person who truly lives out the coherence between political choice and actions, the word, for Cabral, was always a dialectical unity between action and reflection, practice and theory. He never allowed himself to be tempted on the one hand by empty words, nor on the other by activism." In sum, the overall theoretical contribution of Cabral is considered substantial by those who have focused on his work (see, for example, Aaby [1978], Bienen [1977], Comitini [1980], Dowbor [1983], Goulet [1977], McCollester [1973], and Urdang [1979]).

Cabral himself was astute about the future. He offered a prophesy about the prospects for African peoples maintaining unity and believed that their solidarity would transcend conflicts between elites:

> My own view is that there are no real conflicts between the peoples of Africa. There are only conflicts between their elites. When the peoples take power into their own hands, as they will with the march of events in this continent, there will remain no great obstacles to effective African solidarity. (Cabral, *Unity and Struggle*, 1979: xvii)

Diplomat in the International Arena

Cabral's international vision embraced strategic and practical considerations. First and foremost, he was interested in exposing the contradictions of imperialist strategies oriented toward leading newly independent countries in Africa and elsewhere from colonialism to neocolonialism and dependency upon the advanced capitalist nations. Benot (1983) argued that the fundamental character of Cabral's thinking was based on an international level in which he grasped the totality of world relations and not simply the particular struggle that confronted him. Thus, the struggle of the peoples of Guinea-Bissau was viewed in the full struggle of the international working-class movement, a perspective Benot affirmed was profoundly Marxist and contributed to the struggles of Third World peoples to overcome imperialism. Davidson captured the essence of this commitment:

> What Cabral said at home was the same in content as what he said abroad, even if the form was often very different. His argument abroad, and he was often a brilliant publicist, was invariably the truth that he drew from his study of reality at home: the same truth, with the same conclusions, that he espoused in the forests of his homeland. (Cabral, *Unity and Struggle*, 1979: xii)

Chaliand (1977–1978) emphasizes Cabral's success in establishing neighborly relations with Senegal and Guinea free from conflict, attaining the support and eventual diplomatic recognition of numerous African governments, and successfully implementing a flexible policy of nonalignment, which allowed for aid and support from government and private sources in the West and the public support of the Soviet Union and the Eastern bloc, Cuba, the People's Republic of China, and other socialist countries. Thus the diplomatic offensive led by Cabral placed substantial pressure on the Portuguese dictatorship, and the proclamation of independence before an agreement with Portugal could be worked out contributed to the fall of the regime itself.

Cabral's extensive travels to different parts of the world included the reunion with Viriato da Cruz, Mário de Andrade, and Marcelino dos Santos in Paris, where the MAC was formed during November 1957 and later the CONCP was instituted, thereby bringing together the diverse interests of those opposed to Portuguese colonialism in Africa. From the early moments of his activism he was in touch with other Africans. During 1957 he briefly and discretely attended the pan-African sessions in Accra. In January 1960 he attended the All African Peoples Organization Conference in Tunis, in March and April he sought support in England and Europe, and in August he led a delegation to the People's Republic of China, which gave his movement its first substantial external assistance. On November 15, 1960, Cabral submitted a memorandum of twelve proposals to the Portuguese government. Thereafter, the record reveals numerous missions: a talk on May 1–3, 1964, to the Frantz Fanon Center in Milán, where he presented his views on class and social structures of Guinea; his important speech during January 1966 in Havana before the Organization for Solidarity with the Peoples of Asia, Africa, and Latin America, where he analyzed the ambivalence of the petty bourgeoisie and set forth views on the armed struggle; a conference on Portuguese colonialism in Khartoum in January 1969; a lecture on national culture at Syracuse University on February 20, 1970; an appearance before the U.S. House of Representatives Subcommittee on African Affairs on February 20, 1970; a visit to Moscow in April 1970 to commemorate the centenary of Lenin's birth; a conference in Rome and a visit with Pope Paul VI in June 1970; an appearance in Stockholm during April 1971; an address to the Eighth Conference of Chiefs of State and African Governments in Addis Ababa during June 1971; and visits to several European capitals in October 1971. In 1972 Cabral received honorary doctorates from Lincoln University in the United States and from the Institute of African Studies of the USSR Academy of Sciences, and he addressed the Organization of African Unity in Rabat in June.

The United Nations also listened to Cabral and gave him its platform. Many of his written statements to various UN agencies are listed in the bibliographic notes at the end of this chapter. Important statements were made in 1968 and 1969, but his activity particularly intensified during 1972, with a statement before the UN Security Council in Addis Ababa in February, a visit to liberated areas in Guinea by a UN Special Commission during April, the recognition of the PAIGC by the UN Decolonization Committee on August 13, support of the UN Security Council, an appearance before the UN Fourth Committee in October, and the condemnation of Portuguese colonialism by the UN Security Council on November 22.

Manuel Duarte (1977) analyzed this activity and the effort by Cabral to transcend a fundamental contradiction. Cabral claimed that his people had established their sovereignty over most of the national territory, with a national assembly and an executive about to proclaim the existence of the state; the problem was whether the people had the right to integrate into the international community. Cabral's fundamental goal was to resolve this contradiction through international recognition of Guinea-Bissau and Cape Verde as sovereign states. In this sense, "Cabral not only was a political genius, profound sociologist, able diplomat, but a coherent and untiring fighter for the advance of an authentic international juridical order" (p. 24).

The Organization of the Guide

Chabal cautioned that biographers and historians may overstate their cases, write from conviction, or give history its teleological shape. Many of the secondary sources cited in the bibliography are written with a sense of conviction; some of them are personal accounts, impressions, or polemics, and I have attempted to identify their orientation in my annotations. My notes introducing the major sections of the bibliography list other useful reference works, as well as their strengths and weaknesses. I also mention accessible collections and archives.

Chabal referred to the archive of documents in the PAIGC headquarters in Bissau. He stated that Guinea-Bissau has yet to establish official archives, although there were plans for such an undertaking during my visit to Bissau in 1975. The researcher should explore archival prospects with Carlos Lopes, who was once the director of the Casa da Cultura, a publicly owned bookshop devoted to diffusing serious literature about Africa and the world, and who presently heads the Instituto Nacional de Estudos e Pesquisa (INEP), the major social science research center in Bissau, which also is accumulating a library of sources. Chabal also referred to the private papers of Ana Maria Cabral, Amílcar's second wife, who now heads the Fundação Amílcar Cabral in Praia, which is systematically building an archive.

Chabal despaired the dearth of meaningful research materials on colonial matters within Portugal, but in fact Cabral's early writings can be found in periodicals such as *Cabo Verde: Boletim de Propaganda* and *Boletim Cultural da Guiné Portuguesa* and in scientific monographs published by the Junta de Investigações do Ultramar. Most of these writings now are found in Lisbon in the Centro de Informação e Documentação Amílcar Cabral (CIDAC), where Chabal undertook the bulk of his research, and in the microfilm of the Chilcote collection at Stanford University library and Wallerstein collection at Yale University library in the United States. In his doctoral dissertation, Joshua Forrest (1987B: xvii, n. 11) stated: "The Archives Nationales de Sénégal house the most complete collection in the world of original French-language documents on Guinea-Bissau's colonial period and of published works on the national liberation struggle and on post-independence politics."

Also, there are memoirs and documents of the colonial experience in the thousands of monographs, anthologies, and periodicals produced after the Portuguese coup of April 25, 1974 (Chilcote, 1987). The Centro de Documentação 25 de Abril at the University of Coimbra has begun to gather an archive of this literature, including ephemeral documents and the personal archives of leading Portuguese participants in the colonial wars. The Salazar and Caetano archives, held at the Biblioteca Nacional in Lisbon, should yield useful information once they are opened to the public. Thus, those interested in delving into Cabral may be surprised to discover that the record is more than a mere substitute "of mindless propaganda for fact," as Chabal appropriately characterized most of the literature throughout the 1926–1974 period in Portugal.

My contribution herein constitutes neither history nor biography. It is simply a guide to the thought and life of an African whose contribution already has been judged as important. My intent is to lead the student and scholar, the curious and conscientious reader, into the sources about Cabral and his place in history. This book also may help to inform the reader about the conditions and circumstances that allowed him to accomplish so much in the short span of his life, which in turn may serve the purpose of comparative study and example.

The organization of my guide, beyond this introductory chapter, focuses on the major themes in the thought of Cabral, with the intent of synthesizing his ideas, identifying the major sources of those ideas, and revealing some of the assessments of journalists and scholars. My purpose is not to interpret and evaluate this thought in a definitive way but to lay bare its essence, for the reader will soon discover its relevance both to the past and to the contemporary world. These essential themes—important in the formation of Cabral's thought—are colonialism and imperialism; nationalism and national liberation; class and class struggle; and state and development. Each theme is the focus of ensuing chapters.

The first of these themes focuses on the questions of colonialism and imperialism, which consume a great deal of attention in Cabral's work. Cabral obviously was familiar with the major theories of colonialism and imperialism, but he was suspicious of ethnocentric perspectives, especially those emanating from Europe, and he favored an understanding based on African reality. Cabral distinguished between classical colonialism and neocolonialism, and he showed how colonialism denies dominated people their historical process of development, whereas imperialism accompanies the introduction and expansion of capitalism along with new relations of production and allows for conflict and class struggle.

Cabral understood nationalism as a European idea and how African socialism adopted nationalism as a viable strategy. He adopted a revolutionary nationalism in which the struggle against colonialism and imperialism is found in cultural reality. Culture, he believed, was thus essential to the national liberation movement—he believed that cultural resistance to colonial domination is based on the participation of the rural and urban working masses and the revolutionary fraction of the petty bourgeoisie. Preservation of cultural values within the struggle for liberation and independence allows for unity among various ethnic and other groups. Liberation involves the freeing of the productive forces from colonialism, disciplined political organization, and economic and social progress.

Cabral looked for divisions and contradictions everywhere—races, religions, ethnic groups, and social classes were examined. Classes and class struggle appear with the development of the productive forces once a certain level of accumulation is attained. History may advance, but it does not begin with the emergence of classes and class struggle nor does it end after the disappearance of classes. The advance of history evolves through at least three stages: a primitive form with a low level of productive forces; a more progressive stage characterized by private appropriation of the means of production; and a higher stage in which private means of appropriation is eliminated along with classes and class struggle, and new and unknown forces appear.

Development thus accompanies a progressive evolution of the forces of production, but Cabral firmly believed that progress requires a steady advance toward new and organic unities of thought and action. Cabral focused on the building of a revolutionary movement in an undeveloped state, the role of the petty bourgeoisie and its manipulation of the state in a revolutionary situation, and awareness of imperialism and colonialism. His conception of the state was drawn from the experience of organizing life in the liberated areas. New political structures appeared, including a national assembly of representatives and the secret ballot.

Cabral cautioned against foreign capital for it could have negative impact on the class structure and lead to an extroverted economy. He advocated self-centered development based on increased productivity with the agricultural base, some industrial production of simple consumer goods, and some exports in order to finance fuel and machinery. Some small national capital could be permitted where the state was unable to manage. The general development strategy combines the meeting of peoples' needs with self-reliance and building from local values. Inherent in this strategy was the notion of political will in a country poor in natural resources and infrastructure and committed to egalitarian distribution of benefits.

The Lessons of Cabral

There are lessons to be learned from Cabral's attention to these major themes. He taught us the strengths and weaknesses of the liberation struggle, illustrating with his revolutionary experience and the armed struggle in Guinea-Bissau and his familiarity with conditions in Cape Verde, but offering insights that may have relevance to colonial and neocolonial situations elsewhere. Further, he transcended Eurocentric interpretations to offer a new approach to imperialism, which he conceptualized as rationalized imperialism. He showed that although Portuguese colonialism failed to introduce any substantial capitalist development in Guinea-Bissau and Cape Verde, it nevertheless was able to perpetuate itself, and that Portuguese political control through colonialism could have as devastating consequences as monopoly capital elsewhere. His analysis avoided the emphasis on exchange and circulation, so prominent in most writings on development and underdevelopment, and instead concentrated on such concepts as mode of production and productive forces long before they were in vogue. In turn, this allowed for analysis of class and class struggle and the placing of such analysis in a historical context.

Cabral's reference to productive forces, relations of production, and modes of production, as well as his attention to combined and uneven development, place his work in a historically materialist framework. Cabral did not proclaim himself a Marxist nor adhere to rigid and orthodox formulations, as evidenced in his rejection of the thesis that history begins with classes (see Rudebeck [1974] for criticism, and Opoku [1978] for defense of this position). But he was faithful both to the Marxist method and to the proposition that good theory not only may be based on the ideas of others but also must be subject to concrete and historical conditions of real experiences that test theory.

Bibliographic Note

Scattered throughout my bibliography of sources by and on Cabral are useful references that emphasize biographical details of Cabral. The reader may want to examine some of the following, which are especially useful: Andrade (1973A, 1973B, 1974A, 1975A, 1975B, 1975C, and particularly 1980); Bragança (1976); Vasco Cabral (1977C, 1982, 1983A, 1984B, 1984D); Chabal (1978, 1980, 1983A); Chaliand (1973A, 1973B, 1977, 1977–1978); Chilcote (1974); Comitini (1980); Davidson (1964, 1979); António Duarte (1983); Eduardo de Sousa Ferreira (1973); Fighters for National Liberation (1983); António de Figueiredo (1973); Foy (1983); Ignatiev (1975A); Jong and Buijtenhuijs (1979); Krautsova (1973); PAIGC (1973A); Aristides Pereira (1983A); and Ulyanovsky (1980, 1984). For impressions by his parents, see Juvenal Cabral (1947) and the obituary of Iva Pinhel Evora (*Nô Pintcha*, No. 356, August 13, 1977; also see No. 225, September 12, 1976). Impressions of Cabral's first wife are in António Duarte (1983). For comparisons of Cabral to Franz Fanon, see Blackey (1974); Jinadu (1978); Lopes (1977); and McCulloch (1983). For details of his assassination, see Amadou (1973); Bragança (1973C, 1976: 22–34); Carvalho (1973B); CIDAC (1973); Crimi (1975); Ignatiev (1975B); Nikanorov (1975); and PAIGC (1973B, 1973C).

For a summary of useful references to Cabral as a poet and student, see Cabral's early poems (1946, 1948, 1949), his notes on poetry (1951), and the outstanding summary and chronology by Osório (1988) along with Moser's (1978, 1981) useful contributions. Cabral's piece on the role of the African student (1953) is early evidence of his commitment to the culture and future of Africa. See also Vasco Cabral and Andrade (1978) for impressions of student days together, and António Duarte (1983) for an interview with Cabral's first wife

The bibliography identifies thirty-one published and unpublished professional papers that present results of Cabral's scientific study as a student and agronomist, including his university thesis (1951) and five monographs usually in collaboration with others (1958, 1959, 1960). The bibliography also identifies twenty-five scientific journal articles (two in 1949; four in 1950; one in 1952; five in 1953; six in 1954; three in 1956; two in 1958; one in 1959; and one in 1960) on soils and soil erosion, climate, pesticides and storage problems, and agricultural commodities (rice, bananas, beet sugar, ground nuts, and so on) and cattle. A very representative selection of these published and unpublished papers was published in Cabral (1988).

Some of the examples above of Cabral as political organizer and mobilizer are drawn from Andrade (1980) and Ignatiev (1975A). Chabal (1983A: chap. 3 and 4) covered mobilization during the armed struggle. Rudebeck (1974) provided the best firsthand account of this mobilization, including its political, social, and economic implications in the liberated areas prior to independence. The major organizational statements of Cabral are found in his collected writings (1976, 1977, 1979), but especially noteworthy are his "Seminário de quadros" on party principles of November 19–24, 1969; and the clarification of the new party structures, September 13–15, 1970. See also the text on the creation of the National Popular Assembly in *Nô Pintcha* (September 24, 1975); a series of reprinted articles in *Nô Pintcha*—on party principles (Nos. 372–385, 1977), and on cooperation with cadres (Nos. 356–368, 1977); on party organization (Nos. 327–334, 1977); and on improving political work (Nos. 392–400, 1977); and a reprinted article on discipline (*O Militante*, No. 7, March–April 1978).

For a summary of sources of Cabral as revolutionary theorist, see the collected works under the title *Unity and Struggle* (1976 and 1977; and 1979) and the various anthologies, including *Revolution in Guinea* (1969 and 1972); *Our People Are Our Mountains* (1971); *Return to the Source* (1973); and *Guinea-Bissau: Toward Final Victor* (1974). Examination of Cabral's texts suggests the possibility of a classification of those written or spoken (taped or transcribed) for internal audiences (for example, the work on party principles, November 19–24, 1969); and those prepared for external audiences such as for press conferences, international meetings, international organizations, and so on (see, for example, the informal meeting in New York with U.S. supporters, transcribed in *O Militante* No. 3 [September–October 1977], 55–59). Among his outstanding theoretical texts was the speech of January 6, 1966, in Havana. Among the important practical texts, see the annual reports on the armed struggle and the eight directives for party workers in 1965 after the First PAIGC Congress at Cassacá. The major secondary sources on the theory of Cabral include Chabal (1981C); Chaliand (1975); Chilcote (1968, 1984); Kofi (1981); Lopes (1984); Luke (1981); Magubane (1971); Marton (1983); McCollester (1973); McCulloch (1983); Nyang (1976); O'Brien (1977); Opoku (1978); Oramas (1978); Ribeiro (1983); Simpósio Internacional Amílcar Cabral (1984); Solodóvnikov (1983); and Suret-Canale (1983).

Cabral was a foremost diplomat in the international arena. The published record of essential documents prepared and presented by Cabral is impressive and voluminous. His speeches and writings are listed in the bibliography under the following dates and places: for communications suggesting resolution of the conflict with the Portuguese government, see the the open note of October 13, 1961; the message to Portuguese troops of February 22, 1963; and a note in *O Militante* (No. 4, November 1977). For presentations at the CONCP, see those at Rabat, February 13, 1963; and at Dar es Salaam, October 3–8, 1965. For views offered at African conferences, see documents, including those at the Third Conference of African Peoples, Cairo, March 23–25, 1961; the Second Conference of Afro-Asian Jurists, October 15–22, 1962; the African Chiefs of State of Union Africaine et Malgache Conference, Quagadougou, March 1963; the First Conference of Chiefs of State, Addis Ababa, May 1963; the First Meeting of the Organization of African Unity (OAU), of June 20, 1963; the Eighth Meeting of the OAU, June 21–23, 1971; and the Ninth Meeting of the OAU, Rabat, June 1972.

Papers and speeches before various international meetings included those at the Centre Franz Fanon, Milán, May 3, 1964; at the First Conference of Peoples of Africa, Asia, and Latin America, Havana, January 1966; Stockholm, April 14, 1970; Rome, June 27–29, 1974; and Finland, October 19–22, 1971. There were also papers published in London under the pseudonym Abel Djassi (1960 and 1961). Additionally, Cabral made appearances in the United States: at Syracuse University on February 20, 1970; at Lincoln University on October 15, 1972; and before the U.S. House of Representatives Subcommittee on Africa, February 26, 1970. There were speeches in the Soviet Union during November 1967, April 1970, and December 1972 (reprinted in Nikanorov, 1975: 31–45).

Documents presented by Cabral to the United Nations include those to the UN Fourth Committee (1961; June 5, 6, and 14, 1962; December 12, 1962; October 31, 1963; May 27, 1964; June 1965; July 7, 1965; and October 16, 1972) and to the Decolonization Committee of 24 (June 1965). There were statements before the UN General Assembly (October 5, 1963) and the UN Security Council (February 1, 1972), as well as to the UN Human Rights Commission (1968) and UNESCO (Paris, July 3–7, 1972). The reader can find many of these documents reproduced in part or entirety in various periodical listings under Cabral's writing in the bibliography.

For a review of Cabral's diplomatic undertakings and the legal context, within international law and the charter of the United Nations, see Manuel Duarte (1977). Benot (1983) provides a useful analysis of Cabral in the international community.

2

Theory of Colonialism and Imperialism

Colonialism and imperialism can be found in a rudimentary form in the Greek and Roman empires. They also appeared in a mercantile "old" form in the sixteenth and seventeenth centuries represented not only by the Spanish exploitation of precious metals in Latin America but by the string of coastal trading points established by Portugal to control traffic in spices, ivory, precious metals, and slaves. The modern usage of these terms dates from the late nineteenth century, with the rise of industrialization in Europe and the search for raw materials and markets in Africa and other parts of the Third World. Since that time, the rise to dominance of the capitalist mode of production and inequalities of wealth and power have characterized development and accumulation throughout most of the world.

Colonialism and imperialism were conspicuous in the late nineteenth century when the European powers carved out their colonial empires in Africa and searched for raw materials, requisite for the evolving industrialization and for markets that could absorb excess production. Their objectives were primarily economic, in the need to bolster the domestic economy, and political, in the sense of assuring imperial stature and dominance among the world powers.

Marx did not employ colonialism and imperialism as terms to explain the dominance of advanced nations over backward areas. He generally used the term colonialism to refer to settlement of uninhabited areas from which indigenous peoples had been driven out, and he did not formally employ the term imperialism. In his writing on Ireland, he attributed poverty and misery there to English external oppression and exploitation. In his writing about India, Marx advanced the notion that whereas merchant capital exploits and destroys without transforming, industrial capital transforms and advances the economy in progressive ways.

These concepts were developed by later writers. For example, the English liberal, J. A. Hobson, in *Imperialism: A Study* (1902) believed that British imperialism could be stemmed by resolving the problem of domestic underconsumption of products destined for foreign markets. Karl Kautsky argued that the class conflicts of capitalism would diminish through peaceful processes. Joseph Schumpeter in *Imperialism: Social Classes* (1919) stressed that imperialism was a precapitalist phenomenon that would disappear with progressive and rational capitalism. Rosa Luxemburg in *The Accumulation of Capital* (1913) elaborated a theory of imperialism that explained continuous capital accumulation and, in particular, the penetration of foreign capital into backward economies. Nikolai Bukharin in *Imperialism and World Economy* (1917) drew his ideas from Rudolf Hilferding's conception of finance capital in *Das Finanzkapital* (1910) and suggested that imperialism was an advanced stage of capitalism. V. I. Lenin in his *Imperialism, the Highest Stage of Capitalism* (1917) was influenced by Hobson, Hilferding, and Marx in his understanding of imperialism and monopoly capitalism, and he was particularly concerned about the growing influence of large banks and rapid concentration of production in large industrial enterprises.

Contemporary thinkers draw their understanding of imperialism from these and perhaps other writers. Paul Baran and Paul Sweezy in *Monopoly Capital* (1966) referred to Hilferding, Luxemburg, and Lenin while emphasizing the role of the giant corporations and their managers. Other perspectives evolved—for example, Immanuel Wallerstein in *The Modern World System* (1974) attributed deteriorating patterns of trade and production in Africa to the capitalist world system, whereas other theorists, such as Pierre Philippe Rey in his *Colonialisme, neo-colonialisme et transition au capitalisme* (1973), characterized underdevelopment in those areas as a reflection of precapitalist economies.

Cabral was also influenced by the classical writers, although he does not tell us who contributed to his ideas of colonialism and imperialism. Certainly Marx and Lenin were important to his thinking. Although their works are not cited by Cabral, their influence is clear in his thinking, as summarized in this chapter.

Portuguese Colonialism and African Resistance

The Portuguese colonial experience in Cape Verde and Guinea-Bissau dates to the discoveries and explorations of the fifteenth century. One purpose was to divert control of West African trade from Muslim to Portuguese merchants and to find Christian allies to overcome Islam. Cape Verde became the key link to Portuguese control over the region. Previously uninhabited, it was colonized and developed into a base for trade in slaves and other commodities with the adjacent mainland. Its hegemony over the Guinea coast contributed to exploitation and abuse there. Although in the latter half of the sixteenth century and throughout the seventeenth century the slave trade filtering through Cacheu and Bissau increased greatly, Portugal faced a period of declining influence and increasing challenge from foreign interests, especially from Dutch, English, and French expeditions. Despite poor colonial administration, the Portuguese managed to hold on to these territories, as control of the Cape Verdes and Bissau reinforced the Portuguese position in West Africa. A period of brief recovery from 1837 to 1859 was associated with the administrator, Honório Pereira Barreto, who stabilized finances and settled many Cape Verdeans and Portuguese in Guinea. Portuguese influence declined somewhat thereafter with the repression of the slave trade, poor agricultural production, and increased foreign competition (there were French and British incursions in the late nineteenth century). At the same time, Portugal was pressed to defend against the ever-increasing attacks of African tribes, especially in Guinea, which had been separated from Cape Verde in 1879 and established as a separate colony.

Portuguese efforts to contain the rebellions involved military occupation and campaigns of "pacification" throughout the last quarter of the nineteenth century and into the twentieth century. Generally, the colonialists were penned inside their cities as the African resistance continued. Stagnation in trade and persistent deficits in the colonial budget were consequences of the turmoil. A column of Angolan recruits was cut down in 1884, expeditions during the ensuing decade failed, and campaigns during 1901, 1903, 1904, and 1907 were only partially successful. During campaigns from 1913 to 1915, Teixeira Pinto achieved acclaim for his suppression of Africans. Nevertheless, the resistance continued, as evidenced by further campaigns in 1917, 1925, and 1936 when the Portuguese finally proclaimed that the rebellions had been pacified.

An account of the African resistance can be obtained only by sifting through Portuguese colonial records and the observations of Portuguese historians and observers. Pélissier (1989) provided the best synthesis of these events from 1841 to 1936. A definitive African perspective has yet to be written, but a tentative sketch of this resistance can be delineated (from Chilcote, 1967: 93–99), including the unsuccessful revolts of African chiefs at Cacheu in 1679; the rebellion seventeen years later of Bibiano Vaz, who sought trade with the English and French; the Papel war of 1696 led by Incinhate, who sought liberalization of trade restrictions and an end to abuses of the slave trade; a Mandinga uprising at Farim in the same year; a Papel revolt under Palanca during 1753 in an effort to keep the Portuguese from rebuilding their fort at Bissau; a Bijagós revolt against the English settlement at Bolama in 1792; a battle between the Papéis and Portuguese at Cacheu during 1824 and 1825; Papel uprisings at Bissau in 1844 and 1846; a Mandinga attack at Farim in 1846; and a Felupe massacre of a Portuguese military column in 1878.

After Guinea became a separate colony, there were other incidents, including a Fula attack on Buba in 1880 by Mamadú Paté and another uprising a year later by Bakar Kidali; the Beafada war at Jabadá in 1882; a

Felupe ambush in 1884; the Fula uprising under Mussa Molo in 1886; rebellions by the Mandingas and Beafadas in 1889; uprisings during 1891 and 1892 and a state of siege at Bissau; an attack by the Papéis and Balantas in December 1893 against the fortress of Pidjiguiti in Bissau and an ensuing battle until the following May; the war of Oio in 1897; the insurgency of the Bijacós on the island of Canhabaque in 1900; a rebellion near Cacheu in 1904; a Manjaco defeat of Portuguese troops at Farim in the same year; African resistance led by Unfali Soncó along the Geba River disrupted navigation and impeded commerce between Bissau and Bafatá until about 1908; a rebellion of the Papéis at Bissau in 1908; and a Balanta attack near Golê in 1909.

African resistance inflicted some loss to advancing Portuguese columns during the four campaigns of Teixeira Pinto during 1912 and 1915. The Fula chieftain, Abdul N'Djai, who had supported these campaigns, was rewarded with the region of Oio but soon thereafter even he defied Portuguese authority until his defeat by another Portuguese expedition in 1919. During 1917, a state of siege was in effect in the Bijacós archipelago and a rebellion took place at Nhambalã; further troubles ensued at Canhabaque in 1925 until 1936.

These events suggest a pattern of resistance throughout most of the colonial period and a foundation for Cabral's national liberation struggle. Cabral refers frequently to this resistance but without delving into historical detail. The PAIGC (1974B) attempt to construct an African history of Guinea-Bissau and Cape Verde includes brief reference to the African resistance during the last decade of the nineteenth century, attributing most of the protests and revolts to the refusal of various tribes to pay taxes demanded by the colonialists.

The present account examines the role of Unfali Soncó and the revolt of 1907–1908 and the resistance to pacification thereafter—events mentioned by Cabral in his writings. The account also identifies other cases of African resistance in West Africa, but it represents only an initial effort to document the overall pattern of African involvement.

Colonialism

Cabral believed that colonialism and imperialism had impeded national consciousness, independence, and real national liberation. People, he thought, not only have a right to their own history, but they must recover their interrupted history: "National liberation is the inalienable right of every people to have its own history" ("Cabral, *Unity and Struggle*, 1979: 143). Cabral wrote that once the people gain control over their mode of production through national liberation, they can transcend the "sad position of being peoples without history." Culture is the vital element in the national liberation process. National liberation is expressed as an act of culture, the political expression of a people undertaking the struggle. Culture thus acts as either a positive or negative influence on people and their conditions.

Where cultural life is strong, new forms of economic, political, and armed resistance may contest foreign domination. Given its tenuous position, foreign domination must either liquidate all the population of a dominated country in order to eliminate all vestiges of resistance or it must "harmonize economic and political domination of these people with their cultural personality" (Cabral, *Return to the Source*, 1973: 40). Whereas the first proposition leaves "a void" and "empties foreign domination of its content and its object," the second has "no practical viability" and has never been "confirmed by history" (p. 40). In order to resolve this predicament, the Portuguese advocated a theory of assimilation with the intent of integrating "civilized" elements of the African population into the colonial superstructure, but this was unsuccessful in thwarting the drive to independence.

Colonial situations lead to "strong, dependent, and reciprocal relationships . . . between the cultural situation and the economic (and political) situation in the behavior of societies" (Cabral, *Return to the Source*, 1973: 41). Thus culture is the conscious consequence of the economic and political activities of that society. Colonizers build a system to repress the cultural life of the colonized people, and in the process they provoke cultural alienation in the population, either by creating a social gap between the indigenous peoples who are assimilated into the colonial society and the popular masses, or by dividing and deepening the divisions in society—between urban and rural petty bourgeoisie, between rural ethnic groups, between peasantry and workers, and so on. The colonizers attempt to repress or inhibit cultural activity of the masses, favoring instead the prestige and cultural influence of those who rule. These rulers include, on the one hand, colonial administrators, civil servants, and merchants, who reflect the values and beliefs of European society; and, on the other, tribal chiefs, who in return for their support receive economic and material privileges, education for their children, and so on.

Culture becomes an element of resistance to foreign domination: "the vigorous manifestation on the ideological or idealist plane of the physical and historical reality of the society that is dominated or to be dominated" (Cabral, *Return to the Source*, 1973: 41). Cultural resistance serves as an incipient phase in the liberation struggle. This resistance evolves in the direction of freeing the African society of its colonial cultural legacy and of developing a popular culture embracing indigenous values—a national culture based on the history of struggle; a scientific struggle commensurate with the requirements necessary for technological progress; and a universal culture for integration in the contemporary world (p. 55).

Cabral devoted much attention to the question of colonialism. Classical colonialism implies direct domination through foreign armed forces, police, administrative agents, and settlers. Direct domination may lead to any of three consequences: total destruction, partial destruction, and ostensible destruction of the local population. In these cases the native or local peoples may be totally or partially replaced by a colonizing population. Where the local peoples are not obliterated, they usually are relegated to special areas and deprived of their normal means of living (Cabral, *Return to the Source*, 1973: 66). Neocolonialism is indirect domination through the political control of local agents, and it is a way of "rationalizing" colonialism. Classical colonialism is traditional and formal, whereas neocolonialism occurs usually after independence has been achieved for a nation.

A summary of this theory of colonialism, drawn from Nyang (1976), advances the arguments that colonialists used violence to take over lands of other peoples; that superior technology allowed colonialism to succeed in its initial phase; and that technology transformed the means of production, stepped up social organization of work, and brought man into a world market. Nyang (1976: 5) suggested, "the processes of colonialism took the African out of his own historical realms and placed him in a Eurocentric historical drama." Thus, the struggle against colonialism becomes a motivating force of history today. Colonialism thus impeded the internal development of Africa, and especially so in the Portuguese case because the colonial power was not strong enough to bring about economic, social, and political development in its own territories. As a weak nation, Portugal could not afford to allow the independence of its colonies and promote neocolonialism thereafter.

Imperialism

These descriptions of colonialism are transposed to an understanding of imperialism. Classical colonialism becomes an imperialism of direct domination, whereas neocolonialism is an imperialism of indirect domination. Imperialism, according to Cabral, is "capital in action," destined to fulfill its historical role of developing the productive forces and transforming the means of production, differentiating classes with the development of a bourgeoisie, and intensifying the class struggle (Cabral, "O imperialismo," n.d.: 1). Specifically, neocolonialism was a strategy in a specific phase of imperialism after World War II. This phase was characterized by monopoly capitalism and the emergence of an international system of multinational corporations. According to Cabral, under neocolonialism imperialism promoted policies of aid in newly independent countries, while emphasizing certain investment in European countries. It was a counterrevolutionary strategy "simultaneously to dominate the working class in all the advanced countries and smother the national liberation movements in all the undeveloped countries" (Cabral, quoted in Nwagor, 1975: 22–23).

In a speech reviewed and analyzed by Andrade (1974B: 21–24), Cabral cited neocolonialism as a sort of "rationalized imperialism" aimed at defeating the international working class as well as the colonized peoples of the world:

> Neocolonialism is at work on two fronts—in Europe as well as in the underdeveloped countries. Its current framework in the underdeveloped countries is the policy of aid, and one of the essential aims of this policy is to create a false bourgeoisie to put a brake on the revolution and to enlarge the possibilities of the petty bourgeoisie as a neutraliser of the revolution; at the same time it invests capital in France, Italy, Belgium, England, and so on. In our opinion the aim of this is to stimulate the growth of a workers' aristocracy, to enlarge the field of action of the petty bourgeoisie so as to block the revolution. (Cabral, *Revolution in Guinea*, 1969: 73)

In contrast to classical colonialism, where transformations in the social structure are not pronounced, neocolonialism makes rather substantial changes (Nwagor, 1975: 18–30).

Cabral understood imperialism to emanate from the economic relations between colonies and metropoles—the result of monopoly capital in the advanced capitalist nations—but he despaired that Portugal was not an imperialist state, despite its pretenses at maintaining an empire of colonies in Africa and elsewhere, and that Portugal had not brought about any significant material transformation in its colonies. In assessing the significance of this idea, McCulloch (1983: 128) suggested that

> Cabral's theory of imperialism, in as much as it is new, is presented in the guise of a metaphor. The outlines of that metaphor can be found in his discussion of modes of production, his typology of historical epochs, and his invention of the concept of an aborted history. When combined, these elements suggest a new direction which the discussion of relations between the First and Third World should take. These new prescriptions for a theory of imperialism arrived as it were prematurely in Cabral's writings and he can do no more than suggest the form a new theory should take.

Cabral looked to a class analysis of the bourgeoisie under neocolonialist domination. A "native pseudo-bourgeoisie" evolves from the petty bourgeoisie of bureaucrats and compradores and gives the illusion of becoming a national bourgeoisie when in fact it is subservient to the ruling class of the dominating country. Therefore, it will tend to become more and more alienated from the slowly developing urbanized working class as well as the agricultural proletariat, once private property in rural farming areas is introduced. When this false bourgeoisie appears under neocolonialism, it is important to realize that the petty bourgeoisie becomes a neutralizing rather than a revolutionary force, and that the revolutionary struggle itself may be slowed or paralyzed.

Cabral explained that in the struggle against imperialism and colonialism, a horizontal structure within an ethnic group such as the Balanta, given the absence of political power composed of national elements, could facilitate the formation of a broad united front, indispensable to the success of the movement of national liberation. He warned that the embryonic character of the working classes and the peasantry (an important force in the revolutionary struggle) may make difficult the task of distinguishing true national independence from fictitious political independence so that only a revolutionary vanguard, usually an active minority, would be conscious of this difference and carry their consciousness through struggle to the popular masses.

Within a neocolonial situation, society usually is structured in a vertical form so that the national state serves to aggravate contradictions and make impossible the formation of a broad national front as under colonialism. On the one hand, part of the nationalist forces is mobilized by material changes brought about through nationalization and the economic initiative in the commercial sector; likewise, psychological change is evident through religious and other forces. On the other hand, the repressive character of the neocolonial state against the forces of national liberation, the sharpening of class contradictions, the legacy of foreign domination, and the impoverishment of the peasantry provoke nationalism and raise the consciousness of the popular masses. In this situation, the dominant class progresses through a phase of "bourgeoisification," whereas the working classes and the peasantry, exploited through the indirect domination of imperialism, open new perspectives in the evolution of national liberation and constitute a true popular vanguard of national liberation struggle. This vanguard, however, must align with other exploited classes, including employed rural workers, sharecroppers, small farmers, and the nationalist petty bourgeoisie. Such an alliance necessitates the organization and mobilization of nationalist forces in a strong and well-structured political organization.

Cabral suggested another distinction. In the colonial situation "in which the nation-state confronts the repressive forces of the bourgeoisie of the colonizing country" there is at least an appearance of a nationalist solution in the form of a national revolution in which a nation emerges from independence. In contrast, where the working classes and their allies struggle simultaneously against the imperialist bourgeoisie and the dominant class against a nationalist solution, the neocolonial situation cannot be resolved by a nationalist solution and can be overcome only by "the destruction of the capitalist structure implanted by imperialism in the national territory, along with a socialist solution" (Cabral, "O imperialismo," n.d. 3–4).

Despite the differences between classical colonialism and

neocolonialism, these two forms of imperialist domination must also be identified as similar phenomena: "both in colonialism and neocolonialism the essential characteristic of imperialist domination remains the same—denial of the historical process of the dominated people, by means of violent usurpation of the freedom of the process of development of the national productive forces" (Cabral, *Unity and Struggle*, 1979: 129–130).

Cabral was especially concerned with a definition of imperialism. Imperialism, he believed, is the monopolistic stage of capitalism, unable to resolve its own contradictions. Historically, it reinforced the colonial position of England and France, isolating Germany from exploitation of the backward countries. This led to the drive of German financial capital, together with Italian and Japanese capital, to expand on their own in search of needed raw materials and surplus profits, thus leading to World War I. The Russian Revolution represented "the first major blow to imperialism," and World War II was the consequence of "antagonisms which characterize the development of imperialism," accompanied not only by the consolidation of socialism in many parts of the world, but by the demand of "dependent peoples for the liberation struggle" (Cabral, *Revolution in Guinea*, 1969: 13–14).

Cabral believed that the basic contradiction in the international system was the struggle of the Third World against imperialism. A particular problem was the perpetuation of Portuguese colonialism, given that Portugal was a poor nation in comparison to the rest of Europe, without the capacity to invest and develop its colonies; Portugal was, in effect, under the authority of bourgeois English domination. This relationship helps to explain the lengthy rule of Portugal in Africa and its inability to effect a neocolonial solution (Lopes, 1984).

What were the characteristics of this imperialism? Given its underdevelopment and backwardness and the dominance of rival imperialist powers, Portugal somehow was able to retain its colonies and empire. Cabral attributed this continuity to the support of England since the Treaty of Methuen of 1703 when Portugal became "a semi-colony of England" and "England had every interest in using the Portuguese colonies, not only to exploit their economic resources, but also to occupy them as support bases on the route to the Orient, and thus to maintain absolute domination in the Indian Ocean." Portugal thus served as an intermediary: "the sometimes envious guardian of the human and material resources of our countries, at the service of world imperialism" (Cabral, *Revolution in Guinea*, 1969: 14). This historical relationship is important in understanding that "Portugal has been no more than the sometimes envious guardian of the human and material resources of our countries, at the service of world imperialism. That is the real reason for the survival of Portuguese colonialism in Africa, and for the possible prolonging of our struggle" (pp. 14–15). Cabral went on to explain that the people were mobilized "on the basis of the daily realities of suffering and exploitation, and now, even the children in Guinea know what colonialism and imperialism are" (Cabral, *Our People Are Our Mountains*, 1971: 22). Andrade (1980: 144) characterized this basic thesis as "imperialist domination found in the historical process of a dominated people."

Essentially, the negation of the free development of the productive forces would allow dominated people to escape from their situation due to the contradictions manifested through class struggle. The denial of historical development of a dominated people also denies their cultural development, and that is why "the history of national liberation struggles shows generally these struggles are preceded by an increase in expression of culture" (Cabral, *Return to the Source*, 1973: 43).

Elsewhere, Cabral elaborated on his characterization of imperialism:

> Where colonization on the whole blocked the historical process of the development of the subjected peoples or else eliminated them radically or progressively, imperialist capital imposed new types of relationships on indigenous society, the structure of which became more complex and it stirred up, fomented, poisoned or resolved contradictions and social conflicts; it introduced together with money and the development of internal and external markets, new elements in the economy, it brought about the birth of new nations from human groups or from peoples who were at different stages of historical development. (Cabral, *Return to the Source*, 1973: 58)

Colonialism thus limits development, whereas imperialism is accompanied by the introduction and expansion of capitalism as well as new relations of production, which in turn stir up conflict and class struggle.

Cabral saw imperialism as fulfilling a particular function within capitalism. Its historical mission involves speeding up development of the productive forces of society, sharpening class differences as the bourgeoisie evolves, intensifying the class struggle, and raising the standard of living. Imperialism in the Portuguese colonies of Africa has not yet fulfilled this mission, however (Cabral, "The Weapon of Theory," in *Unity and Struggle*, 1979: pp. 127–128).

There are two principal impacts of imperialism: direct domination through classical colonialism, in which administrative agents and police dominate the people, and indirect domination through neocolonialism, in which indigenous elements wield power (Cabral, *Revolution in Guinea*, 1969: 80–81; and Cabral, *Unity and Struggle*, 1979: 127–129).

How then could Africans confront Portuguese colonialism and imperialism? Cabral suggested three courses of action. One involved a change in the position of the Portuguese government. Another was pressure through the United Nations. And finally, there was the struggle by the people using their own means and resorting to violence. All approaches were attempted. Ultimately, it was through a people's struggle that imperialism was weakened and through the inevitable collapse of the Portuguese dictatorship that formal independence was recognized. The United Nations, through a series of resolutions, was able to mobilize international sentiment in favor of the African revolutionaries (Cabral, *Return to the Source*, 1973: 20).

McCulloch (1983: 123) believed that Cabral's description of colonialism and imperialism is "far closer to the reality of the past two decades and it is far more subtle in account for the changes which have subsequently become obvious in social structure and economic formations than anything suggested in the writings of his contemporaries." Hobson, Hilferding, Lenin, and Luxemburg offered Eurocentric theories of imperialism based on the European experience; Cabral presented a new approach to imperialism by emphasizing "the age of rationalized imperialism." The experience of Cabral illustrates the strengths and weaknesses of liberation struggles in the face of the failure of Portuguese colonialism to implement any substantial capitalist development in the African colonies. Cabral was able to relate this failure of Portuguese colonialism to the conditions of his struggle and to find a correct revolutionary strategy. McCulloch suggested that two lessons stand out in Cabral's interpretation: economic and political control are not one and the same, and the absence of capitalist penetration can lead to as negative an impact as the consequences of capital. However, he also believed that Cabral overlooked the connection between neocolonial social structures and the interests of international capital:

> This weakness is expressed in the form of a paradox: on the one hand, Cabral argues that, because of the contradictions inherent in imperialism, the evolution of capitalism has led directly to the growth of African nationalism; yet, counterbalanced against this, he also presumes that neocolonialism is a necessary and logical outgrowth of classical colonialism. Therefore imperialism is simultaneously highly adaptive to change and self-destructive. This leaves unanswered the most important question as to how and under what specific conditions antinationalist movements can avoid the trap of neocolonial dependence. (McCulloch, 1983: 120–121)

Bibliographic Note

For historical details of Portuguese discovery, exploration, and colonization, see the references in Chilcote (1967: 138–139), and for a general background and the best overall coverage of any work, see the studies by Davidson (1988) on Cape Verde and Galli and Jones (1987) on Guinea-Bissau. The PAIGC history of Guinea (PAIGC, 1974B) includes but a sketch of the African resistance to Portuguese colonialism. Chilcote (1967: 93–99) delved through the Portuguese chronicles and records of the colonial experience in order to piece together some of the major historical points of African response to the Portuguese presence in Guinea and Cape Verde. However, Pélissier (1989) provided the best overall synthesis for the 1841–1936 period of Portuguese campaigns and African resistance. McCulloch (1983: 116) identified three major writings by Cabral that deal with imperialism: "Death Pangs of Imperialism" (July 1961); his Havana speech "Weapon of Theory" (January 1966); and his 1971 Helsinki speech. Other writings that focus on colonialism and imperialism include his widely known report under the pseudonym Abel Djassi (1961). Articles on colonialism are in *Partisans* (1962), *Africa Quarterly* (1966), and *Pensamiento Crítico* (1970). Additional material includes Cabral's "O imperialismo" (n.d.), which dwells on direct and indirect forms of imperialism, and his brief piece in *Afrique-Asie* (May 1972). There are a few critical assessments of his theory of colonialism and imperialism, including Ahlsen (1972); McCulloch (1981); Nyang (1976); and Nwagor (1975).

3

Theory of Revolutionary Nationalism and National Liberation

A Guinean scholar has suggested that the four most important sources in the thought of Cabral are a concept of imperialist domination (including direct political domination and neocolonialism); a concept of history in which class struggle is a determinant force; a concept of the petty bourgeoisie as decisive in the transformation of relations of production and the political conduct of the African revolution; and a concept of a national liberation struggle in a cultural context (Lopes, 1982: 126–127, and 1987B: 52). The first three of these concepts are the focus of other chapters, but here I draw out the essence of Cabral's thinking on nationalism and national liberation, with attention to the notion of culture.

Nationalism and Revolutionary Nationalism

Nationalism is understood in a variety of ways. In general, it is a manifestation of commitment to a particular community, usually a nation-state. Patriotism involves allegiance to symbols of the past such as the flag, anthem, heroes, and language, but nationalism has a broader scope. In an exhaustive probe of definition and typology, Anthony Smith in his *Theories of Nationalism* (1983) distinguished between nationalism and national sentiment, on the one hand, and nation and nation-state, on the other. A comprehensive search of the literature thus provides little consensus over the meaning of nationalism, whether the term implies a devotion to one's nation, a set of aspirations for independence and unity of the nation, a form of socialism based on the nationalization of private or foreign capital, or whatever. The concepts of nation, nationality, and nationalism have different and confusing meanings in Europe and elsewhere. Sometimes the terms nation, nationality, people, and nation-state are taken as synonyms or to mean different things in different situations.

Lenin considered nationalism "a broad and very deep ideological current."

Accepting this view, Horace Davis in his *Nationalism and Socialism* (1967) suggested that nationalism is both a negative and a positive force—negative in obscuring "some of history's greatest crimes" and positive in giving impetus to progressive movements. Davis believed that for Marx, nationalism was "the necessary condition and prerequisite for the true internationalism which he envisaged for the future" (p. 6). Marx and Engels, he argued, based their internationalism on nations, but were convinced that nations had to pass through a stage of capitalism before reaching socialism. They recognized that some nations were stronger than others, and believed for some years that imperialism, despite its devastation, would bring capitalist development in its wake. They also distinguished between nation, in the sense of a people of a sovereign state, and nationality, for those who have a common language and background but not a state and thus are without history. They preferred the former terminology and believed that the struggle of the proletariat could be organized on a national basis, not that of nationality. They also were interested in the bourgeoisie as a progressive force in many countries in Europe. The working class could support this national bourgeoisie in its struggle against imperialism, and when the workers became strong enough, they would take the lead.

The Russian Revolution was accompanied by a new emphasis on nationalism as thinking shifted attention from imperialism as set forth by Lenin and Bukharin to the idea that nationalist movements should be supported when they oppose imperialism as well as oppression and exploitation at home. Marxists like Lenin never fully accepted the principle of self-determination, and Rosa Luxemburg rejected it altogether. Stalin, in contrast, gave credence to the idea that socialism could evolve through the revolutionary experience of a single country like Russia—this in opposition to Trotsky, who argued that only a permanent revolution could bring about effective socialism and the fall of the capitalist system.

The idea of self-determination was adopted by African socialists, who were influenced by the European theories before them. Nationalism was integrated into the appeals of Marxists and Marxist-Leninists. Kwame Nkrumah insisted that socialism must relate to the African situation. Sekou Touré believed that a Marxism applied to the mobilization of African peoples was particularly African in conception and reality. These African leaders tied their independence movements to African nationalism.

Two waves of African socialism have appeared since World War II, according to Tetteh A. Kofi. The first wave included Nyerere and Léopold Senghor, whose African socialism was based on a foundation of traditional culture, and Nkrumah and Touré, who attempted to mold an African socialism from some Marxist-Leninist ideas. All of them understood African socialism to be rooted in communal land ownership, egalitarian society, and networks of reciprocal social obligations; their weakness, Kofi believed, was their use of socialism for nationalism and industrialization. He concluded that "the failure of the regimes of African Socialism to achieve a successful socialist transformation of the African communalistic mode of production was due to their rejection of class antagonisms in social transformation" (Kofi, 1981: 856). John Saul argued that the failure of these regimes was due to their Africanization of existing colonial structures, external dependence, and the emergence of a petty-bourgeois hierarchy that controls the state, usually through a single party and a vague ideology of nationalism. Consequently, development is impeded (Saul, 1973: 303).

The second wave of socialist ideology in Africa was represented by the armed struggle of Lusophone countries to liberate themselves from Portuguese colonialism. Their struggle opposed imperialism, and their ideology was more clearly Marxist-Leninist: "It was Cabral more than Nkrumah or Touré or any other African leader who concretized African realities into the framework of Marxism-Leninism. Cabral developed not only the theory and tactics of wars of liberation from colonial rule but also was the one who looked beyond the seizure of power" (Kofi, 1981: 856). In contrast to the earlier forms of African socialism, Saul referred to the more militant movements of Cabral and others as embracing "revolutionary" or "insurgent" nationalism (Saul, 1983: 303). Basil Davidson (1973D: 284) also characterized Cabral's nationalism as revolutionary: "His work and thought have taken shape at a time when the reformist nationalism of the black world is giving way, through sheer incapacity, to a revolutionary nationalism." This notion of revolutionary nationalism can be understood through examination of Cabral's writing and, in particular, several important themes.

That the struggle against colonialism and imperialism is found in cultural reality constitutes an initial theme. Lopes has reminded us that Cabral proved that revolutionary practice was not possible without recognizing the reality of a social formation through the elaboration of a theory adapted to reality (Lopes, 1982: 101). Cabral argued that this reality "is dictated by our economic condition, by our situation of economic underdevelopment" (Cabral, "Party Principles and Political Practice," in *Unity and Struggle*, 1979: 57). This relationship between culture and the economic condition gives rise to national liberation as an act of culture. Culture thus serves as an element of resistance to foreign domination: "Culture is the vigorous manifestation, on the ideological or idealist level, of the material and historical reality of the society that is dominated or to be dominated" (Cabral, "National Liberation and Culture," in *Unity and Struggle*, 1979: 141).

A second theme in the discourse on revolutionary nationalism emerges in the belief that culture is part of the history of people and the daily struggles of life. Unaffected by class and individual interests, it is not independent of people's economic and political life. According to Opoku (1978: 55): "Culture . . . grows and stagnates with the growth and stagnation of the whole society." Cabral stressed this linking of culture and society, and had a materialist concept of culture: "Culture has a material basis at the level of the forces of production and of the mode of production. It is rooted in the milieu's material reality where it develops and reflects the organic nature of society" (Cabral, "National Liberation and Culture" in *Unity and Culture*, 1979: 140–141).

Finally, Cabral envisaged culture as evolving on four levels: the development of a popular culture, comprising all positive values of the indigenous peoples; the development of a national culture, drawn from history and the successes of the liberation struggle itself; the development of a scientific culture, based on the technological needs for progress; and finally, the development of a universal culture, premised on the striving for humanism, solidarity, and respect for people (Cabral, *Return to the Source*, 1973: 55).

Another theme relates to the duality between the culture imposed by Portuguese colonialism and the traditional culture (Andrade and França, 1977: 6). This duality is suggested in the poetry of Cabral in which he found "harmony" between the expression of the poet and the action of the militant. Here Cabral was able to base his pedagogy of national liberation on the double plane of politics and culture and the struggle for a reafricanization. The national liberation movement also draws upon the cultural resistance that permeated past and present society—its superstitions, religious order, family customs, rituals, and beliefs that Africans held in the face of colonialism (Andrade and França, 1977: 12).

Cabral defined cultural resistance at many levels: a popular culture developed through positive values; a national culture based on history and the successes of struggle, political and moral conscience of the people and patriotism, and dedicated to sacrifice and the cause of independence, justice, and progress; a scientific and technological culture compatible with the needs of progress; and a universal culture tending toward a progressive integration in the present world and the elevation of sentiments of humanism and solidarity. He felt that the realization of these objectives would make possible the armed liberation struggle within the concrete conditions of African life while confronting imperialism (Andrade and França, 1977: 14).

Although Portugal faced the power of the imperialist nations and was dependent on them for its survival, it was able to maintain its colonies in Africa until, ultimately, the dependent peoples of Africa awakened and initiated the liberation struggle against imperialism:

> There can be no doubt that, even more than the class struggle in the capitalist countries and the antagonism between these countries and the socialist world, the liberation struggle of the colonial peoples is the essential characteristic, and we would say the prime motive force, of the advance of history in our times: and it is to this struggle, to this conflict on three continents that our national liberation struggle against

Portuguese colonialism is linked. (Speech to the Third Conference of the African Peoples, Cairo, March 25–31, 1961, in Cabral, *Revolution in Guinea*, 1969: 14)

Resistance shapes a fourth theme in Cabral's writings on revolutionary nationalism. Imperialism, accompanied by cultural oppression, may lead to the destruction of the culture of dominated peoples, thereby necessitating their resistance to colonial and foreign domination. Cabral understood the long tradition of resistance in Africa and its emergence in Guinea-Bissau as a response to Portuguese colonialism carried on from the early appearance of Portuguese traders and settlers to the Portuguese pacification campaigns. This resistance assumed the form of overt spontaneous uprisings as well as passive resistance such as tax evasion, reduction in cash-crop production, and so on. Thus, national liberation struggles often are preceded by cultural resistance:

> The foundation of national liberation lies in the inalienable right of every people to have their own history. . . . The aim of national liberation is therefore to regain this right, usurped by imperialist domination, namely: the liberation of productive forces and consequently of the ability freely to determine the mode of production most appropriate to the evolution of the liberated people, necessarily opens up new prospects for the cultural process of the society in question, by returning to it all its capacity to create progress. (Cabral, *Unity and Struggle*, 1979: 143)

National liberation is an act of culture—a response to outside domination and to the material conditions of life. The important question for Cabral was transforming a contentious nationalism into a revolutionary nationalism in order to overcome colonialism and establish its own state (Bragança, 1976: 12).

National Liberation Struggle

Revolutionary nationalism directly impacts the national liberation struggle in at least five ways in the thought of Cabral. First, this struggle involves two phases, one against the Portuguese ruling colonialist classes, and another against the internal forces that preclude the people attaining liberty, independence, and justice (Cabral, *Unity and Struggle*, 1979: 79). This struggle involves "cultural combat" against colonial domination, and is based on the culture of the rural and urban working masses as well as the revolutionary fraction of the petty bourgeoisie. Culture assumes importance in the national liberation movement, which must "be able to preserve the positive cultural values of every well-defined group, of every category, and to achieve the confluence of these values in the service of the struggle, giving it a new dimension—the national dimension" (p. 48). Thus, the values of these people must be preserved and developed within a national context; this promotes unity and harmony among the various groups and allows for identification with common objectives in the pursuit of liberty and progress.

Second, an elaboration of a theory of national liberation, which Nyang (1976) synthesized from the writings of Cabral, relates to culture, regained history, the embryonic class structure, and neocolonialism. Culture is a weapon against the imperialist power—popular culture serves the struggle for freedom and liberation, and national culture serves the new nations through political and moral awareness and consciousness. Culture thus becomes the instrument through which people reclaim their history and as such it is a function of history and the development of the productive forces of a society. Cabral did not emphasize racial determinants of culture, as do the advocates of negritude, but he saw culture as independent of race. Instead Cabral emphasized the class character of culture as determined by the uneven development of culture in society. Differences in levels of culture explain why some classes and individuals favor or oppose the liberation movement or why some are conscious of problems and are willing to accept change and progress whereas others remain insensitive to the vicissitudes of society. This is true, for example, of ethnic groups with a vertical social structure, such as the Fula ruling class.

Cabral analyzed the relationship of the African petty bourgeoisie and the African masses, identifying the contradictions in both groups but arguing for the need to counterpose African culture against European culture in the struggle against colonialism, but not as an argument in favor of the uniqueness of black culture. The petty bourgeoisie is paradoxical in its ambivalent orientations, yet it is the main hope for mobilizing and organizing the masses because colonialism did not allow the development of a national bourgeoisie or a vanguard working class; here Cabral opposed Fanon's advocacy of the peasantry as the revolutionary class and the lumpenproletariat (Cabral called them the "declassé") as an ally of the peasantry in the struggle against colonialism, and he was unaccepting of the Marxian notion that the proletariat is necessary to lead the class struggle. In this sense, the term nation-class comes into play as a sociopolitical and socioeconomic category so that a broad alliance of alienated classes and forces can join together to oppose the systematic manipulation of African history brought about by colonialism. National liberation is seen in terms of struggle between the nation-class and the colonial state-class. Nyang (1976: 19) found this concept to be "post-Marxist in the sense that he creates a nation class out of the diverse African groups who were willy-nilly brought under one imperial roof." The liberation struggle thus is a national task of all groups led by a petty bourgeoisie, fortified by its education, which can tend to turn toward reafricanization and revolution or away from the struggle to enhance its own interests and bourgeoisification.

Third, a number of principles must be observed in a national liberation struggle, in Cabral's view. Thus, national liberation is a political struggle, its strategy determined by conditions in the colony. A national liberation struggle also needs a strong, well-organized party with a politically educated leadership to lead a broad alliance comprising a majority of the African population. Further, the struggle is internal, initially within the countryside and gravitating to the urban centers. The struggle also is against the colonial policymakers and their system, not against the people of the metropole.

Cabral suggested some of these principles in a series of lectures to party cadres in November 1969 (Cabral, *Unity and Struggle*, 1979). Fundamentally, the struggle must evolve around unity and struggle: "Those who had the idea of unity, because union makes for strength, put the question of unity into the spirit and letter of our struggle, because they knew that there was much division in our midst" (p. 30). Additionally, the struggle must relate to reality: "Man is part of reality, reality exists independently of man's will. To the extent to which he acquires consciousness of reality, to the extent in which reality influences his consciousness, or creates his consciousness, man can acquire the potential to transform reality, little by little" (p. 44–45). The leadership must be one and united under the party: "The leadership of the party is the strength of our people. . . .We cannot allow any division among us. When we speak of the higher leadership of the Party, we are speaking of leadership at any echelon" (p. 74). The struggle will be of the people, by the people, and for the people: "A basic principle for our struggle is that it is the struggle of our people, and that it is our people who must wage it, and its result is for our people" (p. 75). Finally, there must be independence in thought and in action: "Our party and its leadership should be independent in its way of tackling questions and of answering them, and in its action inside or outside our land" (p. 79).

This led Cabral to the "universal scientific laws of revolution." In agricultural countries, the struggle takes place in the countryside where peasants can be mobilized: "Maybe you begin in the towns, but you recognize that this is not good. You pass to the countryside to mobilize the peasants. You recognize that the peasants are very difficult to mobilize under certain conditions, but you launch the armed struggle and step by step you approach the towns in order to finish the colonists" (Cabral, "Connecting the Struggle," in *Return to the Source*, 1973: 87–89). Further, the colonial power first disperses its forces in order to control a country, but when national forces attack, the colonial power must concentrate, leaving vast areas in control of the national forces, which can administer and create new structures. Finally, depending on the process of development and on political aims, including ideological commitment oriented to ridding certain conditions—for example exploitation—it is possible to jump from feudal or semifeudal tribal societies to socialism (pp. 87–89).

Fourth, the movement of national liberation is born precisely in a nationalist conception. Cabral believed that the existence of diverse ethnic groups impeded the formation of a national conscience, and therefore it was necessary to mobilize all elements of the population without ethnic or class distinction. The result was essentially a peasant movement led by the petty bourgeoisie with working-class elements in support. Andrade (1980: 144, 145, 147) analyzed this process as completely altering the social forces. Lopes (1982: 106–109) explained this change in several ways. First, imperialism must be ended and socialism consolidated without reverting to imperialist domination through neocolonialism and capitalism, for Cabral had realized that there were only two courses in the Portuguese situation— return to imperialist domination under colonialism, neocolonialism, and capitalism, or take the path of socialism. Second, all political struggles are class struggles to achieve economic emancipation. Third, the strongest force would consist of the petty bourgeoisie and salaried workers who have a revolutionary conscience. The petty bourgeoisie would not own the means of production, which are indirectly controlled by the state. Thus an ambivalence evolves as the state represents the interests of a class and indirectly controls the means of production. This could only be resolved by having the petty bourgeoisie "commit suicide" in the sense that it renounce its desire to control the means of production.

Fifth, Cabral recognized that culture is but a reflection of the level of productive forces and mode of production of any society. Thus, the chief goal of the liberation movement is not only national independence and the crushing of colonialism, but the "complete liberation of the productive forces and the construction of economic, social and cultural progress of the people" (Cabral, *Unity and Struggle*, 1979: 52). Armed struggle will bring about this liberation, but armed struggle necessitates a strong, disciplined political organization. The features of the liberation struggle include "the practice of democracy, of criticism and self-criticism, the increasing responsibility of populations for the direction of their lives, literacy work, creation of schools and health services, training of cadres from peasant and worker backgrounds— and many other achievements." In this way "the armed liberation struggle is not only a product of culture but also a determinant of culture" (p. 54).

The armed struggle showed Cabral the need to minimize casualties rather than maximize destruction of the enemy. Military actions must be carefully coordinated with political work, and the military wing of the party (army, militia, and guerrilla units) must remain under the control of the political leadership. More difficult than liberating areas was their administration and development. Nyang (1976) demonstrated that Cabral's theory of armed struggle did not necessarily imply that armed struggle was the weapon essential in the liberation. Further, military liberation was not essential to national liberation. (This explains the lengths to which Cabral went to communicate to the Portuguese his goals, but these were not viewed as realistic at the time by the Portuguese.) If armed struggle were the only way for Guineans to reclaim their history (p. 8), it would involve both political and military effort; the political struggle lays the conscious basis and will to move forward, and the social struggle implies the protection and defense of basic rights—the provision of needs for those who struggle militarily for liberation of the country. Thus, Cabral did not believe in important ideas from outside, so internal conditions determined the course of the armed struggle. Foco theory (relating to the center of guerrilla operations rather than the traditional military base) was not the concern here, but in liberated areas it was necessary to begin the process of dealing with the social, political, and economic needs of people. Cabral believed that armed struggle must be fought within the country to be liberated, and that guerrilla units should be given autonomy to control their own resources so as to work more efficiently.

The revolutionary struggle relates to certain economic, cultural, social, political, and geographic conditions. In Guinea-Bissau, these conditions may differ from those in other countries. For example, although Cabral recognized the guerrilla manuals of Mao and Ché Guevara, he proclaimed that because there were no mountains in his country, "the mountains are the people." Social structure and classes were well defined in Vietnam, but there was no proletariat or national bourgeoisie in Guinea-Bissau. In addition, the political struggle must be dialectically combined with the armed struggle, not separate from it. Finally, there must be a broad front of unity, under the aegis of the party and led by a united vanguard, in the process of national liberation. There are two situations in the struggle—the colonial and the neocolonial. In the former, a national solution is necessary: "the national class fights the repressive forces of the bourgeoisie of the colonizing country . . . the nation gains its independence and theoretically adopts the economic structure it finds most attractive." The neocolonial situation necessitates a socialist solution "in which the class of workers and its allies fight simultaneously the imperialist bourgeoisie and the native ruling class" in a struggle to destroy "the capitalist structure implanted in the national soil by imperialism" (Cabral, *Unity and Struggle*, 1979: 133).

Assessments

Scholars and critics have written more on Cabral's theory of revolutionary nationalism and the liberation struggle than on any other topic in reference to Guinea and Cape Verde. McCulloch (1983: 35) affirmed that: "In 1956 as now Guiné had virtually no working class, no industry, no mountains for a guerrilla force in which to hide and only a handful of western education intellectuals. Despite these handicaps, the PAIGC was probably the most successful of all the nationalist liberation movements of the decade." Nyang (1976: 11) went further by proclaiming that "Guineans are the first Africans to truly liberate themselves." Beyond these statements of approbation, other insights and understandings can be drawn from scholars and journalists who have studied Guinea and Cape Verde at close hand.

Carlos Lopes, for instance, has written about the importance of focusing on the concept of nation and the impact of national integration on the process of state building. Although Cabral believed that national integration would serve to break down ethnic differences, Lopes warned that although integration could occur through phases of consolidation, assimilation, and national unification, the raising of national consciousness could lead to a contradictory outcome by inciting ethnic group separatism. To avoid this possibility, Cabral believed that awareness of historical reality would strengthen the national liberation movement in its struggle against imperialism (Lopes, 1983; 1987B: 127ff). Carlos Lopes also reminded us of Cabral's notion of nation-class as a concept that "encapsulates African resistance as a whole to the colonial state" so that class contradictions in African society become secondary to the principal contradiction between the Guinean nation and colonial state. Theoretically, the idea of the Guinean nation is founded on the thought of the national liberation movement and on the cultural, political, social, and economic reality of the ethnic groups in the social formation (Lopes, 1987B: 13–14).

Delving into "the cultural problematic," Lopes argues that for Cabral cultural resistance and the ideological superstructure of the population are intimately linked by a modern nationalism. Culture is a form of historical resistance to foreign penetration, and the struggle of national liberation opposes the historical negation imposed by colonial occupation. Culture has a class dimension, reflected in the identity crisis of the African petty bourgeoisie, who is judged on the one hand as superior to the people because of assimilation into the culture of the colonizer, and on the other is marginalized and alienated by the European colonizer. Within this class, however, there may be consciousness of the nation, a national identity, and a propensity toward reafricanization that can be realized through armed struggle. Thus, the national liberation movement is the means for affirming a national culture, once colonialism is defeated (Lopes, 1984: 77–79).

Enthusiasm for the thinking of Cabral has been expressed by Jinadu (1978: 135) who agreed that "material modes of production are best viewed in the larger context of culture as a way of life, to which reference can then be made with regard to institutional design." Lyon (1980: 162) provided analysis supporting Cabral's notion that colonial rule "incited ethnic antagonism rather than inherent cultural and political differences." Lyon delved into basic ethnic differences that impacted the liberation struggle and persisted in the period after independence. That many Fula and Manjaco people remained outside the liberation struggle partially explained their resistance to PAIGC rule after 1974. He suggested that in the postindependence phase of national liberation the PAIGC was unable to transcend nationalism and achieve the ethnic unity Cabral felt was necessary. In fact, Lyon affirmed that Cabral and the PAIGC offered no real answer to the question how this objective could be achieved (p. 166). Saul (1973) identified Cabral's experience as counter to the more commonplace trend throughout Africa during the 1950s and 1960s when neocolonialism established itself, in the name of nationalism and socialism, as a way of Africanizing the former colonial structures to stifle development rather than liberate productive forces and human energies. Cabral understood that both in colonialism and neocolonialism the character of imperialism tends to persist. Only when national liberation frees the productive forces from all foreign domination can the normal development of a people occur. Another analysis (IDAC, Institute of Cultural Action: 1976) explained how for Cabral the people are the only entity that is able to preserve and create culture, that is to make history by making the transition from cultural resistance to new forms of struggle (political, economic, and military).

Davidson showed how in the face of a declining reformist nationalism throughout the world, Cabral was able to push a revolutionary nationalism in which colonized peoples must overcome their allegiance to the history of others, find their own history, and evolve their own development. Quoting Cabral, Davidson (1974C: 300) characterized a true liberation as

> a veritable forced march on the road of cultural progress [involving] the practice of democracy, criticism and self-criticism, the growing responsibility of populations in the management of their life, the learning of literacy, the creation of schools and medical services, the formation of cadres who come from peasant and worker backgrounds . . . then we see that armed struggle for liberation isn't only a cultural fact but also a factor of culture.

Mesquitela Lima (1980) elaborated on the notion of "revolutionary culture" as it evolved in the thought of Cabral and suggested that all struggle is born within a specific cultural and social situation in which every person wants to be free. Thus when Cabral affirms that the liberation struggle is an act of culture, his notion of culture has profound meaning. Paulo Freire (1978: 14) extended this analysis by relating the process of decolonizing and reafricanizing the minds of the people to the need for a radical transformation of the educational system inherited from the colonizers involving

> the actual negation of every authentic representation of national peoples—their history, their culture, their language. The history of those colonized was thought to have begun with the civilizing presence of the colonizers. The culture of the colonized was a reflection of their barbaric way of seeing the world. Culture belonged only to the colonizers.

Cabral's thinking is not without criticism, however. Chabal (1981: 50–

51) believed that Cabral wrote systematically and in detail only on the subject of culture and national liberation. Despite his enthusiasm for Cabral and his contributions, McCulloch (1983: 91) wrote that

> it is ironic that Cabral's writings on culture and identity should be so obviously flawed without those flaws surfacing in his theory of class. The fact that these errors can co-exist with his compelling class analysis of Guiné indicates that the question of identity and culture are not critical to his theory in the way that Cabral, and his predecessors, thought them to be. In a practical sense these issues have been superseded in Cabral's work.

Bibliographic Notes

Cabral's writings on nationalism and national liberation are extensive, including an early assessment, *Rapport général sur la lutte de libération nationale* (July 1961); *Palavras de ordem gerais* (1965); his Havana speech of January 1966; the Seminário de Quadros, November 19–24, 1969; excerpts from *Nô Pintcha*, Nos. 391–407 (1977), Nos. 439–476 (1978), and Nos. 575–579 (1979); his UNESCO speech in Paris in July 1972; and the Lincoln University speech in 1972. Specifically related to the concepts of nationalism and revolutionary nationalism are writings by Lopes (1983); Davidson (1983, 1984, 1986); Obichere (1973); and Zartman (1968). Analyses on the concept and practice of national liberation include Chabal (1981B); Chaliand (1964, 1967A, 1969); Ehnmark and Hermasson (1973); Emília (1975); Escobar et al. (1976); Faber and Mettas (1962); Gjerstad and Sarrazin (1975); Houser (1975); Ledda (1967, 1970); Lobban (1973, 1974); Lopes (1987B); Lyon (1980); Martíchine (1981); Melo et al. (1974); Moita (1983); OSPAAL (1966); Pierson-Mathy (1980); Olivio Pires (1983); Urdang (1979); Whitaker (1970); Woollacott (1983); and Zeigler (1983A, 1983B). For poems of the resistance, see Dickinson (1980). Reports and analyses of the armed struggle include Afrique-Asie (1974); Agarychev (1970); Andrade (1985); Andrade and Boal (1974); Andreassen and Dahl (1971); the memoirs of Luís Cabral (1984); Carlos Cardoso (1984); Cornwall (1972); Crimi and Lucas (1970); Davidson (1969, 1970, 1974A, 1974B, 1975); Goldfield (1973); Mendy (1967); Nzongola-Ntalaja (1983); and Pinto (1972). For articles on the role of culture and national liberation, see Alegre (1983); Almeyra (1978); Andrade (1983A); Andrade and França (1977). On the idea of culture in the thought of Cabral after independence, see Arruda (1978); Maria Dulce Almada Duarte (1978, 1983); Glisenti (1983); Houtart and Lemercinier (1983); Hubbard (1973); Hunt (1985); Jinadu (1978); Lima (1980); Marton (1980, 1982); Morgado (1974); Opoku (1978).

4

Theory of Class and Class Struggle

Cabral's theory of class and class struggle was particularly relevant to his revolutionary struggle but also has implications for struggle elsewhere. With dialectical method as the basis of his analysis, Cabral suggested categories of class and an approach to the study of class struggle: "Class and class struggle are themselves the result of the development of productive forces in conjunction with the system of ownership of the means of production" (Cabral, *Unity and Struggle*, 1979: 125). However, Cabral questioned the assumption of European Marxists that class struggle is the sole determinant in the evolution of history. To accept such a proposition, he argued, would place outside of history the many human groups dependent on nomadic and sedentary agriculture—especially in Africa, Asia, and Latin America—at a time they were also subject to imperialism. There is history for people who have not experienced class struggle, and history has continuity after the disappearance of class struggle and classes: "Man will outlive classes and will continue to produce and to make history, since he can never free himself from the burden of his needs, of hand and brain, which are the basis of the development of productive forces" (p. 125). Thus, before and after the class struggle some other motive force exists and that is the mode of production, seen as the level of productive forces and the system of ownership; the mode of production thus is the motive force of history: "The level of productive forces, the essential determinant of the content and form of class struggle, is the true and permanent motive force of history" (p. 125).

Cabral was particularly concerned about identifying various social classes and assessing their revolutionary potential. Marx had provided an in-depth analysis of social divisions in mid-nineteenth-century France. In *Class Struggles in France* (1850) and *Eighteenth Brumaire* (1852), Marx recognized many classes in an emerging society that had yet to mature into full-blown capitalists. The class struggle was not limited to a clearly defined ruling bourgeoisie and an exploited proletariat, and other classes had to be considered in a class analysis of French society. For Cabral, the situation in Guinea-

Bissau and Cape Verde was radically different. Colonialism and imperialism had left their mark, but capitalism was barely present, especially in Guinea-Bissau. Given this state of underdevelopment, the bourgeoisie was recognizable in the colonial administration and in small urban and rural bourgeois elements, and a small proletariat was found among disparate groups of semiskilled and skilled workers, generally in Bissau.

Conceptions of Class and Class Struggle

A conception of class and class struggle emerges rather prominently in a series of Cabral's writings. The elements of this conception are analyzed in five steps by examining Cabral's thinking in chronological order from 1964 until 1972.

Cabral's early elaboration appears in "Brief Analysis of the Social Structure in Guinea," presented at a seminar in the Frantz Franon Center in Milán in May 1964 (Cabral, *Revolution in Guinea*, 1969, 1972: 56–75). Cabral showed that the social situation differs in rural and urban areas. Two groups predominated in rural areas: the Fulas, who were semifeudal and Moslem with a hierarchical structure; and the Balantas, who were animist with a horizontal structure lacking state organization. The Fulas were stratified into chiefs and nobles at the top, artisans and itinerant traders below them, and peasants, who were required to work for the chiefs for part of the year and had no rights, at the bottom. In contrast, the Balantas lacked stratification. There was a council of elders that made decisions, property belonged to the village, and each family worked a plot of land for subsistence. There were also small African farm owners—a small group active in the liberation struggle. Europeans were distinguishable from Africans in the towns, the former classified along lines similar to their counterparts in Portugal and comprising high officials and managers of enterprises, middle officials, small European traders, members of the liberal professions, and skilled workers. The Africans included a petty bourgeois of higher and middle officials, members of liberal professions, petty officials employed in commerce, others in commerce working without contract, and some small farmers; a group of wage earners employed in commerce, including dockworkers, boat people, and domestic servants; and a group of déclassés of beggars, prostitutes, and unemployed young people connected to the petty bourgeoisie and workers' families. The African petty bourgeoisie divided into three groups: one group of higher officials and some members of liberal professions being compromised with colonialism, another with nationalist sentiments favorable to national liberation, and a third between these two groups that was indecisive. The majority of wage earners were committed to the revolution, although they tended to defend their own material interests. Many of the déclassé beggars and prostitutes worked for the Portuguese police, but the younger element of déclassés tended to support the revolution. The liberation struggle counted on the peasantry, especially the Balantas who historically had been more inclined to resist the Portuguese; the peasantry, however, was a "physical force" and not a "revolutionary force": "it is almost the whole of the population, it controls the nation's wealth, it is the peasantry which produces; but we know from experience what trouble we had convincing the peasantry to fight" (p. 61).

Cabral also focused on class and class struggle in perhaps his most important speech, delivered to the First Solidarity Conference of the Peoples of Africa, Asia and Latin America in Havana on January 6, 1966 (Cabral, "The Weapon of Theory," in *Unity and Struggle*, 1979: 119–137). He explained that the phenomenon of class evolves from the level of the productive forces and system of ownership of means of production in a deliberate and uneven but progressive and continuous process. Imperialism may serve to accelerate this process, but in Guinea capitalism under Portuguese rule had not fulfilled its historical mission of accumulation so that the forces of production had not achieved a high level of development nor allowed a national bourgeoisie or fully developed working class to evolve. In this situation, a class analysis necessarily must focus on the role of the petty bourgeoisie, which will be "the only social stratum capable both of having consciousness . . . of the reality of imperialist domination and of handling the State apparatus inherited from that domination" (p. 134). The inevitability of this situation, Cabral said, is "yet another weakness of the national liberation movement" (p. 135). Because of its political consciousness and education, the "revolutionary" sector of the petty bourgeoisie assumes the leadership of the struggle against foreign domination. This role must be shared with the enlightened sectors of workers and some elements of "the national pseudo-bourgeoisie inspired by patriotic sentiment" (p. 135). The petty bourgeoisie, however, is a service class not directly involved in the process of production. Historically, it has not held political power because the foundation of the state is in the economic capacity of the ruling class. In the colonial or neocolonial society that capacity is found within imperialist capital and the domestic class of workers. Thus the petty bourgeoisie must not allow itself to transform into a pseudonational bourgeoisie. Instead, it must struggle against the temptation to become bourgeois, join with the revolution, and as a class it must "be capable of commiting suicide as a class, to be restored to life in the condition of a revolutionary worker completely identified with the deepest aspirations of the people." Herein is the dilemma of the petty bourgeoisie in the liberation struggle: "to betray the revolution or commit suicide as a class" (p. 136).

A third effort at delineating Cabral's perspective on class is drawn from two discussions with party cadres—one from his intervention in a meeting of party cadres on July 20, 1968 (Cabral, *A arma da teoria*, 1977: 13–15), and the other from the first of a series of lectures in creole before PAIGC cadres, on November 19–24, 1969 (Cabral, "Party Principles and Political Practice," in *Unity and Struggle*, 1979: 28–44). Emphasizing division and contradiction in Guinean society, Cabral stressed the need for unity and struggle against the bourgeois colonialists in his lectures before party cadres. His attention focused on three "categories" of persons within the petty bourgeoisie: a small but powerful group that favored the colonialists; another group that favored liberation but was unable to commit to the struggle; and a third group that is ready to die for the liberation cause. He also identified a majority of salaried workers in sympathy with the struggle, including carpenters, masons, mechanics, and drivers. Additionally, there were the idle persons who collaborated with the secret police, as well as the unemployed youth who were in contact with the colonialists but were ready to join the struggle. Finally, there were the peasants, including the Balanta, who had no state, and the Fula and Manjaco, who were vertically structured into a ruling class of chiefs and religious leaders, an artisan class, and a peasant class.

Cabral also analyzed social classes in the urban areas and in the countryside of Cape Verde; further he distinguished between islands with and without agriculture as well as islands of large and small property owners. The principal classes comprised large property owners, small property owners, and renters or sharecroppers. Descendants of the large property owners, known as *morgados*, inherited the lands granted to Europeans and progressively lost many of their lands and influence under the colonial consolidation of the Salazar regime. In the face of the colonial banks, only a small number of *morgados* survived, being for the most part the white and mestizo descendants of the old European property owners and subservient to the colonial regime. (See Carreira [1977] for a historical analysis of landowners and slaves, their miscegenation, and ensuing social class formation and emigration.) Many merchants also owned agricultural properties and tended to practice usury, their commercial life being somewhat insignificant.

Small property owners of one to three hectares of land were numerous and diversified, some living in poverty and others able to sustain themselves. Some favored liberation with hopes of expanding their land, whereas others opposed the liberation struggle, fearing any social and political change and the threat of losing their land; yet a third group was indecisive as to whether to support national liberation. The small property owner in the countryside assumed the behavior of the petty bourgeoisie.

The renter paid a fixed price to the property owner in exchange for the right to cultivate it. Faced often with drought and periodic economic crises, the renter also was vulnerable and consequently favored the liberation struggle. No rural proletariat existed on the Cape Verdes, as salaried rural workers were insufficient to constitute a class of any importance.

Within the urban areas, the social structure divided into a portion of the population tied to the countryside and another portion with origins in Europe. A social pyramid existed within the cities, composed from top down of high European functionaries, high Cape Verdean functionaries, a small number of relatively wealthy merchants and industrialists, employees in the public and commercial sectors, salaried workers, and unemployed people. Except for the Europeans, one could not speak of a bourgeoisie in the urban areas. The Cape Verdean functionaries did not possess capital, and, given their unproductive status, they tended to integrate into the petty bourgeoisie. Within the colonial administration only a few Europeans were sympathetic to nationalist sentiments, the Cape Verdean functionaries were inclined to sympathize, and the petty bourgeoisie remained ambiguous over its nationalist sentiments. The small group of merchants and industrialists really did not constitute a class; their capital was not derived from local sources but was dependent on the metropolitan bourgeoisie. Although their life-style was bourgeois, they did not constitute a "national bourgeoisie," but "represented an intrusion of the Portuguese bourgeoisie in the archipelago, under the direction of autonomous elements" (Cabral, *A arma da teoria*, 1977: 15). Only a handful of persons might have sentiments in favor of national liberation, seeing in that outcome the possibility of breaking their dependence and developing their own property in realization of their bourgeois ambitions.

The dominant class was the colonial class, comprising a bourgeoisie residing within Portugal with its representatives controlling the repressive apparatus of the colonial state within the archipelago. Thus, according to Cabral, "the social struggle coincided with the national struggle in the Cape Verdes" (Cabral, *A arma da teoria*, 1977: 15) because the overthrow of the colonial state imposed by the Portuguese bourgeoisie necessitated both national and social liberation.

The petty bourgeoisie was composed of the employees of the public and commercial sectors, high school students, and professional people, many of them with popular and mass origins and suffering from colonial oppression and a hierarchy that relegated Cape Verdeans to a status lower than that of Europeans. Two types were evident: a conservative petty bourgeoisie and a rebellious petty bourgeoisie. Within the latter type were revolutionaries and those who identified with the popular masses. No true proletariat existed because there was no sufficiently developed infrastructure for the formation of a working class, although there were salaried workers and employees who were clearly proletarian and also willing to serve the liberation struggle.

A different treatment of class was included in Cabral's speech at Syracuse University on February 20, 1970 (Cabral, "National Liberation and Culture," in *Return to the Source*, 1973: 39–56; Cabral, *Unity and Struggle*, 1979: 138–154). An analysis of social structure helps in understanding the revolutionary potential of the national liberation movement. Culture has a mass character, but it is fragmented and unevenly developed among all sectors of society. For example, culture is more evenly distributed in horizontal social structure, but it is differentiated in vertical society where economic interests and distinctions are apparent. In support of the colonialists are some high officials and intellectuals in the liberal professions, assimilated people, and representatives of the ruling class from rural areas. The petty bourgeoisie, assimilated into the colonial system and somewhat privileged by its position, must integrate itself back into African life through contact with the masses. Thus, in the first phase of the liberation struggle the rural and urban working masses, including the revolutionary wing of the petty bourgeoisie, are ready for "a cultural conversion" or a "reafricanization." The leaders of the liberation movement, drawn from the petty bourgeois intellectuals or clerks or from the urban workers, wage earners, and chauffeurs, must live with the rural peasant population.

Finally, Cabral's speech at Lincoln University on October 15, 1972, also was important (Cabral, "Identity and Dignity in the Context of the National Liberation Struggle," in *Return to the Source*, 1979: 57–69). In the course of two or three generations of colonization, a ruling class of civil servants, merchants, professional people, and urban and rural landowners emerged out of the foreign domination. This ruling class was indispensable to the system of colonial exploitation, yet it stood between the masses of the working class in town and country and a small number of representatives of the foreign ruling class. The "marginal character" of this petty bourgeoisie made them conscious of the need to rediscover their identity and "return to the source," which implied their negation of the culture of the dominant power over that of the dominated people and a commitment to join the liberation struggle. That commitment varied according each of the three factions of the petty bourgeoisie: the minority who depended on the dominant colonial class; the minority who shared in the leadership of the liberation movement; and the majority who were undecided.

Of these five pronouncements, four were presented in international settings, with the Milán talk in 1964 providing detailed urban and rural categories of class and ethnic groups, including emphasis on the petty bourgeoisie and the peasantry in Guinea. Cabral's Havana speech in 1966 also identified major categories of class, emphasized the role of class struggle, and focused on the contradictory role of the petty bourgeoisie in the revolution. The Syracuse speech in 1970 stressed the role of the petty bourgeoisie and workers, but elaborated on the relationship of culture to class and class struggle, and the talk at Lincoln University in 1972 analyzed the impact of colonialism upon the African petty bourgeoisie and the need for this class to rediscover its African roots and commitment to the liberation struggle. In contrast to his analyses before international audiences, which tended toward theoretical, usually abstract, more intellectually appealing, and sometimes schematic presentations, his talks before party cadres delineated a rather exhaustive pattern of class categories illustrated with abundant examples.

Whereas in international situations Cabral tended to examine Guinea, before party cadres he delved into differences in class composition in both Guinea and Cape Verde, comparing and contrasting the two settings in order to expose contradictions between dominant class and the dominated, between urban and rural situations, between ethnic groupings, between workers and peasants, and, in particular, analyzing fractions of the petty bourgeoisie and its role in the revolutionary process. But these differences seem more apparent than real, and one must be impressed with the clarity and concreteness with which he was able to communicate his ideas at both levels as he emphasized the similarity and compatibility of the struggle in Guinea and Cape Verde.

Major Themes

Having identified the major writings and the evolution of his theory, I now rework the discussion around a synthesis of some of the major themes that run through the thinking of Cabral on class and struggle. First, Cabral looked for divisions and contradictions everywhere in society: races, religions, ethnic groups, and social classes were taken into account (see Table 4.1). White European colonialists supported a continued Portuguese presence and domination in the colonies, whereas black Africans tended to support the liberation struggle. Catholics and Protestants generally backed the colonial regime and were supported by some Muslim elements, whereas most Africans of animist persuasion turned to the liberation effort. Among the various tribes in Guinea-Bissau, the Fula and Manjaco were vertically organized in structure with chiefs and religious leaders constituting a sort of ruling class at the top, often imposed by the Portuguese, whereas the Balantas were organized horizontally with autonomous families sharing collectively in the work. The rulers of the Fula and Manjaco were inclined to support the colonialists, while the Balantas could be counted on to support the liberation struggle. Once these contradictions and divisions were apparent, it was possible to organize the liberation struggle around the idea of unity. The principal contradiction lay in the struggle against Portuguese colonialism, and organization to overcome this contradiction would resolve all other contradictions during the struggle.

Second, drawing upon his own experience, Cabral affirmed that revolution cannot be practiced without a revolutionary theory and that the formation of classes and class struggle is dependent on the level of productive forces and ownership over the means of production. The development of the productive forces, he believed, occurs gradually and unevenly but also progressively, and, once a certain level of accumulation is attained, qualitative changes also appear with classes and class struggle. Classes do not appear as a generalized phenomenon. External factors—for example, forms of imperialist domination—may speed up or deter this development. Rapid

Table 4.1 Contradictions in Colonial Portuguese African Society

Contradiction	Portuguese Society	African Society
Race	White Colonizers	Africans
Religion	Catholics and Protestants	Animists
Ethnic Group Support	Fulas, Manjaco indigenous chiefs, Mandinga	Balantas
Class	Large landowners Colonial capitalists	Small proletariat Some rural and urban petty bourgeoisie
	Colonial civil servants	Some African civil servants
	Unemployed and idle (agents for police)	Most peasants

advances may be the consequence of "abrupt transformations" or revolutions. But history does not begin with the appearance of classes and class struggle, for that would place many peoples outside history. The real motor of history therefore is not class struggle but the mode of production, identifiable by the level of productive forces and the system of ownership. History, however, has continuity even after the disappearance of classes and class struggle: "Eternity is not of this world, but man will outlive classes and will continue to produce and to make history, since he can never free himself from the burden of his needs, of hand and brain, which are the basis of the development of productive forces" (Cabral, *Unity and Struggle*, 1979: 125).

Third, history is seen as evolving through at least three stages: (1) a primitive form with a low level of productive forces, no private appropriation of means of production, and, consequently, no class struggle; (2) a more progressive stage characterized by private appropriation of the means of production, conflicts of interest, and the possibility of class struggle; and (3) a higher stage in which a certain level of productive forces is accompanied by the elimination of private appropriation of the means of production, class and class struggle terminate, and new and unknown forces appear. Cabral labeled these stages, respectively (1) communal agricultural and cattle-raising societies in which the social structure is horizontal and without a state; (2) agrarian feudal or assimilated and agro-industrial societies with vertical structure and the presence of a state; and (3) socialist and communist societies in which the state tends to disappear and social structure evolves horizontally. Given the uneven development of societies, these stages may be combined, and thus history need not be viewed exclusively in terms of any single mode of production. Further, no particular sequence of stages is necessary—a leap in the historical process to the creation of socialist societies is possible, but such "progress depends on the specific possibilities for the development of the society's productive forces and is mainly conditional on the nature of the political power ruling that society, that is on the type of State or, if we like, on the nature of the dominant class or classes within society" (Cabral, *Unity and Struggle*, 1979: 126).

Fourth, although identification of classes does not ensure a successful class analysis, it does allow recognition of elements that must be combined in the class struggle, and Cabral did not hesitate to set forth categories of class so as to formulate appropriate strategies in the winning of revolution. A class analysis is possible once capitalism has permitted the development of the productive forces, the maturing of a bourgeoisie, and the intensification of the class struggle. Imperialism and the movement of capital in its last stage affect these conditions and stimulate the development of certain class forces. In most dominated countries, advanced capitalism operates to multiply surplus values. In some cases a local minority emerges with a privileged standard of living, whereas in other cases a local bourgeoisie is established. Generally, according to Cabral, in a colonial situation the introduction of money and urbanization can alter the composition of social classes. Native ruling classes lose prestige in the face of the increasing outside influence; some peasant populations move from the countryside to urban centers; and new classes such as salaried workers, state employees, and merchants and professionals evolve. In the countryside, a class of small bourgeois farmers may arise. Finally, emerging from a small bourgeoisie of bureaucrats and compradores in the trading system is a native pseudobourgeoisie; in addition, private agricultural property is expanded along with the creation of an agricultural proletariat of wage-earning workers. Native elements may dominate the state power, thereby creating the illusion that a national bourgeoisie is fulfilling its anticipated progressive role of promoting capitalist development. But, argued Cabral, this national bourgeoisie cannot freely guide the development of the productive forces because it is subject to the ruling classes of the dominating countries. A nationalist solution to development cannot be achieved without destruction of the structure of capitalism imposed upon the dependent nation by imperialism.

In Guinea-Bissau, a small colonial capitalist class dominated through political, economic, and military power and cooptation of fractions of certain classes. In the towns, this class of Europeans comprised high officials and managers of enterprises; medium officials, small traders, and merchants and professional people; and skilled workers. Cabral emphasized how this colonial class perpetuated exploitation and repressed the cultural life of Africans through policies of assimilation and division between the indigenous elites and popular masses. The continuing rule of this class was partially dependent on the actions of an African urban petty bourgeoisie, including some higher officials, middle officials and members of liberal professions, and petty officials and commercial employees. Together with small rural farm owners, these Africans constituted a class that assimilated the colonizing mentality and considered itself superior, but it was torn between continued subjection to imperialist capital and the possibility of evolving into a pseudonational bourgeoisie—thereby denying the goal of national liberation—or rejecting bourgeois inclinations, raising revolutionary consciousness, and following the revolutionary struggle. This choice, according to Cabral, was decisive: to betray the revolution or to abolish itself as a class. Once this "marginal" class was aware of this paradox, it was possible to return to its roots to identify with the aspirations of the mass of the people. Below the African petty bourgeoisie were the wage earners, including dockworkers, boatmen who transport goods and agricultural produce, domestic servants, and people who work in small repair shops, but they were not yet a proletariat or working class because of the low development of the forces of production.

Fifth, Cabral elaborated on the PAIGC motto, "Unity and Struggle"— unity in order to attain strength and confront internal contradictions and struggle to overcome colonial domination. Cabral then explained this motto in terms of class contradictions. On one side was the white colonial class of Portuguese who politically are unable to oppose any regime and persist in their defense of colonialism. On the other side were the Africans, led by the petty bourgeoisie, itself divided, with one group who wanted the colonialists to leave but were afraid to express their sentiments through action and a smaller group that struggled against colonialism. There were also the salaried workers, a majority of whom sympathized with the struggle and a minority who sympathized with colonialism; these workers were carpenters, masons, mechanics, drivers, and sailors. In Guinea-Bissau, between the petty bourgeoisie and workers were young people recently arrived from rural areas who did not work but were connected to petty bourgeois or workers' families and proved to be useful in the liberation struggle. In addition, there was a group of part-time or idle workers who come in contact with the Portuguese. They may have been prestigious football players, impressed by material possessions but humiliated by their relations with the colonialists; thus, many of them turned to the revolution.

The class structure differed in Cape Verde. There were large and small landowners, although the former lost most of their land through drought and poor colonial administration. There was a class of tenant farmers, dependent on the large landowners and the banks, and sharecroppers. There also were a small number of agricultural workers; unfortunately not enough to form a class. Cabral assumed that the large landowners would support the colonialists, and the small landowners would divide their support between the colonialists and those struggling for change; they were similar to the rural small bourgeoisie in Guinea-Bissau.

Given these different class structures, Cabral attempted to show that the apparent contradictions between life in Cape Verde and Guinea-Bissau were minimal. Cape Verdeans were more educated and had served the colonial administration in Guinea. However, the people in both countries were similarly exploited, and class behavior did not differ much:

> But if we study the question closely, we see that the general tendency of this Guinean petty bourgeoisie is to coexist easily with the Cape Verdean petty bourgeoisie. The general tendency is for them to understand each other, alongside the Portuguese. And we have never seen in the bush, for example, any contradiction between Cape Verdeans and Guineans. (Cabral, *Unity and Struggle*, 1979: 41)

Assessments

My synthesis thus far has revealed the categories of class, the approach to a class analysis, and the implications of class struggle found in the writings of Cabral. Many persons who have written about Cabral have not overlooked his class analysis. Therefore, my concluding discussion incorporates their interpretations and assesses the significance of his theoretical contribution by emphasizing several points.

First, the writers who have succeeded in popularizing the revolution in Guinea and in graphically portraying the leadership role of Cabral tended to stress organizational rather than theoretical aspects of the revolution. In his very early account, Gerald Chaliand devoted a few useful pages to the question of social classes in the towns and countryside; these classes are identified but not explicitly integrated with the account of his personal experience and impressions in Guinea (Chaliand, 1969: 12–21). Likewise, Basil Davidson in his pioneering study (1969: especially 73–77) concentrated on firsthand impressions. Lars Rudebeck (1974) devoted a chapter to the ideology and goals of the PAIGC by concentrating on Cabral's thought, including the emphasis on class and class struggle; and he explored these concepts in later papers (Rudebeck 1979A, 1983). The great value in all these works, however, is in their personal impressions of the revolutionary struggle. In particular, the three observers emphasized the organization of party and revolution. They at least implicitly remind us that the organizational success of the revolution was tied to the thinking of Cabral and the revolutionary leadership, and Davidson stressed the relationship of theory and the experience of the evolving struggle.

Second, some writers are concerned with the degree to which Cabral departed from classical Marxism. Cabral's references to productive forces, relations of production, and modes of production, and his emphasis on combined and uneven development through history clearly place his analysis within a dialectical and historically materialist framework. Freire (1978: 8) lends support to the idea of class analysis in understanding Guinea:

> Only through such praxis—in which those who help and those who are

being helped help each other simultaneously—can the act of helping become free from the distortion in which the helper dominates the helped. For this reason there can be no real help between dominating and dominated classes, nor between "imperial" and so-called "dependent" societies. These relationship can never be understood except in the light of class analysis.

Yet class struggle does not necessarily determine the course of all history, according to Cabral. Rudebeck (1974: 75) quarreled with Cabral's interpretation of history and questioned whether he was true to dialectics, but affirmed that Cabral derived his theory from the concrete struggle against colonialism and imperialism:

> If we accept the view that the origin of social classes is found in the interaction between the productive forces at a given level and the relations of production . . . then we may also accept the formal logic of Cabral's reasoning, when he argues that the mode of production is a more basic factor than the class struggle itself, and that consequently the level of development of the productive forces ought to be designated as "the true and permanent motive force of history.

McCulloch explained why class analysis is not utilized much in the African setting by suggesting the small size of the middle classes in relation to the peasantry as a factor and the source of wealth for the new rulers after independence. "It is not ownership of the means of production but, rather, position within the instrumentalities of the state that has been the chief source of wealth" (McCulloch, 1983: 59). Also, a focus on ethnicity obscures attention to classes as well as communal ownership and a lack of industry, whereas the rhetoric of nationalism in the African context tends to perpetuate the myth of a classless society, past and present. Cabral contended with the assumption of European scholars that Africa was a continent without history; in this context, according to McCulloch, Cabral attempted to reconstruct theory to deal with real conditions: "no one has made a more adventurous attempt than Cabral to explore the influence of colonialism through the creation of classes" (p. 62).

Opoku (1978: 48) reminded us that Cabral really was not contending with orthodox Marxist interpretations in his rejection of the thesis that history begins with classes; further, he showed that Cabral would likely accept the thesis, set forth by Engels, that the state becomes necessary as an instrument of a ruling class as class struggle evolves through history. Such observations suggest that Cabral was both faithful to Marxist method and the proposition that good theory not only may be based on the ideas of others but must be subject to concrete and historical conditions of real experiences in which theory is being tested. Praxis, or the dialectical interaction between theory and practice, most certainly guided Cabral in his thinking and action.

Third, this attention to the mode of production leads to Cabral's view of three stages in history. Rudebeck (1974: 77) commented:

> In the three-step scheme of Cabral, traditional agricultural societies have a place of their own and are not regarded simply as pre-stages to feudalism. Instead, feudal and bourgeois societies are regarded as sub-stages of one and the same general stage, i.e., the stage of private appropriation of the means of production. Thus, we again see that Cabral is anxious to do justice to a historical perspective differing from the one-eyed occidental perspective, but without abandoning the theoretical tools of Marxism. . . . He presumes that man through history strives to achieve the total and free development of his possibilities of life.

Fourth, Cabral combined an analysis of materialist modes of production with the idea of culture. Jinadu focused on this theme in an effort to confront the erroneous thesis that African political thought is without substance and significance. Jinadu (1978: 135) explained Cabral's contribution: "It is that the material modes of production are best viewed in the larger context of culture as a way of life, to which reference can then be made with regard to institutional design. For, in the final analysis, political systems are also cultural artifacts." With his observation that an increase in expression of culture generally precedes national liberation struggles, Cabral denied "the alleged antithesis between revolutionary struggle and cultural nationalism" (p. 125). This is a sensitive theoretical area, which Cabral dealt with in some detail, inspired in part by the thought of his Mozambican comrade, Eduardo Mondlane. Cabral focused on "dependent and reciprocal relations between the national liberation struggle and culture" in his Syracuse speech in 1970. And, of course, it is a theme that has interested Mário de Andrade (1983A).

Fifth, Rudebeck (1984A, 1984B) argued that the class character of the mobilization initiated and organized by the PAIGC was guided by Cabral's understanding of the political potential for resistance of various classes and strata. It was not class based in the sense of anticipating the takeover of political and economic power by the surplus-producing class, which was essentially peasant. The PAIGC was anticolonial, nationalist, and national liberationist, and united around the idea of transcending class divisions in society. In his distinction between the Fulas and Balantas, Cabral separated class from classless society, vertical from horizontal lines. This vertical-horizontal distinction served as a powerful analytical tool and allowed for understanding the dynamic dimension of peasant society. Lopes (1982) referred to the two "logics" as the conflict of "ethnic rationality" as opposed to "state rationality"; this conflict was limited by pacts between the colonial state and the Fula chiefs. The least modern groups (Balanta) were found by Cabral to be most receptive to the idea of national liberation, a contradiction necessitating further analysis. Rudebeck stated that focus on the vertical structure of the Fulas obscures their respective class position vis-à-vis the state, be it colonial or postcolonial. Cabral analyzed internal class structure of peasant relations without direct reference to the impact of colonialism; he charged the radical "petty bourgeois" party and state leadership with the task of national development. The question of specific power relations was left open or vaguely or ideally addressed, and still is today. The focus on vertical and horizontal relationships allowed Cabral to avoid introducing peasant conservatism into the passive class struggle. The peasantry thus was a "physical" rather than "revolutionary" force, although the peasants were virtually the only surplus producers in the country. His class basis of the national liberation movement was based on this type of analysis.

Sixth, there is interest in Cabral's unique contribution to a theory of the petty bourgeoisie within an African situation. Chaliand (1977–1978: 4) asserted that "Cabral made an original theoretical contribution on the scope and limits of class struggle in African societies, on the role and ambivalence of the petite bourgeoisie at the head of the national liberation movement." Opoku (1978: 47) argued that the bourgeoisie and proletariat are missing in Cabral's analysis, unlike the attention given to those classes in modern thought. But this is more a reflection of the low level of productive forces within Guinea than some radical modification of class analysis. Cabral referred to wage-earning workers rather than proletariat, but in discussing the dockworkers and people who transport merchandise up and down the rivers, he noted their class consciousness and initiative in launching strikes and how, without any trade union leadership, they formed a nucleus with other wage-earning groups in the towns. Thus, he exclaimed, "we found our little proletariat" (Cabral, *Revolution in Guinea*, 1969: 66).

Aquino Bragança argued that Cabral saw no social class as being in conditions of fighting against Portugal, and thus he conceived a strategy that allowed him to create an instrument—a clandestine political formation—that would alter the situation (Bragança, 1976: 7). He reminded us that the petty bourgeoisie was caught between its ambivalence of seeking radical options that would modify its status quo or be satisfied with reformism that would allow it certain privileges under colonialism (p. 9). In 1961, only fourteen Guineans had obtained a university education in Portugal, a small fraction integrated to the colonial apparatus in contrast to the majority of assimilados or small state functionaries or those salaried by the European private sector. This African group, because of its organizational capacity, represented the future leadership of the modern African state—a majority timidly prepared to seek independence. Cabral discovered that most salaried persons were employees of the port and maritime transport (agricultural products) who constituted "a hegemonic fraction" of the Guinean petty bourgeoisie. This faction was conscious of its role and organized "nationalist" unions and the first strikes during 1956–1959, which served as a prelude to the armed struggle a few years later (p. 11). By 1964 Cabral had to ask the petty bourgeoisie to abandon its power to the workers and peasants, and for this reason, according to Rudebeck, the mobilization for revolution was organized around a political and cultural basis, and not a class basis. After independence and the coup of November 1980, it was apparent that the underlying class struggle had not been resolved by the success of the revolution:

> The latent class struggle manifested itself in a continuous tug of war between different tendencies within the PAIGC and in the social and political life of Guinea-Bissau. There was debate and even confrontation over different conceptions of development. The conflicting tendencies concern such things as large-scale commercial export agriculture versus production of food for the people, attempts to have advanced and very expensive industrialization projects versus more modest industrial production for consumption by the masses, elite-oriented training in the schools versus broad political orientation and participation in productive work, Guinean nationalism versus union with Cape Verde in the long term perspective of wider African unity. A persistent structural tendency, furthermore, seems to have been that the gap between the people and state was widening. (Rudebeck, 1981B: 5)

There also is the question of the working class and its role in the class struggle: "The working class, its political consciousness, and culture occupy the place of a myth in Cabral's theory, which contains the wish for the arrival of a world not yet formed and perhaps not even possible in some black African states" (McCulloch, 1983: 73).

Finally, there is attention to the role of the peasantry. How can national liberation and independence be achieved without a developed working class, and how can the peasantry be utilized in the struggle? O'Brien (1977: 4–5) affirmed that the peasants of Guinea were not wage laborers nor did they enter into

> unmediated relations of production with capital. . . . The determination of what was to be produced, of the size of output and of the division of labour was left to the peasants. . . . The surplus value obtained from the peasantry by the Portuguese was extracted by indirect mechanisms. . . . Once this surplus product or surplus labour had been extracted from the peasant system, it entered the hands of capitalists, for whom it became abstract surplus value which behaved as capital in the capitalist economy. . . . Specifically, it re-entered the colonial economy, most importantly for the peasantry, in the forms of commodities they required and the physical and organizational apparatus necessary to maintain and reproduce the conditions of their subjection to the capitalist system. The peasant production process was therefore integrated into and participated in the expanded reproduction of capital.

O'Brien suggested that this proletarian character does not make the peasantry a proletariat because of its contradictory class determination. Although this explains the necessity of focusing on the petty bourgeoisie in a class explanation of potential revolutionary conditions in Guinea, O'Brien initiated a provocative inquiry into the potential revolutionary role of the peasantry, and his analysis was inspired by Cabral's thinking and the successful revolution in Guinea.

McCulloch identified several elements in Cabral's conception of class. First, he focused on a group's position within the dominant ownership of production, but noted that this notion causes problems—for example, in analyzing the peasant ownership of land that they work for groundnut cultivation for export and also for subsistence and limited exchange of foodstuffs. Second, the element of culture in Cabral's definition of class, especially as related to the peasantry and the petty bourgeoisie. (The peasantry resided in rural ethnic communities without state organization, except for the Fulas, so that their affinity to traditional culture could serve the opposition movement to colonial rule. The material advantages of the petty bourgeoisie were offset by their living within two cultures.) Both groups share a sense of servility in the colonial society so that there is a natural affinity between them, just as, for the same reason, there were no major contradictions between peoples of rural and urban areas (McCulloch, 1983: 64). Third, classes appear and evolve through the conflict between the level of forces of production and ownership of means of production, so that "once a certain level in the accumulation of a material surplus is achieved in primitive communalist societies, then a qualitative jump occurs and classes appear" (p. 65).

Aaby (1978: 12–13) looked at the Balanta peasantry as "a gerontocratic, segmentary, patrilineal clan system" and "a stable low-productive male dominated society" and argued that their social patterns of accumulation are organized around the procuring of wives and cattle. A structural transformation would not result in Balanta society because "no surplus is invested in the development of productive forces."

McCollester and most other writers have acknowledged the weakness of the peasantry as a revolutionary force, given that its basic structure remained intact, but its role in cultural resistance was tied to its defense of indigenous culture in the face of the colonizer's "civilizing mission." It was this aspect that interested Cabral and should be studied in more depth (McCollester, 1973: 16).

McCulloch (1983: 69) suggested two reasons for Cabral's explanation of the peasantry being unable to act as a revolutionary class: first, "the erosion of national culture and the detachment of that culture from the ongoing activity of tribal and national life"; and second, "the narrowness and brutality of village life, which ties the individual so much to blind necessity strangles any initiative for change." He concludes that "Cabral makes little effort to sort out these two elements, thereby leaving his account of the peasantry rather ambiguous."

Other observers have insisted on rethinking the role of the peasantry. Rudebeck (1983) drew upon the work of Lopes (1982) in writing that

Cabral's distinction between horizontal and vertical organization of peasant groupings may have led other observers to a misconception of the role of the Fulas, for example, whose lack of active participation in the armed struggle may have been due to their cultural autonomy, which kept them from complete assimilation by the colonial power and discouraged them from nationalist militancy. Rudebeck also reflected on the class basis of the liberation struggle and the awareness of peasants of their exploitation under Portuguese colonialism, and their consequent willingness to give their surplus to the institutions of the independent state emerging from their struggle. Lopes (1986) has used the term "class" to explain stratification, the relations of production, and exploitation; he identified a crisis of identity in the postcolonial period attributable to the lack of a national project and the failure to substitute a model of accumulation for the pluralist class interests that characterized the national liberation struggle. Lopes also referred to Cabral's distinction of horizontal societies (decentralized economic structures typical of the Balantas) and vertical societies (centralized power and advanced social stratification typical of the Fulas and Mandingas) and argued that the creole language serves to unify the heterogeneous ethnic groupings. He focused on the primitive modes of production characterized by the organization of work divided between an individual base (the small family) and a collective base (the large family or clan where the means of work is found on the land collectively owned by the clan and available to all according to rules that distribute parcels to families). Under these conditions, he noted, there are no mercantile exchanges, and distribution of products is subject to lineage rules (Lopes, 1986: 20–21).

Sigrist (1980) examined the role of the Balantas in the colonial resistance with detailed referencing to the thought of Cabral and showed that the revolution was carried out by subsistence peasants under intellectual leadership, whose origins related not to collectivist agriculture but to a more developed commercial system in the Cape Verdes. Although Sigrist claimed that Cabral was politicized by Portuguese Marxists, she acknowledged that he avoided the Eurocentric influences and instead emphasized concrete analyses.

Forrest (1987A), however, argued that Cabral's emphasis on class was misleading because politics in Guinea today depends largely on institutional, ethnic, and leadership competition; power struggles at the top prevail rather than village committees and democratic participation, and the peasantry has rejected the state economic sector in favor of unofficial economic activities. Consequently, "neither class nor ideology are important in explaining political conflict in the centralized political arena of post-colonial Guinea-Bissau" (Forrest, 1987B: xxii). Furthermore, Galli and Jones (1987: 192–193) believed that the desire by Cabral to unify diverse ethnic elements resulted in inflexible political structures along Leninist lines that undermined individual peasant initiative.

My discussion has synthesized Cabral's thinking on class and class struggle and has explored some of the implications of his ideas. Among the themes of interest in this discussion were Cabral's preoccupation with organization and its significance in the revolution; his theoretical orientation within the Marxist tradition and the extent to which he pursued traditional or new conceptions, derived from his revolutionary experience; his emphasis on the revolutionary potential of the petty bourgeoisie, given the weaknesses of the bourgeoisie and proletariat; and his attention to the peasantry and its cultural resistance as a prelude to the revolution. All of these themes may be relevant in the study of other questions such as strategies to be employed in the armed struggle, the possible revolutionary alliances and united fronts, and the forming of the revolutionary vanguard. Issues of how to institutionalize the revolution, once in power, how to provide for the needs and demands of the people, and how to ensure participatory democracy also may be significant. We need to look more deeply into these important themes, questions, and issues. The thought and experience of Cabral thus serve as a foundation and springboard for such an endeavor.

Bibliographic Note

The principal writings of Cabral in which there is extensive discussion of class and class struggle include his talks in Milán (1964), Havana (1966), Syracuse (1970), and Lincoln University (1972), in addition to his discussions with party cadres (1968 and 1969). There are, of course, hundreds of references to the question of class, and the reader should peruse the bibliography for clues to these references suggested in my annotations. Also see Chilcote (1983) for a discussion on class and class struggle and consult additional essays in *Simpósio Internacional Amílcar Cabral* (1984). Additionally, consult McCulloch (1983) and Chabal (1983A) for syntheses and critiques of Cabral's thinking. For useful overviews of class and its implications in the analysis of Cabral, see McCollester (1973); O'Brien (1977); Opoku (1978); Rudebeck (1974, 1979A, 1981B, 1983, 1984A, 1984B); Sigrist (1979, 1980). Consult Andrade (1983A) and Jinadu (1978) on class and culture and Lopes (1987A) on class and nation. On the peasantry, see Aaby (1978); Galli (1986, 1987); Galli and Jones (1987); and Hochet (1983). On the role of intellectuals, see Benot (1981) and Lopes (1977). On classes and social structure in Cape Verde, see Carreira (1977). On women, consult Urdang (1975A, 1975B, and especially 1979). On the concept of the petty bourgeoisie, see Bragança (1976); McCulloch (1983); Lopes (1982, 1987B); and Wallerstein (1983).

5

Theory of State
and Development

Amílcar Cabral did not elaborate a definitive theory of state and development, although it is possible to understand his conception of these terms by examining his writings and their interpretation by others. This chapter first looks at some general theories about the state as a backdrop to a discussion of what Cabral had to tell us about his own theoretical and practical experience. Next the chapter delves into his understandings of development through the process of nation-building before and after independence. Assessments by observers and critics are brought together as a means for evaluating Cabral's contributions.

Radical understandings of the state draw upon the thought of Hegel, Marx, Engels, and Lenin and also focus on conceptions of Marx in order to interpret the role of the state in the contemporary world. Hegel and Marx noted a fundamental contradiction between the state and the civil society of citizens. Marx attempted, however, to separate his understanding of the state from an idealistic or abstract conception and to root it in a materialistic conception. In the *Manifesto* (1848), Marx and Engels saw the state as mediating conflicts within the dominant or ruling class; the state acts in the interests of this class as its instrument. In *State and Revolution* (1917), Lenin outlined several stages through which the state evolves and eventually disappears with communism. Among the perspectives in the contemporary literature, a pluralist view sees the state as a marketplace through which filter demands and interests of competing groups and individuals; an instrumentalist view links state policies to the interests of the ruling class; and a structuralist view emphasizes the autonomy of agencies or apparatuses rather than the struggle of individuals and classes. This dispersion of perspectives suggests that there is no consensus over a theory of state, and readers who may wish to delve into these and other views, should consult Martin Conroy, *The State and Political Theory* (1984) and Bob Jessop, *The Capitalist State* (1982).

Some scholars have affirmed that Cabral contributed substantially to a conception of the state. For example, Henry Bienen (1977: 558) stated that: "With regard to Africa, it has been Amílcar Cabral, more than any other leader, who explicitly takes up the development of the state, and what it means to build a revolutionary movement in a very undeveloped and ethnically heterogeneous colonial society." Cabral envisaged society, and African society in particular, as advancing through three stages, from a communal agricultural and cattle-raising society horizontally formed without a state and social classes to agrarian feudal or agro-industrial societies with social structure vertically developed within a state to a socialist and communist society in which the state, class, and class struggle gradually disappear. There was no specific timetable for progress through these stages, he believed, but progress depended on the possibilities for the development of the society's productive forces, the type of the state, and the nature of the dominant class or classes within society. The possibility of a leap in the historical process depended on how man mastered nature and "the creation of socialist states" (Cabral, "Weapon of Theory," in *Unity and Struggle* 1979: 125–126).

The central problem for Cabral was the state in the colonial situation. The class struggle in Guinea-Bissau was mitigated during the colonial period, and the colonial state was prominent: "What commands history in the colonial situation is not the class struggle. . . . In the colonial period it is the colonial state which commands history" (Cabral, *Revolution in Guinea*, 1972: 69). This focus allowed Cabral to examine the African petty bourgeoisie and its manipulation of the state apparatus, its awareness of imperialism and neocolonialism, and its prospects for destroying the colonial regime and building new structures after independence. Cabral's conception of the state can be drawn from the experience of organizing life in the liberated zones during the colonial period. Cabral stated: "The position of the people of Guinea and Cabo Verde has for some time been comparable to that of an independent State part of whose national territory—namely the urban centres—is occupied by foreign military forces" (Cabral, *Return to the Source*, 1973: 26). What, then, was the nature of this independent state? How was it institutionalized during the liberation period, and what was its impact upon the struggle for independence?

Building a State in Liberated Areas

Cabral described the process of building the state independent of the colonial form. Whereas other African countries preserved the structures of the colonial state, in Guinea-Bissau the state was being created in relation to particular conditions: "Our fortune is that we are creating the state through the struggle." Referring to the popular tribunals established in liberated zones, Cabral argued that Guineans had not copied the Portuguese or any other system: "Ours is a new judicial system, totally different from any other system, born in a country through struggle. It is similar to other systems, like the one in Vietnam, but it is also different because it corresponds to the conditions of our country" (Cabral, *Return to the Source*, 1973: 84).

Once some of the country was liberated and Cabral's forces controlled the liberated zones, freedom and sovereignty were enjoyed by the people. Cabral turned attention to development of the state: "We have our state, we have a strong political organization, a developing administration, and we have created many services" (Cabral, *Unity and Struggle*, 1979: 79). These services included working with the people to raise production, ensuring diversification of crops, improving distribution systems, establishing people's stores, improving education along with the building of schools, and establishing health-care centers and clinics.

After independence, the problem would be assimilation of the new structures in the liberated zones with those in the Portuguese colonial enclaves. Village committees, people's courts, people's stores, health clinics, and rural schools were to serve as the models for the new integrated society, whereas the land, the Portuguese-controlled trading companies, and the few factories had to be brought under national direction. Self-centered development rather than the adoption of a state bureaucratic model would be emphasized at the outset of independence. This involved increased production in agriculture and some exports in order to finance fuel and machinery, as well as some manufacture of simple consumer goods, such as tools, soap, cooking oil, and so on. (This process was described by Peter Aaby [1978].)

The revolutionary party was decisive in establishing a state in liberated areas parallel to the colonial state. At a PAIGC congress in 1964, the party was reorganized along decentralized lines so that power could be transferred to local bodies and special administrative committees in the liberated zones (Cabral, *Unity and Struggle*, 1979: 178). Cabral saw the party as instrumental in the direction of the emerging state. He viewed the party as the state during the liberation period: "As the party functions as a state in the process of development. . . . The fundamental characteristic of a state is its ability to suppress those who act against the interests of that state. Our interests, the interests of our party, which directs our state, these interests are also the interests of our people" (Cabral, *Palavras de ordem gerais*, 1965: 18). Rudebeck (1974: 96) commented that this definition was similar to the Marxist instrumentalist view of the state and to the Weberian notion of the state legitimately in control of physical force.

If the party functions as the state, then what are its goals? In his *Alguns princípios do partido* (1974), Cabral stressed that the guiding principle of the party was unity and struggle: union leads to strength in the face of adversity and a propensity to divide. Unity is a means, not an end. Struggle is a condition of every human being, and all of us struggle. For Cabral, the party was to consist of a limited number of persons and to be disciplined, with consensus and commitment to principles and the objective of national liberation. Its strength derived from its principle of internal revolutionary democracy in which party members should be critical and self-critical and open about explaining party objectives and principles to the masses. There should be no division between those responsible for political and military decisions. A basic principle was democratic centralism. The political norms thus included criticism and self-criticism, collective leadership, democratic centralism, and revolutionary democracy. Mobilization implied control, efficiency, conscious planning, and guidance along with participation, spontaneity, and democracy (Rudebeck, 1974: 144–145).

The early history of the PAIGC can be divided into seven periods, all important in understanding the building of an independent state during the liberation struggle through the transition to the forming of the state after independence: (1) the period from the founding of the party in 1956 to the organization of workers in Bissau, Bolama, and Bafatá, the successful strikes of sailors during July 1959, and the massacre of stevedores on the Pidjiguiti wharf on August 3, 1959, resulting in an adjustment of strategy and shift of attention from urban to rural areas; (2) an active phase of preparation of the masses for armed struggle and warning to the Portuguese and to the world that independence for Guinea and Cape Verde was necessary; (3) the liberation struggle, formally commencing with an attack on the barracks at Tite on August 23, 1963; (4) realization of the Congress of Cassacá and the victorious battle on the island of Como during February 1964, resulting in a restructuring of the party and the armed forces so as to form a regular army and to establish administrative organization in the liberated zones; (5) the making of political decisions about 1970 and 1971 to improve political work, consolidate the structures of the state, and develop the armed struggle, leading to the creation of the National Popular Assembly and elections for its membership in August–October 1972, and the repulsion of a Portuguese attack during March and April 1972; (6) the first meeting of the Popular National Assembly and proclamation of the independent state of Guinea-Bissau on September 24, 1973; and (7) negotiations with the Portuguese to establish formal independence for Cape Verde (July 1975) and the convocation of the Third Party Congress in July 1977 to consolidate the party structure in relation to the two countries (Aristides Pereira, 1976A).

The institutions that comprised this independent state prior to the victory of the liberation struggle included the party as the principal organization of the mobilization effort (see Rudebeck [1974] for the most detailed description). In the liberated zones, the building of a state involved new political structures, including the Conselho Superior da Luta (CSL) or "Highest Council of the Struggle," with a broad membership of about seventy and roughly corresponding to a central committee that had existed before the 1970 reorganization of the party. The council was expected to meet at least once a year after its initial meeting in August 1971, when Cabral proclaimed it "the highest organ of our struggle" (quoted in Rudebeck, 1974: 110). Within the CSL was a twenty-four–person executive committee, including members of the seven-member war council; the executive committee was equivalent to the Political Bureau prior to the 1970 changes.

Until his assassination, Amílcar Cabral was secretary general of the party, Aristides Pereira was vice–secretary general of the party, and Luís Cabral was responsible for national reconstruction. The three constituted a powerful three-man permanent commission at the top. After Cabral's death, the permanent commission evolved into a four-person permanent secretariat, including Pereira as secretary general, Luís Cabral as vice–secretary general, and Francisco Mendes (Chico) and João Bernardo Vieira (Nino) as secretaries. Rudebeck (1974: 107) referred to this as "the party within the party," implying that some persons within the party had special responsibilities and tasks and constituted "the backbone of an emerging state." There were important party congresses in 1964 and 1973, but it was "doubtful if the PAIGC leadership during the period . . . even seriously considered the party congress as their highest organ, except in a very formal sense" (pp. 107–109).

Two national committees administered the war effort: liberated areas in the north and south were each headed by a twelve-person national committee. A three-person permanent commission existed within each committee, made up of a political commissar, security commissar, and commissar for national reconstruction in the liberated areas, especially with regard to education and health. These committees were established in 1970 with plans to meet four times annually. Each liberated area was divided into four regions, and each region into four sectors or zones. Between the sector and zone and the village level was a section level. Five members comprised the village committee.

The major military organization was the Forças Armadas Revolucionárias do Povo (FARP), representing the last of the four phases in military activity during the liberation period: (1) the initial guerrilla phase in 1962 led by a small group of persons of petty bourgeois origins; (2) evolution of the guerrilla struggle with peasant participation in 1963; (3) a guerrilla army of several thousand that by 1964 had transformed itself more into a regular army (from local guerrilla warfare to coordinated mobile warfare); and (4) the FARP, which was able to launch assaults on urban centers leading to final victory (Davidson, 1969: 91). By 1970, the military struggle was organized into three fronts—eastern, northern, and southern—each with a commander responsible to the council of war. The basic army unit or *bigrupo* comprised thirty-two to forty members with considerable autonomy under the dual leadership of a military chief and a political commissar. In 1972, the military was reorganized: the three fronts devolved into small Frentes de Luta and the army into army corps each with a commander. Although the *bigrupo* remained intact, the village militia became the Forças Armadas Locais (FAL) or Local Armed Forces. During the struggle, political positions were considered more important than military posts, and there was no specific military hierarchy until after independence. Remuneration was low, but military personnel had access to state-allocated rice rations and benefited from a high degree of literacy due to literacy campaigns.

The judicial system in 1968 comprised popularly elected courts, Tribunas do Povo, each with three members and serving four to eleven villages. These courts had responsibility for offenses that could not result in jailing of the accused. Above this was a zone court at the regional level to deal with offenses punishable by imprisonment of up to four years. The supreme court was the five-member Tribunal de Guerra.

Cabral proclaimed that the supreme organ of the people was the Assembleia Nacional Popular (ANP), or National Popular Assembly, the key organ in the new state: "The ANP as the highest sovereign organ of the people will meet and proclaim the national state of Guinea, providing it with an executive and a constitution for our African Nation" (Cabral, "O estado da Guiné-Bissau," 1971: 6). Regional councils, elected by secret ballot in the liberated areas, elected 80 of the 120 members of assembly, the remaining seats being chosen among members of the party. On September 24, 1973, the first assembly convened in the region of Boé and announced the establishment of a new state whose form became clearer in the following year with formal independence. The executive was placed in the Conselho do Estado, a fifteen-person group elected by the assembly with its president serving as commander-in-chief and responsible for international relations. There also was a cabinet or Conselho dos Comissários de Estado.

Rudebeck has assessed the significance of these changes. Up to 1973, the party was conceived as the state. The idea of a state separate from the party was not expressed in any party documents prior to 1971, except in the original party program. In 1972 Rudebeck analyzed a distinction between candidates on single lists of party cadres representing about one-third of the assembly members; the other two-thirds were representatives of the people. He referred to changes in 1970, which clarified the division of labor and responsibility at higher organizational levels: changes at lower levels were insignificant, at middle levels they involved some reshuffling and renaming, but at the higher level these changes resulted in organs that were to prevail after independence (Rudebeck, 1974: 107–109).

Transition from Liberation Struggle to Building a State

In an analysis of the transition of the state from control over liberated zones to administration of the newly independent country, Rudebeck (1984A) showed how at the time of independence in 1974 state power resided in the liberated rural zones and the official strategy was aimed at satisfying the popular needs through allocation of internal resources, for the most part within agriculture. Yet after independence, political mobilization declined due to policies leading to substituting international aid as a means for ensuring popular support. Political power became centralized within Bissau, which had historically been the colonial base, so that a policy of rural development became increasingly less possible. This culminated in the coup of November 1980 in which the new regime promised but did not implement policies to correct the errors of the past.

Rudebeck identified some important theses in a retrospective view of these developments. First, the struggle for national liberation prior to independence involved many classes and was only minimally based on the class interests of the African peasantry to transform the economy into a popularly ruled national economy able to sustain the production of surplus for national development. He went on to suggest that class divisions are rooted in relations of production and the productive process whereby surplus is appropriated by some for the purpose of exploiting others. However, people are also divided culturally by ethnicity in which language, religion, and custom are manifested in common identities through which national unity can be expressed. Thus class and culture are foundations for politics and political struggle. It was also evident that resistance to colonialism allowed ethnic groups to join forces and to transcend ethnic differences and seek unity through a sense of nationality.

Once colonialism ended, class consciousness and class struggle appeared in manifest forms. Class struggle in Cape Verde was developing independently of class struggle in Guinea-Bissau. Rudebeck felt that Cabral's distinction of vertical and horizontal lines for ethnic groupings was useful in understanding the propensity of Fula chieftains to exploit the labor of peasants and to retain their power and social position, whereas the Balantas were largely "stateless" and egalitarian with little central authority. Furthermore, application of this distinction may obscure the tendency to oppose all traditional peasants, whether they be vertically or horizontally organized, and to maintain in the national period the pattern of centralized state authority evident in the colonial period.

A further thesis suggested that nationalism was nurtured not only by resistance to colonialism but through the national liberation movement. The Balantas, Rudebeck argued, fought for freedom to live without a state, whereas the Fulas, who already had their own state with ties to the colonial state, were interested in the autonomy of their own culture and exploitation of the peasantry. Political consciousness of all Africans in the liberated areas during the period of armed struggle was due to the goal of national unity and the fact that cultural and ethnic identity was not threatened. Thus the transformation to a nationally integrated mode of production could be achieved only by the struggle of people to control and direct the transformation and overcome the opposition to the peasantry. Class struggle would overcome this contradiction.

Cabral's characterization of the vertical and horizontal forms of political organization within the peasantry explained his emphasis on forms of peasant resistance rather than on passive class struggle and explains why he called the peasantry a "physical force" rather than a "revolutionary force." Rudebeck believed that Cabral understood this ambiguity even though he ultimately had to rely on petty bourgeois leadership to make a conscious choice to abandon power to workers and peasants and achieve people's power. Further, the people were mobilized politically for national liberation, not primarily on a class basis but on a cultural basis. This pertained to the African petty bourgeoisie, who ultimately had to join with the peasantry to organize the national liberation. Although the national liberation struggle provided for a unity between these two classes, once independence was achieved a class contradiction would inevitably become apparent. This opposition between the petty bourgeoisie and the peasantry would prove to be more important than that between the Fula chief and the exploited peasant.

In liberated zones the traditional mode of production was reinforced by a return to self-reliance and self-sufficiency as well as reaction to the exploitative colonial system. But after independence an integrated system of production and national self-reliance did not necessarily ensue—a contradiction inherent in the strategy of the PAIGC, which was tied to the interests of both the petty bourgeois leadership and the peasantry. "The dynamic of the national struggle was political, social, cultural, rather than immediately directed at the productive base of Guinean society" (Rudebeck, 1984A: 6). Furthermore, this contradiction concerned Cabral, who envisaged people's power as rooted in the elected assemblies of the people who would limit and control the functions of the state, whereas the party role would be that of an ideological guide. This would entail that the people or peasantry become a "revolutionary force" rather than the "physical force" Cabral had characterized them as in 1964.

Finally, the class basis of the state determines the orientation of developmental policies. However, once popular support was no longer essential in maintaining the power of the revolutionary leadership, the democratic institutions of the party and the state were unable to ensure the popular orientation of developmental policies. Therefore, the emerging power base of the regime within the state apparatus, in combination with foreign support, was unable to pressure the leadership to implement their officially proclaimed strategy of autonomous development oriented to the satisfaction of people's needs based on their own work. Thus, the problem rests with the fundamental difficulty of convincing peasants to produce for national accumulation and of finding the means to convince leadership to pursue their autonomous strategy of satisfying the needs of people. (These propositions are summarized from Rudebeck [1982, 1983].)

Building the State After Independence

Cabral once observed:

> We have to face the question whether or not socialism can be established immediately after the liberation. This depends on the instruments used to effect the transition to socialism; the essential factor is the nature of the state, bearing in mind that after the liberation there will be people controlling the policy, the prisons, the army, and so on, and a great deal depends on who they are and what they try to do with these instruments. Thus we return again to the problem of which class is the agent of history and who are the inheritors of the colonial state in our specific conditions. (Cabral, *Revolution in Guinea*, New York, 1969: 72)

In this insightful passage, Cabral was raising questions about the viability of the petty bourgeoisie and its prospects to bring about "national democracy."

In the aftermath of independence, the institutional structure was adapted to the new situation. According to Chabal (1983: 124), the unilateral declaration of independence by the PAIGC in 1973 was "directly inspired by Cabral's view of the national liberation struggle and by his understanding of international politics." The party continued to be a major force. Perceived as "the basic institution of sovereignty," the party congress represented an important opportunity for institutional changes. The first congress (1964) had resulted in a restructuring of the party, the second congress (September 1973) had proclaimed the formation of the new independent state, and the third congress (November 1977) set forth policy for the postindependence period prior to the November 1980 coup. Delegates were selected by a preparatory commission, itself appointed by the CSL. The party statutes of 1973 and 1977 were premised on a democratization of the party in towns and villages.

Although there was no official or autonomous peasant organization and peasants lacked power or means to negotiate with the government over their problems and interests, peasants were formally represented through the village committees. The workers União Nacional dos Trabalhadores da Guiné (UNTG) had been founded in 1961 as an early opposition force to the colonial state. After independence, it was mainly concentrated in Bissau due to lack of organization elsewhere, and it did not hold its first congress until 1978. The youth organization, Juventude Africana de Amílcar Cabral (JAAC), was formed at the time of independence for youth aged sixteen to thirty, but did not hold its first congress until 1979. With its strong control in Bissau, JAAC served to draw the youth toward the party. The Abel Djassi Pioneers, formed in 1966, served the needs of children under age fifteen. Women were organized under the União Democrática das Mulheres (da Guiné e Cabo Verde), the successor to the PAIGC Commission of Women run by Carmen Pereira.

Assessing the Theories on State and Development

Cabral favored direct democracy through decentralized regional assemblies (Rudebeck, 1984A, 1984B: 9; Galli and Jones, 1987: 72). However, once the PAIGC achieved independence after Cabral's death, it was caught up in the problem of Bissau as it took over the colonial administrative machinery. State personnel were concentrated in Bissau rather than among the rural population in the countryside. The party leadership was concerned about control in the former center of Portuguese colonialism, and so the party became absorbed in transferring power from the liberated areas to Bissau. This involved the takeover of the colonial bureaucracy, the move of party cadres to Bissau, and an effort to win over the population there. Petty bourgeois sympathizers and collaborators of the PAIGC who had worked in Bissau in the colonial administration were unwilling, however, to break from their former status as privileged persons. Davidson (1981: 166–167) called them not a class but a social grouping unwilling to sacrifice their personal interests for the revolutionary cause. Lopes (1982: 181) showed that the party leadership was not prepared for the transition, that there was a commonality of interests between "two currents of the petty bourgeoisie" in the PAIGC leadership and in the colonial administration. Lopes referred to tribal, clientele, social, and friendly ties that resulted in demobilization and a tendency to take over, but not radically transform, the former colonial state apparatus (p. 223). Galli and Jones (1987: 74) commented: "The transition to state power was thus defined in terms of taking over the state apparatus from those who had held control rather than in terms of turning it over to popular control." They went on to discuss the process of state building whereby party officials doubled as state officials without a system of checks and balances; this involved state organs at the national, regional, and sectoral levels: "The overlap between party and state was undesirable in particular because it allowed a small number of officials to have a monopoly over both party and state structures in the region and thereby created considerable opportunity for abuse of the population" (Galli and Jones, 1987: 78).

One of the revolutionary leaders, Vasco Cabral (1980: 9), once reminded his peers that the party should be strengthened through the principles of Amílcar Cabral. But many years after the death of Cabral, it was also clear that the party then was no longer waging a liberation struggle against colonialism in search of independence; it was caught up in other priorities and needs of state building while facing a continuing threat from imperialism and underdevelopment. It was obvious, however, that the principle of unity in the struggle against the enemies of imperialism and development was undermined by internal disputes within the party, culminating ultimately in the ouster of Luís Cabral as head of state in November 1980.

Amílcar Cabral had warned about the latent class struggle during the liberation period and in the period after independence: "What commands history in the colonial situation is not the class struggle. I do not mean that the class struggle in Guinea stopped completely during the colonial period; it continued, but in a muted way. In the colonial period it is the colonial state which commands history" (Cabral, *Revolution in Guinea*, 1972: 69). Here Cabral focused on the petty bourgeoisie because of the undeveloped working class and a peasantry that had not achieved any revolutionary potential. Bienen (1977: 564) explained the role of the petty bourgeoisie after independence: "Only the petty bourgeoisie can be aware of the reality of imperialist domination, and at the same time be able to direct the state apparatus."

Chabal (1983) referred to Cabral's vision of a state structure in pursuit of socialism without recourse to political repression. His notion of socialism would be determined by the limits of Guinea's internal resources and external constraints, not by some outside model. Industrial development was not a priority. Some modernization of agriculture would be possible if realized within the perspective of villagers who envisaged socialism as beneficial to their interests. "We thus have no good reason to doubt his repeated forecast that the development of an independent Guinea would differ little in orientation and priority from that of the liberated areas during the war" (p. 155). The key to his notion of "revolutionary democracy" was a balance between party rule and popularly elected state institutions (p. 158).

However, problems appeared with the formation of the new state. As one party observer reminds us, the state is always the instrument of one class for the exploitation of another (Lopes, 1982: 53). The coming together of different ethnic groups characterized the phase of armed struggle in Guinea, and today the state continues to be caught up in the legacy of colonialism by not applying any of the experiences that emanated from the liberation struggle.

Because the state is the locus of struggle among different class interests, it helps to examine the struggle through three types of states: (1) the Fula or Mandinga state tied to traditional structures and characterized by a tributary mode of production; (2) the colonial state that functioned under the capitalist mode of production; and (3) the independent state that emerged from the liberation struggle. The independent state draws its character from the earlier state forms and its rationalization evolves either through its legacy to the lessons of the liberation struggle or through its neocolonial dependency on the institutional apparatus of the colonial state (Lopes, 1982: 56–57).

The early impact of capitalism in Guinea was attributable to the Salazar regime and the Portuguese financial bourgeoisie that after 1928 pushed its interests through the commercial monopoly of Companhia União Fabril (CUF), while at the same time the regime continued with its repression of internal resistance, dating to the revolts of 1907–1909 under Unfali Soncó and the Beafadas and the pacification campaigns of 1913 onward. Lopes (1982: 66–68) contrasted the experience of the colonial apparatus to the new African state that emerged during the liberation struggle at the Congress of

Cassacá in 1964 in which the party first formulated a state structure for the liberated areas. With the reforms of 1970 and elections for the National Popular Assembly, the new state evolved through a Conselho do Estado and Conselho dos Comissários do Estado. Small reforms of the government in 1977 and 1978 were unsuccessful as governmental organization "followed the play of internal forces . . . and democratic principles were undermined by internal struggles and conflicts of interests among militants of different social origins" (p. 73).

These tensions culminated in the 1980 coup. The inner circle of concentrated power under Luís Cabral included José Araújo, who was responsible for party organization, and Armando Ramos, head of trade. The period was characterized by tight control, censorship, and repression. Some 100 persons had been executed without trial in 1974 and 1975 for collaboration with the Portuguese during the armed struggle, but several hundred others may have been executed without trial about 1978 and 1979, possibly including rival nationalists who had returned from exile in Senegal and others who were implicated in the abortive November 1978 coup. During the 1980 coup, former PAIGC leader Rafael Barbosa, who had been imprisoned for collaboration with the Portuguese, was released and managed to give a speech on radio denouncing the Cape Verdean influence, thereby appealing to racist sentiments. There were three factions in the power struggle—a military faction led by Nino Vieira; a "national revolutionary" wing led by Vasco Cabral, which wanted to restore the PAIGC as an independent political force; and a right wing led by Victor Saúde Maria, which opposed the party and favored tribalism.

Aristides Pereira and Cape Verdean leadership opposed the coup and immediately severed diplomatic ties, changing the name of the Cape Verdean wing of the party to the PAICV (Partido Africano da Independência de Cabo Verde). Vieira convoked an extraordinary party congress in November 1981 and retained the party name PAIGC, but excluded Pereira and those who had participated in the PAICV. Diplomatic relations were finally restored in 1982, but bitterness continued thereafter. The congress reflected a power struggle among the party factions. When Saúde Maria failed in his attempt to control the party, he was not appointed to a post as deputy secretary general. Vasco Cabral became secretary of the central committee with powers to revitalize the party.

Although Ribeiro (1983) emphasized the idea of unity based on the relationship of Cape Verde to Guinea-Bissau, and identified the national, historical, economic, geographical, and national liberation contexts, he said nothing about the November 1980 coup and its consequences and impact on such a unity. A deeper analysis of internal conflicts reveals some of the problem. Chabal (1983: 129) affirmed, for instance, that the PAIGC was unable to combine political democracy with an economic development policy that benefits the countryside, so Luís Cabral resorted to silencing criticisms of his government. Consequently, a power struggle ensued within the party between those who favored Amílcar Cabral's policy of developing the countryside and those who, with Luís Cabral, preferred a more rapid, centralized and urban industrial development.

In the aftermath of the coup, McCulloch (1983: 34) concluded, "The revolution in Guiné has, at least for time being, gone sour," and he blamed the problem "on foreign aid and political nepotism." Lopes (1987B: 132) attributed the coup to vagueness in the party "concept of revolutionary national democracy" which had "amounted to a storehouse of contradictory thoughts. The absence of discipline and political coherence encouraged demobilization, provoked by Bissau."

A further problem was the difference between the Cape Verdean and Guinean wings of the party because the Cape Verdeans were more politically and ideologically developed than the Guineans. Because the main cadres and party militants were Guineans and the armed struggle took place in Guinea-Bissau, it might be assumed that party principles and ideas had spread from Bissau to Praia, but the effect was different because of "political commandism" among "the higher calibre cadres" in Cape Verde, many of whom had served in Bissau. Lopes argued that policies had openly favored Cape Verdeans, who received rapid promotions. Furthermore, the state structures of Cape Verde were more operational because of the tradition of Cape Verdean experience in the colonial administration. The Cape Verdean government relegated the Guineans to a secondary level in order to deal with the flank of Cape Verdean petty bourgeoisie and pressure from the powerful emigré communities in the United States, Portugal, and Senegal. Lopes (1987B: 137) believed that the "exaggerated nationalism" of Cape Verdean leaders had led to separatism and that "Luiz Cabral's political practice must be seen as the result of his ideological weakness and within a context of class struggle in which he allowed himself to be carried along by his own petty-bourgeois background."

Rudebeck (1981A: 3–4) suggested that although the original leaders of the liberation movement were in control of the new state apparatus,

> they had only crushed the colonial state apparatus very partially, and the alternative constructed in the liberation areas during the struggle was not able to outdo the colonial state in carrying out traditional state functions. For every day that passed the PAIGC leadership depended more and more for running their independent state on the technocratic and education competence of the non-revolutionary petty bourgeoisie, at the same time as necessary finance proved to be more easily available by international aid than by persuading traditional peasants to abandon their ancient mode of production in order to produce a surplus for national development.

This problem was due to limited state investment in agriculture and consequently to a failure of agricultural surplus as the regime depended more and more on foreign aid: "The regime's petty bourgeois and internationalized class basis did not force it to implement the radical development strategy to which it was politically and ideologically committed" (p. 4) so that after 1980 the structural situation of the new regime was very much the same: "Its class basis is as petty bourgeois and internationalized as that of its predecessor . . . while its professed ideology is as radically nationalist" (pp. 4–5).

There also were substantial organizational problems in the party and mass organizations, according to Galli and Jones (1987: 86):

> The mass organizations were designed to mobilize support for government and party and to channel the energies and enthusiasms of the people exclusively in directions acceptable to the leadership. They were not intended to be the means by which the people could control the leadership or even influence their decisions.

Galli and Jones set forth an indictment of the state apparatus, emphasizing the tight control of the party over election procedures in 1972, 1976, and 1984 and deploring the lack of alternative candidates.

Candidates for regional councils and the National Popular Assembly were put forward at the village level, discussed at the regional level, and forwarded to the national electoral commissions. In 1984, for example, 84 percent of the eligible voters voted for the final list of candidates in Bissau in contrast to the 50 and 56 percent, respectively, in Bafatá and Gabú—a reflection of the lack of peasant support from local leaders hostile to the PAIGC. The ANP itself was the only forum where party policies could be debated, but after 1979 it was not very effective. The Extraordinary Session of November 7–10, 1980, was called to ratify a new constitution and ensure unity between Cape Verde and Guinea-Bissau. The constitution reflected differences between the executives of the two countries and allowed Cape Verdeans to hold office in Guinea. Some 200 Cape Verdeans held important positions in Guinea by 1980, many from the previous colonial administration, and Luís Cabral refused to permit amendments that could rectify the imbalance.

Galli and Jones (1987: 93–94) showed the deterioration in relations between party and state officials and the people by suggesting that the party served as an instrument for direction from the government:

> The party had atrophied. . . . The mass organizations were too tightly constrained by the leadership to be able to articulate at a national level the aspirations and grievances of the populations they were meant to represent. The Assembly had no effective power to change policies set by government leaders. But it was the major disaffection within the top leadership that set in motion the chain of events which followed.

Galli and Jones went on to note the relatively low number of peasants and women delegates in the ANP and their peripheral roles within the party. They also deplored tight control of UNTG cadres in Bissau.

Clearly, if we are to accept the indictment of Galli and Jones, the problems of the new state and the party were but a reflection of Cabral's own warnings on what might happen. McCulloch (1983: 92) considered Cabral's delineation of the state in colonial and postcolonial Africa as "highly innovative" and "when his writings are viewed in terms of the direction which political theory has taken since his death . . . his . . . reflections on the state identify him as the forerunner of most contemporary theorizing on post-colonial society." Cabral's attention to the role of the state in the transition from colonialism to independence focused on imperialism, and in the period from 1964 to 1972 his view changed from seeing the state "predominantly as a neutral instrument necessary to the functioning of any national polity to seeing it as an essentially repressive instrument devoted to the domination of one class by another" (p. 93). McCulloch believed that in his earlier essays Cabral emphasized that while the petty bourgeoisie was the only indigenous class capable of running the institutions of the state, it could not on its own hold state power: "The African petty bourgeoisie cannot be successful as the servant of Portuguese or international capital" and the postcolonial state would have to be semiautonomous (p. 94). Cabral saw the instruments of the state, especially the army and the police, as decisive in the period after independence: "In these early essays Cabral does not in general identify the state with the repressive role which is characteristic of the Leninist conception of state power" (p. 95). McCulloch noted that in later writings Cabral saw the state as simply carrying out its prescribed functions, but his informal talk in New York (1972) his conception of the state was premised on the total destruction of all colonial institutions so that the state was then viewed as a repressive apparatus (p. 96). Cabral was impressed with the state structures established in the liberated zones, but believed that there was no guarantee of a successful transition in the independence period. The state must function without serving as the instrument of class domination. It becomes semiautonomous. In this sense, McCulloch believed that Cabral was expressing a view based on his particular experience and was not tied to the "limitations of much recent literature on the autonomous or overdeveloped state . . . linked with the vulgarity of Lenin's pioneering work" (p. 98). He concluded that in supporting the petty bourgeoisie as the only class capable of operating the state apparatus, Cabral also recognized that the possibilities for a socialist transformation might be "lessoned by the character of the post-colonial state and its domination by petty-bourgeois elements" (p. 98). McCulloch concluded with an assessment: "Cabral's exposition on the state and his account of the petty bourgeoisie sit rather uncomfortable side by side. The threads which could join together these dimensions in his work are present, but because of the frailty of his account of ideology and class consciousness they remain separate" (p. 99).

Toward a Model of Development

Development for Cabral represented an evolution of the productive forces and the relations of production in a harmonious social division, without exploitation. Given that the level of the relations of production in Guinea was so low, no privileged class would control the means of production. There were three great classes: the peasants constituting about three-fourths of the population; the salaried workers, including public functionaries; and the petty bourgeoisie. The petty bourgeoisie was divided into two parts: the commercial bourgeoisie and the bureaucratic bourgeoisie, tied to the state and made up of technocrats and high administrative functionaries from the colonial period. This latter stratum controlled the state apparatus and implemented policies and strategies of development.

The state acts in several areas as synthesized from Lopes (1982: 118–119): in the political sphere, it integrates all social levels; on the social level, its integration is achieved through provision of social services; on the administrative level, it coordinates the different ministries throughout the regions of the country; and in the cultural sphere, it raises the national conscience through the means of mass communication.

Cabral's vision of the future society implied the liberation of people from oppression, exploitation, and poverty; this was no idealistic dream, but was based on the recognition that the transformation of society entailed many difficulties. Cabral was aware of the impact of neocolonialism on other African countries, and he was conscious of the need to implement social, economic, and political changes after independence. The transformation therefore included the construction of a radically different and new social, political, and economic order in the liberated zones prior to independence, including schools and health centers, production and distribution of foodstuffs, and the guaranteeing of people's support and participation. He consciously began the task of organizing the foundations of the new state that would emerge after independence. He viewed the role of the party as essential in the initial phase; through the party political training would take place for the cadres who would carry on with the administration of the state. He was concerned that these cadres be conscious of the party principles and that the party serve as the link between the people and the leadership. He viewed the village council as a grassroots base of society. During the liberation struggle and until the 1972 elections the party represented the state structure; thereafter, the National Popular Assembly would assume the political functions of policymaking. After independence, the party would be linked with the new state.

Cabral talked about the "new man" and a "new society." Rapid industrialization would not necessarily be the course of development after independence in a society whose resources largely related to agriculture. Indeed, agriculture would serve as the basis for providing for basic needs of people as well as generating a surplus for the construction of light industry and infrastructure.

The model of development that appeared to evolve during the liberation and postindependence periods was not based on traditional approaches or on ideas imported from outside Guinea and Cape Verde. Rudebeck (1981B: 2) believed that the social formation of Guinea was "characterized by a traditional peasant mode of production but linked to the world market by way of a state enjoying some autonomy." The strategy of the leadership after independence, however, was "socialist-oriented," although the term did not appear in official documents.

Denis Goulet (1977) suggested that in the case of Guinea-Bissau, an alternative development strategy was in effect. This strategy combined meeting basic needs with stimulating self-reliance and building from local values. Goulet emphasized that this strategy was particularly applicable to Guinea-Bissau because it was very poor in resources and infrastructure, committed to an egalitarian distribution of benefits, willing to pursue its drive toward socialism while tolerating collaboration with capitalist partners who tolerate the country's autonomy, and oriented to establishing institutions around local needs and values. The key to successful development in the country was "political will," an idea inherent in the thinking of Cabral and the experience of revolutionary struggle. Goulet was optimistic about the prospects for development. Goulet described how the PAIGC during the 1964 to 1973 period was able to combine revolutionary activity jointly with an institutional role in society, involving the building of new loyalties across ethnic lines and focusing on the evolving new nation; providing basic services such as food, health, education, and so on in liberated areas; mobilizing the peasantry into a force for change; and diffusing new values during the liberation phase that could aid the developmental strategy after independence (p. 5). He noted qualities of discipline, seriousness of purpose, decentralization of decisions, constant learning, and self-improvement as useful in formulating a developmental strategy: "Societies adopt alternative development strategies favoring basic needs, self-reliance, and local values when their political leaders make these priorities the substantive agenda of their dialogue with the population" (p. 8). The hope inspired by the country's performance in its first years of independence, he believed, was traceable to the vital link among self-reliance, meeting basic needs, and building on local values established by the popularly supported political party, first in practice, and only afterward in theory.

This notion of development is clearly found in the thought and experience of Cabral. Kofi (1981) identified principles that constituted Cabral's theory of development in Guinea-Bissau. Traditional elements were to be assimilated into a cohesive unit whereby guerrillas and peasants cooperate in raising national consciousness and breaking down old tribal structures. Imperialism and colonialism had to be eliminated. The militant revolutionary struggle was premised on the integration of all Africans into a national revolutionary party. After independence development would be based on democratic centralism. Kofi characterized Cabral's view of development as "developmental nationalism": "his singular theoretical contribution lies in what is to be done after the war of liberation" (p. 858).

Cabral's theory of the social evolution and development of Guinea-Bissau thus included building unity among traditional elements, ending colonialism and imperialism, assuring independence by means of armed struggle if necessary, and implementing structural development after independence. While his untimely death precluded his working out a detailed theory for transition to socialism after independence, we are aware of certain principles relating to the role of the petty bourgeois leadership and its need to overcome conflict with the direct producers of peasantry and workers, and the necessity of class struggle and finding a balance in socialist relations and forces of production to ensure a smooth transition.

McCulloch (1983: 101–102) compared the focus of Cabral on production to that of French anthropologists:

> Meillassoux and Terry fall into the trap of abandoning Marxism in the process of seeking to apply a rigorous Marxist analysis to lineage-based societies. Cabral, on the contrary, endorsed the productive forces thesis in the hope of gaining some respite from the pull of orthodox Marxism which he felt to be such a dead weight on the back of revolutionary theory in Africa.

McCulloch analyzed the differences in two major writings of Cabral ("Weapon of Theory" [1966] and "National Liberation and Culture" [1970]) and noted a shift from an emphasis on the class struggle in the earlier essay to a view in the later essay in which Cabral had "completely abandoned the role of class struggle as the motive force of history" and came "perilously close to that strain in African socialism in which class theory is seen as being largely irrelevant to African history" (McCulloch, 1983: 105). McCulloch, however, saw the thesis of a progressive evolution of the productive forces as an advance in contradiction of underdevelopment theory that stresses uneven levels of technology and degenerative patterns of change.

> Cabral arrived at his productive forces thesis, subliminally or even accidentally. It does not fit in directly with his general theory of imperialism nor with his analysis of the class struggle in Africa. If it did, then it would satisfy a number of questions which Cabral's theory as it stands cannot answer. The reason for this gap is in part due to the fact that Cabral's writings pose a number of problems concerning historical change, the nature of the imperialist relationship and the possibilities

for post-colonial development which fall beyond the scope of Cabral's own work. (McCulloch, 1983: 109)

In contrast to the pessimism of McCulloch, Luke (1981: 329) affirmed that Cabral's theory of socialist development "provides an attractive alternative to African societies intent upon a socialist mode of development." A close look at what ensued after the death of Cabral, however, reveals serious developmental problems, especially in Guinea. Okafor (1988) has attributed the devastation of the economy to the reliance of the government on international assistance and the undermining of its own developmental priorities to conform to demands of the donors as well as mismanagement of agricultural credit. Rudebeck (1974: 83) has observed that Cabral did not work out the problem of how a small and poor country like Guinea could escape underdevelopment: "By extending his argument logically, however, we may conclude that a common international strategy for revolutionary countries is a precondition for the fulfillment of third-world national liberation in the direction of socialism."

Galli and Jones (1987: 47) criticized Cabral for his "evolutionary view of human history," and Galli (1987) disputed his assumption that "Guinean peasants were culture-bound subsistence producers of relatively low productivity" (p. 87) and that "colonialism had had a negative impact of underdeveloping rather than developing indigenous agriculture" (p. 89). She also questioned the PAIGC adoption of a model of primitive socialist accumulation as the development strategy for Guinea-Bissau because historically and presently Guineans have been capable of generating large surpluses with inadequate infrastructure of roads and waterways, lack of subsidies for technical inputs, and so on. However, Chabal (1983: 165) has argued that Cabral would have pursued and implemented "a systematic policy of agricultural development in a far more energetic and determined fashion."

Bibliographic Note

Cabral's writings do not explicitly elaborate a theory of the state, and it is necessary to look carefully at his ideas on organizing the vanguard party, its relationship to the state established in liberated areas prior to independence, and the emergence of a state after independence. The lectures in the Seminário de Quadros, November 19–24, 1969, for example, reveal the principles of party organization and activity. For analysis on Cabral's conception of the state, see Agüero (1983); Andrade (1977A); Andreini and Lambert (1978) for nation-building; Belchior (1973) on the peoples congresses in liberated areas; Bienen (1977); Campbell (1977); Chabal (1983B); Davidson (1973C, 1974B, 1977A, 1977B, 1978A, 1978B); Forrest (1987A), who questions Cabral's emphasis on class and ideology; Galli (1987) and Galli and Jones (1987) on contradictions in the new state; Gamacchio (1985); Lopes (1982, 1986, 1987B); Mendonça (1982) on nation-building in Cape Verde; Moita (1976); Murteira (1978); Obichere

(1975); Pierson-Mathy (1980); and Washington (1976, 1980). For sources on development, see Jorge Cabral (1984); Luís Cabral (1978A) on the state after independence; Vasco Cabral (1973C) on the party and state, and (1977B, 1984C) on the Congress of Cassacá; Davidson (1973D, 1981D); Falola (1983); Goulet (1977, 1978A); Luke (1981); Okafor (1988); Rudebeck (1972, 1973, 1974) for development in the liberated zones as well as other sources, and (1979A, 1979B, 1981A, 1982, 1984A, 1984B); and Schiefer (1984).

Conclusion

This guide to the thought of Amílcar Cabral has examined his role as poet, student, agronomist, fighter, theorist, and diplomat. Cabral was viewed as a disciplined intellectual, productive scholar, and revolutionary theoretician, as well as an efficient organizer, mobilizer, and unifier. My study leads the reader into the sources about him and his place in history, delves into the conditions and circumstances that permitted his many accomplishments in a short span of life, and synthesizes his principal ideas. I organized the discussion around four major themes.

The first, on colonialism and imperialism, reveals that dominated people are denied their historical process of development under colonialism and that imperialism associates with the expansion of capitalism. Cabral related culture to the historical resistance of African peoples to the Portuguese presence. This resistance served as the foundation for the liberation movement which, Cabral understood as the struggle of a people to recover their own interrupted history. The struggle against colonialism thus serves as a motor force of contemporary history. As the initial political expression of a people, culture spawns new forms of resistance. Cabral distinguished between colonialism and neocolonialism—the former involving direct domination and the latter indirect domination. Classical colonialism becomes the imperialism of direct domination, and neocolonialism the imperialism of indirect domination. Neocolonialism was implemented as a counterrevolutionary strategy after World War II in a phase of monopoly capitalism and multinational corporations. Cabral defined imperialism as the monopolistic stage of capitalism, unable to resolve its own contradictions. He believed that the fundamental contradiction of the international system was the struggle of the Third World against imperialism. Whereas colonialism blocked the historical development of subjected peoples, imperialism, accompanied by the penetration and expansion of capitalism, imposed a complex structure on indigenous society and stirred up new conflicts. Thus, imperialism fulfills a historical mission by speeding up the development of the productive forces of society, intensifying the class struggle, and raising the standard of living.

Second, Cabral showed how African socialism adopted the European idea of nationalism as a strategy in the struggle against colonialism and imperialism, and he argued that culture was essential to the national liberation movement. His theory of revolutionary nationalism and national liberation was premised on the relationship between culture and the economic condition, which gives rise to national liberation. He believed that the armed liberation struggle would emanate from the development of a popular culture of positive values—a national culture based on history and the successes of struggle; political and moral conscience of the people dedicated to sacrifice and the cause of independence, justice, and progress; scientific culture compatible with the needs of progress; and universal culture in the direction of world integration and the elevation of humanism and solidarity. He delineated a duality between the culture imposed by Portuguese colonialism and the traditional culture.

Third, Cabral applied a theory of class and class struggle to his historical perspective, but he questioned the European assumption that class struggle is the only determinant in the evolution of history because this would place outside of history the lives of many peoples, especially in Africa, Asia, and Latin America at a time they were also subject to imperialism. Cabral noted divisions and contradictions everywhere in society, involving races, religions, ethnic groups, and social classes. Classes are the consequence of the development of the productive forces and the dominant mode of production, but man will outlive history and continue to produce and make history. Cabral identified at least three stages in the development of the productive forces: a primitive form lacking private appropriation of the means of production and consequently no class struggle; a more progressive stage characterized by private appropriation of the means of production, conflicts of interest, and the possibility of class struggle; and a higher stage in which private appropriation is eliminated, class struggle diminishes, and unknown forces appear. He believed that these stages were not mutually exclusive and could be combined in the uneven development of societies. Further, no particular sequence of stages is necessary, and a leap to the formation of a socialist society is possible. Cabral also identified various social classes, with attention to the revolutionary potential of the petty bourgeoisie and the peasantry.

Finally, although he did not elaborate a definitive theory of state and development, Cabral was concerned with the evolution of the revolutionary state in the liberated zones and in the period after independence. He recognized the problem of assimilating the new structures in the liberated zones with those in the Portuguese colonial enclaves. Village committees, people's courts, people's stores, health clinics, and rural schools would serve the new integrated society. Development would become self-centered rather subject to the bureaucratic model, but the revolutionary party would be decisive in the process of state building in the liberated areas. The party was instrumental in the emerging state during the liberation period, and the party would guide the people through the principles of unity and struggle—unity implying strength in the face of adversity and struggle serving as a fundamental condition of all peoples. Cabral also envisaged development as representing the evolution of the productive forces and relations of production in a harmonious social division without exploitation. He recognized that the liberation of people from oppression, exploitation, and poverty involved many difficulties. He looked to agricultural development rather than rapid industrialization as the basis for providing for basic needs of the people and generating some surplus for infrastructure and light industry.

I have identified the principal elements of the thought of Amílcar Cabral, and it should be clear that his contribution has been substantial in terms of the range and diversity of ideas as well as innovation and application of theory to the historical experience. As we advance into the 1990s, however, Africa remains largely poor and unstable—in particular, the former Portuguese colonies including Angola, Cape Verde, Guinea-Bissau, and Mozambique.

Further, the recent changes in the socialist world—in particular, the decline of Marxism-Leninism and the orthodox vanguard parties and command economies of Eastern Europe—have resulted in a reassessment of socialism and Marxism. I do not see these developments as diminishing the contributions of Cabral. Indeed, he anticipated some of these problems, even in the midst of his own revolutionary struggle.

First, Cabral demonstrated the importance of organizing the vanguard party in the revolutionary period as the means of establishing government and providing for basic human needs in liberated areas, mobilizing the diverse ethnic peoples, and raising revolutionary consciousness. Under Cabral and the revolutionary leadership, the PAIGC not only challenged and ultimately defeated Portuguese colonialism and imperialism but dedicated itself to forming alternative political and economic institutions. Cabral taught us the strengths and weaknesses of the liberation struggle and offered insights that may have relevance to colonial and neocolonial situations elsewhere. His approach has served revolutionary causes elsewhere in the Third World, especially in Central America.

Second, Cabral applied an independent Marxist analysis and original thinking to the struggle for independence, and showed that success was not dependent on following or replicating the old formulas of the Soviet Union and its allies or any other revolutionary situation. He transcended Eurocentric conceptions to offer a new approach to imperialism (rationalized imperialism) and to nationalism (revolutionary nationalism). Cabral placed his analysis within a historically materialist framework, but he did not advocate rigid formulations nor proclaim himself a Marxist, although he was influenced by the Marxist method and the belief that good theory is based on concrete and historical conditions and experience.

Finally, Cabral showed how his example as organizer and unifier along with personal determination and commitment could influence and motivate the mass revolutionary movement.

Photographs

Amílcar Cabral, speech in Rome,where he received an honorary doctorate

Luís Cabral, half-brother of Amílcar and president of Guinea-Bissau from 1975 to the November 14, 1980, coup (photo by Frances B. Chilcote, August 1975)

Chica Vaz, deputy of the Popular National Assembly, 1974

Children at school in a liberated zone of Guinea-Bissau, circa 1972

From the left, Aristedes Pereira and Nino Vieria, who became, respectively, presidents of Cape Verde (1975 to present) and Guinea-Bissau (November 14, 1980 to present)

Children in a liberated zone of Guinea-Bissau learning to handle arms, circa 1973

A Portuguese air force bombing of a village in a liberated zone

PAIGC marines at attention, circa 1973

FARP action on the Northern Front, 1973

Representatives of the region of Balana-Quitafine at the Popular National Assembly during 1973

Carmen Pereira

Aristides Pereira, speech to the Popular National Assembly, 1973

Representatives at the Popular National Assembly in 1973. In the center foreground is Vasco Cabral, economist

PAIGC soldiers alongside a poster of Amílcar Cabral after his death

Appendix: Perspectives of the Revolutionary Vanguard

The limitations of field research in the midst of a revolutionary struggle certainly are obvious to anyone who has attempted to delve into particular cases once a revolutionary or national liberation movement has come to power. The dearth of serious published systematic studies of revolutions attests to this problem, and although at the outset of my study I was confident of my prospects, I encountered nearly insurmountable obstacles.

The Partido Africano da Independência da Guiné e Cabo Verde proclaimed victory and independence from Portuguese rule on September 24, 1973, signifying that Cabral's premature death eight months earlier was not in vain. The guerrilla movement indeed did control the outlying rural areas and some small towns, but formal independence was not possible until the coup of April 25, 1974, dissolved the old Portuguese dictatorship and a treaty of September 1974 formally recognized the break.

During the interim of informal and formal independence, I resolved to study the degree of political socialization that Cabral and the PAIGC leadership had brought to liberated zones during the revolutionary struggle. I was interested in identifying and analyzing perspectives of the revolutionary vanguard of leaders who had joined Cabral—some as early as 1956 with the founding of the PAIGC, but most in the early 1960s with the initiation of the rebellion. I desired to compare and contrast their perspectives with those of the new generation—the sons and daughters of a revolution in power, initially in liberated zones where schools were established to bring education and a revolutionary consciousness to the African population, but now in urban areas still permeated by the legacy of Portuguese colonialism.

My research proposal included objectives and major questions for field research, identification of methods, and a timeline for the study. My funding was secured in mid-1974, but I postponed travel and field work for a year due to the complications caused by the Portuguese withdrawal and the assumption of power by the revolutionaries over all the country. This necessitated the revolutionaries to move to the capital, Bissau, and resolve the contradictions inherent in the process of assimilating colonial and revolutionary values. The delay also facilitated a visit to Cape Verde after formal independence was declared on July 5, 1975.

The investigation thus was carried out in the wake of independence during August and September 1975. The visit allowed for direct impressions of the capitals, Bissau and Praia, and the outlying towns and rural interior. Some of these impressions are in the journal notes of my wife, Frances, who accompanied and assisted me in the interviews and research.

In Cape Verde we felt both desperation and hope: the dry island of Sal and its strategic airstrip that once served Portuguese and U.S. interests in Africa and continued to service South African air traffic; rainfall on the island of Santiago and the temporary escape from years of drought; determined and optimistic government officials who were committed to bring relief to centuries of human misery and to provide for basic needs of the people; a visit to the town of Santa Catarina where Cabral once lived and a look at the primary school he had attended in Praia; and a tour of the infamous concentration camp of Tarrafal.

We interviewed several high officials in the government, and years later I also met Miranda who in 1968 was sent by Cabral to Cape Verde to organize resistance among the people. Miranda was arrested nine months later, detained six years at Tarrafal, and eventually released five days after independence. Before returning to Cape Verde, Miranda spent two years in prison with Rafael Barbosa, one of the initial participants in the internal opposition, who later collaborated with the Portuguese while in prison and reappeared briefly during the coup of November 14, 1980. Miranda was a popular PAIGC leader from the island of Santa Antão (interview in Praia, January 20, 1983).

The visit to Bissau was marked by many interviews with party officials, including President Luís Cabral, who had invited us to the country. Bissau was a distinctly colonial city, small and rustic in appearance. We also visited the interior, traveling along the paved road to Bafatá, birthplace of Amílcar Cabral. This road bisects the country and was strategically important for the Portuguese occupation forces and their control of the principal urban towns during the war. At Bafatá we were received by the head of the region, Chico Bá, who recounted his experience in the struggle and analyzed the problems of agriculture, health, and education that impacted his region. He explained that the region had remained under Portuguese control prior to independence, and this necessitated hard work to educate the people politically. Additionally, large numbers of refugees were returning to the area. The main goals involved planning for the future, diversification of crops, and organization of cooperatives.

At Gabú, a town of seven thousand inhabitants an hour to the east of Bafatá, we were entertained by Lay Seck, president of the region, who spoke of his involvement in the war but concentrated on the problems of the region, including lack of food, even though it was a cattle-producing area; deficient medical assistance; and the need to raise educational standards in an area of Moslem influence. In the rural areas, we saw many *tabancas*, or small villages, with circular huts with woven walls and thatched roofs where peasants cultivated rice and maize together with other vegetables. The resourcefulness and hard work of these people impressed us, and we believed that under the guidance of the party they were capable of resolving problems at the local level.

Research Questions and Methods

Soon after our arrival in Bissau, it became apparent that interviews with school children were not possible due principally to the assimilation of the rural liberation zones into national life; a tendency at the educational level to defer to Portuguese colonial practice; and the lack of policy oriented to resolving discrepancies between colonial and revolutionary educational methods, practices, and materials. We had arrived too late to seriously examine the impact of political socialization in liberated zones and too early to learn of new directions in education. Thus, we concentrated on interviews with the revolutionary leaders in an effort to learn of their background and participation, revolutionary commitment, awareness of historical conditions, and perspectives for nation-building.

My method was informal in-depth interviews accompanied by a structural format of themes related to historical experience, probing for a personal account of involvement in the revolution, and identification of some biographical characteristics. Often the interviews began with a personal account of participation in the struggle for independence because respondents were usually comfortable in discussing their roles. In the process of each interview, I attempted to learn the age, birthplace, ethnic affiliation, educational level, class origins, and parental background of the interviewee; additionally, I identified past and current political responsibilities and goals. Depending on the knowledge and awareness of the respondent, I also delved into their perspectives on a number of themes: Portuguese imperialism, its stages and impact; the legacy of colonialism and neocolonialism and past and present relations of dependency and their consequences; types and examples of classes and class conflicts; cases of historical resistance to Portuguese rule; decisive events in the struggle for independence; and the role of institutional life, especially in the agricultural units, government and party, revolutionary army, and schools and services.

Difficulties and Results

During August and September 1975 I interviewed twenty-one persons in
Cape Verde and Guinea-Bissau, including twenty leaders of the PAIGC. (The
interview with Braime is not included. It reflects his impressions and
involvement in the 1959 Pidjiguiti strike and massacre, and specific
questions were not directed to him because he was not part of the
revolutionary leadership.) Two of these leaders were founders of the party. All
but two of the respondents had participated in the war to liberate Guinea-
Bissau from Portuguese colonialism; three of them returned to Praia after
independence to become officials in the Cape Verde government, and five of
them joined the government of Guinea-Bissau. Information on all Cape
Verdeans interviewed is given in Tables A.1 and A.2. One of the Guinean
respondents was born in Angola and active in the struggle there, but had
joined the PAIGC in 1967.

The following interviews are edited for style and content only to the
extent of excluding material not relevant to the questions and themes of
participation in the revolutionary struggle. A brief biographical note precedes
each interview and, where possible, identifies what has happened to the
respondent since 1975. Content generally is presented in verbatim form so
that there be no alteration of the meaning intended by respondents. Roughly
an hour in length, each interview was recorded on cassette tape. Interviewing
was intensive, in-depth, and probed a number of themes. The results are
organized around two aspects. Table A.1 provides personal information such
as age, birthplace, tribal affiliation, education, and social class. Table A.2
summarizes perspectives of such themes as Portuguese imperialism, past and
present dependency through the legacy of colonialism and neocolonialism,
class and class conflict, historical resistance, and the status of the
revolutionary organizations.

The interviews, however, are uneven, due in part to political conditions
so soon after independence, especially in Bissau where suspicions and distrust
were obvious and certainly not unexpected, given the past evidence of
penetration of the Portuguese secret police agents into the ranks of the
PAIGC, the murder of Cabral, rumored differences between Cape Verdeans
and Guineans, party infighting and potential personality conflicts, and
possible deficiencies in administering the state apparatus after independence.
(These problems surfaced in the November 1980 coup that deposed Luís
Cabral.)

I also experienced problems of differences in educational background and
experience. Some respondents were unable to articulate perspectives around
some of the historical themes. They had not conceptualized the general
historical experience, and tended to reflect views drawn from personal
experience. Some of them focused on problems related to their administrative
responsibilities, and seemed unable and sometimes simply unwilling to delve

into the past. None of the interviews matched the sophistication in analysis, articulation of theoretical and conceptual position, or basic knowledge and understanding of Amílcar Cabral, and this should be clear to the reader who compares their responses to his writings and speeches.

Finally, a brief synthesis of these interviews is possible. It is unnecessary to isolate individual differences that are apparent from interview to interview, but some patterns and common characteristics are apparent. Although the interviews clearly reflect individual and personal views and thoughts, it should also be apparent that they represent a sense of collectivity and solidarity over the accomplishments and objectives of the revolution. Time constraints allowed only two weeks for interviews in Cape Verde and a month in Guinea-Bissau. I feel that at the time the interviews represented the views of the party and government. The interviews are representative in the sense that they include leaders from different sectors. Not all important leaders are included in the following set, although on other occasions I have talked with Amílcar Cabral, Aristides Pereira, and Pedro Pires. Others not included were busy and unavailable or traveling.

The profile of data in Table A.1 reveals that all but one of the respondents were male, and, with the exception of three Cape Verdeans who

Table A.1 Revolutionary Leadership Profile, 1975

Characteristics	Cape Verdeans ($N=8$)	Guineans ($N=12$)	Total
Sex (female/male)	0/8	1/11	1/19
Age			
30 and under	3	3	
31–35	5	5	
36–40	2	6	8
Over 40	3	1	4
Ethnic origin			
Pepel	3	3	
Balanta	2	2	
Other or not identified	6	6	
Mulatto	8	1	9
Education			
Primary	5	5	
Secondary	3	6	9
University	5	1	6
Social class/occupation			
when entered struggle			
Petty bourgeoisie			
Functionary	2	5	7
Commerce	3	4	7
Professional or other	2	1	3
Peasantry	1	2	3
Participation in armed struggle			
Prior to 1965	4	10	14
1966 to 1973	3	1	4
Postindependence	1	1	2

were 30 years of age or younger, most were older, including the five high Guinea-Bissau officials of Cape Verdean origin. Some of the Guineans were quick to identify their tribal affiliation whereas others, often of petty bourgeois background, offered no such distinction. As might be expected, given their access to educational facilities, the Cape Verdeans tended to be higher educated than their Guinean counterparts, with the exception of one who was of Angolan origin. Social class origins were identifiable from parental occupation and respondent vocation when participation in the liberation struggle began. Most of the leadership identified its direct participation to the period before 1965. Some of the older leaders who had not been educated beyond primary school were articulate and sophisticated in elaborating their perspectives, and they tended to attribute their education not to schooling but to learning gained from the revolutionary process.

The perspectives summarized in Table A.2 focus on four ideas, emphasized in the writings and speeches of Amílcar Cabral. First, half the

Table A.2 Revolutionary Leadership Perspectives, 1975

Perspectives	Cape Verdeans (N=8)	Guineans (N=12)	Total
Imperialism Overview			
Theoretical and substantive	1		1
Substantive	5	4	9
Simplistic	2	8	10
Stages of imperialism			
Clear conception	2		2
Some detail	2	1	3
No understanding	4	11	15
Dependency overview			
Theoretical and substantive	1		1
Substantive	2		2
Simplistic	5	10	15
No understanding		2	2
Dependency after independence			
Broken	5	10	15
Inevitable or necessary		1	1
Insignificant	3	1	4
Social classes overview			
Theoretical and conceptual	3	4	7
Dichotomy colonial/exploited	2	4	6
No delineation/liberation front	2	3	5
No understanding	1	1	2
Social classes after independence			
Differentiated	2	1	3
Moderately different	4		4
Disappeared or never existed	2	9	11
No understanding		2	2
Historical Resistance			
Sophisticated view	6	4	10
Impressionist view	1	7	8
No understanding	1	1	2

leaders articulated clear and detailed understanding of imperialism in its historical and theoretical context, yet only one-fourth attempted to conceptualize imperialism in terms of stages or essential epoches of confrontation between colonizer and colonized. Because both independent countries had experienced centuries of colonial rule and surely looked to Portugal and other nations for support in their nation-building and reconstruction, I asked the leaders to discuss their views of dependency. Only one offered any conceptualization of dependency, whereas three provided substantive detail and example of past and anticipated problems. However, most respondents believed that independence assured their nations of sovereignty and autonomy, and that neutrality and nonalignment should be followed in relationships with friendly and supportive nations. Half of the respondents were able to provide sophisticated interpretation of historical moments of African resistance that shaped their struggle for independence before 1960. Finally, it was interesting to note that one-third of the leaders offered a class analysis somewhat similar to that of Amílcar Cabral a decade earlier, and another third of them simply distinguished between classes of Portuguese exploiters and African exploited. More than half of the respondents insisted that social classes in their countries had disappeared through the revolutionary process or that they had never existed.

— 1 —
Luís Cabral

Luís Cabral was the half-brother of Amílcar Cabral. He was one of the six founders of the PAIGC, a party leader, and after independence and the assassination of Amílcar, he became president of the Council of State, a post held until November 1980 when he was ousted in a coup. Thereafter, he lived in Cuba until early in 1983 when he returned to the Cape Verdes. This interview was given on August 27, 1975, in Bissau. The interview recounts details of his involvement in the formation of a clandestine opposition party and in organized labor. A second part emphasizes his attention to problems in his country immediately after independence as well as his perspectives on class struggle, imperialism, and dependence of Guinea-Bissau on the outside world.

Can you tell us something about your personal experiences in the struggle for freedom of your country? How was it that you first became involved?

It is always difficult to talk about oneself. Well, I first became involved because of my brother Amílcar. We had a special relationship ever since the time we were very young. When he returned from Portugal to work in Guinea, he felt that it was necessary to create a party. As you know in Portugal the older students from the colonies formed an anticolonial movement, the Movimento Anti-Colonialista (MAC). The members of this movement included Agostino Neto and Mário de Andrade of Angola, Marcelino dos Santos of Mozambique, Amílcar, and others from São Tomé and Príncipe. Their idea was to create an organization in each colony. So we began by selecting persons known for their African nationalism. We created some legal cultural organizations through which we engaged in political work, even though we had no authorization to do this. These persons worked clandestinely as a group. With this as a base, we began to work in 1955 and 1956. In 1956 from this group, six people founded the Partido Africano da Independência da Guiné e Cabo Verde (PAIGC). At this time, Amílcar was living outside of the country in Portugal and Angola, but he came here once in a while, and as brothers we maintained contact through regular correspondence. Realistically, we couldn't do very much at this time because everybody had to work at their jobs.

In Bissau, during 1954 and 1956 some of us were influential in labor circles. Africans paid dues to the "official" *sindicatos* (labor unions) but they were not considered members and could not be elected to the leadership. At that time, I was a member of the Conselho Geral dos Sindicatos. Unfortunately, after founding the party, we verified that elements of the party in the Sindicato were also connected with the police and the politics of the Portuguese. So we had to become clandestine.

In 1958 the Republic of Guinée (Conakry) became independent. The following year there was a strike of stevedores in the port of Bissau with elements connected to the party. And immediately following the strike in September 1959 Amílcar came here from Angola. He analyzed the situation, and in discussion we decided to abandon all manifestations against the Portuguese. We began to gather facts and recruit members. We decided to concentrate our attention in the *mato* (rural forested areas), where the people lived totally separate from colonial life and resisted the Portuguese presence. At this time some of us left Bissau and established contact with the people. In 1960 there were denouncements, several of our comrades were taken prisoners, but we still maintained relations with some Portuguese friends. Also Aristides Pereira, who was head of the telegraph and telephone service here in Bissau, listened to a conversation from Lisbon to Bissau in which Portuguese officials discussed my imprisonment. Forewarned, I managed to flee to Senegal without being taken prisoner. From there I went to Conakry and then to France to participate in a meeting with Portuguese anticolonists. It was necessary also to attend the Pan-African conference in Tunis. Once having participated in the conference, however, I could no longer return to Portugal, for Portuguese officials knew who participated in the conference as well as those individuals from the colonies who opposed Portuguese policies.

In 1960 various people of the party were taken prisoner here: Fernando Fortes and even my brother, António Cabral, who was expelled and sent to Portugal. It was a mixup. He was older than I but younger than Amílcar. He was a functionary in the bank at that time. There were many others who were taken prisoner or who left.

Why did this happen in 1960?

After the strike (Pidjiguiti) and because of the independence of Guinée. In 1959 the Portuguese sent agents of political police (known as Polícia Internacional e Defesa do Estado—PIDE) to Bissau. They arbitrarily seized many people and especially those who manifested their nationalism.

During the years from 1954 to 1960, how did you operate within the Portuguese society?

We started by participating in the political life of the Portuguese by promoting candidates of the Portuguese opposition—for example, Norton dos Matos and Craveiro Lopes. At that time there was a Portuguese current in

Guinea associated with us. There was also Fausto Teixeira. They were opposed to fascism, and we were able to work with them within the framework of the struggle of antifascism. It was only in 1954 and 1955 that Amílcar gave us a new direction—that our struggle was not only against fascism, and that we could not condition independence on those opposing Portuguese fascism. We were struggling against colonialism and against fascism but essentially the struggle was directly against colonialism.

Was the turning point Pidjiguiti?

There was clandestine work before that. The real work began only after the independence of the Republic of Guinée. That event had its impact here in this country. It was then that 200 agents of the PIDE were sent here. So, because of the strikes and demonstrations, the PIDE analyzed the political situation. The massacre of 1959 reflected this. . . .

Was Pidjiguiti spontaneous or was it directed by the party?

You could not say that it was really directed by the party, but it was related to the political work of the party. People acted in a much more organized and conscious way than they did previously because there had been work by the party. At this time I was working in the Casa do Gouvêa. My colleague, Carlos Corrêa, also worked in the Gouvêa (now he is under-commissioner of agriculture). He was taken prisoner on August 3 and was only freed because we intervened along with the management of the company. But then Lisbon ordered him imprisoned and sent to Portugal. Since we had access to the telegraph and telephone system of Lisbon and Bissau, he fled that night for Senegal. So that in the morning when the PIDE went to the Gouvêa to take him, he was gone.

Where were you born?

Here in Bissau on April 11, 1931. My father was Cape Verdean and a primary teacher here in Bissau. My mother was Portuguese. My father spent much of his life here in Guinea. He was educated after my birth. Then he went to Cape Verde. He was a functionary and primary teacher and spent all his youth here. When I was very young, about three years old, we went to Cape Verde. I went to primary school in Praia. I went to secondary school in Praia and São Vicente. After the death of my father in 1951, I returned in 1952 with Amílcar. Amílcar was born here also—in Bafatá. Amílcar went to primary and secondary school in Cape Verde and continued his studies in Portugal. When I came here I started to work in Gouvêa (I always worked there). I finished my secondary studies here in Guinea and worked here too. This was how Amílcar and I planned it.

Amílcar had problems here. An informer, Amelio Ovim [name inaudible], a well-known councilman and captain, denounced Amílcar as a subversive in 1954. So Amílcar asked who denounced him. But they told him only that it was a man of authority. They did not take him, but he had to leave and so he went to Angola where he remained in contact with us and came back regularly.

What happened in 1960?

We left Guinea in order to build the party. I worked ten months in Senegal, and Amílcar worked in Conakry. We maintained the party. We established the Southern Front. In 1966 I went to the Northern Front. I was a member of the permanent secretariat of the party. After Amílcar's death we had the second congress. Later we established the National Assembly.

Could you say that your struggle was one of class struggle?

We don't see it in that way—in the past it was a struggle for national independence. Our party served as a front (you can't look at it in the context of a European party in which a party defends a class interest and there are several parties, each with its limited area). This is not the case here, our party is a national liberation front. To progress we must group together within the party all the honest forces of the country which want to participate in the struggle.

But isn't the objective to establish a proletariat?

That depends on what development takes place. It is not our objective to have large national capitalists. We struggled for independence. We can have certain private initiatives, but they must be within the limits of our poverty. We cannot allow private interests to work against the interests of the large masses of people.

Is the objective to achieve a classless society?

No, we can't say this. Our slogan is not to give examples of one sect or another, it is not to call us certain names that come from one place or another. We are not going to make great leaps forward without first doing the groundwork. Our desire is to achieve objective realities within our objective of creating a just society without exploitation and with justice. . . . Others can see us as we are.

The merchants who were here and worked together with the Portuguese, did they remain?

Yes, they remained. We believe that the merchants have a following in the city. We do not feel that we should act against them simply because they were here during the colonial period. But today, on the other hand, the state must organize for the country, including imports. As for imports, we do not have great resources to spend outside the country and we must import that which is most essential for our economy. We must also control prices so that they are fair. But private enterprise will continue for years, while the state will serve a complementary role in the areas of greatest importance to the country. Our people's stores had an important role during the period of our struggle and still continue to be important. They have overcome tremendous obstacles and now provide for the massive needs of Bissau. During the struggle we had considerable experience in supplying the liberated zones. Arriving in Bissau, in several months we were able to gain control of essential national commerce, forcing the merchants to sell products at a set profit.

Amílcar Cabral identified your struggle as anti-imperialist. Would you continue to call it that?

Yes, our constitution (our state) is anticolonial and anti-imperialist. We fought against colonialism, and we will continue to struggle against all aspects of domination. We are preoccupied with national interests. We will work mutually with other countries, but we will not let anyone interfere in our internal affairs.

Given lack of resources, doesn't the country remain dependent on the outside world?

Even if one had all necessary resources, no one country can exist in isolation. But we are in Africa and we must establish relations with the African community of nations as well as the rest of the world. . . . We are a people who wish to integrate into our African world. This cooperation is indispensable for our development. Because of the struggle that we have experienced, no people or state has the right to dominate us, but the state must be free and sovereign and able to develop itself on equal terms.

Do you see a contradiction between the dependency of the country on the outside world, and the anti-imperialist struggle?

No, the imperialists may have intentions, but for us everything depends on the internal conditions of our country. And we are a people who have struggled for many years, as you know. Today our country is totally free politically, and it wants to build an independent economy, but in cooperation with other peoples. . . . In no way will we subject ourselves to others. We are a people who love our independence and would resist any attempt to diminish the conquests we have achieved.

What is going to happen to the Casa Gouvêa and the "old" CUF [the Portuguese monopoly which dominated in Guinea-Bissau]?

Casa Gouvêa still is controlled by Portuguese interests. We have not yet come to the end of our negotiations with Portugal—our last meeting with them was in July. We will meet again with them to resolve this and other cases, including the bank. We have established our Banco Nacional de Guiné-Bissau. . . . After resolving the bank situation, we will deal with the Gouvêa case. The Gouvêa cannot continue here in its present form. We will not nationalize it. We will find a new structure, probably establishing a "mixed" state-private enterprise. Perhaps there will be separation of industrial and commercial activities. We have to end its monopoly over most of our economy in transport, commerce, and insurance. All this will be discussed. The only thing that is more or less clear is that we will have a large mixed enterprise—Gouvêa and the state for industry and for processing of agricultural goods.

When Portugal took over the Companhia União Fabril, didn't Gouvêa pass to the public sector?

No, part of it remains under private control among interests in Portugal. CUF only had part interest in the company—its administration.

What will be the relation of Guinea to Cape Verde? Will a federation be created or will the two countries unite to form a single nation?

The party is going to meet before the end of the year in a congress to resolve the question. We are going to restructure the party. Then we have to formulate a constitution. And the two national assemblies will get together and discuss it. The dominant thinking in the party is to establish a federation. Two states with a great deal of autonomy and one federal government that will coordinate the action of the two states.

2

Fernando Fortes

Fernando Fortes was born in São Vicente, in the Cape Verde Islands. His parents were Cape Verdean, but in 1947 he went to Bissau. There he was active among students and workers; in the early 1950s he joined Amílcar Cabral in organizing a number of opposition movements, and in 1956 he was one of six founders of the PAIGC. This interview, in Bissau on August 25, 1975, focused on this early experience. At the time Fortes was commissioner of telecommunications. After the 1980 coup, Fortes left Bissau to reside in the Cape Verdes. He died in Moscow early in 1983.

I have been in Bissau since 1947, but I was born in São Vicente. My parents are also from São Vicente. In 1947, when I was seventeen years old, I came to Bissau to work. In 1947 there was already some political resistance among students in São Vicente due to the Second World War. São Vicente suffered the consequences of that war; there were rationings and disturbances of the people. The port of São Vicente was very busy as a connecting point between traffic from Europe to South America; traffic of people, goods, and foodstuff. There were many English companies in São Vicente.

In Cape Verde there were also grave problems due to the war, especially food shortages for the population as a whole. During this time the process of national consciousness began to emerge. The students formed groups to study books secretly and to debate issues. Our study group was small and restricted. Some of my friends were tortured and jailed by the Portuguese fascists; others were killed. Comrade Cabral was the oldest in our group. When I entered the lycée in São Vicente he was already doing advanced work. He also attended the lycée in São Vicente. I met him the very first days of my experience at the lycée. Cabral had already an excellent and known reputation in the lycée as an exceptional student, as a colleague always ready to help others, and he tutored classes for free in his house. In 1943–44 he went to the island of São Tiago, where his parents lived, and he stayed there to work.

I finished the lycée in São Vicente in June 1947, and in November 1947 I came to Bissau. Here in Bissau my friends formed a cultural group to keep in touch with literature, cultural events, and to facilitate an analysis of current problems. Other groups began to form and spread; the UPG [the Union of Guinean People], the MING [Movement for the National

Independence of Guinea]—all these groups formed in 1953 and 1954 before the PAIGC. Since my arrival in Bissau I worked for the postal service. Comrade Cabral worked as an agronomist. I had the opportunity to work together and live with comrade Aristides Pereira until 1960 when he left. Cabral attended some of our group meetings, and he called our attention to the African reality. All our meetings were secret because any form of association or meeting was illegal. He worked hard with us and was our political teacher.

At this time we decided to go underground, and after a meeting with Cabral, we decided to form the PAIGC; this meeting occurred December 19. We decided our main task was to inform and educate the people. We never wanted to impose our views on others or force them to accept our explanations. Explain and educate patiently. We began to infiltrate the workers' union. Our group consisted of four people: Amílcar Cabral, Luís Cabral, Aristides Pereira, and myself. Our main activity was the political education of the people, and we infiltrated the workers' union and the municipal assembly in 1957 and 1958.

During the event of August 3, 1959, when the stevedores asked for wage increases, there was a violent reaction by the government and officially fifty people were killed by the soldiers. There were about two hundred wounded. Personally, I believe more than eighty people were killed. The wage increase demand by the sailors was a result of the political education of the party, but we never expected such violence and bloodshed to occur. The party did not expect the incident to take the dimension that it took; the group called Cabral from Angola to come back to Bissau. He arrived the 26th of September and we immediately had a meeting. We considered the Pidjiguiti incident of August 3 as a declaration of war. There was no other solution.

At the meeting with Amílcar, we all decided that he should not come back to Bissau anymore for his frequent visits—he should stay away. Comrade Luís Cabral left for Senegal, where his wife's family lived; later he went to Conakry. Aristides left in 1960. I stayed here to direct the mobilization of the interior (the countryside), and I could only leave this area after receiving orders from the outside. So I stayed behind and conducted the mobilization efforts in region "Zero," the region of Bissau.

When the police and army were tightening their grip on our group, we decided to ask for orders from Conakry. But on February 6, 1961, before receiving any further orders, I was arrested. In August 1961, I was tried and sentenced to jail with maximum security, but because of my family's efforts, I was put on conditional liberty here in Bissau in 1963. In 1964 we continued with the party's work until early 1966 (March of 1966) when I was arrested again and held until March of 1967. Then I was sent to Angola. From March to August 1967 I was in jail in Luanda; after August I was sent to a concentration camp until 1971. So from August 1967 until 1971 I was in the concentration camp. Then I stayed another three years in residence in

Luanda without permission to leave. Every week I had to report to the police. After February 25, I did not report anymore to the police, but left Luanda in July to come back to Bissau. I arrived and went to Conakry. I was very happy to come back to Bissau knowing that I could not be arrested anymore. I was very happy to see my comrades whom I thought I would never see again. I was very happy to hug Aristides Pereira in Conakry at the PAIGC.

Now we are in another phase of our struggle. This is a different stage. It will require great sacrifice and a total dedication to the party work. I have a responsibility to those comrades who helped form the party and who were killed. I have a responsibility to give my best to the party as one of the founders of the party. We want to build a different society, a different man.

——— 3 ———

Felinto Vaz Martins

At the time of this interview, August 22, 1975, Martins was commissioner of industry. He was born in Bolama about 1939 and received some secondary education in Bissau. His parents were of the Pepel tribe and were peasant farmers. His father died in the struggle, and one sister also participated. He lived in Portugal for two years until the outbreak of war in Angola in 1961, when he fled to Switzerland. While in Switzerland he studied and worked for seven years, acquiring technical training. He returned to Guinea-Bissau immediately after Cabral's death in early 1973. A portion of the interview, dealing with details of industry, has been omitted.

What are your perspectives on the imperialism that has affected your country in the past and present?

This is a political question. We consist here of a department that is essentially technical in nature. The party is responsible for expressing the political orientation of the state. We want to have good international relations with all countries of the world. We do not want to interfere in the foreign affairs of other countries. We are interested in the course of international relations and want to be aware of international events, but we do not want to interfere in the affairs of other states. This is our policy of nonalignment. We are a part of the Third World and are allied to the countries of the Third World.

About the past, before independence, what are your perspectives on imperialism and colonialism?

We were always honest, never diplomatic. We told about things as we perceived them and we always condemned everything that was against the people—everything that belonged to colonialism, neocolonialism, and imperialism in a general sense. We condemned the ideas, but we respected the people. Our government can condemn a certain action taken, but it respects the individual(s) who implemented it. We fight against ideas that go against man, but we do not go against man. This is a basic tenet of our fight.

The country has suffered a lot in the past and lacks resources. Is the country dependent upon the international system?

There is no truly independent country. Even political independence is relative, so much so for economic independence. The latter does not exist. The advanced developed countries depend on the less developing countries vis-à-vis the supply of primary products, and we depend on the advanced countries for the supply of infrastructure, technological know-how, and financial assistance. There is no absolute independence, but we are striving to obtain the necessary relative political economic independence. We are proud of our past struggle that we won with arms against an enemy much more powerful than ourselves. We are ready for the great sacrifice to preserve this independence which cost us dearly.

The existing dependence does not represent a contradiction of the revolutionary process in which you are involved?

We don't believe so, because in the context of events in the world it is a necessary relationship between and among nations; this does not constitute dependency per se. It is a relation among nations of good understanding (of good faith). From the beginning the party established those general guidelines. In the current phase of economic takeoff we are economically dependent on certain countries which are assisting us. Some countries are helping us in an honest and open way, but we always emphasize that such aid should not be accompanied by a political counterpart. We have good relations with Portugal; it is in our interest to maintain good relations with Portugal. We continue to have economic relations with Portugal. On this western coast our country was an enclave with economic ties to Portugal. In this initial phase of relations we are trying to diversify our sources of primary necessities. However, we are tied to Portugal. Foreign observers are surprised to learn the extent of our ties to Portugal. One of the results of the independence war was that this country is isolated from Africa. This will continue for some time to come. We are expanding to become part of Africa economically. We do not want to be isolated, we want to be part of the Third World.

To continue to develop the energy and industry sectors, will you establish new relations with other countries or can you sustain present relations?

We need relations with other countries for the supply of equipment and machinery. We have projects—hydraulic industry—which in the takeoff phase need assistance from friendly nations that want to see us develop and grow. The existing industry here was a processing industry with links to the agricultural product. Everything was imported from Portugal and exported to Portugal. We need to begin planning in order to enact and implement worthwhile projects.

What countries do you have relations with?

We are beginning some planning projects with the help of those same countries which assisted us during the revolutionary struggle: Sweden, the Soviet Union, and Portugal. We were enemies of Portugal, but now we are friends. Some technical international agencies of the United Nations have also assisted us.

What are your perspectives on social classes in the past and currently?

There were three social classes: (1) the *"indigenas"*—*indigena* means that which is natural. The term was prejoratively used to mean those who were ignorant without knowledge of anything; (2) the "assimilated," those who evolved and to whom certain duties in the Portuguese administrative apparatus were entrusted; (3) the "Portuguese," who were effectively the masters. Clearly the policy of the PAIGC was to abolish all classes; every person is considered a citizen. All people are equal vis-à-vis the law and the state organisms. There are no social classes. It is the people for the people (the motto of our struggle).

So today there are no social classes? What about social conflicts?

The conflicts which may exist are conflicts evident everywhere. For example, in the sector of employment we have a lot of difficulties. During the revolutionary struggle the Portuguese had a great number of native soldiers and civilians who where fighting against us. The civilians were mechanics, electricians, etc. . . . who repaired the Portuguese war machine. After the struggle the soldiers and civilians were de-mobilized and were unemployed. The conflict that exists is the lack of jobs for these people. These people were in the majority peasants who came to the urban centers to flee the war and acquired professional training here. Now our problem is the social rehabilitation of these people. Our country does not have current capabilities to absorb all this mass. There are plans for the creation of cooperatives of various natures: construction, agricultural, and textile cooperatives. The military forces have plans to create cooperatives where the military men can work and help effectively in this economic struggle we are facing.

Could you verify resistance movements in the past which served as a lesson to your struggle? Resistance movements against colonialism?

A clear case is that of Pidjiguiti. Those who resisted were the first victims of our fight; our political party was still a clandestine party. The Pidjiguiti marked a turning point in our fighting strategy against the Portuguese. The men, I personally witnessed, were killed barbarically; fifty people were killed. We realized by the act of Pidjiguiti that a dialogue with Portugal was impossible. It also influenced our comrade Amílcar Cabral to move the struggle to the countryside. Initially, he wanted to make the struggle in the cities, through strikes. This urban struggle would have been too great a sacrifice for our cadres. The struggle should begin in the countryside, and then move toward the cities. That is why Cabral decided to go out and work and raise consciousness among the people. Cabral wanted to show the people that it was their fight, not a fight for Cabral or his men. There are several incidents of comrades who were caught and killed during the fight. The revolutionary struggle was indispensable. We could not dialogue with Portugal, although in this phase of the struggle there was always a willingness on our part to dialogue with Portugal. We were not military men but militants with arms. Arms to defend a cause we believed just, for the liberty of our land and the social welfare of our people.

––––– 4 –––––

Paulo Correia

Paulo Correia was president of the Comité do Estado of the Region of Bissau, a second vice president of the National Assembly, and a member of the Conselho Executivo de Luta (CEL) at the time of this interview on August 23, 1975. Born in Cadé, Nuacru, in 1942 of parents from the Balanta tribe, he entered the party in 1961 and joined the fighting in early 1963. He was a commander of the Eastern Front during the armed struggle. He also served as a first vice-president of the Council of State.

After independence we divided the country into regions, and within each region there are sectors, the latter are further divided into sections. In each section there is a "communidade de base." Here in Bissau we have sixteen base committees and two sections. These committees have the function of organizing the people, to allow the expression of different opinions, and to provide a channel so that these opinions of the people reach the government. Likewise, the committees provide a channel for government policies to reach the people. Here in Bissau we have to work to politically educate the people about our party political line. The region of Bissau was the headquarters of the enemy camp, and during the struggle it was hard for the party to infiltrate this region. We had to work hard mainly underground.

Today our main problem is unemployment. We do not have the means to provide jobs for everyone. We have also financial problems. During the liberation struggle many peasants came to the city and were employed by the colonial government in jobs supporting the Portuguese war machine. After the struggle these peasants could not find city jobs, and today this group constitutes the bulk of the unemployed. Now we have also a problem of shortages of goods and foodstuff. During the war many goods were imported but now we cannot afford to buy imported goods and foodstuff, such as rice and grains. Bissau has a population of 85,000 people.

What is your view of imperialism?
Our economic difficulties are a result of the war and the imperial-colonial policy of Portugal. The colonial rule of Portugal inhibited and distorted our national consciousness and identity. The imperialist policy had the objective of dividing and exploiting the people and the country. The imperialist

administration attempted to create and intensify tensions among the people so that they could not unite and fight the Portuguese domination. The party sought to educate the people so that they could come together and unite against the Portuguese. We demonstrated successfully that the Portuguese were our single common enemy. We could not fight one another, but we had to fight the foreign enemy. Today, there is no longer imperialism in our country, although there is international imperialism.

Is economic dependency a problem?

Our liberation struggle and the objective of the party was the complete and immediate independence of Bissau and Cape Verde. We have succeeded in the political independence of these countries. Now we face a struggle of national economic reconstruction.

What about social classes?

In comparison with other countries, we do not have class structures here. The small bourgeoisie also suffered from Portuguese colonial domination, so during the war this class did not give us trouble. Today, we have no classes here, and we have no class contradictions.

What resistance movements were important in the past?

From the very beginning of Portuguese colonial rule our people resisted the Portuguese. This resistance took many different forms. There were some instances of armed struggle, but with the Portuguese policy of divide and rule, the resistance took the form of political and cultural resistance. When our national liberation struggle began, the people had a clearer perspective of the resistance. Pidjiguiti, the third of August incident, marked the first resistance since the formation of the party. Many parents sacrificed their lives in order to protect their sons who were fighting in the struggle. The Portuguese began to kill the parents of guerrilla fighters, until those parents themselves took up arms and joined the fight.

How did you come to participate in the struggle?

I became involved in the struggle in 1960 along with other comrades. I had participated in the Portuguese military service. In 1960 we began underground meetings and activities for the party. In 1961, when the Portuguese army began to crack down on underground activists, I was forced to leave to the southern region. In the southern region I worked in the mobilization effort in the countryside. I was born in Cadé, Nuacru in 1942. In 1958 I went to Bolama, and then I came to Bissau. My father is a peasant; both my parents are from the "Bala" tribe. My father had two years of elementary school education. I have elementary education. In 1960 I was almost arrested here in Bissau, but I fled to the south. We were attacked and persecuted many times by the enemy during the day, and at night we went to talk to the people in the countryside. The population fed and clothed us. In early 1963 I entered the armed struggle. We had very few weapons. In my first struggle with the enemy troops, we fought with swords. I was wounded in this struggle. Later we found more weapons, guns, grenades. We were constantly marching day after day. We had logistic problems of finding food and transportation. Finding food was our major difficulty.

—— 5 ——

Domingos Brito Dos Santos

Born in Bissau, Brito joined the struggle in 1963 by directing the PAIGC school in Conakry. He also organized schools in the liberated zones. At the time of this interview in Bissau on August 25, 1975, he was a member of the Conselho Superior de Luta and the secretary-general of the Commissary of Education and Culture. The interview emphasizes issues and problems of education before and after independence.

In every developmental effort of a country, education is of high priority because of the need to educate cadres to carry on the objectives of our struggle and of Comrade Amílcar Cabral. Even during the struggle for national liberation we were able to build schools and educate our cadres in the liberated zones. Since 1964 we have been able to provide schools in the liberated zones despite the difficulties of the war. Of course, today the situation is different and more complex.

Today the whole country is liberated, and we have to deal with a whole range of developmental problems, particularly in education. Therefore, our problems have become greater and more complex. We had a sad legacy from the period of colonialism; the colonial administration did not build any infrastructure in this country. Even in education there were not enough trained teachers to teach the children. We have to deal with these difficulties and try to overcome them gradually. At this moment we have about 80,000 students in all the schools of the country, and more than 10,000 students in the lycées, the technical school, the secondary school. This year we opened two more lycées, one in Bafatá and one in Cachungo. This represents an effort to decentralize the great number of students located here in Bissau.

During the war, many of the students fled from zones where there was concentrated fighting and came to Bissau. Now we have to deal with this situation and decentralize education—provide new schools in other regions, so that these students can go back to their homelands and regions. We also want to build preparatory schools in all the regions, but this is not yet possible because of the situation of our overall economy.

To build schools we need to have a certain type of economy and development which we do not yet have. Our economy is based on agriculture, and our agriculture is based on primitive methods. We need to develop our agriculture and modernize our methods; we need new agricultural tools and machines. We need money to buy these new machines. Thus, we need the technical and financial assistance from abroad to help us develop our agriculture and economy. We have received aid from several countries which feel a solidarity with our struggle and country. Solidarity groups in several countries have given us aid, particularly in the field of education.

Right now, the schools are closed for vacation, but we have a seminar for teachers. This seminar is a means of improving the skills of our teachers. We have built a center for the improvement of our teachers, their skills and knowledge; this center will also improve the administrations of the schools. There is also the Institute of Friendship, which is an organization in charge of the boarding schools (*internatos*) and is subsidized by the state. Many friendly countries have given us scholarships to send our students abroad for higher education. These students will go to college and technical schools to learn different skills so that when they return to Bissau they will help us in our developmental efforts. The students who are going abroad will stay away for four or five years, and this constitutes a large sacrifice for our country, which needs their skills. However, we have several students who are finishing their education abroad and will be returning home this year.

During the war, in the liberated zones, we have 156 schools with about 14,600 students. We do not have data available for the number of schools and students in those areas occupied by the Portuguese. Today, in all the country we have about 80,000 students in the primary schools. We have about 2,000 primary school teachers and about 70 secondary school teachers; there are two centers which educate the teachers, one in Bolama and one in Bissau. This year we are at the planning stage to develop an educational system responsive to the developmental needs of our country. In cooperation with other ministries and commissaries we are trying to find out how many technical people are needed in agriculture and in other economic sectors. We do not have any industries or factories here, but the government will build factories in the future, and we have to train personnel accordingly. Therefore, together with other commissaries, we are trying to predict the future needs of each sector of the economy and direct our educational efforts to fulfill those needs in order to develop the country. We are gathering information and data about our population in order to start this planning; we do not yet know what is the total population of our country. We have also started a literacy program for adults throughout the country; during the colonial period 99 percent of our adult population was illiterate. This is an extremely important problem; we have begun to use the literacy campaign methods developed by Paulo Freire.

As to the overall general educational structure, the educational themes vary according to the levels of the classes. In the more advanced sixth grade level, the teachers are teaching mathematics, reading skills, Portuguese language, physics, biology, and politics. The political education follows the political lines of our party, its objectives and programs. In the fourth grade everything is taught except physics and chemistry. In the third grade everything is taught except geography and biology. In the second grade reading and mathematics are taught. In the first grade students learn reading skills and penmanship. In the lycée level, we are still using the Portuguese textbooks, but we modify the curriculum to teach African history, African geography, and our political struggle for liberation, instead of Portuguese history and geography. We use Portuguese textbooks because we have not had the time and resources to develop our own books. In the primary schools we use both Portuguese and the party textbooks. We adapt the Portuguese textbooks to our reality and needs.

I went to fight in Conakry in 1963 and stayed away from Bissau for twelve years; I just came back this year. I am originally from Bissau, and before participating in the struggle I worked in the business sector. But like many other comrades, I had the consciousness and awareness to abandon my work and join the struggle. I went to Conakry in 1963. For many years I was the director of the Piloto school and the Institute of Friendship. I was the first founder of all the schools of the PAIGC during the struggle; I founded all the schools of the party in the liberated zones. Apart from the armed struggle, we needed to educate our cadres. The armed struggle was essential to liberate our country from the enemy, but it was equally important to educate our cadres alongside the armed struggle. The education of the cadres had to accompany the armed struggle. The Piloto school was the central organization which unified all the other schools in the liberated zones; the Piloto school developed the programs to be taught in the other schools. The Piloto school was the model school of the party. That was my main participation in the struggle to help formulate the educational programs for the cadres. I abandoned my job to join the struggle because I was aware of the exploitation of our people by the Portuguese colonial rule and I realized that it was my duty to contribute to the struggle. In Bissau I went to primary school and in the party I had my political formation.

—— 6 ——
Manuel Boal

Born in Angola and later a student in Portugal, Boal became a medical doctor after studies in Paris. He worked for the MPLA in Angola, and later joined the PAIGC struggle in Guinea-Bissau. In Conakry he coordinated the distribution of medical supplies to the liberated zones. After independence, he came to Bissau and assumed the position of secretary-general of the Commissary of Health. The following interview focuses on his experience in health in Guinea-Bissau and was conducted in Bissau on August 26, 1975.

Our current situation has not differed very much from the situation we encountered after the war, but there are some problems we are already tackling. During the national liberation struggle there were two systems of medical assistance in this country—one operating under the Portuguese in the occupied zones, and the other operating by the party in the liberated zones. In the liberated zones, the system was characterized by its decentralized nature. We had in every zone a hospital with a surgeon and medical personnel, capable to provide the basic medical assistance to the population in the zone. The hospital was located in the jungle and had straw beds. We provided medical assistance not only to our combatants but to the whole population. We provided all types of services from general check-up to hospitalization and surgery. The hospital had usually twenty beds. To complement the regional hospitals, we had sanitation posts serviced by nurses with straw beds. The posts were located close to the more numerous villages. As you know, our country is divided into regions, and the regions divided into sectors. In some sectors, we were able to provide a smaller hospital run by a doctor or medical assistant; the medical assistant is a technician in medicine. The more numerous cadres and units had two or three nurses that followed them in the combat zones. This was the basic infrastructure of our medical assistance; our equipment was very restricted both in number and quality.

The whole medical assistance was given free to both the cadres and the whole population. Moreover, the surgeons, doctors, nurses, and medical personnel worked without remuneration, but were fed and provided for by the party. Although medical assistance to the population was free, it is important to know that it was the population that provided support, clothes, and food to the hospitals. The population gave rice and other foodstuff to the hospitals.

The population transported medical supplies from the borders to the regional hospitals. In some cases when patients had serious problems, the population transported these patients from the regional hospitals to our hospitals near the borders. The party had two hospitals near the borders of Guinea and another inside Senegal. The hospital on the Senegalese border was called the "Home of the PAIGC." These three hospitals were equipped with laboratories, X-ray machines, electricity. These hospitals were able to attend the more serious patients and the wounded soldiers. This was our medical assistance in the liberated zones.

In the occupied zones the Portuguese controlled the infrastructure of the medical assistance. Their infrastructure was more centralized because their services were centered in Bissau. They had forty-seven doctors here in Bissau working in big hospitals with a thousand beds. Another forty-seven doctors were spread out in the occupied zones, following the units of combat; their services were more limited and were restricted to providing assistance to those directly participating in the war. All serious cases and the wounded were transported by helicopter to Bissau.

After the national liberation struggle, when we arrived here in Bissau, we had to adapt the existing situation to our new perspective. First of all, we had learned the advantages of a decentralized structure of medical assistance during our struggle. Secondly, in this stage of national reconstruction and peace, the existing concentration of medical staff, equipment, and hospitals in Bissau could no longer be justified and represented an injustice to the people living in the other regions of the country. Also, this concentration caused innumerable problems for Bissau, such as greater traffic congestion. Because of all these factors, we decided to decentralize the medical assistance; we wanted to localize medical services by creating in each region an autonomous network of medical assistance to the population. Therefore, we revitalized the hospitals in each region. With the help of foreign aid and technical assistance we were able to open those hospitals that were already in existence during the time of the Portuguese.

At this moment we have functioning three regional hospitals with more than a hundred beds each; these hospitals perform surgeries, X-ray services, and laboratory examinations. These three hospitals are that of Bafatá, Bolama, and Cachungo. Our country has eight regions, and we want to build hospitals in all the regions. However, to build a regional hospital is very expensive; such a hospital costs about seven million dollars to build, and, of course, upon completion we would have to continue to finance and maintain it. This is a very expensive and impossible task for us at the moment.

The three regional hospitals of Bafatá, Bolama, and Cachungo are open now because those hospitals were already in existence during the struggle. Therefore, our economic situation now does not allow us to build a regional hospital in each of the five remaining regions of the country. However, our objective still continues to be the decentralization of medial assistance and the establishment of an autonomous network of medical assistance in each and every region of the country. Given our limitations and our objectives, we decided that in those regions where there were already hospital facilities we would naturally make use of them in order to establish the autonomous network of medical assistance. In those regions which lacked such facilities, we would attempt to build the work from "the basic to the center," that is, to build small hospital units of twenty beds and sanitation posts. Later, as our economic and budgetary conditions permit, we will build the regional hospitals of a hundred beds.

Therefore, we are moving progressively towards decentralization and regionalization of medical assistance. We have three regional hospitals with a hundred beds each, and we have smaller hospital units of twenty beds each in the other regions. This decentralized system helps us provide assistance to a large number of our population throughout our country and alleviates the congestion problem here in Bissau. The hospital facilities here in Bissau are sophisticated and more comparable to those in Europe; these hospitals provide specialized treatment to serious cases. Therefore, those cases too serious to be treated in the regional hospitals are sent here to Bissau for treatment, and this will continue to be so in the future.

During the national liberation struggle, the liberated zones were divided into ten regions. We had five regional hospitals and seven sectoral hospitals (smaller units).

In terms of medical supplies and equipment, we will follow the same perspective and program. First, we equip those medical facilities already in existence and functioning. We will provide the basic supplies to the smaller hospitals in each region. Progressively and gradually, we will try to supply all facilities equally and in response to particular needs. In terms of medical personnel, this is particularly a serious problem. We have approximately a population of 600,000 to 800,000 people. We have currently a total of ten doctors in all of the country; about sixty-one nurses, about three hundred sixty medical assistants, and about a hundred nurse assistants. Therefore, we have very few medical personnel. We have about one doctor for every 80,000 people, and this is insufficient. We had to ask for technical assistance from foreign countries to fill this gap in personnel. We also opened two schools to educate nurses; one school is in Bolama to educate auxiliary nurses; the other is here in Bissau to educate nurses.

This problem of personnel cannot be resolved from one day to the next, and therefore we will continue to depend on foreign medical technical assistance, particularly senior medical staff, for a long time in the future. Right now, we have Portuguese, Cuban, and Soviet doctors here; currently, we have about forty foreign medical doctors and technicians. The Soviet Union and Cuba have always helped us by providing doctors and staff during the national liberation struggle. After the war, Portugal sent doctors and technicians. After all, we were never anti-Portuguese, we were anticolonialism. We also have scholarships to send our people to study medicine abroad.

Another problem in this stage of national reconstruction is the provision of medical supplies. We had to ask urgent assistance from the United Nations Commission for Refugees, because at the end of the war about 40,000 to 50,000 refugees returned to the country. The UN Commission gave us a substantial amount of aid, including medical supplies. We also asked assistance to UNICEF, and they have sent us the first shipment of medical supplies. UNICEF has assured us of a $300,000 fund per year. Both UNICEF and the UN Commission have already sent us foodstuff, clothes, and medical supplies. The socialist countries, the USSR, and Sweden have continually provided us with medical assistance and supplies. Our country is in a stage of national reconstruction. At the moment we need foreign assistance because in all sectors of our economy we have problems of insufficient equipment, supplies, and the infrastructure to build our economy. Hopefully, within three to four years we will not have to rely so much on foreign assistance and we will be more self-sufficient in resolving our problems.

Our budget for 1975–1976 is in the process of being approved by the government and the Ministry of Finances. There has been a restructuring of salary levels: the minimum wage has been raised and the very high salaries are being cut.

We have a campaign to vaccinate the population against the measles. Other diseases we have to fight against are malaria, tuberculosis, parasitic diseases.

My generation and the previous generation have always been sensitized to the need for emancipation of our country. I am from Angola. I studied in Portugal, and in 1961 I fled from Lisbon with other comrades. I went to Paris and studied in 1967 and earned a degree in pediatrics. But before going to Paris in 1967, I worked for the MPLA in the Congo, and then came to participate in the PAIGC struggle. I was hesitant whether to stay here or go back to the MPLA, but after the death of Amílcar I decided to stay here. After fleeing from Lisbon in 1961, I went to "Quinxa's" until 1963, and then went to Senegal to start my study of pediatrics. At this time I joined the PAIGC. I went to finish my studies in Paris in 1967. After 1967 I was working for the PAIGC as a MPLA militant; there was an agreement between the MPLA and the PAIGC. After the death of Cabral I decided to stay permanently in the PAIGC. In Conakry I coordinated the transport of medical supplies to the countryside in the liberated zones and I also made inspection visits to the hospitals in the countryside. I founded two centers for the preparation of nurses in the countryside; one center opened in 1971 and the other opened in 1972. I was director of the centers during the war of liberation.

I arrived in Bissau in September of 1974. My current position is secretary-general of the Commissary of Health. I am a militant of the

PAIGC. In principle, I am going to stay permanently here in Bissau. Currently I have no plans of returning to Angola. In my participation in the struggle I learned to respect the people. In my student days, a nation of people was an abstract concept. However, during the struggle I came to live with the people in the countryside. I learned to be more humble. I learned to listen to the people and to try to understand the people. I learned that it is very important to come into contact with the people. It was a period of re-education for me; a re-evaluation of my values. Now I believe that it is possible to create a new man; a lot of work is necessary both in terms of the party and individually. Our best education is to come into close contact with the mass of people. The important thing is for the militant to always be a militant.

It is too early to talk about social classes in our country. The party and the people want to create a new man in our society.

I do not think we are economically dependent on any country. We are willing to cooperate with all countries, so long as these countries recognize our independence and sovereignty. We ask for assistance from abroad, but we only accept aid that is not attached to conditions.

----- **7** -----

Juvencio Gomes

Gomes was born in February 1944 in Brubaque of poor parents from the Pepel tribe. At the time of the interview, August 22, 1975, he was president of the Municipal Chamber of Bissau and a member of the Superior Council of Struggle of the Party. He recounts his experience in revolution, emphasizing that his education was obtained during the struggle after finishing primary school.

What is your perspective about the imperialism of the past, and how it has affected the situation here in Guinea-Bissau?

Like many of my comrades, I went to work for the PAIGC party full of enthusiasm and militancy. In this context of militancy, we had concrete objectives during our struggle for national liberation, which culminated with the total independence of Guinea-Bissau and Cape Verde. Our struggle was a struggle in its totality; that is, it was a struggle not only for independence, but it was also a struggle for the creation of a new life in Guinea-Bissau and Cape Verde. In this context of a new life in Guinea the political formation was and still is the basis for the militant to know and understand the reasons for our struggle and the objectives of the struggle. Alongside the political formation [education] there was also a cultural formation during our struggle. We had to make our struggle for national liberation against Portuguese colonialism an armed struggle because that was the only alternative that was allowed us. Our party reached the conclusion that armed struggle was the only solution for our liberation against colonialism. In this context we consider the armed struggle as a part of our political struggle. In our political struggle we believe that the Portuguese colonialism represents an interest— that is, represents the economic domination of a people over another people. Better yet, of a determined class of a people over another people.

From the beginning of the armed struggle, comrade Amílcar Cabral, secretary-general of the party, distinguished concretely between the Portuguese colonialism and the Portuguese people. We know that Portuguese colonialism represented the economic interest of certain distinctive Portuguese social classes, which sought to maintain its domination over our people. The colonialism not only represented the interest of a certain Portuguese class, but also the interest of other bourgeoisie classes in other capitalist countries. Therefore, Portuguese colonialism was a fraction of the global imperialism. In this context, our struggle was not only directed against Portuguese colonialism, but also was part of the overall struggle against imperialism. During the armed struggle Portuguese colonialism was assisted by its imperialist allies in America, Great Britain, Western Germany, etc. . . . Overall, our struggle was against imperialist domination.

In terms of our struggle, even during the armed phase, as we were winning over new regions (territories), we then began to create new structures, such as schools, hospitals, and stores for the people. Thus, we began to create a new life for our people. The party's committees were organized together with the popular masses. Therefore, there was a truly popular mass power with structures serving the population. As the struggle developed and evolved, so too these structures developed apart from the armed struggle. In this way our party during the struggle was able to form hundreds of cadres, which were distributed through all aspects of our national life, our struggle, according to their formations.

In comparison to our lack of resources at the moment we can say that we already have a tradition of struggle in the context of reconstruction of a new life, a new society, based upon the principles of our party, that is, to serve the interests of our people. Thus, as militants of the party we always put the interests of the people as our first priority. It was our people, in particular our people in the countryside, who suffered most from the colonial domination. It is necessary to make sure that these people achieve the fruits of their sacrifice. We have to guarantee the creation of "bases" which in the future will allow a development program congruent with our economic potentiality. A development program which will guarantee the building of schools, cultural centers, hospitals; that is, the building of an infrastructure that will de facto serve the people and free them from underdevelopment.

In the past, the country suffered greatly from the exploitation of colonialism and now it is independent. In your opinion, is the country still facing the problem of dependency upon the international economic system?

At the moment we consider our independence a political and juridical independence. Economically we are still dependent. In order to consolidate our political independence it is necessary to have our economic independence as well. Currently, we are receiving assistance from international organizations, from friendly nations, and even from certain countries which in the past had indifferent attitudes toward our struggle for national liberation. Our policy, defined by the party and which the government is following, is a policy of opening (*abertura*), that is, it is a policy of understanding towards all countries of the world, all peoples. All countries that want to help us may do so as long as they follow the most basic tenets of relations between two countries. Economically we are not yet liberated, and therefore we need to struggle for that objective. We need to identify that which we need to do during this initial phase and that which we can do at the moment. We have to plan an economic development program based on a realistic assessment of our current potentialities.

Could you identify the social classes and the conflicts between them?

Our struggle was a struggle for liberation; however, in order to carry it on our party had to study and identify the social structure of our people. Our party arrived at the conclusion that in our country there are different groups and that it was necessary to define them as classes or *camadas* (levels) so that we could identify which classes were favorable or opposed to our struggle for liberation. In the social structure, in its totality, there are the ethnic groups whose existence until now was the basis of the colonial domination. The thrust of colonialism and of imperialism is "divide and conquer," and thus, they preserved and tried to deepen the divisions in the heart of our people. The Portuguese tried to exploit to the fullest the tribal and ethnic divisions within our country.

Could you identify these divisions?

We have ethnic groups in great quantity here, by the hundreds. We have Fulas, Mandingas, Pepéis, Manjacos, Balantas. Each one of these ethnic groups has its own rituals and traditions. In order to maintain their presence and domination over our people, the colonialists tried to exploit these ethnic rituals and tried to create contradictions among the ethnic groups. In the past, the Fulas and Mandingas did not live here, because they are originally from North Africa. In the Fula society there was a whole hierarchical structure of the state and of social classes, such as the nobles, workers, peasants, traders, and kings. The Manjacos also had a similar hierarchical structure. In relation to the other tribes in our country, the Fulas and Manjacos were different from the Balantas and other tribes originally from Guinea-Bissau which did not have such hierarchical structures. Thus, these hierarchical structures were imposed by the colonialists upon our people of the Balanta ethnicity. Originally the Balanta society was a horizontal society in which there were no chiefs. Each problem was resolved by the council of elders.

Thus, as one can see, some ethnic groups were more advanced than others. The colonialists exploited such schisms in order to perpetrate and create more divisions and contradictions. They tried to make and maintain each tribe isolated from one another and tried to make each tribe defend only its immediate interests without any regard or consciousness that Guinea-Bissau is a whole country in its totality. The Portuguese tried to prevent our people from acquiring a national consciousness. Such consciousness was only raised by our party during the struggle for liberation. In every and all colonized countries in Africa, in the cities and in the countrysides, the imperialist forces did not allow the building of a working class. Such a strategy allowed the colonialists to maintain the least expensive unskilled labor and also a market for their products. In our case, those products came from Portugal. Through economic development, with the formation of industry and of a working class, the colonialists would lose a source of raw materials, which would in turn permit them to compete effectively with other capitalist countries. In our case, Portuguese colonialism did not build any industrial infrastructure here. There were only some small industries, such as manufacturing plants, that worked perhaps one month per year. For example, the Casa da Gouvêa has a small processing industry for the making of peanut oil. The plant worked only two to three months per year and waited the rest of the year for a new harvest. All this did not permit the development and formation of a working class.

Can we say that there is no working class?

There is no working class, a proletariat, in our country. However, we do have salaried workers; therefore, a working class in the process of development. In the city we still have the petty bourgeoisie. For the most part, the bourgeoisie was composed of the Portuguese colonialists. As to the "nationals," there was a petty bourgeoisie. This bourgeoisie was, and still is, a *comprador* bourgeoisie, that is, some national commercial businessmen buy everything from abroad. Within our political objective of building a just society, we have to take this petty bourgeoisie into account, which, for the most part, are merchants or the old colonial administrators who, during the colonial times, were able to accumulate some riches and thus transformed themselves into the petty bourgeoisie. And thus, still today there is a whole thinking to be changed, and this is not easy. However, in this new phase we need to take into account these classes so that we are able to concretely define them and place them in their respective place.

Can we say that the revolution will lead to a classless society?

We believe that in our struggle for liberation it was our people who fought and who contributed to make this independence a reality. Therefore, today all our people live in misery and now our struggle has to defend and uphold the interest of our people. Our objective is to defend the interests of the people. We are grateful to our people, because they fought for our independence. It was our people who gave their sons to serve in all the fronts.

Can you identify certain resistance movements against the colonialism in the past?

In the past, one of the key points in the resistance movement before the armed struggle was the third of August incident. After Pidjiguiti, the party's executive committee made an analysis and concluded that it would be impossible to make a victorious struggle in the city. There were a great number of elements in our population that were in favor of independence, but in the city the colonial government was much too strong. During the colonial rule it was in the city that they were able to introduce their culture. In the countryside our people resisted and were able to preserve their own culture. Therefore, through this analysis the conclusion was reached that only through our people in the countryside could the party have strength. I would like to point out that the present moment is more than a proof of this. That is, it was the people in the countryside who accepted the struggle from its very first moments and it was our people in the countryside who fought the struggle here in Bissau. So here we have a relationship between the past and the present, with the movement of armed struggle that at this time we consider the past. The preservation of their own culture by our people, the resistance against the economic domination in the countryside—all this contributed so that our party could find the massive support of our population. In the past there were confrontations and wars of resistance. There was a tradition of armed struggle by our people—that is, a tradition of armed resistance against colonial domination. The last instance of resistance was in the late 1930s during the war of the Canhabague in the Island of Pixavóz. In Bissau, in 1915, there was an armed confrontation between our people against the colonial presence. There were many other such cases.

What are the major institutions today and what problems do they face?

At this moment the most important problem we are facing is the economic problem. You are from a highly developed country, and therefore must know what makes a people economically developed. In our case the Portuguese colonialism did not leave us anything. The colonialists did not build any infrastructure. Our people lived and live from agricultural work, which they do with rudimentary means. There is no industry here left behind by colonialism. Now we are in a planning stage. Our comrade, the president of the State Council, has already described the plans and studies to assist us with the takeoff period of economic development. At the moment the basis for all this is agriculture.

How did you participate in the struggle?

I went to the armed struggle at the age of ninteeen. I was born in Brubaque in February 1944. During the time I spent in the struggle, I was with the fronts in the mata, and thus, I gave my contribution along with all the other militants. I worked in several fronts; e.g., the North, South, and West. Most recently I worked in the Navy. In 1973 I was wounded during an aerial attack in the northern region, and afterwards, upon healing, I was transferred to the midwest in the Mandinga zone. There I worked as political military commissar; afterwards I went to work as political administrative commissar in the south of the country. By April 25 we had won total liberation. I joined the Navy in February of 1973 immediately after the murder of our comrade Amílcar. I was called to work as political commissar of the Navy. Soon after, there was the 25th of April 1974, and in June 1974 I was transferred here, after the first contact between our party's delegation. I was sent here as representative of our party's directorate to deal with the representative of the Portuguese government during the stage of evacuation of the colonial army. Now, within the government apparatus I am president of the Municipal Chamber of Bissau. I am a member of the Superor Council of Struggle of the Party.

I did my primary education in Brubaque and afterwards I joined the struggle. I am from a poor family that had no possibilities of providing me with an education. After finishing primary school I started to work with a teacher. Afterwards I came to Bissau to register at the lycée here in Bissau, but already at this time I was active in the party and worked underground. I could not continue my studies because of my activity inside the party. I had to go fight. Fortunately, the struggle for me was a school, an education. Through the struggle I gained understanding of fundamental concepts, which is the critical knowledge, the knowledge of human rights, the rights of a people, and all this permitted me to gain certain experience. My father is a carpenter and he has primary education. Both my father and mother are natives of the Pepel ethnic group. My mother is part Pepel and part Mandinga. During the colonial rule intermarriages between the different ethnic groups were not allowed. Now these intermarriages are allowed and will continue to be so for future generations. There is a new consciousness, a new life experience. I was the only one in my family who participated in the struggle. I am the only son and have three older sisters. During the struggle, few women left the city to join the struggle, particularly here in Bissau.

8

Carmen Pereira

Born in Bissau in 1936, Carmen Pereira is the leading advocate of women's rights and participation in Guinea-Bissau. With a secondary education and experience in the revolutionary struggle as a coordinator of health care on the Southern Front, she emerged in the top party leadership. The interview was held in Bissau on August 26, 1975.

During the colonial period women had very little participatory role in society. They had little educational opportunity and access. The general attitude was that women should stay home and do domestic work. With the national liberation struggle, women found it necessary to take an active role in the party's organizations in order to fight against the Portuguese colonialism. As Amílcar Cabral said, "The women had two struggles for which they had to fight: the liberation of their country and their own emancipation." During the struggle the women played an important role as messengers, contacts, nurses, teachers, and trained militants. A women's organization, the União Democrática das Mulheres, was created, but it was closed in 1966 because the women were working in the liberated zones under PAIGC instructions. The women were members of the party, and they attended other women's organizations as representatives of the party. The women were involved in all kinds of activities: nursing, teaching, radio broadcasting, in the village committees, and as political commissaries in all the fronts.

During the formation of the state many women participated as members of the National Assembly and the State Council. There are three women in the State Council. After independence the party created a commission to study and analyze the formation of a national women's committee. This commission consists of ten women who all fought as militants in the armed struggle. At the moment the commission's objective is to create a women's committee of the PAIGC. It is a difficult task to educate the women as to the meaning and objectives of a women's organization. At this moment the commission's members are traveling to the different regions of the country, entering into contact with the presidents of the regions, the village base committees (*comunidades de base*) and party structures in an attempt to educate and politicize the masses.

We also have contact with international women's organizations and congresses.

The women have suffered particularly in the area of education. Most of them are illiterate, particularly in the rural areas. We are planning a literacy campaign to address this problem. Today women constitute about 30 percent of the students in the primary schools. We want women to be able to participate fully in the reconstruction process. About 20 percent of the labor force are women. We have one woman in the executive committee of the party and there are two women in the Conselho Superior de Luta.

Discussion about the distinction in life-style between rural and urban families.

There is a distinction in life-style between the peasant families and the urban families. In the countryside, the peasant family consists of a husband with two or three wives. This is a necessity of life, because all the agricultural productive work is done by hand and the husband needs more than one wife to help him. The wife is financially and economically dependent on the husband, because all income derived from the land is shared by all in the family. Rural life is very hard and demands hard work. It is different than the urban environment. In the urban family structure the wife demands that the husband have only herself as his wife. Both spouses work, the wife is usually a clerk or secretary. Therefore, the rural and urban environments demand different family structures. In the education and politicization of the women we must be attentive to these differences. Certain husbands resist women's emancipation. Especially the Muslim religion has a very narrow perspective on the role of women in society. Muslim husbands want their wives to stay home and not participate in other activities.

However, during the struggle, the party overcame all these difficulties, and now one can see women participating at all levels of society. In every village community there are two or three women activists in the village committees. The village committees have a total of five members, two or three of which are women. The women talk in the committee meetings and express their opinions. This can be easily verified in the liberated zones. In the once-occupied ones women are still hesitant to speak in public. They are embarrassed because they were never allowed to speak freely, and this is a new experience for them. We have to work especially hard in the occupied zones to educate and politicize the women as to the need of creating a women's organization within the party structure. The other ethnic tribal groups did not resist the reality of women's emancipation and organization, only the Muslims.

Before the armed struggle in the countryside there were regions where women worked longer and harder than men. The men stayed home, and the women would do the agricultural work and in the afternoon they would return to cook dinner for the men. The men were the dominant figures in those families and the women had to follow their orders. During the armed struggle, the party's political commissaries in the liberated zones would travel from village to village and hold meetings to explain to the men that everyone in the village had to work. The commissaries tried to make them understand that both the men and women had to work the land, and that it was wrong for the men to stay home while the women worked. In the liberated zones the men began to understand the need for them to work with the women in order to increase productivity and to produce more. Often the party's political commissaries would go to a village and work in the field to demonstrate to the husbands that they should work too.

During the armed struggle the party had a day-care center and a boarding school in Conakry. These two schools provided services for the orphans of the war and provided care for the children whose mothers were fighting in the armed struggle. Since national liberation, we have created boarding schools and day-care centers in Bissau and the other regions.

Tell us about your life and participation in the struggle.

I was born in Bissau in 1936, but my family is from Bolama. My father was a lawyer; he completed his studies in Portugal. My mother did domestic work. I went to primary and secondary schools here in Bissau. I first heard of the PAIGC in 1962. I saw the flag of the party and a picture of Cabral, and I listened to some comrades. I decided to join the comrades at the Senegalese border. At that time life was difficult for the nationalists who decided to fight against the Portuguese colonialism. At the border we had no money or resources to buy food and other necessities. I was a seamstress and was able to work for a year to save money for us to live at the border. The party sent me to Conakry and then to the USSR where I spent ten months on a political education internship. In 1965 I went back to the USSR and took a group of nurses for them to complete a nursing course. When I returned to Conakry in 1966, I was transferred to the Southern Front and was in charge of health conditions at the front. Later I worked there as political commissar for a year and a half. Later I became a member of the Executive Committee of Struggle (Conselho Executivo de Luta), and was political commissar in a region for a year. In 1971 I was in charge of directing the reconstruction effort at the front. I became vice president of the National Assembly, then I was elected a member of the State Council. Afterwards, with the proclamation of the state, I assumed the position of political commissar of the Southern Front and represented the secretary-general of the front. Now I am a member of the commission of the organization of the party and am working with the general secretariat of the party. I have learned since 1962. I was a shy person, but I learned from the political education internship, the effort of the party, working together with the comrades, the seminar and conversations with Cabral, and the assistance of Aristides Pereira. With the help of my comrades I accomplished all my missions in the struggle. I gave all my life to the PAIGC, because I know how much the PAIGC did for our country, for our people, and for me personally.

How do you view imperialism?

The Portuguese imperialism has ended. Now we are concerned with working with the population in the occupied zones to educate and politicize the mass about the party's objectives. We have to educate the people in order to advance our economic reconstruction. There are no social classes in Bissau.

—— 9 ——

Augusto Pereira da Graça, "Neco"

*Born in Farim on August 5, 1939, of peasant parents, Neco joined
the party and liberation struggle in 1960. At the time of this
interview, on August 26, 1975, he was secretary-general of the
youth organization, JAAC.*

The main objective of our party was the total liberation of our country;
this objective was concretized on July 5, 1975. Today we have entered a new
phase of national reconstruction. Our task is one of economic development.

After the proclamation of the state, the PAIGC created a Commissary of
Youth and Recreation. The commissary is responsible for the orientation,
organization, and supervision of all youth activities in the country. On
September 12, 1974, about 600 youths held a meeting in Boé to organize the
Juventude Africana Amílcar Cabral (JAAC). JAAC enabled the youth from
the liberated zones and the occupied zones to come together. During the war
the country was divided into two sectors: one that was occupied by the enemy
and the other called the liberated zones. On April 25, a center was created in
Boé where the youngsters who lived in the occupied zones could come to live
and learn the truth about our struggle against the Portuguese colonialism—to
become politicized. Six hundred youth and their mothers lived in the center,
and it was out of this experience that JAAC was created. JAAC was designed
to educate the youth politically and to get them involved in the
reconstruction effort.

JAAC is linked to the party's organizations and the Commissary of
Youth and Recreation. JAAC members are between the ages of fifteen and
twenty-five. In order to become a member of JAAC, a youngster is first
accepted as a candidate for full membership. He must be at least fifteen years
old and must prove his militancy. A youth cannot enter the party without
being a member of JAAC. At the moment there is not yet a JAAC at the
national level, only at the regional levels. In each region there is a JAAC
commission of five members. Both men and women are members of
JAAC.

The Organizaçá de Pioneiros is another youth organization geared toward
the political development of younger children. To be a Pioneiro one must be
ten years old or older. Members are between ten and fifteen years old.
Pioneiro organizations and JAAC have been created in all the regions of the

country. All student activities, youth organizations and Pioneiros are under the supervisory umbrella of JAAC.

Immediately after independence our greatest problem was the education and politicization of the youth who had lived in the occupied zones under Portuguese colonial rule. Some urban students were influenced and adhered to the principle of Portuguese colonial rule. Therefore, the party's effort focused on the politicization of these youths. Those in the rural areas suffered most from colonial exploitation, and thus, they adhered more readily to the party's orientation and activities.

Tell us about your involvement in the struggle.

I was born in the northern region of Farim on the fifth of August of 1939. I attended primary and secondary schools in Farim and later in Bissau. My parents were peasants, and they had no formal education. Both of them were involved in the struggle as militants. I did not finish my secondary studies because the party needed full-time militants. In 1960 I went to work for the party doing clandestine activities in Bissorã for two years. I was arrested twice by the Portuguese military forces. The first time I was held for fifteen days under house arrest. This was in 1960. In 1962 I was arrested again and this time I was deported to Cape Verde in the "Caravalo" prison. I was in prison for seven years under the worst possible conditions. I was tortured and almost killed; it was a miracle that I survived. However, this experience served to strengthen my revolutionary spirit and my determination to continue fighting against Portuguese exploitation. The prison years were a further preparation for the struggle. In 1972 I went to Guinea. I did mobilization work; that is, I explained to the people the creation of the party, the PAIGC objectives, the situation created by colonial rule. The Portuguese not only exploited our land, our resources, and our people, but they did not promote any development of the country. They did not build infrastructure, factories, industry. I mobilized the people by pointing out to them the effects of colonialism in our country.

What is your view of imperialism?

Our struggle against Portuguese imperialism is over and imperialism has ended here in Bissau. However, we must always be alert to external interests and influences. We want relations with all countries and we need trade, aid, and foreign assistance. However, we will never compromise our independence and our principles.

What about dependence?

We do not consider ourselves dependent upon any country. We have economic difficulties, and we need foreign assistance to develop our country. That does not constitute dependency.

How do you view the class struggle?

The Portuguese attempted to weaken our country and people by instigating tribal rivalry. Today we do not have this problem of tribal divisions. We cannot rebuild and develop the country if we are divided into tribes. The party's objective is to unify the population; we are all Guineans and we all have to work together to rebuild the country. The party has achieved this unification through its mobilization and politicization efforts. The question of classes is irrelevant to Bissau, because we have no social classes here.

—— 10 ——
Francisco Coutinho

*At the time of this interview, on August 26, 1975, Coutinho was
director of the people's stores (Armazens do Povo). Born in São
Vicente in the Cape Verdes, he studied there, and later reached Bissau
where he served the Portuguese colonial administration as a
functionary. Later he went to Portugal and entered private business,
and returned to Bissau about the time of independence. In 1982 he
was implicated and imprisoned for illicit handling of the people's
store.*

During the struggle there was a need to coordinate the goods and
foodstuffs that our party received. This led to the formation of people's
stores. Now these stores are going through a transformation; the stores are
following a policy of adapting to the present realities of our situation. These
stores constitute a state enterprise with all the duties and rights accorded to a
private company. The objective is to stabilize the local market and to
cooperate in the control of prices; thus, this state company acts as a means of
equilibrium stabilizing the market and prices. During the national liberation
struggle there were twenty-four stores; today the company has about eighty-
one establishments spread all over the country. Each establishment has its
autonomous authority in the distribution of goods within each region. We are
creating this network of people's stores in all the regions to avoid a
centralization of the economy as a whole, because such centralization creates
problems. However, the overall policies to be followed by the people's stores
in all the regions are decided and formulated by the general directorate with
the assistance of the general counsel.

When we arrived in Bissau, the government decided to open people's
stores in order to avoid speculation over prices of primary goods and
foodstuffs. We have now in Bissau about twenty stores. This transition of
the people's stores from the liberated zones to the urban centers was not
difficult because it meant an overall expansion of the network of stores and
activities and not an overall structure change. However, we had to change the
system of exchange. During the struggle the markets operated under a barter
system. The peasants and other groups would come to the market to
exchange their products for foodstuff and essential goods. Under the present
system the people bring their products to the stores and receive money for

them, and then they use the money to purchase what they need. Everyone has access to the stores. Those who cannot purchase the goods and foodstuff are given the essential items by the government. The stores have all primary goods including clothes, shoes, textiles. Some of the goods and foodstuff are imported from Portugal, Europe, and USSR. We import rice and sugar from the country that gives us the best deal. We need about 30,000 tons of rice to feed all the regions per year, and we need about 2,500 tons of sugar annually. In the near future, we will be able to produce enough rice and sugar to feed our people and also to export. We need about 2,000 tons of flour. Our country has plenty of fruit. We are exporting lumber at the moment; the export policies are in the administrative jurisdiction of the Ministry of Commerce. The people's stores oversee only the internal commerce of the country. The stores also have to compete with the other existing private firms in the purchase of goods in the internal market. The government has fixed prices for essential goods and foodstuff in order to stabilize prices and avoid speculation. Only the people's stores can import foodstuff and primary goods. Other goods which are not considered critical are imported and sold by the private firms. The two major private firms are the Simões Gouveia and the Ultramarina.

What about your involvement in the independence struggle?

I was born in São Vicente, Cape Verde; my parents are from Cape Verde. My father was a policeman and my mother did domestic work. I attended primary school and the lycée in Cape Verde. In 1951 I came to Bissau and worked as a functionary in the Portuguese colonial government performing different administistative tasks. In 1971 I went to Portugal for vacation and decided not to return to Bissau. I left public office and started a private business. In 1974 I returned to Bissau to help the PAIGC in its efforts to rebuild the country and the economy. Each day I learn how important it is to work together as a people for the national reconstruction effort.

What is your view of your country's dependency on other nations?

We are not dependent on any country. We need to import certain goods to help us in our economic development, but all countries, rich and poor, import goods to help their economy. This is not dependency but international trade and relations.

—— **11** ——

Manuel Dos Santos, "Manecas"

Manecas was head of the Commissary of Information and Tourism at the time of this interview in Bissau, on August 27, 1975. He was born on October 30, 1942, in São Vicente, where he went to school. Later he studied engineering in Lisbon. During the armed struggle he was political commissar of the Northern Front and commander of the Comando Abel Djassi. Later he served as commissar of transport and tourism (1978–1984) and minister of social equipment.

Our commissary is concerned with tourism and information. However, our tourism service is of secondary importance at the moment. Most of our efforts are concentrated on information. Information means above all the information and awareness of our people. We want to inform our people of external developments that are related to our development, and we want to make a clear analysis of our problems. We want to inform our people of our clear objectives, situation, and capabilities. We operate a radio station that transmits some programs of political and cultural character. We also publish a newspaper which represents our political line. We want to create a service to collect news from the countryside because it is important for us to be aware of the problems of the interior. We want to expand our news services. We would also like to import new films from abroad. During the struggle in 1972, two of our militants were cameramen and they made some documentaries about the struggle. These have not yet been finished; they need to be edited. Our problem is the limited financial resources of the country. We would like the communication system to expand, but we do not have the financial resources to invest in these projects. There is one radio station in the country. We want to decentralize the radio programming and create regional radio stations with their own local programs. Guinea has three distinct regions with their own distinct characteristics. The radio is the best tool available to reach out to the people.

How did you become involved in the liberation struggle?
I was born in São Vicente in Cape Verde. I did primary school and lycée there. In 1957 Comrade Abílio Duarte went to Cape Verde with instructions from the party to mobilize the people. It was then that I made my first

contact with the party. I finished the lycée, and in 1959 I went to Portugal to study engineering. Some students in Lisbon kept in contact with the party, and there we formed the first party cell among the students in Lisbon. We succeeded in mobilizing some students. In 1964 I had to enlist in the Portuguese military service, but instead I ran away and went to France. In France I contacted the party. During the war I was in all of the fronts: north, south, west. My father was an officer in the merchant navy; he has now retired. He attended the lycée in Cape Verde. I have a brother and sister who work in Cape Verde. I was twenty-one years old when I began fighting, and I learned everything in the party. I went once to Cuba and twice to the Soviet Union for military specialization.

What is your understanding of classes and class struggle in Guinea-Bissau?

Our national liberation struggle was not a class struggle. We do not have distinct classes in Guinea: we do not have a bourgeoisie, a proletariat. The peasants are the major group in the country. The local merchants are mostly Portuguese and Lebanese, but they are few and of no potential significance.

What is your view of imperialism?

We need to develop our economy in order to have economic as well as political independence. Guinea is an integral part of the African movement, and as long as our African neighbors suffer colonial and imperialist exploitation, then the fight for liberation against imperialism is not over.

Is depending on the outside world important for your country?

Contradictions always exist. Our greatest problem is one of production and economic development. We need to develop our agriculture. At the moment we have to address these realities and we need foreign technical and financial assistance to begin this task of national reconstruction. This does not constitute dependency.

—— 12 ——

José Araújo

At the time of this interview in Bissau on August 28, 1975, Araújo was commissar of state without portfolio. Born in Praia, Cape Verde, he spent much of his life in Angola, where his father served the colonial administration. He studied in Angola and later completed his studies in law in Lisbon.

What is the relation between the state and the PAIGC?

We have to talk about our most recent historical past to understand the relation and linkages between the state and the party. The situation that exists today was generated by the national liberation struggle, and the struggle was directed by the party, which mobilized the people and engaged in armed struggle. During the armed struggle the liberated zones were created. Months after the struggle began, in 1964 there was the first congress of the party, which had to deal with the problem of administration. At this moment the scheme there was established, the embryo of what our future state would be, our first republic. There were liberated areas and populations which no longer depended on the colonial state, and these zones and people had to be administered. Thus, the party made several decisions, concluding that these zones and people had to be administered by party organs and structures. This situation evolved over the years. As more zones and people were liberated and came under the party's administration, the structures created to administer these areas also evolved and became consolidated, and thus there occurred the transformation of the party into a party-state. The PAIGC no longer functioned solely as a party, but it exercised the authority and functions of a state organ and apparatus. Cabral made this "contestação," which led to the declaration of the Republic of Guinea-Bissau, that is, the proclamation of the state. Given the situation that arose out of the struggle against colonialism, the country was no longer a colony.

In contrast to the liberated zones, the occupied zones were administered by the Portuguese military: the doctors were military, the president of the assembly was military, all the secretaries of the government were military. Thus, in the occupied zones there was an authentic military administration of the people. During the struggle the country was no longer a colony, it was a territory occupied militarily by the Portuguese. In the liberated zones there evolved democratic structures and institutions of an independent state. In order to complete this transformation, elections were held in the liberated zones to create the Popular Assembly as an instrument to give sovereign rights to the people. When the state was proclaimed, the party, which was a party-state, evolved and separated the distinction between the structures of the state and the structures of the party; and thus created the proper structures for the state, such as the Popular Assembly and an executive organ. This separation was inevitable, because there is de facto a specialization of functions among the state and the party. The PAIGC still preserved its place in society, because the party is not an instrument of the state, but it is an integral part of our society.

The PAIGC has the leadership role in our society. It is still dominant in relation to the state, because it created the state structures. Our constitution points out that the party has a political leadership role in society. The party has the right to select the candidates for the National Popular Assembly, which, according to our constitution, holds all governing rights. The party selects the candidates for the National Assembly and the people vote among the candidates for the assembly. It is impossible for a person to campaign for a seat in the National Assembly without the approval of the party. This is a reality that may not suit other cultures and societies, but it is a reality here as a result of the whole process of the national liberation struggle. The party directed the struggle and it has the right to defend the "victories" of that struggle. The assembly consists of people selected by the party. The party has a dominant role in terms of mass organizations; these organizations are strictly connected to the party. The mass organizations are the Juventude Amílcar Cabral Youth Organization, a women's group and committee, and the unions. The party structures will be revised. At the moment the party has a congress which meets every three years. The congress elects the Superior Council of Struggle, which is a large organ with eighty-five people. The Executive Committee of Struggle is a permanent and large body with twenty-five people. Within the executive committee there is a secretariat of four members: General-Secretary Aristides, and Luís Cabral, secretary. The congress is meeting every three years; the superior council meets more than once a year. During the struggle there was a war council, which no longer exists today; however, there is a military council.

How did you become involved in the liberation struggle?
I am from Praia, Cape Verde. My father was a government functionary, and in 1942 he was transferred to Angola; I was eight years old then. I grew up in Angola where I finished primary school and the lycée in Luanda. In 1953 I went to Portugal to study law. After I finished my law studies, I entered the Portuguese military service. I was in the armed forces for one and one-half years between 1958 and 1960. In 1961 I left Portugal. In terms of the struggle I gained my awareness at the lycée in Angola. Many of my Angolan friends at the lycée are now in the MPLA forces. In 1955–1956 I

met Amílcar in Portugal. In 1957 I saw Amilcar; we both returned from Angola. In 1960, however, I had more contacts with my Angolan friends than with other Cape Verdeans. I was active with other students at the Casa de Estudantes. I was contacted by my Angolan friends to fight in the MPLA. In 1961 I left Portugal with a group of students. By then I had married and had a son of three months. I went to Conakry and there made my first contact with the PAIGC. It was then that I decided to fight for my country. I entered the party and went to Dakar for a year and a half. When the struggle began in 1963 I was in Dakar; afterwards I went to Conakry where I worked in the general secretariat. In 1970 I entered the executive committee; I went to the south as political commissary of the Southern Front. I was there until November 1972. I became sick and went to Função. At the time of the proclamation of the republic I was part of the first executive; I was the commissary of state in charge of the general secretariat. Afterwards there was the 25th of April. I was at the meetings in London and Algiers; when the Portuguese army were evacuated, there was a meeting of the party directorate and the Council of the State, and at this time there was a restructuring of the first executive, and I became a commissary of state without portfolio.

What are your perspectives on imperialism?

Throughout the world there is confrontation. The small countries have to be alert to the ambitions and interests of other countries. We, as a small country and as a country which wants peace and a better living standard for its people, cannot accept imperialism. In the confrontation between imperialism and anti-imperialism we have to choose the anti-imperialist side. We think this is of benefit to all countries. This question has nothing to do with our fight because we did not consider Portugal as imperialist; Portugal was a part of the world system of imperialism.

What about depending on the outside world?

We define our foreign policy as a neutralist one. We are convinced that the best way to maintain our independence is to follow a pure neutral line. If we side with one position or another, we compromise our independence. We need foreign assistance and relations in order to build the country. We need to find common interests with other countries and seek cooperation. We are open to all countries seeking forms of mutual cooperation.

What about social clases and the class struggle?

The classes here are different from the classes in other countries. Here we have people with different social status. We do not regard the party as a class party because we have people of all social status and origins in the party. There was, and is, no capitalist class in this country. The problem could be posed if we were to allow such exploitative classes to form here, but that is not our interest and program. Our effort has been to favor those people who have been most exploited and disfavored. For example, we have incurred great expenses with the boarding schools in which the students do not pay anything, especially those in the countryside. Our effort is to improve the living standards of our people. There is no proletariat in this country because there is no industrialization. The merchant sector here is all foreign, either Portuguese or Arabic, and they have no political impact on the country. Neither numerically nor economically do these groups have an impact politically.

—— **13** ——

Pascoal Alves

Alves was the secretary-general of the UNTG labor movement at the time of this interview in Bissau on August 29, 1975.

During the Portuguese colonial rule there was no mass union movement; there was a labor organization under the auspices and direction of the government and only privileged workers, merchants, and clerks belong to it. Luís Cabral was involved in the creation of the union movement before the war broke out; he gave the political orientation to it. He introduced the idea of strike to help the workers in their demand for wages and better working conditions.

How did you become involved in the liberation struggle?
I entered the fight after the third of August, 1959; I joined some comrades in Conakry. I took part in two union seminars in Conakry in 1961; Luís Cabral was the head of our union. In Conakry I entered the movement organization that existed. Then Cabral expanded and organized the party out of the movement. I did more political work in the front. Only in 1973 did I assume the leadership of the union movement. I did not participate in the Pidjiguiti incident in 1959 because I was then twenty-two years old and did not work. I saw the incident of Pidjiguiti, but did not participate in it. Pidjiguiti was a turning point because it created the conditions for the struggle and for the labor movement.

I was born in Bolama. My father was in charge of a store that was owned by a French company. I did my studies in Bissau where I attended primary school only. My father also had primary education and belonged to the Pepel tribe. We went to Conakry in 1959–61.

In 1962 we began to mobilize the people for armed struggle. Throughout the war I was working in the front. In 1960–61 in Conakry I was political leader in the house where all the militants lived. In 1963 I went to the countryside, the Southern Front; afterwards I returned to Conakry. Then I did an internship in Czechoslovakia for six months. I returned to the countryside in the Northern Front. In 1964–65 I went to the Southern Front, and later to the Western Front for eight months. Later I went to Angola, and then I spent two years in the USSR. In 1970 I returned and went to the Northern Front and I was political commissary for all the Northern Front. I returned to

Bissau in 1974. During the struggle I served as political commissar in the armed forces, because along with the armed struggle there must be political education. The political education involved explaining to the militants the political thought of the party, the principles of the struggle, discipline, and political consciousness. Before picking up arms, the militant has to understand the reasons and the principles of the struggle. As a political commissar, I taught groups of twenty-five militants; each group of twenty-five militants had one political commissary and one military commissary.

During the struggle our constant mission was to attack the Portuguese camps and to trap the Portuguese. There were great logistical difficulties because we did everything on foot. There were long marches and there were long distances, sometimes involving eight to ten hours of marching. We had difficulty in finding things to eat so sometimes we went hungry for a day or two. During the rainy season we had to cross the rivers and swam with our weapons on our backs. About two hundred men were involved with me in the Western Front in Daboe.

My most difficult experience was in Kedaviny, where I spent a year and a half. There was constant bombardment night and day for a whole year. Kedaviny is in the southern region.

During the war our union maintained relations with other international organizations, and through our union we received aid from other international organizations. Concretely, all militants were workers. Only now we are taking serious steps to develop our union. At the moment we are preparing to revise the statute of the union which was created during the war and was geared toward the necessities of the struggle. We want to develop the union according to the different professions and sectors, but this is still too early because we have no industry, no factories. There are a few companies. Now we are organizing the union based on workers' committees in the workplace. In each workplace and company we form a workers' committee; the workers meet and select four to five people to be their representatives in the workplace. The workers' committee is directly related to the UNTG. Each committee is responsible for defending the interests of the workers, for supervising working conditions, and for maintaining good working relations. The union has a national committee which must be elected by the labor congress; the latter has not yet been formed. Our national committee is composed of eleven members, and each member will have a specific function—general secretary, treasurer, secretary of different activities and sectors. The workers and their representatives will attend the labor congress. The companies with five workers or less will have one representative. Now we have about seventy-six of these committees in Bissau.

The labor congress to be held will revise the statute. In the countryside we want to create a rural syndicate subordinated and affiliated to the central union of UNTG. The peasants have to be educated to the significance of the union. It is difficult to create cooperatives in the countryside, because we need to first educate the population. During the struggle we did educate those peasants who worked with us, and some consumption cooperatives existed in the northern region. The future cooperatives have to be linked to the union.

What are your views on social classes and class struggle?

Guinea-Bissau never had a proletariat, and this task is one for the future. Our struggle was not a class struggle.

And imperialism?

During the struggle we fought Portugal and its allies which gave it military aid. But that struggle is over. Today we do not call Portugal an enemy.

Is dependency a problem?

We need to complete our political independence with our economic independence. We need the assistance of other countries, but we are not dependent on any country.

— 14 —

Lay Seck

This interview was held in Gabú on August 31, 1975. At the time Seck was president of the region of Boé. Seck, born in Bolama on June 18, 1940, participated in the liberation struggle over a long period.

The greatest problem we are facing is the lack of food. During the war all the people were military, and the food came from abroad. The Portuguese government would buy rice at the international market for 14 escudos and bring it to the region and sell it for 7 escudos. The Portuguese government needed these people to fight. After the war, there was no food production and we lacked rice, our main foodstuff. The region of Boé has 75,000 people, and Gabú has 7,000. Other difficulties are medical assistance to the population, lack of transportation, the rebuilding of roads, assistance to children.

In the past this city had a hospital with only one nurse and eighteen beds but without a doctor; now we have built a hospital of fifty beds, and we have eight Soviet doctors to help us.

We have sanitary stations. We have schools, but the children are spread out and it's difficult to transport them; most of our children have only one year of primary school. Here in the city we have five primary schools with four years of schooling. This year we will offer two years of lycée. We have adequate number of primary teachers here. We use both "old" and new books; we use Portuguese textbooks, but we have new books from the liberated zone that teach African history and geography. The schools in the liberated zones continue to work.

We have good relations with the local population. We entered this city in September 1974, little by little, after the Portuguese troops had left. After we settled here, we formed the party's base committee, which has five members who are elected by the people. Each village in the region has a party base committee. Each section has a representative of security, health, and education. The sections have representatives in the region. The sectors and regional party committees' members are picked by the party; the people vote only for the base committees in their villages. We have five sectors and fifteen sections; each sector has three sections; each section has several dozen villages. The region's administrative structure is connected with the party, because the region's administrator has to be a militant of the party. The party comes first. Each person who is handicapped or disabled is given assistance by the state. Now we have to give social assistance to our militants who fought in the war.

We have two tribes: Mandinga and Fula. They are both Muslim tribes. They are primarily peasants. During the war the Fulas were friends of the Portuguese, and the Mandingas did not have any contacts with them. Our main concern is to unite the people as Guineans, so we do not dwell on tribal problems. They have no class structure within the tribe. Here in Guinea there is no land property; the land is for all the people. We do not have social classes here. Before there was the traditional chief tribal family; that was the only class here. The Portuguese here are poor and do not constitute a class. In all the region of Guinea there are no classes. The class is the party, and we have to have good militants. We do not want the formation of any class here. Our struggle was a struggle against the domination and exploitation of man and by man. We fought the fascist Portuguese government and not the Portuguese people.

How did you participate in the liberation struggle?

It is difficult to explain the revolutionary experience because that experience arises from a principle. I have experience of the struggle because I spent most of my life in the struggle from twenty to thirty-five years of age. In the war the experience of the struggle came day after day; each day brought a new experience, a new problem to be solved: a tactical attack, bombardment, defense. Our experience also develops from our living with the people.

I was born in Bolama. My father was Sengalese and my mother was Bolama from the tribe of Djabu. Bolama has a history of resistance and many of its people were involved in the armed struggle. I went to primary school in Bolama. In 1960 I went to Conakry to enter the struggle, and I went to the Southern Front to work in mass mobilization, then I came to Bissau. Until 1960–1964 I was involved in armed struggle in the Northern Front, then in the Southern Front I was on the front lines where there was a lot of fighting. I was wounded and returned to Conakry. From 1964 to 1967 I was in Havana, and after 1967 I returned to the Southern Front. In 1975 I returned to Bissau.

My most difficult time was in Conokaré, where there were Portuguese troops. The region had a lot of rice, and the population welcomed us. After each attack we would rest in the village. The Portuguese invaded the region with troops, helicopters, and they told the population that Amílcar was assassinated in Conakry. I knew that the death of Amílcar would not destroy the party, because the party is not only Amílcar. He himself prepared the party to survive this condition; he prepared the party for the day of his absence. We always expected this situation. In the north I fought in Morés, a very bombarded area. In 1964–65 the Portuguese launched their heaviest fighting. From 1963 to 1975 we fought a guerrilla fight; we tried to raise our efforts proportional to Portuguese strengths.

Please describe the organization of your region.

Our greatest problem is the cultivation of rice. We need technological aid (tractors) to help us in production, and then we will be able to export it. Right now our rice comes from Europe through Portugal. We need financial assistance to the region. The priorities of the region are food, hygiene posts, and schools. We have had assistance from the UN to help with the refugee problem; we have 30,000 refugees in the region. In terms of health, we need ambulances and medical supplies. We need school supplies for the children: notebooks, etc. . . . There is a popular tribunal in the city and there is a justice tribunal for the region; they have small courts in the villages. We have a death penalty only by sentence of the war tribunal. Each committee has a responsibility for the popular tribunal. Each tribe has its own laws, and the court respects these tribal justice traditions.

Is religion of importance?

Religion is independent of politics. In this region the majority of people are Muslims, but there are a few Catholics. The party does not want to interfere with the religious freedom of our people; the party wants to support and approve of all religions, Muslim and Catholic.

—— **15** ——

Chico Bá

Chico Bá had had a long history of active involvement in the liberation struggle. At the time of this interview, in Bafatá on August 31, 1975, he was president of the region of Bafatá.

The economic situation is not a problem only for this region, but for the whole country. Our agriculture is geared primarily toward development; this is the plan for the whole country. The economic situation of the region is very weak. The war situation did not permit any development here. The Portuguese military authorities did not allow the peasants to work on the land and produce; the population was allowed only to cultivate those areas where the authorities could supervise and maintain control. The authorities claimed that if the people worked beyond the limited areas, they might come in contact with the guerrillas. All this caused a decrease in production, which is now reflected in the slow progress of the region. This region is primarily producing peanuts because that is what the colonialists wanted to export. The peanut is the raw material for the production of oil. The Portuguese gave attention to those products that were most profitable. In second place came the production of corn, but this production was not sufficient for local consumption.

Our region has a population of about 95,000. The population lived off imported foodstuffs, primarily rice. There is also sugarcane production, but it is for making alcohol; we have three or four industries to transform sugarcane into alcohol. Our future plan is to diversify production to plant beans, vegetables, rice. We want to produce three to four harvests of rice annually. The state is financing this project with the technical assistance of friendly countries with long experience in rice production. In two to three years we hope to stop importing rice, because we have sufficient resources to do so. We need some technological assistance, such as an irrigation system.

Bafatá is one of the richest economic regions in the country. During the struggle this region was not directly involved and affected by the war. There were some military operations and incursions here, but to a much lesser extent than in other areas.

During the war the Portuguese had to do everything to keep this region and its population stabilized and under their control. Most foodstuffs and primary necessities were all imported. Some of the commercial firms had to reduce their commerce, but they were still in operation. During the colonial administration there were lands divided among property owners, but according to the new law passed by the National Popular Assembly of Bissau, the land belongs to the people, to the state. In this context no one can cultivate the land to sell products or to rent, since all land belongs to the state. The land belongs to the people. We are thinking of establishing some cooperatives on an experimental basis. Traditionally, the land is cultivated by the family or by the village. However, we want to educate and develop a spirit of mutual cooperation among the people, so they will understand that the development of production depends essentially on mutual cooperation.

We are organizing the first few cooperatives. In this region we have three big cooperatives of production. We have a production site run by the state, which is situated along the river Geba near a village called Balamin, an experimental center founded by Cabral with the objective of promoting agricultural production and developing an irrigation system. This center was founded before the war by Comrade Cabral, and during the struggle the Portuguese used it as a training camp for its troops. Now it is operating under the supervision of national and foreign agricultural experts and irrigation technicians. The plan is to further expand the production cooperatives, but it is a difficult task to politically educate the population to change their attitude toward working the land, to teach them to work collectively and to assist one another.

In this region the population was divided: some were under the Portuguese control, and others were on our side. It was difficult for the party to consolidate its power and authority. It was difficult for the population to understand the party and its political line; the people were a bit confused in their interpretation of the party. It was natural for this confusion to happen. Here we have Fula, Mandinga, and Balanta tribes, and it is our task to integrate and unite the people.

What about social classes and class struggle?

There are no social classes as such in Guinea; it is inconvenient to use such a concept. The majority of our people are peasants, and the peasant is the most important group in our country. There were groups of people who worked with the Portuguese and who attempted to prevent the unification of our people. Within the tribes there were and are hierarchical structures which can be interpreted as the beginnings of a class structure, but these were only present within the tribes, such as the Fulas. There is no proletariat here, because the workers come to the city during the dry seasons to work and save money, and they go back to their villages to work the land during the rainy seasons. There is no fixed, organized, and developed proletariat. The objective of the society is to achieve a classless society, but we have not reached this objective yet. We have to develop industries in order to create a proletariat. There is also a large number of refugees in this region, about 5,000 now.

The base committees were developed and organized by the party in the villages and in the city; they are party committees. These committees establish a linkage between the government and the masses, in relation to the needs of the government and in relation to the mass support of the people for the government's development program. This region has six sectors with about two hundred sections; each sector has a committee and assembly. Each sector's committee gives direction and leadership to the sections' committees, which in turn inform and educate the people. The popular assemblies at the sectional level meet once a week. Each committee has to have at least two to three women participants; the party wants to improve and expand the role of women in the society.

How did you participate in the liberation struggle?

I was born in Bissau into a family of five brothers; one died. My father paid for my studies. In 1956 when the party was formed, I had just finished primary school. I went to the lycée until 1959, and then I entered the party. I did some underground activities until 1962. I fled from Bissau to the north and went completely underground. In November 1962 when I returned to Bissau to do some underground work, I was arrested and held until January 1964. I fled from prison in 1964 and went to join the armed struggle in the countryside. I worked as a militant in several activities: education, health, etc. . . .

In 1965–66 I began to assume high positions in the party. I began to direct political activities in the northern region until 1971. In 1971 I was elected a member of the Conselho Nacional de Luta, which assumed the responsibility of reconstruction of the northern region. In 1972 I was transferred to the south as political commissary of the Southern Front until April 1974. In April 1974 I was transferred to the western region as political commissary.

I am a member of the Executive Committee of the Struggle and a leader of the party. In 1971 and 1972 I was in Moresco in the northern region when the Portuguese launched an offensive. The Portuguese failed because the population gave important support to the popular forces. The battle began the week of the nineteenth to twenty-fifth of December. We succeeded in driving the Portuguese out of the region. In June and July 1974 I came here to do political work and entered in contact with the Portuguese military during the transition period. Now I take part in every base community debate and in popular assemblies, listening to the people and teaching them how to debate. My wife participated in the struggle as a nurse.

—— 16 ——
Otto Schacht

Having entered the liberation struggle in the early 1960s, Schacht later studied engineering in Czechoslovakia and also spent some time in Sweden. Born in Farim in 1938, he went to school in Bissau and Portugal. His mother was from Bissau, his father was Portuguese. At the time of this interview, in Bissau on September 5, 1975, he was commissar of communication and transportation.

We have finished the first phase of the armed struggle. Now this new phase of national reconstruction is much more difficult because it requires more sacrifice and greater will. We have made many mistakes in this phase because of our inexperience in this kind of struggle, which is different from the armed struggle familiar to our militants. National reconstruction is our task now.

Our commissary deals with the areas of communication and transport. The commissary is divided into two different directions, each having a certain number of services under its guidance. For example, the communication sector is in charge of civil aeronautics; the transport sector is in charge of four different departments: merchant marine, automobile, air transportation, and traffic. All these sectors are represented in the commissary. We want to coordinate all transportation activities within the country. In air transportation we have two airlines which operate within the country—small planes holding five to ten passengers. For the moment this is sufficient to satisfy our needs. We have one main airport in Bissau, but throughout the country there are several landing strips for these planes. We want to improve the runways and maybe create another airport. Unfortunately, of all the old Portuguese colonies, Bissau was the only one which lacked any infrastructure in regards to air transportation. The old colonial government left us nothing, no airplanes, nothing. To make international flights, the only airplane we have is a DC-3. In Angola, Mozambique, and Cape Verde there is an air transportation infrastructure. We are waiting for two more DC-3s which were offered by the Portuguese Air Force. We are in urgent need of these planes to facilitate the transportation of people and goods.

In terms of ground transportation, we do not yet have a state company of transportation. We do not have the financial capability to invest in a fleet of trucks for transportation. There is a private bus company called Boa Viagem that serves Bissau with five buses. The population needs adequate transportation. It is difficult to create a transportation system in the countryside and on our islands. Our ultimate goal is to establish a state transportation company.

Guinea abounds in rivers, which are all open to navigation, and river transportation is the cheapest form of transport in the country and around the world. However, we do not have the boats to make use of this fluvial system. This lack of river transportation is greatly felt. The old colonial administration did not leave behind any operating boats. Boats which carry people and cargo now consist of a total of four. There are private companies which have cargo boats. We attend to the administration of the ports, the loading and unloading of cargo, and the warehouses. Bissau is the main port, but we have other facilities in the other islands which were shut down during the revolutionary struggle, and which still remain closed.

How did you become involved in the liberation struggle?

In 1962 I fled from the old colony of Guinea and got involved in the PAIGC activities. I fought as a militant in Dakar, Conakry, then the party decided to send me to continue my studies. In 1964 I went to Czechoslovakia to study electronics, where I stayed until 1969. In 1969 I went to Sweden to do an internship related to my profession, and then I returned in 1972 to Conakry to participate in the fight once more. I went to fight in the east Boé. I was at the Military School of the Belasie as a teacher until 1974.

I was born in Farim in 1938; I went to primary school in Bissau and the lycée in Portugal. My mother was from Bissau and my father was Portuguese. He was a functionary at the customs department. When the Pidjiguiti incident occurred, I was in Lisbon, Portugal; I was at the time doing military duty in the Portuguese Air Force. After completing the lycée I was called to serve in the Portuguese military until 1962. I returned to Guinea from Portugal in 1962 and stayed in Guinea. While I was serving in the Portuguese Air Force the Portuguese arrested me, and I was in prison for three months.

What are your views of imperialism?

Our national liberation struggle clearly lies within the context of international imperialism. We have contributed to the global struggle against imperialism, colonialism, and neocolonialism; we fought for nineteen years against colonialism. Personally, I believe that colonialism is an integral part of imperialism.

Is Guinea dependent on the outside world?

We depend on our own resources and on our people. We have received assistance from other countries, but this assistance was given with no compromises attached nor obligations. Our economic and political policy is one of "nonalignment," because we are not dependent upon any country; we do trade and have relations with those countries with whom we have an understanding and with whom we want to deal. We do not feel dependent on anybody except ourselves. I think that in the future the country can develop self-sufficiently. Guinea is essentially an agricultural country and we are rich in agricultural resources. We have fishing resources; our coasts are the best fishing coasts in all of Africa. Many countries have asked for fishing licenses to use our coastal areas. We have the capability to develop minerals from the subsoil. It is my opinion that we have the resources to be economically independent of any country. Guinea is very rich in rice, and now we are exporting the rice, which is our basic foodstuff. New agricultural technology will increase our agricultural production.

In our current national reconstruction phase all economic sectors are of equal importance and priority. We have to create an infrastructure in which all sectors develop proportionally.

What about social classes and the class struggle?

The colonial administration particularly emphasized tribal divisions and sectarianism, making certain ethnic groups believe that they were superior to others and thus creating rivalry. This became the focal point of our struggle, that is, to end such tribal rivalry and division. We are all Guineans, and our party's theme is unity, struggle, and progress. This is the basis of our thinking: the unity of our people, and the unity with Cape Verde and Guinea because we are all one people. National unity within Guinea has already been achieved, and in the future we are working toward the unification of Guinea and Cape Verde into a single country and one people.

Our struggle was one of liberation. Here there were no classes in the European sense, and thus a class struggle along European lines of thought did not take place. Here, there were the Portuguese and the rest of the population; there were only the colonialist class and the lumpen. There were no industries and factories, thus no working class. I believe that we have to build a proletariat here because we are all workers now.

—— 17 ——
Joseph Turpin

This interview with Turpin was obtained on September 6, 1975, in Bissau. At the time he was secretary-general of foreign affairs and commerce.

What are your perspectives on imperialism?

During the national liberation struggle we had great difficulty with the imperialist-colonialist world class, because the imperialist countries gave military, economic, political, and moral support to our Portuguese colonialist enemies. The imperialist-colonialist-capitalist countries were against the aspirations of our people and our struggle. Today our liberation struggle has come to an end, but we still have our development struggle to face. We are a small country aware of our limited resources and capabilities. In our liberation struggle our objectives were our people's independence and dignity. However, now we have to turn our efforts toward economic development without compromising our independence and principles. In our present situation we cannot and do not want to abstain from relations with other countries. We are open to all countries and to international trade. The concern of the PAIGC and the government is to not condemn Portuguese colonialism and its allies at this stage; our main task is to face our current situation and to improve the living standards of our people.

What about Guinea's dependence on the other nations?

In the history of the development of all countries there is always an interrelationship or interdependence. There is a necessary cooperation between the more advanced industrial countries and the less developed ones. This cooperation between developed and underdeveloped, capitalist and socialist countries is a necessity and a reality. We are underdeveloped and lack resources, and thus this cooperation is indispensable. We cannot say we are self-sufficient in our development efforts, but we are independent in our thinking and in our actions within our national territory. Political independence alone will not end the misery of our people; work, aid, and foreign technical assistance will create a basis to improve the living conditions of our people. In this context we are interrelated with other countries. No country in the world can call itself self-sufficient in its economic production and trade. Even the United States, the world's economic power, has the need to cooperate with other countries in order to have access to raw materials and markets. This does not mean that the independence of the United States is at stake. Likewise, our interrelationship with other countries will not place our independence in jeopardy or at stake. We need foreign aid and cooperation to help our economic takeoff.

What about social classes and the class struggle?

If I recall correctly, Comrade Cabral presented his views on social classes in Havana. Certain theories explain that during a revolutionary struggle the working class is the one which has greater consciousness and thus plays the dynamic role in the revolution. Amílcar explained these theories as they manifested themselves in the reality of Guinea. Guinea does not have a working class because of the absence of industries and factories. Guinea has a peasant class, which played a central role in the PAIGC and in the revolutionary struggle. The peasant class took up arms to fight for independence. The intellectuals, from the petty-bourgeoisie families, directed and oriented the struggle. In terms of class struggle there were groups which were against our ideas and political thinking, but this problem has been resolved. Those people have either accepted our present reality or have chosen to leave the country. At the moment our country has a rural population of about 90 percent. However, we want to diversify the economy and build factories and industries. We want to create the conditions for the development of a working class. In reference to Guinea we cannot talk about a class struggle because the party has unified the people. The peasant class can be the embryo for a future working class without any divergence between them. Our main priority is to improve the living conditions of our people—to fight against poverty, hunger, and illiteracy.

How did you become involved in the liberation struggle?

Personally, I see a revolution as a change, a transformation from one situation to another. We fought against the Portuguese colonial domination in order to gain our independence. This is revolutionary. We are living in misery, our people are tired, and we need food, factories, and other conditions to make our country prosper. This process of creating an infrastructure and conditions is a revolutionary process.

I do not like to talk about myself, because one person does not make a revolution, and I alone did not make the struggle. My parents are from Bolama, but I was born in Guinea. I participated in various revolutionary activities in the liberated zones of the north, south, and west. I went abroad for party work and attended some UN General Assembly meetings.

—— 18 ——

André Corsino Tolentino

This interview was held in Praia on August 16, 1975. At the time Tolentino was secretary of state for foreign affairs in the government of Cape Verde. He was born on the island of Santo Antão, received his early education on São Vicente, and studied at the Technical University of Lisbon.

Concerning the general characteristics of the imperialist colonialist domination, we can say that here in Cape Verde to a certain extent we experienced the extreme of the imperialist-colonialist domination. There are certain characteristics of this domination that are unique to the Cape Verde situation. One example was the absence of classical raw materials, which would have allowed for the rapid and easy "enrichment" of the colonialists and which would have also called for the migration of a great number of those from the metropolis to the islands of Cape Verde. This concentration of colonialists would have in turn created certain material conditions for their own convenience and service. Thus, a certain minimal administrative and productive infrastructure would be created to ensure the well-being and support of the colonialists from the metropolis. However, with the arrival of national independence, with the creation of a more just society as a consequence of a true struggle for liberation, these same structures would serve the people of Cape Verde at this moment.

What actually happened, according to the historical facts, was that the islands of Cape Verde were found uninhabited and were occupied primarily by individuals who were exiled from Portugal and by individuals accused of petty crimes. Therefore, individuals considered "undesirables" in Portugal were sent to the Cape Verde islands. However, from the very beginning the islands played an important role in the discoveries of Portuguese colonial domination. The islands served as an important point of departure. The colonialists began to build a minimum support structure. With the discovery and occupation of Brazil by Portugal, Cape Verde served as an intermediary between the African coast, the west coast of Africa, and the coast of Brazil. The slaves who were gathered in the west African coast were sent to Brazil. However, the slaves were first trained here in Cape Verde before leaving for Brazil. They were trained in different activities such as agriculture, cattle raising, disciplined work. And thus, there was a whole process of occupation and population of Cape Verde. Therefore, the Europeans and the Africans coexisted as masters and slaves. But with time and in response to the necessities imposed by the nature of the islands, there was a certain racial mixture. This "fusion" had its problems, conflicts, and sanctions. However, this tendency toward racial mixture predominated and persisted, and the majority of the population is "mixed" (*mestiça*). At least it is much more integrated than the other territories which were dominated by Portugal.

There was also a tradition of exportation or "re-exportation" of the labor force in Cape Verde to Brazil and to Portugal itself. There was a traditional emigration of the population abroad. Above all this, emigration was a consequence of a gradual deterioration of the natural environment and conditions of the country—a consequence of the lack of governmental measures geared toward the creation and development of material infrastructure designed to support and maintain the archipelago and its population. It is a consequence of the lack of productive infrastructure designed to retain the labor force in Cape Verde. This is a unique characteristic of Cape Verde. What did the Portuguese in their colonialism and imperialism take from Cape Verde? They took our labor force and used it in the other colonies, particularly in São Tomé and Angola. From the beginning there was a greater literacy in Cape Verde than in the other colonies. The Cape Verdeans were used to serving the colonialist interests, and there was a policy to grant a kind of fictitious privilege to the Cape Verdeans, precisely to use them as instruments of domination in other colonies.

Another aspect of Portuguese imperialism was the use and defense of the strategic position Cape Verde provided to Portugal. There was an intense effort to include these islands strategically as a departure point toward the rest of Africa. That is why today we try to warn all Africans to guard the true independence of this continent by not allowing any foreign powers to establish bases here in Africa.

A third characteristic of the imperialist domination is reflected in the kinds of relationships that were established between the dominant social class here in Cape Verde and the colonial government. In the very beginning of colonization, during the sixteenth and seventeenth centuries, the Portuguese government had a policy of giving the islands to particular families. Thus, São Tiago Island was given to two families who made the island their private domain and established a feudal socioeconomic system. This tradition is important to our understanding today since each island belonged to one or two families, the owners of the islands who had full economic, political, and administrative powers. And with time, their children inherited the lands, and thus a new propertied class emerged. And the children of the original slaves worked as slaves for the owners' children. And thus feudal class relations were established. These characteristics are still in existence today, and among the priorities of our program is land reform, which will restructure the exploitation of land to serve the interest of our free men.

How do you see your country's dependence on other nations?

Our foreign policy is one of nonalignment. It is true that within the nonaligned countries we can observe a variety of tendencies. Here in Cape Verde we will follow a serious nonaligned policy, since we choose nonalignment not as a convenient means to avoid confrontations. Here we believe that nonalignment can really have significant impact as long as the countries within this movement take their independence and destiny seriously and organize themselves in such a way as to present solutions to problems and to address the two superpowers as a cohesive force, organized and conscious of their desired goals. It is in this context that we follow a nonaligned policy.

Our program of development is a modest one. It is a program that takes into account our natural resources and it is a program that relies heavily on the capability of our people. Thus, it is oriented toward serving the needs of the majority of our people.

In terms of foreign relations we all know that independence is relative. We achieved our independence because we had to assure our sovereignty, and we had to make known the interests and wants of our people. Once sovereignty is achieved, we have to live in an interdependent world. A world not dominated by one power or the other, but an interdependence in which everyone participates in and contributes to according to their capabilities. However, we want to do everything to avoid any intervention by any superpower in our internal affairs. We want to have relations and to cooperate with every country which wishes to cooperate with us, without attempting or wanting to dominate us. There are people who regard us simply as a military base. We want to end this thinking, we want others to understand that here in Cape Verde live our people. That instead of being a strategic location, we are a people, and we want to be recognized and treated as such. Therefore, we are very wary of those who want to obtain concessions from us as a precondition for giving us aid, while at the same time violating our independence.

What about current economic relations and conditions?

Independence is always relative, because it would be absurd for us to cut economic relations with the world economy. Even the great industrial powers cannot afford to cut economic ties. So we are all interdependent. What we want is that in this existing interdependence, relations be based on justice and not on exploitation. We believe we share common goals and common characteristics with other countries in the world. We are willing to establish the best relations possible with all the countries in the world. However, if there are countries whose governments intend to violate our sovereignty or want concessions which would jeopardize our sovereignty, then in this case we say "stop" and do not want any relations. From our program of national development, from our struggle, well-informed people know or may deduce where our friendship lies . . . who our friends were during the national liberation struggle, and therefore, with whom there are certain kinds of "privileged" relations. All this can be deduced from our struggle and our current program of development.

What about social classes and the class struggle?

At the very beginning the classes were very distinct: first, the Portuguese colonialists; second, the landowners; third, the slaves who worked the land. Later, there was a process in which intermediary groups were created as the landowners legally recognized their "mulato" sons, giving them land. As commerce developed, Cape Verde and Guinea were dominated together; a commercial circuit was established between the metropolis [Portugal], Guinea and Cape Verde, and Brazil. The Portuguese traded raw materials, textiles, and certain merchandise, and they bought or traded slaves on the coast of Guinea. The slaves were then brought to Cape Verde to be trained and "disciplined" before being sent to Brazil. From Brazil cotton and sugar went to Portugal. Thus, the triangle Portugal, Guinea and Cape Verde, and Brazil was formed.

The development of commerce brought forth the commercial class. Four classes were then discernible: the slaves, the propertied class, the commercial class, and the Portuguese colonialists. The petty bourgeoisie, predominantly occupied with commercial activities, was often owner of land or property. There was also the administrative class, the functionaries, which consisted mostly of the Portuguese, and the literate natives or "mulatos." The latter were the middle or lower administrative personnel, which as a group competed alongside the merchant class for privileges and resources. The landowners' sons were the professionals—the lawyers, doctors—those who studied in Portugal and in Europe. There was also the peasantry. We had here a very complex and confusing system of land exploitation in Cape Verde. Let me give an example. The landowner gives his son a huge piece of land (a *morcadio*). The son goes to study abroad or decides to emigrate to the city because he feels that managing the land is beneath the privileged class. Thus he moves to the city and gives responsibility of the land to a *rendeiro* (leaser or rentier) who also has resources. Frequently the land is too big to be worked by a single person; thus, the rentier contracts a piece of the land to a third person. The rentier as a middleman (an *intermediário*) makes a lot of money, because he can rent the land to the third party for a big sum. Now, the third person who contracts the land hires the labor force, the peasants, to work the land. The peasants may work the land for themselves or parcel out the land to *milheiros*. Thus, the land is divided out among all these people. To work *milheiro* means that at the end of the year the peasant gives half of his production (work) to the rentier. It is a complex process.

Were resistance movements of importance?

There was a case unique to Cape Verde. During the national liberation struggle the petty bourgeoisie played a very important role. The petty bourgeoisie consisted of those who were able to study abroad and thus acquire certain intellectual skills. These people had access to the press and intellectual circles abroad, and they came into contact with leaders of the liberation movement. The dynamic organizing nucleus of the struggle for liberation of Cape Verde came from the petty bourgeoisie—that is, they were the sons of the merchant class and the sons of the propertied class. The petty bourgeoisie was not necessarily revolutionary, but at the same time this class perceived itself as exploited and dominated by the Portuguese colonialists, the white man. The white man symbolized power, a superior race, and Western civilization. Therefore, the "mulato," even when economically privileged, was immediately a victim of discrimination, and thus, the mulato (the petty bourgeoisie) felt the necessity to liberate himself. Perhaps this petty bourgeoisie does not conform to the scheme presented by Comrade Cabral about the role of the bourgeoisie. But this is how I see the role played by the petty bourgeoisie in Cape Verde.

The petty bourgeoisie faced an interesting situation in the revolutionary process: either it would side with the popular masses or it would side with the colonial forces. In actuality, as a nationalist bourgeoisie, it opted to fight along with the masses. With the raising of the national consciousness of the masses and the coming together of forces, the bourgeoisie disappeared as a class as it began to defend the interests of the popular masses. The program of reforms put forth by the party had a natural relationship to the peasants and the workers. The party's objectives identified with the objectives of the peasants and the workers. Of course there were some big landowners and other privileged Tolentino property owners who attempted to resist the liberation movement and the mobilization of the masses. Particularly after the twenty-fifth of April, they formed a group called União Democrática de Cape Verde and União dos Povos (UPIC). However, they lacked the support of the masses. Eventually, those opposed to the national struggle left to go to Brazil. It is interesting and significant that they went to Brazil, since that gives us a clue as to their ideology. Some fled to the United States. These people who have left have made *no* drain on our effort of nation-building and development.

After the Second World War was there resistance?

During the war Cape Verde was used as a naval base, particularly the Island of São Vicente. There was widespread discontent and demonstrations by the people of the island against the sending of workers to work at the "Roxa" (rock) of São Tomé. These demonstrations were local, dispersed, and without great repercussion.

What about the current revolutionary institutions?

Naturally, the party prevails as the supreme organization. There is also the "Lei Nacional" (national law), which is a revolutionary institution. At the moment we are studying the formation of a workers' union in Cape Verde. We also want to create consumer cooperatives at the national level since at the moment we are heavily dependent on imports. We are attempting to control the price of imports and we want to eliminate the series of intermediaries in the commercial circuit. Thus, the immediate organization of a system of cooperatives is extremely important for the overall administration of the economy. The ministries of government are headed by our comrades who fought for our liberation. The revolutionary struggle creates a new man who learns to have a real-life perspective on things.

How did you become involved in the liberation struggle?

I am twenty-nine years old, born on the island of Santo Antão. My parents were peasants who owned land; they had an elementary education. I went to elementary school on the island of Santo Antão, secondary school on the island of São Vicente, and I attended the Technical University of Lisbon for a year and a half. In Lisbon I had the opportunity to meet and to debate with other students from Cape Verde and the other colonies. I began to acquire a globalist perspective on liberation movements. Paradoxically, my stay in Lisbon provided me the opportunity to begin my political formation. In 1968 I was forced to leave Portugal along with other friends. I went to Belgium and attended the University of Bayern. In 1969 I went to Guinea-Bissau to work in the countryside. I served for a while in the navy, and worked in the preparation of the military cadres in the western region of Bissau. For a brief period of time I directed the school for the preparation of the cadres. Then I went to Western Europe for a while. In 1974 I returned to Cape Verde to participate in the first official party delegation after the twenty-fifth of April Portuguese revolution. I worked on the island of Santo Antão as political organizer until the elections. Currently, I work as secretary of state in the area of foreign relations, and I am a representative in a district. Almost all my family participated directly and indirectly in the liberation struggle; my brothers work actively in the party.

—— 19 ——

Fernando Lopes

At the time of this interview, in Praia on August 16, 1975, Lopes was a labor leader and member of the party executive in Cape Verde. Born in São Tiago Island in 1947, he attended the University of Lisbon.

Here in Cape Verde before the twenty-fifth of April there was no possibility of any type of mass organization. There were fascist unions, which had no mass and popular representation and which in reality were another instrument of control and repression of the workers. In our political program, we advocate the existence of mass organizations for the defense of the interests of the masses, and thus, the freedom of union organization and the right to form other organizations which are *not* outside or contradictory to our liberation process.

In this context, from the beginning of our presence here in Cape Verde, the party picked some of its organizers to work jointly with the local workers to explain to them union organization. The party organizers explained the necessity of having their own organization to defend their professional and general interests. Therefore, a commission was created here in Cape Verde for the establishment of the unions, which was also called Grupo de Ação Sindicato. There were difficulties at first, because the workers thought of the union as something to which they had to pay money without receiving any benefits. This general distrust of union organization was only transcended because the Grupo de Ação Sindicato consisted of members of the party who were trusted by the workers, but even so it was difficult to explain to the people the advantages and benefits of unions. Thus, the first phase consisted of this educational campaign.

Afterwards, there were elections in each workplace to select those most capable of working with the Grupo de Ação Sindicato to help plan for more unions. The elections were held in the transition period in Cape Verde. The commission went to each workplace and set a table. Depending on the particular local and technical conditions, the election process would vary between the raising of hands to the presentation of lists of candidates. Because of the composition of the labor force (some seasonal temporary workers, some fourteen-year-old workers, and some very old workers), an eligibility standard had to be developed for the selection of the union delegates. After the elections, several meetings of union delegates took place in order to train these people on the minimum basics of unionization. The delegates did not have any knowledge of union techniques and of the particular role of the unions at the moment of transition in Cape Verde. The commission attempted to give the basic union training for these delegates so that they would use their acquired skills in their workplace.

What about social classes and the class struggle?

Here in Cape Verde, even in reference to the colonial period, it is difficult to define the social classes. The classes are usually defined in terms of the relations of ownership or lack of ownership of the means of production. But here in Cape Verde what happens? The means of production, if they existed—in whose hands were they? In the countryside there were the big landowners who were descendants of Portuguese or were native Portuguese themselves and who were very big property holders. There were also smaller landowners and the rentiers. The rentiers were those who did not own any land, but that rented the land from the big landowner in order to cultivate it. The rentier paid part of his production in kind or paid a sum of money. The big landowners usually lived in Portugal or lived in the city. Therefore, there was no kind of capitalist agricultural enterprise, with the agricultural entrepreneur overseeing the agricultural activities. However, these big landowners still received big profits by renting to others. This situation has changed, because during the national liberation struggle the peasants took over and occupied those lands on which they had been working and whose owners were absent in Portugal. At this moment these lands are managed by a commission of old rentiers who do not have private ownership of these lands. About five properties are in this situation of being administered by the commission. The owners were Portuguese families who did not care about the lands and who now live in Portugal. One of the properties was owned by a Portuguese involved in counterrevolutionary activities here in Cape Verde. His land was occupied for political reasons. He was arrested by the Portuguese authorities and deported from Cape Verde.

In the city, during the colonial period, the majority of people were lumpen-proletariat; they emigrated from the countryside and from the other islands looking for jobs; they now live in the outskirts of the city. They have seasonal work, and when jobs are not available there are problems with delinquency and petty crimes. Therefore, there was this lumpen-proletariat class. The percentage of permanent workers with permanent skills (the carpenters, bricklayers, mechanics, dockers) was about one to two percent of the total work force. There was the governing administrative class; within this class there were the top administrators and the lower echelon of funcionaries. The top administrators cooperated with the colonial regime. With the successful accomplishments of the revolution, very few of them remained in Cape Verde. Therefore, in the city there were the workers, the lumpen-proletariat, the administrative class, and the merchants. The merchants have closer ties with Portugal than with the domestic economy of Cape Verde. They are economically dependent on the Portuguese industries. There is no industrial production here, so the merchants import everything that they sell here, and they live more off the circulation of money than anything else. At first the merchants were hostile to the revolutionary movement, because they thought that communism would take over. But later they began to understand that, given our concrete conditions, we could not afford to follow such a political course in relation to our difficult situation—we could not afford to take a step back in order to advance two steps afterwards. There are other underdeveloped countries which, because of their resources and capabilities, can afford to take a revolutionary step (even if it means "retarding" technical processes and social conditions) and move forward later.

As you know, there was an attempt to create "false" movements here in Cape Verde. These movements were supported by the top administrative class and the merchants, without any support from the masses. These groups disappeared by themselves. We had our underground organization here, with experienced cadres, and we went about organizing our party. In November and December we began our process of occupying lands and the radio station at São Vicente. This was immediately before the signing of the agreements on independence with the Portuguese authorities. This was the moment of greatest confrontation, and also the time that we made our "popular prisons." This was the time when we discovered counterrevolutionary plots, and we decided to mobilize the people, "putting them in the street" to identify the opposition and capture them. Of course, because of the spontaneous outburst of the population, there were innocent people who were captured but later set free. We conducted a "politics" of constant internal pressures until the signing of the agreements.

What are your perspectives of imperialism?

We have to follow a foreign policy congruent with our needs and capabilities. Our policy is that of nonalignment. Given the principles of our revolutionary struggle and given our present economic conditions we cannot align ourselves with any military bloc. We want relations with every country as long as our sovereignty is respected. We support other liberation movements existing in Africa and in other parts of the world. Our support can only be that of political support because we have no other capabilities. We welcome relations with any country that wants to cooperate and aid in our economic goals. Our economic situation is chaotic; there are no financial or technical means for an economic takeoff. The Portuguese government has followed through with its financial obligations to us. At the moment we need foreign assistance to help us plan an economic development program according to our available resources. We have to build the country. How?

Even if we wanted to, it is absolutely impossible to avoid foreign investment. However, we have to regulate these investments in accordance with our interests. We are a small country working toward the development of our people. Other countries should respect our sovereignty and not interfere in our internal affairs.

How did you participate in the liberation struggle?

I was born on São Tiago Island in 1947. I attended the University of Lisbon in Portugal and studied history, particularly African history. Currently, I am a member of the national directorate of the party in Cape Verde, and I also work with mass organizations. I did not participate in the fighting in Guinea. My parents were born in Cape Verde; my father was a merchant. My father had only an elementary education. I am now a deputy from the São Domingos district.

—— 20 ——

Carlos Nunes Fernandes Dos Reis

Reis was born in 1946 in São Vicente and studied social science in Portugal. At the time of this interview, in Praia on August 17, 1975, he was minister of education in the government of Cape Verde.

Our society was subjected to a colonial rule which for many years used the educational policy and programs to alienate the people—a form of mental isolation and alienation of the youth from their land, their culture, and their problems. One of our central concerns is to reformulate such thinking and attitude. In the creation of a new man, Comrade Cabral has said education plays an important role. We have to design new educational methods for teachers to communicate with their students; the preparation of the teachers themselves; the content of the educational programs. For example, under the colonial rule our elementary school children had to memorize the names of the railroad stations in Portugal. They had to memorize the railroad tracks in the north and south of Portugal without even knowing what a railroad track looked like. This is an excellent example of the educational programs under the colonial administration.

Even under and during the six-month transitional government in which we participated, the reformulation of education was an urgent matter. We began to reformulate the programs at the elementary level to the educational problems of the Cape Verdean people so that the educated youth could discuss this situation and its solution in the school. In this way, the schools would reverse their role of alienating the people. We already have established commissions to elaborate the new programs, we have some textbooks which have been chosen to be used; and we have elaborated others to be sent abroad to be edited and published. One of our difficulties at the moment is to publish the books which we are elaborating. We hope to be able to publish the books in Portugal, but so far we have no assurances of such prospects. As you know, the new Portuguese government was formed very recently and Portugal is focusing its attention on its own current problems. However, we do hope to edit and publish some books in Portugal.

The commissions have been formed to a certain extent according to the geographical features and divisions of Cape Verde. We have commissions in Praia and in São Vicente. One commission coordinates the books and programs for primary schools and the other formulates the curricula for the secondary schools. The commissions focus on the particular educational disciplines: language (Portuguese, French, English), science, physics, mathematics, geography. Our priority is to concentrate on the elementary level, because this is the area in which we are able to advance most rapidly. In this area it is important to advance with the new reading materials; elaborate texts which explain and illustrate the reality of Cape Verde—texts which will focus on our land, our animals, our people, our potentials. In other disciplines, such as science and math, we can adapt books and programs from other countries. Thus, in relation to education our greatest difficulty is the elaboration of educational programs and materials.

This is intimately interlinked to another problem which is the preparation of the teachers themselves. At this moment we have in Cape Verde 1,200 elementary teachers. The majority of our teachers never received a specific educational training; most have four years of primary school. A third of our teachers have only four years of primary school and are called "monitors," without any real possibility of greater educational proficiency.

Our lycées traditionally focus on the formation of intellectuals. They study Greek and Latin. Very few study the problems related to Cape Verde— problems of development, of agriculture, of fishing. This is also one of our concerns. During the years of colonial administration, it was necessary to intensify the political campaign of the party. The denunciation of Portuguese colonialism at an international level, particularly since 1965, forced the colonial government to formulate last-minute solutions which culminated in an increase in the number of classes, the greater percentage of which were not state classes.

In an attempt to find hasty solutions at the last minute, in this period there was a school established for the preparation of teachers, Escola Magisterio Primário, but its orientation and the conditions imposed on students never permitted serious work. This is reflected in the number of people who were prepared in that school, since it is the only school here in the Praia. The program is of two years duration and about a dozen people are graduated annually. This is a ridiculously low number of trained teachers given the current needs of the country. Thus, we want to restructure the school, restructure its programs, and create new conditions to allow more people to participate in teacher education. Another school is the Escola de Proveitação do Professor do Posto. A professor do posto is a rural teacher. This school attempts to provide additional instruction to rural teachers to supplement their four years of primary school and to help them solve immediate problems relating to rural education. This school functions in the countryside of São Tiago. We want to establish this same kind of school in the countryside of Santo Antáo. This project depends on technical assistance from other organizations. We have a project to create another school in São Tiago to prepare elementary teachers.

Around the twenty-fifth of April, a bit more than 65,000 students were at the elementary level. When we add students from private schools and the lycées, the overall number does not reach 70,000. This brings up the degree of illiteracy (70%) in Cape Verde, and this is the fundamental problem of our educational situation. We cannot advance the educational program toward a specialized education until we have advanced simultaneously the overall educational capability of the whole population. We not only have to create the future engineers and doctors, but also the literate farmers and fishermen so that the latter will use both their mental and physical capabilities. Thus, the fight against illiteracy is a priority in this ministry. There are less than 70,000 children in school, but our population is young; more than 50 percent of the population is less than fifteen years old. The number of children younger than fifteen years old is more than 150,000. There are a great number of children without access to schools. There is no doubt that we will need the assistance of international organizations and foreign countries. It is urgent for us to create more schools.

The established educational commissions are linked to the regional party organizations and councils in all the islands. Educational brigades have been created to combat illiteracy among the adult population and to reach out to those children previously denied access to schools.

At the secondary level there are two lycées, one in São Vicente and one here at Praia. There is also a technical school in São Vicente. We have asked assistance from the UN organization to help us restructure the program and orientation of this technical school.

We have established several projects with the United Nations. We have two projects of "recycling teachers," which consist of the collaboration of Portuguese experts and the UNESCO. There are alternative educational methods to encourage greater participation of the student and his family in the educational process. We want to reach out to the rural population. This project will take place here at the Praia with about three hundred teachers and in São Vicente with a hundred teachers. It will involve both elementary- and secondary-level teachers.

How do you see imperialism in a historical context?

We think that the state is an instrument of execution of the party's program, and the party's program is profoundly anti-imperialist. Our fight against colonialism is a part of the international anti-imperialist struggle of all oppressed people in the world. We have to talk about our struggle, the resistance of our people against colonialism.

What about dependency on other countries?

We do not associate our struggle against imperialism with the need to cut ties with foreign countries. There is no such need to cut foreign relations. We need to be realistic and pragmatic; given our resources and problems, we need to have ties with all countries in the world. We are aware of our need of foreign assistance, particularly in this takeoff economic phase of national reconstruction. All we want is that our principles, our independence, our struggle be acknowledged and respected.

What are your perspectives of social classes and class struggle?

The colonial society here in Cape Verde had a specific character, although it had been molded within the general lines of colonial administration common in all parts of the world. It had unique features. One such feature was the attempt to utilize the Cape Verdean population itself as the backbone of the colonial system itself. Cape Verde was used as a "link" in the Portuguese strategic scheme as such; Cape Verde did not need to develop. For many years Portugal used to export Cape Verdean labor and middle-level functionaries to other colonies. The Portuguese attempted to prepare colonial administrative cadres in Cape Verde to export these to other colonies. This was done with two objectives: first, to create a false image of Cape Verdeans in the other colonies, thus dividing the colonial peoples and trying to break up African unity; secondly, to deprive Cape Verde of its best people who could help in the development of the country. There was a twofold intention: to prepare Cape Verdean cadres for export and to prevent at any cost the development of Cape Verde by creating an abyss between the Cape Verdean cadres and the illiterate Cape Verdean population.

With the development of our struggle we tried to break this thinking, alienation, and social organization in the sense that we brought together the student, the functionary, the worker, and the peasant who side by side picked up arms in Guinea; they struggled and identified themselves as Africans, as people, as militants of the PAIGC. These cadres are here in Cape Verde identifying themselves with the Cape Verdean people, with the working class, with the misery and exploitation of our people. The birth of our struggle, the organization of the PAIGC, and the process of the struggle itself served as a "coup" to this social stratification instituted by the colonial administration and which our party has been eliminating.

Today, there is no special social stratification. Naturally, there are the state administrators, and there are a great number of illiterates who cannot have access to certain work. There has been an identification of the privileged classes with the misery of the population. After independence, students, clerks, and others went to the countryside to work alongside the peasants in order to help in production and to identify with the peasants. There is no longer a sharp division between different social classes but instead an identification of classes with one another. This identification implies the elimination of social stratification.

Were resistance movements essential to the liberation struggle?

The episodes of resistance of our people were spread out among the other colonies due to the emigrant nature of our people—being constantly forced to emigrate to other colonies, particularly Angola and São Tomé. In São Tomé in 1953 there was a massacre of São Tomé and Cape Verdean workers; Cape Verdeans were working with the São Tomeans in the cacau plantations. In Angola, Cape Verdeans also resisted colonial exploitation alongside the Angolan people. There were isolated episodes here in Cape Verde, which nevertheless marked our culture distinctively. Rebelados—a part of our people who never accepted in any form the colonial intervention—lived independently; they refused to answer questions in the colonial courts. They never accepted aid from the Portuguese (but they accepted aid from PAIGC). Despite Portuguese persecution, the rebelados succeeded in maintaining intact their culture, their self-sufficiency, and their resistance. There are personalities who became known as nationalists in our history. Neco Lalima, who was a rabelado, was murdered for his resistance. Captain Ambrósio celebrated the resistance in São Vicente and died in exile in Angola.

How did you participate in the liberation struggle?

I was born in São Vicente, went to the lycée in São Vicente, and later went to Portugal to study social sciences. In 1968 I left Portugal and returned to Cape Verde and went in 1969 to Guinea to participate in the struggle. First, I participated in the Escola Piloto and later joined the Navy cadre in combat struggle. I stayed four years in Portugal but did not finish my studies. According to Portuguese law, after completion of one's studies the student had to enter immediately the colonial military service; I was doing underground work for PAIGC along with other students. I was in Guinea from 1969 to 1974. I returned to Cape Verde in 1974 and participated in the transitional government. My parents were born in São Vicente and São Antão. My father was a merchant and died while he was very young. My parents had a primary education. My mother did not participate in the struggle.

An Annotated Bibliography

This annotated bibliography is composed of three principal sections. The first chronologically lists books and collections of writing, pamphlets, and mimeographed documents published under the name of Amílcar Cabral. The second section consists of periodical articles published under Cabral's name; they are also listed chronologically. The third section includes general works on Guinea-Bissau and Cape Verde with reference to Cabral; it identifies books and monographs, chapters in books, pamphlets, periodical articles, and ephemera in a single alphabetized list.

—— 1 ——

Books, Collections of Writings, Pamphlets, and Ephemera by Amílcar Cabral

The following list includes books and collections of writings, pamphlets, and mimeographed primary documents under Cabral's name and published by the Partido Africano da Independência da Guiné e Cabo Verde and by the United Nations. Entries are listed under a yearly date of publication and alphabetically within each year, which roughly coincides with date of presentation; annotations clarify these dates.

Many items are documentary ephemera and can be found in the Ronald H. Chilcote Collection on Portuguese Africa, available on microfilm in the libraries of Stanford University and the University of California, Riverside; and in the Immanuel Wallerstein Collection, available on microfilm at Yale University Library and the Cooperative Africana Microform Project, Center for Research Libraries, Chicago, Illinois. Thus these materials are generally accessible to the reader.

Additionally, I specifically refer to the location of documents and unpublished manuscripts available at the CIDAC (Centro de Informação e Documentação Amílcar Cabral) in Lisbon, where much material is systematically coded and organized. The Instituto de Investigação Científico e Tropical (IICT) in Lisbon maintains a section on Cabral in its reference catalogue, including the references to his agrarian writings that appear in Cabral (1988); beyond these writings the IICT lists several hundred additional references to Cabral, most of which are not in its library, but I have listed those that I have not consulted by referring to the IICT.

The Fundação Amílcar Cabral is building an archive of documents on and about Cabral; according to Ana Maria Cabral, the Fundação is preparing a bibliography of these works (letter 57/CD/89, Praia, September 11, 1989).

Related documents not listed below may be found in Chilcote (1972). Some documents listed below are cited in the sources mentioned in the introduction to the third section (see below).

No Date

"As caractéristicas essenciais do nosso tempo. A agonia do imperialismo. O caso português." No Place: Texto 3, Grupo de Trabalho sobre Colonialismo. P. 1, mimeo.
Brief indictment of Portuguese imperialism.

"Das possibilidades do cultivo industrial da cana-sacarina na Guiné. Estudo informativo." No Place. Typescript.
Cited in Cabral (1988: 51).

"Excertos da entrevista dada por Amílcar Cabral, secretário geral do PAIGC à revista 'Tricontinental.'" No Place. Pp. 2, mimeo.
Excerpts from an interview in the Cuban journal *Tricontinental.*

"O imperialismo." No Place. Pp. 7, mimeo.
Emphasis on two forms of imperialism: the first on direct domination, the second on indirect domination. Examines colonialism and neocolonialism, the role of violence, and the role of the petty bourgeoisie. (See CIDAC: GB Partido I-6.)

"Intervention d'Amílcar Cabral, Secrétaire Général du PAIGC au 6ème Congrès de l'UPS." Dakar.
Cited in IICT reference catalogue.

"Luta do povo, pelo povo, para o povo." No Place. Pp. 5, mimeo.
Cabral's name does not appear on the document, but it is his text. Focus on people's struggle. (See CIDAC: GB Partido I-5.)

"O papel da pequena burguesia." No Place. Pp. 4, mimeo.
Focus on the petty bourgeoisie. (See CIDAC: GB Partido I-7.)

"Para a melhoria da acção das nossas forças armadas." Conakry, mimeo.
Cited in IICT reference catalogue.

"Para a reorganização dos exércitos nacionais populares (EP)." No Place, mimeo.
Cited in IICT reference catalogue.

"Princípios. O nosso partido e a luta devem ser dirigidos pelos melhores filhos do nosso povo." No Place. Pp. 11, mimeo.
Text on the role of the party in the revolutionary struggle. (See CIDAC GB Partido I-38.)

Richtlignen voor de PAIGC. No Place. (Guidelines for the PAIGC, Determined in 1965.)

"Saudação do camarada Amílcar Cabral." Conakry, mimeo.
Cited in the IICT reference catalogue.

Unidade e luta. Luanda: Edição do PAIGC em Angola. Pp. 26.
(See CIDAC: GB Pensamento Político I-3.)

(with A. Castanheira). "Projecto de estudos solos de Cabo Verde." Sacavem: Estação Agronómica Nacional, Sacavém. Typescript.
Not cited in Cabral (1988) but listed in the reference catalogue of the IICT.

(with Aristides Pereira). "Rapport sur la lutte de libération des peuples de la Guinée Portugaise et des Iles du Cap Vert." [Conakry]: PAIGC. Pp. 4, mimeo.
Six-point statement on the liberation struggle.

1942?

"Fidemar." Mindelo?
An unpublished story written just before his eighteenth birthday. Fidemar (Son of the Sea) is portrayed "as a 'revolutionary' who claimed the right of all 'to liberty and life' and who finished up departing from his island in the hope of returning strengthened in order to liberate it" (Quoted in Andrade, "Biographical Notes," in Cabral, *Unity and Struggle* [1979], xix–xx).

1942–1943

Poems of Adolescence.
Unpublished poems written in Mindelo, São Vicente. Osório (1988: 21–29) lists thirty-one poems and has published many of them with annotations. Generally signed under the pseudonym Larbac. One of these poems (No. 14) is entitled "Restauração" and perhaps the poem "1 de Dezembro" was awarded a first prize in a contest of the Liceu Gil Eanes on December 5, 1942 (noted in *Notícias de Cabo Verde* No. 219 [December 5, 1942]). Poem No. 28 "Que Fazer?" is described as probably a poem of transition from lyrical themes of love in a period of adolescence to an effort to relate to "social contradiction although not dialectically" (Osório, 1988: 27). Poem No. 31, "Eu sou tudo e sou nada," is dated 1944 and was published in *O Militante* No. 2 (August 1977), 44, and also in *Raizes* Nos. 17–20 (January–December 1981), 20.

1944–1949

Poems of Youth.
Unpublished poems listed by Osório (1988: 29–33). Includes No. 32, "A Ilha" (1945).

1949

"Tragi-comédia em quatro actos." Lisbon, [1949].
A group of thirteen poems of his "Livro de curso," cited by Osório (1988: 32).

1951

"Estudo da erodibilidade de alguns solos do Alentejo." Sacavém: Estação Agronómica Nacional, 1951.
Cited by IICT as distributed in Lisbon. A study of soils in the Alentejo.

"Estudo do clima da região de Cuba em relação à defesa da terra." Sacavém: Estação Agronómica Nacional, 1951.
Also cited in the reference catalogue of IICT as distributed in Lisbon. Cited in Cabral (1988: 49). Climatic study in the Cuba region of the Alentejo.

"O problema da erosão do solo. Conbribuição para o seu estudo na região de Cuba (Alentejo)." Unpublished Thesis, Instituto Superior de Agronomia, Universidade Técnica de Lisboa, 1951. Pp. 133, typescript.
Published in Cabral (1988: 81–176). Study of soil erosion in the region of Cuba in the Alentejo.

(with A. Diniz). "Projecto de estudos dos solos de Cabo Verde." Sacavém: Estação Agronómica Nacional, 1951. Typescript.
Soil studies of Cape Verde.

1953

"Das possibilidades do cultivo industrial das jutas na Guiné. Estudo informativo." Bissau: Repartição dos Serviços Agrícolas, 1953. Typescript.
Cited in Cabral (1988: 49). Study of the jute industry in Guinea.

1954

"A participação portuguesa na Conferência Mancarra-Milhos (Bambey, Senegal)." Bissau, 1954.
Cited in Cabral (1988: 50) as published in *Boletim Cultural da Guiné Portuguesa* but no specific reference given.

"O problema do arroz na Guiné. Estudo informativo." Bissau: Inspecção do Comércio Geral, 1954. Typescript.
Cited in Cabral (1988: 50) and in the IICT reference catalogue. On the problem of rice in Guinea.

1955

"Das possibilidades do cultivo industrial da cana sacarina na Guiné. Estudo informativo (privado)." No Place, 1955. Typescript.
Cited in IICT reference catalogue.

"Notas acerca de alguns solos da Guiné Portuguesa." Lisbon: Lição proferida na Cadeira de Pedologia e Conservação do Solo do Instituto Superior de Agronomia. Typescript.
Text of a lecture on soils in Guinea. Cited in Cabral (1988: 50).

(with A. Nobre da Veiga). "Plano para a recuperação de terrenos para a agricultura da Guiné." Bissau: Repartição Provincial dos Serviços Agrícolas e Florestais, 1955.
Text of a plan on the recuperation of agricultural lands in Guinea. Cited in Cabral (1988: 50).

1956

"Estudo do microclima dos ambientes rel[e]cionados com os produtos armazenados." Lisbon: Brigada de Estudos da Defesa Fitos-sanitária dos Produtos Ultramarinos, 1956.
Not listed in Cabral (1988) but cited in the IICT reference catalogue.

"Sobre a acuidade do problema do armazenamento no arquipélago de Cabo Verde." Summary in Vol. 4, pp. 75–76, sixth Conferência Internacional do Africanistas Ocidentais, 1956.
Reprinted in Cabral (1988: 445). Summary of a paper on storage problems in Cape Verde.

(with others). "Carta de solos da propriedade do Cassequel." Lisbon: Sociedade Agrícola do Cassequel, 1956. Pp. 179, mimeo.
Excerpt published in Cabral (1988: 447–449).

1957

"Das possibilidades de exploração racional de pastagens nas Ilhas Bijagós (Guiné Portuguesa)." Lisbon: Sociedade Comercial para o Fomento da Agricultura e da Indústria na Guiné, 1957.

Paper on the possibility of cattle grazing in the Bijagós Islands.

"As possibilidades de cultura da bananeira na Guiné Portuguesa." Lisbon: Sociedade Comercial para o Fomento da Agricultura e da Indústria na Guiné, 1957. Cited in Cabral (1988: 50). On the prospects for banana production in Guinea.

(with others). "Carta de solos da Fazenda Tentativa." Lisbon: Companhia do Assúcar de Angola, 1957. Pp. 231, mimeo.
Written in Lisbon, November 28, 1956. Excerpt reprinted in Cabral (1988: 451–453).

1958

Acerca de uma classificação fitossanitária. Lisbon: Ensaios e Documentos (51), Junta de Investigacões do Ultramar, 1958. Pp. 96.
Reprinted in Cabral (1988: 469–515). Effort to classify pests that affect agricultural storage areas.

Infestação entomológico em alguns armazéns de cereais. Lisbon, 1958.
Coauthored with M. I. Moreira. Cited in Marrocu (1985). A study of pests in agricultural storage areas.

"Locais essenciais no exame fitossanitário de porões de navios mercantes." Lisbon, 1958.
On the problem of pests. Cited in Cabral (1988: 50).

"Reconhecimento agrológica da Fazenda Longa-Nhia." Lisbon: Companhia Angolana de Agricultura, 1958. Pp. 48, mimeo.
Study cited in Cabral (1988: 50).

(with A. S. Carvalho). *Resultados de algumas inspecções a armazéns de cereais.* Lisbon, 1958.
Cited in Marrocu (1985) and in Cabral (1988: 51).

(with Alice Costa). "Deterioração e conspiracação em alguns armazéns de cereais." Lisbon, 1958.
Paper on problems of storage of cereals; cited in Cabral (1988: 50).

(with Maria Irene Moreira). "Infestação entomológica em alguns armazéns de cereais." Lisbon, 1958.
On problems of storing cereals. Cited in Cabral (1988: 50).

(with others). "Carta de solos da Fazenda S. Francisco." Lisbon: Companhia do Assúcar de Angola, 1958. Pp. 213.
Distributed March 29, 1958. Excerpt published in Cabral (1988: 517–519).

1959

"Da cultura industrial da beterraba sacarina." Lisbon: Entreposto Mercantil, 1959. Pp. 61, mimeo.
Study of beet sugar written in Lisbon in 1958. Reprinted in Cabral (1988: 611–642).

"Da cultura industrial da beterraba sacarina." Lisbon: Entreposto Mercantil, 1959. Pp. 107, mimeo.
Another study of beet sugar. Reprinted in Cabral (1988: 643–696).

"Estudo preliminar dos solos de Longa-Nhia (Angola)." Lisbon: Companhia Angolana de Agricultura, 1959.

Study of soils in Longa-Nhia, Angola. Cited in Cabral (1988: 51).

(with J. V. Botelho da Costa and Ario Azevedo). "Os solos e a cultura do café nas roças do Amboim e do Seles." Lisbon: Companhia Angolana de Agricultura, 1959. Pp. 226, mimeo.
Study of coffee in regions of Angola. A portion reprinted in Cabral (1988: 697–700).

(with M. Irene Moreira, Alice G. Costa, and A. S. de Carvalho). *Para a caracterização das condições fitossanitárias do armazenamento*. Lisbon: Estudos, Ensaiose Documentos (66), Junta de Investigações do Ultramar, 1959. Pp. 141.
Reprinted in Cabral (1988: 537–609). This collection of essays includes a series of five studies by Cabral and others on the problems of pests and storage of agricultural products.

1960

"Memorandum à Assembleia Geral da Organização das Nações Unidas." Conakry: PAIGC, December 1, 1960.
Cited by McCarthy (1977: item 1623).

"Memorandum enviado ao Governo Português pelo Partido Africano da Independência." Conakry, November 15, 1960. Mimeo.
Cited in the reference catalogue of the IICT. An appeal to the Portuguese government.

"Messagem aos colonos portugueses da Guiné e Cabo Verde." Conakry, October 1960. Mimeo.
Cited in the reference catalogue of the IICT. An appeal to Portuguese settlers in Guinea and Cape Verde.

(under Abel Djassi, pseudonym). "Portuguese Colonialism on Trial for the First Time—A Statement to the Press and Radio." London: Frente Revolucionária Africana para a Independência Nacional das Colónias Portuguesas, March 3, 1960. Pp. 2, mimeo.
Brief denunciation of Portuguese colonialism.

(with Ario Azezedo et al.). "Carta de solos da Fazenda Longa-Nhia." Lisbon: Companhia Angolana de Agricultura, 1960. Pp. 181, mimeo.
Soil study on the Fazenda Longa-Nhia in Angola. Partly reprinted in Cabral (1988: 779ff.).

(with Armando Ramos, Adriane Araújo, Richard Turpin, and Inácio Silva). "Proclamação." Conakry: Movimento de Libertação da Guiné e Cabo Verde, November 1960. Pp. 2, mimeo.

(with A. J. Soares de Gouveia). *Condições fitossantárias de produtos ultramarinos em armazéns do porto de Lisboa (Alcântara Norte)*. Lisbon: Estudos, Ensaios e Documentos (68), Junta de Investigações do Ultramar, 1960. Pp. 119.
Reprinted in Cabral (1988: 701–766).

(with others). "Comunicado aos povos da Guiné e Cabo Verde." [Conakry]: PAIGC, December 1960. Pp. 2, mimeo.
Communiqué to the peoples of Guinea and Cape Verde on the international support for the PAIGC cause.

(with others). "Frente de Libertação da Guiné e Cabo Verde. Partido Africano da Independência." [Conakry]: Partido Africano da Independência, October 1960. Pp. 2, mimeo.
A call upon Portuguese settlers to assume a position of neutrality.

1961

"Appel à l'unité et à l'action directe." Conakry, April 23, 1961, mimeo.
Cited in Marrocu (1985) and in the reference catalogue of the IICT.

"Communiqué à la presse." Conakry: Partido Africano da Independência da Guiné e Cabo Verde, June 9, 1961. P. 1, mimeo.
Press communiqué. Alleges the colonial regime is preparing a war of extermination.

"Un crime de colonialisme (fondements juridiques de notre lutte armée de libération nationale). Extrait du rapport présenté par le camarade Amílcar Cabral, au Comité Spécial de l'ONU pour les territoires administrés par le Portugal." Conakry: Partido Africano da Independência da Guiné e Cabo Verde, 1961.
Extract from his report to the UN Special Committee. Cited in McCarthy (1977: 1662).

"Déclaration proposant la réalisation immédiate de mesures concrètes pour la liquidation pacifique de la domination coloniale en Guinée 'portugaise' et aux Iles du Cap Vert." Conakry: Partido Africano da Independência da Guiné e Cabo Verde, October 13, 1961. P. 1, mimeo.
Concrete proposals for ending Portuguese colonialism.

"Discurso proferido pelo Delegado da Guiné 'Portuguesa' e das Ilhas de Cabo Verde, Amílcar Cabral (Abel Djassi), Secretário Geral do Partido Africano da Independência." Conakry and Cairo: Partido Africano da Independência da Guiné e Cabo Verde, March 25–31, 1961. Pp. 3, mimeo.
Reprinted in Cabral, *Obras escolhidas* (1976: I, 189–191) under the title "As lições positivas e negativas da revolução africana." Speech to the third Conferência dos Povos Africanos in Cairo. The reference catalogue of IICT lists "'Une crise de connaissance,' Cairo: Third Conference of African People."

"Intervention par Amílcar Cabral, secrétaire général du PAIGC." Accra, June 1961.
Identified in the reference catalogue of the IICT and cited in Marrocu (1985).

"Memorandum à Assembléia Geral da Organização das Nações Unidas." Conakry: Partido Africano da Independência da Guiné e Cabo Verde, September 26, 1961. Pp. 2, mimeo.
Memorandum to the United Nations. Describes colonial repression in Guinea-Bissau.

"Mémorandum aux Nations Unies (Extrait concernant les propositions concrètes soumises à l'Assemblée Générale)." [Conakry: Partido Africano da Independência da Guiné e Cabo Verde], September 1961.
Extract from the September 26, 1961, memorandum to the United Nations.

"Memorandum to the UN General Assembly." Conakry, September 26, 1961. Mimeo.
Cited in the reference catalogue of the IICT.

"Note à la presse." Dakar: Partido Africano da Independência da Guiné e Cabo Verde, October 13, 1961. Pp. 2, mimeo.
Press release.

"Note ouverte au gouvernement portugais." Conakry: Partido Africano da Independência da Guiné e Cabo Verde, October 13, 1961. Pp. 2, mimeo.
Note to the Portuguese government calling for negotiations for independence.

Rapport général sur la lutte de libération nationale. Conakry: Partido Africano da Independência da la Guinée "Portugaise" et des Iles du Cap-Vert, July 1961. Pp. 38.

Cited in Marrocu (1985) as *Relatório geral sobre a luta de libertação nacional*, Dakar: Conferência das Organizações Nacionalistas da Guiné e das Ilhas de Cabo Verde, July 1961. Reprinted in Cabral, *Obras escolhidas* (1976: I, 67–77 and 192–194). An assessment of the liberation struggle in Guinea-Bissau.

"Rapport sur la lutte de libération des peuples de la Guinée 'Portugaise' et des Iles du Cap-Vert." Cairo: Partido Africano da Independência da Guiné e Cabo Verde, March 23–25, 1961. Pp. 5, mimeo.

Brief report of successes in Guinea-Bissau, submitted to the third Conférence des Peuples Africains.

"Texto integral do discurso do nosso camarada Amílcar Cabral (Sessão Extraordinária do Conselho de Solidariedade dos Povos Afroasiáticos)." Cairo, January 22, 1961. Mimeo.

Text to the Cairo meeting of the Council of Solidarity with Afro-Asian Peoples. Cited in the reference catalogue of the IICT.

(under Abel Djassi, pseudonym). *The Facts About Portugal's African Colonies.* Introduction by Basil Davidson, dated June 1960. London: Union of Democratic Control, [1961]. Pp. 20.

Offers details of economic misery, forced labor, illiteracy, and other problems under Portuguese colonial rule, refers to the African awakening, and identifies the major liberation movements.

(with Aristides Pereira). "Communiqué à la presse." Conakry: Partido Africano da Independência da Guiné e Cabo Verde, January 28, 1961. P. 1, mimeo.

Condemnation of the Salazar regime and an appeal for cooperation with the democratic opposition.

(with Aristides Pereira). "Rapport sur la lutte de libération des peuples de la Guinée Portugaise et des Iles du Cap-Vert." Cairo: Partido Africano da Independência da Guiné e Cabo Verde, March 23–25, 1961. Pp. 5, mimeo.

Report to the third Conférence des Peuples Africains.

1962–1972

"Communiqué." Conakry, Dakar, and Rabat: Partido Africano da Independência da Guiné e Cabo Verde.

Mimeographed series issued by the PAIGC and signed by Amílcar Cabral as secretary general.

Conakry series: March 24, 1962, 2 pp.; April 5, 1962, 1 p.; August 3, 1962, 1 p.; March 25, 1963, 1 p.; March 30, 1963, 1 p.; April 5, 1963, 1 p.; April 22, 1963, 1 p.; June 5, 1963, 1 p.; June 12, 1963, 1 p.; July 1, 1963, 1 p.; July 3, 1963, 1 p.; July 25, 1963, 1 p.; July 26, 1963, 1 p.; July 27, 1963, 2 pp.; July 29, 1963, 2 pp.; September 17, 1963, 1 p.; October 4, 1963, 1 p.; October 26, 1963, 1 p.; October 30, 1963, 2 pp.; November 26, 1963, 1 p.; January 14, 1964, 2 pp.; January 28(?), 1964, 1 p.; January 30, 1964, 1 p.; March 27, 1964, 2 pp.; April 3, 1964, 2 pp.; April 10, 1964, 2 pp.; April 14, 1964, 1 p.; April 20, 1964, 1 p. plus "Annexe," 2 pp.; April 22, 1964, 1 p.; April 24, 1964, 1 p.; April 27, 1964, 1 p.; April 29, 1964, 1 p.; June 1, 1964, 1 p.; June 3, 1964, 1 p.; June 5, 1964, 1 p.; June 9, 1964, 1 p.; June 19, 1964, 2 pp.; June 23, 1964, 2 pp.; June 29, 1964, 2 pp., including "Annexe"; July 2, 1964, 2pp.; July 15, 1964, 2 pp.; July 20, 1964, 1 p.; July 22, 1964, 2 pp.; August 31, 1964, 2 pp.; September 2, 1964, 1 p. and attached "Fiche Biographique" of Chantre Forte; September 4, 1964, 1 p.; September 14, 1964, 1 p.;

September 16, 1964, 1 p.; September 18, 1964, 1 p.; September 21, 1964, 1 p.; June 8(?), 1965, 1 p.; June 10, 1965, 1 p.; July 2, 1965, 1 p.; July 16, 1965, 1 p.; July 20, 1965, 1 p.; July 27, 1965, 1 p.; July 29, 1965, 1 p.; August 3, 1965, 1 p.; September 13, 1965, 2 pp.; September 20, 1965, 1 p.; November 4, 1965, 2 pp.; November 5, 1965, 2 pp.; November 9, 1965, 1 p.; November 11, 1965, 1 p.; January 14, 1966, 1 p.; March 4, 1966, 1 p.; March 7, 1966, 1 p.; March 22, 1966, 1 p.; March 24, 1966, 1 p.; March 30, 1966, 1 p.; June 1, 1966, 2 pp.; June 3, 1966, 1 p.; June 9, 1966, 1 p.; June 19, 1966, 1 p.; August 4, 1966, 2 pp.; August 12, 1966, 1 p.; September 1, 1966, 1 p.; April 18, 1967, 2 pp.; April 20, 1967, 2 pp.; April 24, 1967, 2 pp.; August 17, 1967, 1 p. ; August 18, 1967, 1 p.; August 24, 1967, 2 pp.; September 4, 1967, 1 p.; October 2, 1967, 3 pp.; October 4, 1967, 2 pp.; January 19, 1968, 1 p.; January 26, 1968, 1 p.; January 30, 1968, 2 pp.; February 6, 1968, 1 p.; February 15, 1968, 1 p.; February 19, 1968, 1 p.; March 1, 1968, 1 p.; March 4, 1968, 1 p.; March 5, 1968, 1 p.; March 22, 1968, 1 p.; April 8, 1968, 2 pp.; April 16, 1968, 1 p.; May 9, 1968, 1 p.; May 16, 1968, 2 pp.; May 20, 1968, 1 p.; May 28, 1968, 2 pp.; June11, 1968, 3 pp.; June 18, 1968, 1 p.; June 24, 1968, 1 p.; June 28, 1968, 1 p.; September 15, 1968, 2 pp.; November 7, 1968, 2 pp.; November 14, 1968, 1 p.; December 3, 1968, 2 pp.; December 17, 1968, 2 pp.; January 17, 1969, 2 pp.; February 9, 1969, 1 p.; March 7, 1969, 2 pp.; March 29, 1969, 3 pp.; April 12, 1969, 2 pp.; April 26, 1969, 2 pp.; May 17, 1969, 3 pp.; June 6, 1969, 2 pp.; September 15, 1969, 2 pp.; December 1, 1969, 2 pp.; February 17, 1970, 2 pp.; March 16, 1970, 2 pp.; April 3, 1970, 2 pp.; November 9, 1970, 2 pp.; January 11, 1971, 2 pp.; January 18, 1971, 2 pp.; September 25, 1972, 1 p.

Algiers series: June 10, 1966, 1 p.

Dakar series: February 7, 1963, 2 pp.; February 12, 1963, 1 p.

Rabat series: February 12, 1963, 1 p.; February 27, 1963, 1 p.; March 1, 1963, 1 p.

1962

"Un crime du colonialisme. (Fondements juridiques de notre lutte armée de libération nationale)." Conakry: Partido Africano da Independência da Guiné e Cabo Verde, 1962, mimeo.
Cited in Marrocu (1985).

"Déclaration." Conakry: Partido Africano da Independência da Guiné e Cabo Verde, October 15, 1962. P. 1, mimeo.

"Déclaration à l'occasion du 3ème anniversaire des grèves de Bissao et du massacre de Pidjiguiti." Conakry: Partido Africano da Independência da Guiné e Cabo Verde, August 3, 1962. Pp. 2, mimeo.
Remembrance of the Pidjiguiti massacre of August 3, 1959.

"Déclaration faite par M. Amílcar Cabral du Parti Africain de l'Indépendance de la Guinée et du Cap-Vert (PAIGC) lors de la 1420ème séance de la Quatrième Commission le 12 de décembre 1962. [Conakry]: Partido Africano da Independência da Guiné e Cabo Verde, December 12, 1962. Pp. 19, mimeo.
Appeal to the Fourth Committee of the United Nations.

"Déclaration sur la situation actuelle de la lutte de libération en Guinée 'Portugaise' et aux Iles du Cap-Vert." Conakry: Partido Africano da Independência da Guiné e Cabo Verde, January 20, 1962. Pp. 2, mimeo.
Declaration on the current situation in the liberation struggle.

"Discours à la deuxième Conférence des Juristes Afro-Asiatiques." Conakry: Partido Africano da Independência da Guiné e Cabo Verde, October 15–22, 1962.

Cited in Marrocu (1985) and identified in the IICT reference catalogue.

"Discours prononcé par M. Amílcar Cabral, chef de la délégation de la Guinée 'Portugaise' et des Iles du Cap-Vert, Secrétaire Général du PAIGC." Conakry: Partido Africano da Independência da Guiné e Cabo Verde, 1962. Pp. 4, mimeo.

Speech to the second Conférence des Juristes Afro-Asiatiques, October 15–22, 1962, Conakry.

"La lutte de libération nationale en Guinée 'Portugaise' et aux Iles du Cap-Vert." [Conakry]: Partido Africano da Independência da Guiné e Cabo Verde, June 1962. Unpaged, mimeo.

Extract from the June 1962 declaration to the UN Special Committee on Portuguese Territories. On the liberation struggle.

"Note à la presse." Dakar: Partido Africano da Independência da Guiné e Cabo Verde, December 26, 1962. P. 1, mimeo.

Reaffirmation of the PAIGC position against Portuguese colonialism.

"Notre peuple et l'Organisation des Nations Unies, Extrait de la déclaration faite par M. Amílcar Cabral, Secrétaire Général du PAIGC, devant la Commission Spéciale de l'ONU pour les territoires administrés par le Portugal, le 6 juin 1962." Conakry: Partido Africano da Independência da Guiné e Cabo Verde, June 6, 1962. Pp. 2, mimeo.

Extract from the June 1962 declaration to the UN Special Committee on Portuguese Territories.

"Nous sommes les combattants anonymes de la cause de l'ONU. Extrait de la déclaration faite par M. Amílcar Cabral, Secrétaire Général du PAIGC lors de la 1420ème séance de la IVème Commission de l'ONU, le 12 décembre 1962." [New York]: Partido Africano da Independência da Guiné e Cabo Verde, December 12, 1962. Pp. 2, mimeo.

Extract from the June 1962 declaration to the Fourth Committee of the United Nations.

"Nouveaux crimes de colonialistes portugais." Conakry: Partido Africano da Independência da Guiné e Cabo Verde, March 24, 1962. Unpaged, mimeo.

Exposé of Portuguese colonial crimes.

"Le peuple de la Guinée 'Portugaise' devant l'Organisation des Nations Unies: présentée au Comité Spécial de l'ONU pour les territoires administrés par le Portugal." Conakry: Partido Africano da Independência da Guiné e Cabo Verde, June 1962. Pp. 85, mimeo.

A full analysis of the situation in Guinea-Bissau to the United Nations Special Committee.

"Pour une solution pacifique du problème de l'accès de la Guinée 'Portugaise' et des Iles du Cap-Vert à l'indépendance nationale." Conakry, June 1962. Unpaged, mimeo.

Extract of June 1962 declaration presented to the UN Special Committee.

"Rapport aux Etats-Unis." Conakry: Partido Africano da Independência da Guiné e Cabo Verde, 1962.

Cited in McCarthy (1977: item 1642) and identified in the IICT reference catalogue.

"La répression coloniale en Guinée 'Portugaise' et aux Iles du Cap-Vert." [Conakry]: Partido Africano da Independência da Guiné e Cabo Verde, June 1962. Unpaged, mimeo.

Extract of the June 1962 declaration to the United Nations. On Portuguese colonial repression in Guinea-Bissau.

Statement, June 5, 1962, in United Nations, General Assembly, Special Committee on Territories under Portuguese Administration, 44th Meeting, Conakry, A/AC.108/28. Pp. 33.

See also other documents A/AC.108/SR.44, Conakry, June 5, 1962; A/AC.108/45, Conakry, June 6, 1962; A/AC.108/SR. 51, Rabat, June 14, 1962. Report on the situation in Guinea-Bissau and Cape Verde.

"Sur une solution pacifique du problème de l'accès de la Guinée Portugaise et des Iles du Cap Vert à l'indépendance." Conakry, 1962, mimeo.

Cited in Marrocu (1985).

"Telegram." Conakry, December 10, 1962, in United Nations, General Assembly, Fourth Committee A/C.4/595, New York.

"Télégramme envoyé au secrétaire général de l'ONU." Conakry: Partido Africano da Independência da Guiné e Cabo Verde, August 5, 1962. P. 1, mimeo.

Denunciation of Portuguese crimes.

1963

"Conférence de presse, donnée par le Secrétaire Général du PAIGC Ingénieur Amílcar Cabral le 24 juin 1963, à Conakry." Conakry: Partido Africano da Independência da Guiné e Cabo Verde, June 24, 1964. Pp. 4, mimeo.

Press conference.

"Déclaration." Dakar: PAIGC, February 15, 1963. Pp. 2, mimeo.

"Déclaration." Rabat: Conférence des Organisations Nationalistes des Coloinies Portugaises, February 13, 1963. Pp. 2, mimeo.

"Déclaration du PAIGC sur l'évacuation par les autorités portugaises des civils européens du sud." Paris: Partido Africano da Independência da Guiné e Cabo Verde. Distributed by Comité de Soutien à l'Angola et aux peuples des colonies portugaises, February 1963. Pp. 2, mimeo.

Because of PAIGC successes, evacuation of Europeans took place in the south of Guinea-Bissau.

"Déclaration sur la situation de la lutte de libération nationale en Guinée 'Portugaise' et aux Iles du Cap Vert." Rabat: Partido Africano da Independência da Guiné e Cabo Verde, January 21, 1963. Pp. 5, mimeo.

Analysis of the situation and lists ten principles for the struggle in 1963.

Letter, October 31, 1963, in United Nations, General Assembly, Fourth Committee A/C.4/618, New York.

"Mémorandum à la XVIIIème session de l'Assemblée Générale de l'Organisation des Nations Unies." Conakry: Partido Africano da Independência da Guiné e Cabo Verde, October 5, 1963. Pp. 5, mimeo.

Memorandum to the UN General Assembly.

"Mémorandum à Ses Excellences les chefs d'Etat de l'Union Africaine et Malgache." Ouagadougou, March 1963. Pp. 14, mimeo plus unpaged annexes.

Six-part analysis of the situation in Guinea-Bissau with an appendix of previously issued documents, including a memorandum to the Portuguese government in December 1960, a memorandum to the United Nations in September 1961, an open note to the Portuguese government in October 1961, and a declaration of January 21, 1963.

"Mémorandum à Son Excellence le Président du Groupe Africain, Assemblée Générale des Nations Unies (ONU), New York." Conakry: Partido Africano da Independência da Guiné e Cabo Verde, October 1963. Pp. 4, mimeo.
Memo to the United Nations on the situation in Guinea-Bissau.

"Mémorandum au Comité de Coordination de l'Aide aux Nationalistes Africains, Organisation de l'Unité Africaine, Dar es Salaam." Conakry and Dar es Salaam: Partido Africano da Independência da Guiné e Cabo Verde, June 20, 1963. Pp. 4, mimeo.
Memorandum to the Organization of African Unity.

"Mensagem dirigida pelo camarada Amílcar Cabral ao Congresso da UGEAN em Rabat." Rabat, August 1963, mimeo.
Cited in Marrocu (1985) and identified in the IICT reference catalogue.

"Message à Ses Excellences les chefs d'état africains." Addis Ababa: Partido Africano da Independência da Guiné e Cabo Verde, May 1963. Pp. 2, mimeo.
Presented to the first Conférence des Chefs d'Etats Africains. The IICT reference catalogue lists a similar document, "Message à la Conférence des Chefs d'Etat Africains." Conakry, 1963, mimeo.

"Message aux soldats, officiers et sergents de l'armée coloniale portugaise." [Conakry]: Partido Africano da Independência da Guiné e Cabo Verde, February 22, 1963. Pp. 4, mimeo.
Message to the Portuguese colonial army.

"Nous avons lutté par des moyens pacifiques. Nous n'avons eu que les massacres et le génocide." Addis Ababa: Partido Africano da Independência da Guiné e Cabo Verde, May 1963. Pp. 5, mimeo.
An appeal for peace and independence presented to the first Conférence des Chefs d'Etat Africains.

"Pourquoi nous avons pris les armes pour libérer notre pays." Addis Ababa: Partido Africano da Independência da Guiné e Cabo Verde, May 1963. Pp. 5, mimeo.
Presented to the first Conférence des Chefs d'Etat Africains.

(with Aristides Pereira). "Comunicado aos combatentes, responsáveis e militantes do partido, a todos os Guineenses e Caboverdianos." Dakar: Partido Africano da Independência da Guiné e Cabo Verde, July 21, 1963, mimeo.
Cited in Marrocu (1985).

(with Aristides Pereira). "Comunicado: o desenvolvimento da luta em Cabo Verde." Dakar: Partido Africano da Independência da Guiné e Cabo Verde, July 21, 1963, mimeo.
Cited in Marrocu (1985).

1964

"About the Development of Our Struggle, 1964." [Conakry]: Partido Africano da Independência da Guiné e Cabo Verde, 1964.

Press conference.

"Brève analyse de la structure sociale de la Guinée 'Portugaise'. Version condensée d'une série d'interventions orales de Amílcar Cabral . . . à un séminaire organisé par le Centre Franz Fanon de Milan a Treviglio du 1er au 3 mai 1964." [Conakry]: Département de Secrétariat, Information, Culture et Formation de Cadres, Collection "Discours et Interventions," Partido Africano da Independência da Guiné e Cabo Verde, May 1964. Pp. 7 (unnumbered), mimeo.

Reprinted in Cabral, *Obras escolhidas* (1976: I, 101–107). Address to the Franz Fanon Center, Milan.

"Communiqué: la bataille de Cafine." Conakry: Partido Africano da Independência da Guiné e Cabo Verde, September 18, 1964. P. 1, mimeo.

Report on the battle of Cafine.

"Communiqué sur le développement de la lutte de libération nationale en Guinée 'Portugaise' et aux Iles du Cap-Vert en 1963." Conakry: Partido Africano da Independência da Guiné e Cabo Verde, January 17, 1964. Pp. 3, mimeo.

General assessment of progress in the armed struggle.

"La développement de la lutte de libération nationale en Guinée 'Portugaise' et aux Iles du Cap-Vert en 1964, par Amílcar Cabral, Secrétaire Général du PAIGC." Conakry: Partido Africano da Independência da Guiné e Cabo Verde, January 17, 1964. Pp. 6, mimeo.

Reprinted in Cabral, *Obras escolhidas* (1976: II, 37–40). Focused on the Battle of Como and the First Congress of the PAIGC.

Petition. United Nations, General Assembly, Special Committee on the Situation with Regard to the Implementation of the Declaration on the Granting of Independence to Colonial Countries and Peoples, A/AC.109/Pet. 274, May 27, 1964.

Appeal for independence.

1965

"L'Afrique et la lutte de libération nationale dans les colonies portugaises," pp. 43–52 in CONCP, *La lutte de libération nationale dans les colonies portugueses*, Algiers: Informations CONCP, 1965.

From IICT reference catalogue.

"Communiqué: la bataille de Cafine." Conakry: Partido Africano da Independência da Guiné e Cabo Verde, July 19, 1965. P. 1, mimeo.

Communiqué on the success of the Battle of Cafine.

"Communiqué: déclaration faite, en exclusif, par le Secrétaire Général du PAIGC, à l'occasion du 3 août, anniversaire du massacre de Pidjiguiti et journée de solidarité avec les peuples de colonies portugaises." Conakry: Partido Africano da Independência da Guiné e Cabo Verde, August 3, 1965. P. 1, mimeo.

Remembrance of the massacre of dockworkers of Pidjiguiti.

"Communiqué: destruction des casernes portugaises de Guiledge et Sanconha." Conakry: Partido Africano da Independência da Guiné e Cabo Verde, September 15, 1965. P. 1, mimeo.

Press release on success in the armed struggle.

"Communiqué: la libération de la région de Boé." Conakry: Partido Africano da Independência da Guiné e Cabo Verde, June 3, 1965. P. 1, mimeo.

Communiqué on the liberation of the Boé region.

"Communiqué sur le développement de la lutte de libération nationale en Guinée 'Portugaise' et aux Iles du Cap-Vert en 1964 (Texte de la Conférence de presse donnée à l'Alger par le Secrétaire Général du PAIGC M. Amílcar Cabral, le 22 mars 1965)." Algiers: Partido Africano da Independência da Guiné e Cabo Verde, March 22, 1965. Pp. 7, mimeo.
Press conference on progress in the struggle for independence.

"Declaration by Amílcar Cabral, Secretary General, to AGP (Guinean Press Agency) on August 3, 1965, on the Occasion of the Anniversary of the Massacre of the Pidjiguiti, and Day of Solidarity with the People of the Portuguese Colonies." Conakry: Partido Africano da Independência da Guiné e Cabo Verde, August 3, 1965. P. 1, mimeo.

"Discours d'ouverture," pp. 65–70 in *La lutte de la libération nationale dans les colonies portugaises*, Algiers: Informations CONCP, 1965.
Cited in IICT reference catalogue.

"Les martyrs et victimes du colonialisme ne sont pas morts: ils ressuscitent chaque jour dans nos coeurs." Conakry: Partido Africano da Independência da Guiné e Cabo Verde, August 3, 1965, mimeo.
Cited in Marrocu (1985) and identified in the IICT reference catalogue.

"Mémorandum présenté au Comité de Décolonisation de l'ONU, à Addis-Abéba, en juin 1965, ..." Addis Ababa: Partido Africano da Independência da Guiné e Cabo Verde, June 1965. Pp. 6, mimeo.
Memorandum to the United Nations Committee on Decolonization.

Palavras de ordem gerais—do Camarada Amílcar Cabral aos responsáveis do Partido. [Conakry]: Partido Africano da Independência da Guiné e Cabo Verde, November 1965. Pp. 35.
Reprinted as *Palavras de ordem gerais.* [Conakry]: Edição da Comissão da Organização, Formação Política e Ideológica, September 1969; also Bolama: Imprensa Nacional da Guiné-Bissau, 1974, pp. 45; and Bissau: Edição do XX Aniversário da Fundação do PAIGC, 1976, pp. 51. Reprinted in Cabral, *Obras escolhidas* (1976: I, 137–164). Eight theses on the preparation and practice of the liberation struggle.

"Palavras de ordem gerais para a inter-região do norte." Dakar and Conakry: Partido Africano da Independência da Guiné e Cabo Verde, November 1965, mimeo.
Cited in Marrocu (1985).

Petition, United Nations, General Assembly, Special Committee on the Situation with Regard to the Implementation of the Declaration on the Granting of Independence to Colonial Countries and Peoples, A/AC.109/Pet. 411, New York, July 7, 1965.
Appeal for independence.

"Sobre a situação da luta e as suas perspectivas." Dakar: Partido Africano da Independência da Guiné e Cabo Verde, November 1965. Pp. 26, mimeo.
Review of substantial progress since the party congress in February 1964.

"A unidade política e moral força principal da nossa luta comum." Dar es Salaam, October 3–8, 1965, mimeo.
Speech presented to the second conference of the CONCP. Cited in Marrocu (1985). Identified in the IICT reference catalogue as also published in Conarky, 1965.

1966

"Fondements et objectifs de la libération nationale. II—Sur la libération nationale." [Conakry]: Département de Secrétariat, Information, Culture et Formation de Cadres, Collection "Discours et Interventions," Partido Africano da Independência da Guiné e Cabo Verde, 1966. Pp. 12, mimeo.

A look at national liberation and revolution in the context of the Guinea experience. The IICT reference catalogue gives this reference but includes the first part, "I—Sur la domination impérialiste."

"Les fondements et les objectifs de la libération nationale en rapport avec la structure social. Extrait du discours prononcé . . . à la 1ère Conférence des Peuples d'Afrique, d'Asie et d'Amérique Latine, La Havana, jan. 3–14, 1966." Conakry: Département de Secrétariat, Information, Culture et Formation de Cadres, Collection "Discours et Interventions," Partido Africano da Independência da Guiné e Cabo Verde, 1966. Pp. 12, mimeo.

Excerpt from speech in Havana, Cuba, January 1966, with emphasis on a class analysis of the Guinea situation.

"Intervention faite à la Première Conférence de la Solidarité des Peuples d'Afrique, d'Asie et d'Amérique Latine." Havana: January 1966.

Speech to the Tricontinental conference. Reprinted in Cabral, *Obras escolhidas* (1976: I, 199–213). Cited in McCarthy (1977: item 1614).

"Mensagem a todos os responsáveis, militantes e combatentes de todas as frentes de luta do nosso grande partido." Conakry: Partido Africano da Independência da Guiné e Cabo Verde, December 20, 1966, mimeo.

Cited in Marrocu (1985) and identified in the IICT reference catalogue.

"Para a reorganização das forças revolucionárias do povo (FARP). Estudo da situação do inimigo, da nossa situação e descrição da nossa organização das FARP." Conakry: Partido Africano da Independência da Guiné e Cabo Verde, November 1966, mimeo.

Cited in Marrocu (1985) and the IICT reference catalogue.

"La situation actuelle de la lutte de libération nationale." Conakry: Partido Africano da Independência da Guiné e Cabo Verde, 1966, mimeo.

Cited in Marrocu (1985) and identified in the IICT reference catalogue.

The Struggle for National Liberation in Guinea (B) and Cape Verde. Havana: OSPAAL, 1966. Pp. 33.

Summary of the report of Cabral to the Executive Secretariat of the OSPAAL, Havana, Cuba. French version is "La lutte de libération nationale en Guinée (B) et Cap Vert." No Place, December. Pp. 34, mimeo.

1967

"Les options de CONCP," in *La conférence de Dar es Salaam*. Algiers: Editions CONCP, August 1967, mimeo.

Cited in the IICT reference catalogue.

"Para o desenvolvimento da nossa luta contra os helicópteros (do camarada Amílcar Cabral aos combatentes responsáveis e militantes do Partido)." Conakry: Partido Africano da Independência da Guiné e Cabo Verde, June 1967, mimeo.

Cited in Marrocu (1985) and in the IICT reference catalogue.

1968

"Les crimes des colonialistes portugais face à la Déclaration Universelle des Droits de l'Homme." [Conakry]: Commission d'Information et Propagande du Comité Central du Partido Africano da Independência da Guiné e Cabo Verde, 1968. Pp. 26, mimeo plus photographs of African victims.

Exposé of Portuguese violations of human rights in paper presented to the UN Commission on Human Rights.

"Declaração do Secretário Geral do Partido, Camarada Amílcar Cabral, no acto de entrega à Cruz Vermelha Internacional de três prisioneiros de guerra portugueses." Dakar: Partido Africano da Independência da Guiné e Cabo Verde, December 19, 1968. Pp. 2, mimeo.

In French as "Déclaration faite par . . . à la Croix Rouge Internationale de trois soldats portugais faits prisonniers par nos forces," Dakar, December 1968. Pp. 2, mimeo. Announcement of release of three prisoners of war to the International Red Cross.

"Mensagem ao povo da Guiné e Cabo Verde, aos quadros, militantes, e combatentes do nosso partido." Conakry: Partido Africano da Independência da Guiné e Cabo Verde, December 30, 1968, mimeo.

Cited in Marrocu (1985) and the IICT reference catalogue.

"National Liberation and Social Structure," pp. 261–269 in William J. Pomeroy (ed.) *Guerrilla Warfare and Marxism: A Collection of Writings from Karl Marx to the Present on Armed Struggles for Liberation and Socialism.* New York: International Publishers, 1968.

Excerpts from Havana address, January 1966.

"Sur la situation de notre lutte de libération nationale." Conakry: Partido Africano da Independência da Guiné e Cabo Verde, March 1968, mimeo.

Cited in Marrocu (1985). Cited by the IICT reference catalogue as "Rapport sur la situation. . . ."

"Texte du message à l'occasion de la journée du 3 août." Conakry: Partido Africano da Independência da Guiné e Cabo Verde, August 1968, mimeo.

Cited in Marrocu (1985).

Die Theorie als Waffe. Berlin: Oberbaum Verlag, 1968. Pp. 71.

Cited in McCarthy (1977: item 1661), Pyhälä and Rylander (No Date), and the IICT reference catalogue.

1969

"Alguns princípios do partido aos camaradas participantes no Seminário de Quadros, realizado de 19 a 24 de Novembro de 1969. 1. Unidade e luta. [Conakry]: Partido Africano da Independência da Guiné e Cabo Verde [1969]. Pp. 26, mimeo.

Focus on party principles, in particular unity and struggle, in a presentation to participants of the Seminário de Quadros.

"Alguns princípios do partido aos camaradas participantes no Seminário de Quadros, realizado de 19 a 24 de Novembro de 1969. 2. Partir da realidade da nossa

terra ser realistas." [Conakry]: Partido Africano da Independência da Guiné e Cabo Verde [1969]. Pp. 31, mimeo.
Focus on party principles, in particular unity and struggle, in a presentation to participants of the Seminário de Quadros.

"Análise dos tipos de resistência . . . Aos camaradas participantes no seminário de quadros realizado de 19 a 24 de Novembro de 1969. 1. Resistência política." [Conakry]: Partido Africano da Independência da Guiné e Cabo Verde [1969]. Pp. 18, mimeo.
Emphasis on political resistance in presentation to participants of the Seminário de Quadros.

"Análise dos tipos de resistência . . . Aos camaradas participantes no seminário de quadros realizado de 19 a 24 de Novembro de 1969. 2. Resistência económica." [Conakry]: Partido Africano da Independência da Guiné e Cabo Verde [1969]. Pp. 25, mimeo.
Emphasis on economic resistance in presentation to participants of the Seminário de Quadros.

"Análise dos tipos de resistência . . . Aos camaradas participantes no seminário de quadros realizado de 19 a 24 de Novembro de 1969. 3. Resistência cultural." [Conakry]: Partido Africano da Independência da Guiné e Cabo Verde [1969]. Pp. 27, mimeo.
Emphasis on cultural resistance. (See CIDAC: GB Partido II-30.)

"Análise dos tipos de resistência . . . Aos camaradas participantes no seminário de quadros realizado de 19 a 24 de Novembro de 1969. 4. Resistência armada." [Conakry]: Partido Africano da Independência da Guiné e Cabo Verde [1969]. Pp. 19, mimeo.
Emphasis on armed resistance in presentation to participants of the Seminário de Quadros.

"En souvenir d'une visite de solidarité." Conakry: Partido Africano da Independência da Guiné e Cabo Verde, November 1969, mimeo.
On the occasion of the visit of Göran Palm and Bertil Malmström to the Pilot School of the PAIGC. Cited in Marrocu (1985).

"Forward," dated Boé, October 1968, pp. 9–15 in Basil Davidson, *The Liberation of Guiné*, Baltimore: Penguin Books, 1969.

"Intervention au cours de la visite effectuée par Göran Palm et Bertil Malmström à l'école pilote du parti." Conakry, 1969, mimeo.
Cited in IICT reference catalogue.

"Mensagem do secretário geral do PAIGC, camarada Amílcar Cabral a 19 de setembro de 1969." [Conakry]: Partido Africano da Independência da Guiné e Cabo Verde, September 1969, mimeo.
Cited in Marrocu (1985).

"Notas ao camarada Oswaldo." Gabu, March 31, 1969, typescript.
Cited in Marrocu (1985).

"Notas para a delegação do BP na frente leste (sectores 1 e 3)." Boé: Partido Africano da Independência da Guiné e Cabo Verde, February 14, 1969, mimeo.
Cited in Marrocu (1985) and the IICT reference catalogue.

"On the Situation of Our Armed Struggle for National Liberation (Report to the OAU Liberation Committee Meeting, Dakar, June 1969)." Dakar, June 1969, mimeo.

Cited in Marrocu (1985) and the IICT reference catalogue.

"Operação 'Tenaz'-B." [Conakry], March 30, 1969, typescript.
Cited in Marrocu (1985).

"Palavras de ordem gerais do camarada Amílcar Cabral aos responsáveis do Partido, Novembro de 1965." Conakry, September 1969, mimeo.
Cited in the IICT reference catalogue.

Revolution in Guinea: An African People's Struggle. London: Stage 1, 1969. Pp. 142.
Published in the United States by Monthly Review Press, 1972. Also *Revolution in Guinea*, Berlin: Oberbaum Verlag, 1970, pp. 150; and *Revolutionen i Guinea*, Copenhagen: Demos, 1973, p. 101. A brief introduction by the editor traces Cabral's activity and is followed by fifteen documents by Cabral plus the PAIGC party program. The documents comprise the speech at the Third Conference of African Peoples, Cairo, March 25–31, 1961; statement to the UN Special Committee, Conakry, June 1962; extracts from a declaration to the UN Fourth Committee, New York, December 12, 1962; extracts from a speech to the Second Conference of Heads of State and Governments of Non-Aligned Countries, 1964; text of seminar at Franz Fanon Center, Milan, May 1–3, 1964; address to CONCP Conference, Dar es Salaam, 1965; party directive, 1965; "Weapon of Theory" speech, Havana, January 1966; declaration to OSPAAL, December 1968; declarations, Dakar, March 3 and December 19, 1968; interview in *Tricontinental*, September 1968; declaration and interview, Khartoum, January 1969; and New Year's message, January 1973.

"Saudação do Camarada Amílcar Cabral aos camaradas participantes no Seminário de Quadros, realizado de 19 a 24 de Novembro de 1969." [Conakry]: Partido Africano da Independência da Guiné e Cabo Verde, [1969]. Pp. 17, mimeo.
Opening remarks to the Seminário de Quadros, November 1969.

"Seminário de quadros, 19–24 de Novembro 1969." Conakry: Partido Africano da Independência da Guiné e Cabo Verde, November 1969, mimeo.
Reprinted in Cabral, *Obras escolhidas* (1976: I, 111–118, and II, 61–67). Cited in Marrocu (1985).

"Situação actual da luta aos camaradas participantes no Seminário de Quadros, realizado de 19 a 24 de Novembro de 1969." [Conakry]: Partido Africano da Independência da Guiné e Cabo Verde [1969]. Pp. 30, mimeo.
An analysis and review of the liberation struggle to participants of the. Seminário de Quadros.

1970

"Démasquons les mensonges et les crimes des colonialistes portugais, renforçons le Parti et la lutte afin d'accélérer la libération totale de notre peuple. Message . . . à notre peuple et à nos combattants et militants, à l'occasion du XIV anniversaire de la fondation du Parti." Conakry: Partido Africano da Independência da Guiné e Cabo Verde, September 1970. Pp. 19, mimeo.
Message on the fourteenth anniversary of the founding of the PAIGC.

"Esclarecimento sobre as novas estruturas da direcção do partido e sobre as funções dos diversos órgãos dirigentes (Intevenção do camarada Amílcar Cabral na reunião de quadros superiores do partido, 13–15 de Setembro 1970)." Conakry: Partido Africano da Independência da Guiné e Cabo Verde, September 15, 1970, mimeo.
Cited in Marrocu (1985) and in the IICT reference catalogue.

"Forças armadas locais—I. Sul do Geba; II. Norte do Geba." Conakry: Partido Africano da Independência da Guiné e Cabo Verde, September–October 1970, mimeo.
Cited in Marrocu (1985) and in the IICT reference catalogue.

"Forças Armadas Revolucionárias do Povo (FARP). Bases e componentes." [Conakry]: Partido Africano da Independência da Guiné e Cabo Verde, September 19, 1970. Pp. 4+5+4, mimeo.
On the organization and structure of the FARP.

Guinée "portugaise": le pouvoir des armes. Paris: Cahiers Libres (162), François Maspero, 1970. Pp. 112.
Collection of five previously published essays from *Partisans, Tricontinental, and Pensamiento Crítico.*

"Intervista a Amílcar Cabral," in B. Crimi and U. Lucas, *Guinea Bissau, una rivoluzione africana.* Milano: Vangelista, May 1970.
Cited in Marrocu (1985).

"Lettera a Bobo (Comando do Sector z, Frente Leste)." Conakry: Partido Africano da Independência da Guiné e Cabo Verde, March 18, 1970, typescript.
Cited in Marrocu (1985).

"Libération nationale et culture. Conférence prononcée au 1er Mémorial dédié au Dr. Eduardo Mondlane, Université de Syracuse (Programme des Etudes de l'Afrique de l'Est)." Syracuse, New York, February 20, 1970.
The IICT reference catalogue also identifies it as distributed in Conakry. Pp. 18, mimeo. Reprinted in Cabral, *Obras escolhidas* (1976: I, 221–233). Published in English as "National Liberation and Culture." Syracuse: Occasional Paper No. 57, Program of Eastern African Studies of the Maxwell School of Citizenship and Public Affairs, Syracuse University, February 20, 1970. Text of speech in memory of Eduardo Mondlane at Syracuse University, where Cabral also received an honorary doctorate. (See CIDAC: GB Cult I-8.)

Liberation Struggle in Portuguese Colonies. New Delhi: All-India Peace Council & Indian Association for Afro-Asian Solidarity, People's Publishing House. Pp. 72.
Includes full text from June 1970 speech to the Rome conference of June 1970 and other addresses.

"Une lumière féconde éclaire le chemin de la lutte. Hommage à Lénine à l'occasion du centenaire de sa naissance." [Conakry]: Edition de la Commission d'Information du PAIGC [1970]. Pp. 14, mimeo.
Reprinted in Cabral, *Obras escolhidas* (1976: I, 214–220). Cabral's address of April 1970 in Alma Ata, commemorating the 100th anniversary of the birth of Lenin.

"Mensagem-relatório do camarada Amílcar Cabral aos quadros, combatentes, e militantes do partido." Conakry: Partido Africano da Independência da Guiné e Cabo Verde, January 1970, mimeo.
Cited in Marrocu (1985).

"Message to the People on the Occasion of the Fourteenth Anniversary of the Foundation of the PAIGC." Conakry: Partido Africano da Independência da Guiné e Cabo Verde, September 1970.
Cited in Marrocu (1985), McCarthy (1977: item 1625), and the IICT reference catalogue.

"Notre lutte est aussi un acte de solidarité. Intervention du Amílcar Cabral . . . Rome, 27–29 June 1970." [Conakry] and Rome: Partido Africano da Independência da Guiné e Cabo Verde, June 1970. Pp. 14, mimeo.

Intervention at the Conférence Internationale des Solidarité avec les Peuples de Colonies Portugaises, Rome, June 27–29, 1970.

"Notre peuple, le gouvernement portugais et l'ONU." [Conakry] and Rome: Partido Africano da Independência da Guiné e Cabo Verde, June 1970. Pp. 13, mimeo.

Reedited text for a solidarity conference in Rome, June 1970, based on a report to the UN Special Committee in 1962.

"Para a reorganização dos exércitos nacionais populares (EP)." [Conakry], December 1970, typescript.

Cited in Marrocu (1985).

"Rapport sur la situation de la lutte: Dix ans après le massacre de Pidjiguiti." [Conakry]: Partido Africano da Independência da Guiné e Cabo Verde, January 1970. Pp. 28, mimeo.

Extensive excerpts from a report on the liberation struggle during 1969.

Report on Portuguese Guinea and the Liberation Movement. Hearing Before the Subcommittee on Africa of the Committee on Foreign Affairs, House of Representatives, 91st Congress, Second Session. Washington D.C., February 26, 1970. Pp. 25.

Testimony by Cabral and his report to the OAU Liberation Committee, Dakar, June 1969.

The Struggle in Guinea. Cambridge, Massachusetts: Africa Research Group, 1970. Pp. 16.

Reprint from *International Socialist Journal* 1 (August 1964), 428–446. Text presented to the Franz Fanon Center, Milan, May 1964. Circulated by the Africa Research Group in 1969, according to the IICT reference catalogue.

"Sobre a utilização do sistema GPAD." Conakry, September 1970. Mimeo.

Identified in the IICT reference catalogue.

"Sur la situation de famine aux Iles du Cap Vert." Stockholm: Partido Africano da Independência da Guiné e Cabo Verde, April 14 [1970]. Pp.5, mimeo.

Portuguese version, "A situação de fome no arquipelago de Cabo Verde, N.D. Pp. 5, mimeo. Review of the famine and hunger in Cape Verde, revealed in a press conference in Stockholm, April 14.

"Sur la situation de notre lutte armée de libération nationale, janvier–septembre 1970." Conakry: PAIGC, October 1970.

On the armed struggle from January to September 1970. Cited in McCarthy (1977: item 1659) and in the IICT reference catalogue.

"Sur les lois portugaises de domination coloniale." [Conakry]: Partido Africano da Independência da Guiné e Cabo Verde, June 1970. Pp. 37, mimeo.

Focus on Portuguese colonial law and practice in the colonies.

1971

"Allocution prononcé par . . . Amílcar Cabral devant la 8 Conférence des Chefs d'Etat et de Gouvernement d'Afrique (séance de clôture)." Addis Ababa: Partido Africano da Independência da Guiné e Cabo Verde, June 21–23, 1971. Pp. 9, mimeo.

Speech to the Organization of African States.

"Avslutande samtal med Cabral 13 november 1969," pp. 117–131 in *Vår kamp, er kamp*. Stockholm: Pan/Nordstedts, 1971.
Cited in Marrocu (1985) and in the IICT reference catalogue.

"A Brief Report on the Situation of the Struggle (January–August 1971)." Conakry: African Party for the Independence of Guinea and Cape Verde (PAIGC), 1971. Pp. 22.
Reprinted in *Ufahamu* 2 (Winter 1972), 5–28, and in Cabral, *Obras escolhidas* (1976: II, 105–114). Analysis of progress in the armed struggle.

"La conscience nouvelle que la lutte a forgé chez les hommes et les peuples de notre pays est l'armée la plus puissante de notre peuple contre les criminels colonialistes portugais. Message du Amílcar Cabral à l'occasion de XV anniversaire de la fondation du Parti." [Conakry]: Partido Africano da Independência da Guiné e Cabo Verde, September 1971. Pp. 6, mimeo.
Speech advocating an awakening of conscience as the arm of the people against Portuguese colonialism.

"A consciência nova que a luta forjou nos homens e mulheres da nossa terra é a arma mais poderosa do nosso povo contra os criminosos colonialistas portugueses (mensagem no XV aniversário da fundação do partido)." Conakry: Partido Africano da Independência da Guiné e Cabo Verde, September 1971.
Cited in McCarthy (1977: item 1590) and in the IICT reference catalogue.

"Discurso de encerramento." Conakry: Partido Africano da Independência da Guiné e Cabo Verde, August 16, 1971, mimeo.
Speech closing the meeting of the CSL. Cited in Marrocu (1985).

"Discurso proferido pelo delegado da Guiné 'Portugesa' e das Ilhas de Cabo Verde, Amílcar Cabral, Secretário Geral do Partido Africano da Independência." Cairo: Partido Africano da Independência da Guiné e Cabo Verde, March 25–31, 1971, mimeo.
Cited in reference catalogue of IICT.

"The Eighth Year of Our Armed Struggle for National Liberation." Conakry: Partido Africano da Independência da Guiné e Cabo Verde, 1971.
Cited in McCarthy (1977: item 1603) and in the IICT reference catalogue.

"Em nome dos movimentos de libertação da Africa." Addis Ababa: Partido Africano da Independência da Guiné e Cabo Verde, June 21–23, 1971, mimeo.
Cited in Marrocu (1985).

"O estado da Guiné-Bissau," December 3, 1971, pp. 5–16 in *Assembleia Nacional Popular, orgão supremo de soberania do povo guineense*. [Bissau]: Edição do Departamento de Informação, Propaganda e Cultura do Secretariado do Comité Central do PAIGC [1984]. Pp. 16.
Includes excerpts from "Mensagem do ano novo." (See CIDAC: GB Estado I-31.)

"On the Situation of Starvation in the Cape Verde Islands." Stockholm and Conakry: Partido Africano da Independência da Guiné e Cabo Verde, April 14, 1971, mimeo.
Cited by Marrocu (1985) and identified in the IICT reference catalogue.

Our People Are Our Mountains. London: Committee for Freedom in Mozambique, Angola, and Guinea, 1971. Pp. 40.
Brief introduction by Basil Davidson followed by speeches by Cabral of October 26, a question-and-answer session of October 27, and a report on the armed struggle dated September 1971, all presented during a visit to London.

"Para a frente! Vamos melhorar e reforçar a nossa acção, tirar o máximo rendimento dos sucessos alcançados no ano findo, obter novas e maiores vitórias e causar ao inimigo perdas mais pesadas em 1971. Mensagem do novo ano do . . . à agressão criminosa dos colonialistas portugueses contra a República da Guiné." [Conakry]: Partido Africano da Independência da Guiné e Cabo Verde, January 1, 1971. Pp. 22, mimeo.

New Year's message and a review of accomplishments of the past year.

"Para a reorganização e a melhoria do trabalho das Brigadas de Acção Política." [Conakry]: Partido Africano da Independência da Guiné e Cabo Verde, February 1971. Pp. 5 plus 2 (appendix), mimeo.

Address to party militants on the reorganization of the Brigadas de Acção Política (See CIDAC: GB Partido III-2.)

"Les patriotes de Bissau et d'autres villes doivent chaque jour mieux s'organiser et agir avec intelligence et sûreté. Message du . . . à l'occasion du 3 août." [Conakry]: Partido Africano da Independência da Guiné e Cabo Verde, August 3, 1971. Pp. 7, mimeo.

Reprinted in Cabral, *Obras escolhidas* (1976: II, 101–04). Message of optimism.

"Rapport bref sur la situation de la lutte (janvier–août 1971)." [Conakry]: Partido Africano da Independência da Guiné e Cabo Verde, September 1971. Pp. 32, mimeo.

Report on the armed struggle during the period January–August 1971.

"Reunião do Conselho Superior da Luta (9 a 16 de Agosto de 1971). Abertura. Sobre a situação da luta. Intervenção do camarada Amílcar Cabral." [Conakry]: Partido Africano da Independência da Guiné e Cabo Verde, August 1971. Pp. 28, mimeo.

Speech to meeting of the Conselho Superior da Luta, August 1971.

"Reunião do Conselho Superior da Luta (9 a 16 de Agosto de 1971). Discurso de encerramento. Intervenção do camarada Amílcar Cabral." [Conakry]: Partido Africano da Independência da Guiné e Cabo Verde, August 1971. Pp. 11, mimeo.

Closing speech to meeting of the Conselho Superior da Luta, August 1971.

"Reunião do Conselho Superior da Luta (9 a 16 de Agosto de 1971). Sobre alguns problemas práticos da nossa vida e da nossa luta. Intervenção do camarada Amílcar Cabral." [Conakry]: Partido Africano da Independência da Guiné e Cabo Verde, August 1971. Pp. 23, mimeo.

Speech to meeting of the Conselho Superior da Luta, August 1971.

"Sobre a agressão da República da Guiné e os acontecimentos ulteriores nesse país." Conakry: Partido Africano da Independência da Guiné e Cabo Verde, August 1971, mimeo.

Cited in Marrocu (1985) and in the IICT reference catalogue.

"Sobre a criação da Assembleia Nacional Popular." [Conakry]: Partido Africano da Independência da Guiné e Cabo Verde, December 3, 1971. Pp. 10.

Also signed by Fidélis C. Almada. Later elaborated January 8, 1973 for the Conselho Superior da Luta.

"Sobre a situação da luta. Sobre alguns problemas práticos da nossa vida e da nossa luta." Conakry: Partido Africano da Independência da Guiné e Cabo Verde, August 9–16, 1971.

On the armed struggle, on practical problems. Cited in McCarthy (1977: item 1651) and in the IICT reference catalogue.

"Sobre alguns problemas práticos da nossa vida e da nossa luta." Conakry: Partido Africano da Independência da Guiné e Cabo Verde, August 9–16, 1971, mimeo.
Report to the CSL. Cited in Marrocu (1985).

"Speech on Behalf of African Liberation Movements at the Closing Session of the 8th Conference of African Heads of State and Government, OAU, Addis Ababa, 21–23 June 1971." Conakry, June 1971, mimeo.
Cited in the IICT reference catalogue.

"Tirons toute les leçons de l'agression criminelle perpétrée par les colonialistes portugais contre le peuple frère de la République de Guinée. Reforçons et développons la lutte pour remporter de plus grandes victoires en 1971. Message du nouvel an du camarade Amílcar Cabral, secrétaire général du parti, 1 er janvier 1971." [Conakry]: Partido Africano da Independência da Guiné e Cabo Verde, January 1, 1971, mimeo.
Cited in Marrocu (1985).

Vår kamp, er kamp. Edited by Göran Palm. Stockholm: Pan/Norstedts, 1971. Pp. 141.
Cited in Pyhälä (No Date).

1972

"Aucune manoeuvre ou crime des colonialistes portugais ne sera à même d'éviter la victoire inéluctable de notre peuple africain. Rapport bref sur la lutte en 1971." [Conakry]: Partido Africano da Independência da Guiné e Cabo Verde, January 1972. Pp. 18, mimeo.
Confidence that the liberation struggle will soon succeed.

"L'aggression terroriste portugaise contre la Mission Spéciale des Nations Unies par. . . ." [Conakry]: Partido Africano da Independência da Guiné e Cabo Verde, April 1972. Pp. 25, mimeo.
Report on Portuguese threats to the UN Special Mission sent to liberated areas of Guinea-Bissau.

"Allocution prononcée par . . . à la 1632ème Séance du Conseil de Sécurité de l'ONU, à Addis-Abéba, le 1er février 1972." [Conakry]: Partido Africano da Independência da Guiné e Cabo Verde, February 1972. Pp. 10, mimeo.
Address to the UN Security Council in Addis Ababa, February 1, 1972.

"Allocution prononcé par Amílcar Cabral au Symposium organisé par le Parti Démocratique de Guinée, au Palais du Peuple de Conakry, à l'occasion de la Journée Kwame Nkrumah, le 14 mai 1972." Conakry: Partido Africano da Independência da Guiné e Cabo Verde, May 1972. Pp. 7, mimeo.
Speech in honor of Nkrumah.

"Carta circular as SEP, n. 803 (Decisão do partido, fundada nas resoluções e moções votadas unanimamente na Assembleia Magna das SEP, Moscovo, 23 de Janeiro e 3 Fevereiro de 1972)." Conakry: Partido Africano da Independência da Guiné e Cabo Verde, July 31, 1972, mimeo.
Cited in Marrocu (1985) and in the IICT reference catalogue.

"Decisão (de 1 de Janeiro de 1972) sobre alguns problemas da nossa vida nas regiões liberadas." Conakry: Partido Africano da Independência da Guiné e Cabo Verde, January 1972, mimeo.

Cited in Marrocu (1985) and in the IICT reference catalogue.

"Discurso proferido na reunião do Conselho Científico do Instituto da Africa da Academia das Ciências da URSS por ocasião da atribuição do diploma 'Honoris Causa. 23 de Dezembro de 1972.'" December 1972. Pp. 9, mimeo.

Excerpts from an anthology of writings by Cabral in Russian edited by V. G. Solodóvnikov. Speech by Cabral on the occasion of receiving an honorary doctorate from the USSR Academy of Sciences.

"Em nome do nosso povo." Addis Ababa: Partido Africano da Independência da Guiné e Cabo Verde, February 1, 1972, mimeo.

Communiqué to the UN committee. Cited in Marrocu (1985).

"Em nome dos movimentos de libertação da Africa. Em nome do nosso povo. Discursos proferidos pelo camarada Amílcar Cabral em Addis-Abeba perante a 8 Conferência dos Chefes de Estado da Africa (Junho de 1971) e perante o Conselho de Segurança da ONU (Fevereiro de 1972)." [Conakry]: Partido' Africano da Independência da Guiné e Cabo Verde, February 1972. Pp. 20, mimeo.

Two speeches, one in Addis Ababa in June 1971 and the other to the UN Security Council in February 1972.

"Hommage à Kwame Nkrumah (allocation prononcée au symposium organisé par le PDG au palais du peuple à Conakry, à l'occasion de la journée Nkrumah, le 13 Mai 1972)." Conakry: Partido Africano da Independência da Guiné e Cabo Verde, May 1972, mimeo.

Cited in Marrocu (1985) and in the IICT reference catalogue.

"Intensificatons l'action sur tous les plans de la lutte pour accélérer la libération de notre peuple et expulser à jamais les colonialistes portugais de notre patrie africaine (message à l'occasion du nouvel an)." Conakry, January 1972, mimeo.

Identified in the IICT reference catalogue.

"Intensificatons l'action sur tous les plans de la lutte pour accélérer la libération de notre peuple et expulser à jamais les colonialistes portugais de notre patrie africaine. Message du Amílcar Cabral, à la 1632ème séance du Conseil de Sécurité de l'ONU, à Addis-Abeba, le 1 février 1972." Addis Ababa, February 1972. Pp. 9, mimeo.

Reprinted in Cabral, *Obras escolhidas* (1976: II, 115–120). Message to the UN Security Council.

"Intervention du secrétaire général du PAIGC, Amílcar Cabral, à la soirée de solidarité du 20 octobre," in *M. Amílcar Cabral . . . a visité la Finlande les 19–22 Octobre 1971*. Helsinki: Comité d'Afrique de Finlande, 1972.

"Interview with Amílcar Cabral," pp. 156–170 in Donald C. Hodges and Robert E. A. Shanab, *NLF: National Liberation Fronts, 1960/1970*. New York: William Morrow, 1972.

Originally from *Tricontinental* No. 8 (September–October 1968), 114–126.

Der Kampf um Guinea-Bissau. Heidelberg, 1972. Pp. 119.

Cited in Pyhälä and Rylander (No Date).

"A libertação da Guiné," *Boletim Anti-Colonial* (December 1972), reprinted as pp. 55–62 in *Boletim Anti-Colonial*. Porto: Afrontamento, 1975.

Interview originally published in October 1971 in *Polémica and Anti-Colonialismo*.

"Mémorandum à l'intention des chefs d'Etat ou de gouvernement d'Afrique (9 ème conférence de l'ONU, Rabat, juin 1972)." Conakry: Partido Africano da Independência da Guiné e Cabo Verde, 1972, mimeo.

Cited in Marrocu (1985) and in the IICT reference catalogue.

"Memorandum for the Attention of the African Heads of State and Government of East Africa." [Conakry]: Partido Africano da Independência da Guiné e Cabo Verde, September 1972, mimeo.
Cited in Marrocu (1985).

"Message au Congrès constitutif de l'USAL (Union Socialiste Arabe de Lybie)." [Conakry]. 1972, mimeo.
Cited in Marrocu (1985).

"Nous allons renforcer notre vigilance pour démasquer et éliminer les agents de l'ennemi, pour défendre le parti et la lutte et pour continuer à vouer à l'échec tous les plans des criminels colonialistes portugais." [Conakry]: Partido Africano da Independência da Guiné e Cabo Verde, March 1972. P. 1, mimeo.
Statement attacking Portuguese colonialism.

"O papel da cultura na luta pela independência." Paris: Partido Africano da Independência da Guiné e Cabo Verde, July 1972.
Cited in Marrocu (1985). Paper presented to UNESCO.

"Le peuple de la Guinée et des Iles du Cap Vert devant l'ONU. Intervention du Secrétaire Général du PAIGC, Amílcar Cabral, devant la Quatrième Commission de l'Assemblée Générale des Nations Unies (XXVIIème Session)." No Place: Partido Africano da Independência da Guiné e Cabo Verde, October 1972. Pp. 24, mimeo.
Portuguese version, "O povo da Guiné e Cabo Verde perante a ONU," Conakry: PAIGC, October 1972, cited in McCarthy (1977: item 1640) and in the IICT reference catalogue. Statement to the UN Fourth Committee. (See CIDAC: GB Pensamento Político I-13.)

"Rapport bref sur la lutte de libération en 1971." Conakry: Partido Africano da Independência da Guiné e Cabo Verde, January 1972.
Report on the armed struggle during 1971. Cited in McCarthy (1977: item 1643).

Revolution in Guinea: Selected Texts by Amílcar Cabral. Translated and edited by Richard Handyside. New York and London: Monthly Review Press, 1972. Pp. 174.
U.S. edition of earlier anthology (1969).

Selected documents, pp. 297–381, in Ronald H. Chilcote, *Emerging Nationalism in Portuguese Africa*. Stanford: Hoover Institution, Stanford University.
Includes by Cabral: "Death Pangs of Imperialism," "The Rise of Nationalism," "In Defense of Land," "On the Contradiction of the 'Peoples' of Guiné," "Agricultural Production in Guiné," "Movimento de Libertação da Guiné e Cabo Verde—Proclamação," "Memorandum to the Portuguese Government," "Declaration on the Present Status of the Fight for Liberation in Portuguese Guiné and in the Cape Verde Islands," "The National Fight for Liberation," "Development in the Struggle for the National Liberation of 'Portuguese' Guiné and the Cape Verde Islands in 1964."

"Une seule solution: l'indépendance. Message du . . . à l'occasion du XVIème anniversaire de la fondation du parti." [Conakry]: Partido Africano da Independência da Guiné e Cabo Verde, September 19, 1972. Pp. 11, mimeo.
Reprinted in Cabral, *Obras escolhidas* (1976: II, 121–126). Speech on the necessity for an immediate independence. (See CIDAC: GB Partido I-34.)

"Speech at the 1632nd Session of the Security Council of the UN, Held in Addis Ababa on 1 February 1972." Conakry, February 1972, mimeo.
Identified in the IICT reference catalogue.

"Sur le rôle de la culture dans la lutte pour l'indépendance." Paris: Partido Africano da Independéncia da Guiné e Cabo Verde, July 3–7, 1972. Pp. 28, mimeo.

Lecture at a UNESCO "Meeting of Experts on the Notions of Race, Identity and Dignity."

"Vamos acelerar a liquidação total do colonialismo português em 1972, para libertarmos o homem africano da Guiné e Cabo Verde de toda a espécie de opressão, para construirmos uma sociedade justa, baseada na nossa própria história e nas realidades da nossa terra, mas aberta a todas as conquistas da humanidade no caminho do progresso. Mensagem do . . . ao nosso povo e aos nosso combatentes e militantes, por ocasião do ano novo." [Conakry]: Partido Africano da Independência da Guiné e Cabo Verde, January 1972. Pp. 10, mimeo.

New Year's message and review of successes during 1971.

"Vamos reforçar a nossa vigilância para desmascarar os agentes do inimigo para defendermos o partido e a luta e para continuarmos a condenar ao fracasso todos os planos dos criminosos colonialistas portugueses." Conakry: Partido Africano da Independência da Guiné e Cabo Verde, March 1972, mimeo.

Cited in Marrocu (1985) and the IICT reference catalogue.

1973

Cabral on Nkrumah. Newark, New Jersey: Jihad Productions, in cooperation with the PAIGC, 1973. Pp. 8.

Frigjoringskamp: teori og praksis. Oslo: Novus, 1973. Pp. 119.

Cited in Pyhälä and Rylander (No Date).

"Mensagem do ano novo," January 1973, pp. 2–4 in *Assembleia Nacional Popular, orgão supremo de soberania do povo guineense*. [Bissau]: Edição do Departamento de Informação, Propaganda e Cultura do Secretariado do Comité Central do PAIGC, [1984].

French edition, "Message du nouvel an de Amílcar Cabral, Secrétaire Général du Parti," [Conakry]: PAIGC, January 1973. Pp. 16, mimeo. Excerpts from New Year's message. (See CIDAC: GB Partido I-33.) Also an untitled and undated text in Portuguese, 19 pp., mimeo. Reprinted in Cabral, *Obras escolhidas* (1976: II, 217–224). The IICT reference catalogue lists a similar entry, "La situation de la lutte du PAIGC en janvier 1973." Conakry, January 1973, mimeo.

Return to the Source: Selected Speeches of Amílcar Cabral. Edited by Africa Information Service. New York: Monthly Review Press, 1973. Pp. 110.

Contains five speeches: Speech of October 16, 1972, to the UN Fourth Committee; the lecture at Syracuse University, February 20, 1970; the address at Lincoln University on October 15, 1972; an informal talk with black Americans on October 20, 1972; and the New Year's message of January 1973.

Revolutsiya v Gvinee. Moscow: Glavnaya Redaktsiya Vostochnoi Literaturi, 1973.

Collection of writings in Russian. Also *Revolutionen i Guinea*. Copenhagen: Demos. Cited in McCarthy (1977: item 1649) and the IICT reference catalogue.

"A sua última mensagem ao povo da Guiné e Cabo Verde (Janeiro de 1973)." 3d ed. No Place: Associação de Caboverdianos e Guineenes, Partido Africano da Independência da Guiné e Cabo Verde, January 1973. Pp. 16, mimeo.

January message.

"Sur la création de l'Assemblée Nationale Populaire en Guinée Bissau. Résultats et bases des élections générales réalisées dans les régions libérées en 1972." [Conakry]: Partido Africano da Independência da Guiné e Cabo Verde, January 8, 1973. Pp. 6 plus 6 pp. of photographs and an appendix of 7 pp., mimeo.

The communiqué is signed by Amílcar Cabral and dated January 8, 1973. The appendix, signed by Amílcar Cabral and Fidelis Cabral, contains results of elections in liberated zones of Guinea-Bissau during 1972.

Uusi tietoisuus—voirakkoin aseemme (New consciousness—our strongest weapon). Helsinki, 1973. Pp. 144.

Collection of speeches and writings edited by Mikko Pyhälä. Cited by Pyhälä and Rylander (No Date).

1974

Alguns princípios do partido. Lisbon: Colecção de Leste a Oeste, Seara Nova, 1974. Pp. 79.

Presented to a Seminário de Quadros of the PAIGC, November 19–24, 1969. Consists of essays "Unidade e luta" and "Partir da realidade da nossa terra ser realistas."

Análise de alguns tipos de resistência. Lisbon: Colecção de Leste a Oeste, Seara Nova, 1974. Pp. 133. Also Bolama: Edição do PAIGC, Imprensa Nacional, 1979. Pp. 139.

Presented to the Seminário de Quadros of the PAIGC, November 1969. Essays on political, economic, cultural, and armed resistance.

(et al.). *De Salazar a los capitanes.* Compiled and edited by Carlos Ossa. Buenos Aires: Grupo Editor de Buenos Aires, 1974. Pp. 110.

Cabral's contribution, pp. 21–12, is from *Tricontinental* No. 33, a critique of António de Spínola and his policies and actions in Guinea-Bissau.

Decisões (de 30 de Agosto de 1970 e 1 de Janeiro de 1972) sobre problemas actuais de nossa vida nas regiões libertadas. Bolama: Imprensa Nacional da Guiné-Bissau, 1974.

Cited in Marrocu (1985) and the IICT reference catalogue.

Guiné-Bissau. Nação africana forjada na luta. Lisbon: Textos Amílcar Cabral (1), Publicações Nova Aurora, 1974. Pp. 175.

Anthology of fourteen texts of Cabral, coordinated by J. Camacho and Joel Silveira. Includes article from *Partisans* (1962); presentation at Milan, May 1964; and the January 1966 Havana speech.

Guiné-Bissau: Toward Final Victory! Selected Speeches and Documents from the PAIGC. Richmond, British Columbia: LSM Press, 1974. Pp. 98.

Introduction by Ole Gjerstad that identifies the roles of Cabral and the PAIGC in the liberation struggle. The documents by Cabral include his speech to the Franz Fanon Center, Milan, May 1–3, 1964; extracts from "Palavras de ordem gerais," 1965; speech to UNESCO, Paris, July 3–7, 1972; statement on elections of August–October 1972, January 8, 1973; extract of discussion in New York, October 20, 1972.

PAIGC unidade e luta. Lisbon: Textos Amílcar Cabral (2), Publicações Nova Aurora, 1974. Pp. 243.

Organized October 1974 by the Grupo de Acção Democrático de Cabo Verde e Guiné, who provide a brief preface to these three principal texts: "Palavras de ordem gerais," November 1965; "Alguns princípios do partido," November 19–24, 1969; and "Análise dos tipos de resistência."

"A resistência cultural (Seminário de Quadros do Partido—Novembro 1969)." Bissau: Serviços de Informação do PAIGC, 1974. Pp. 13, mimeo.
Speech abridged from the Creole, given November 19–24, 1969. (See CIDAC: GB Partido I-2.)

Textos políticos. Porto: CEC, 1974. Pp. 64.
Excerpts and selections from twelve documents during the period 1962 to 1973. Appeared after the Portuguese coup of April 25, 1974, in a new edition, Porto: Afrontamento, 1974. Pp. 51. Reprinted edition of "a clandestine publication" organized by Luís Moita and Maria do Rosário Moita and the group responsible for publishing *Boletim Anti-Colonial.* Organized into four parts: the history of struggle for liberation, the organization of a national liberation movement, anticolonial policy, and Cabral's last speech of January 1, 1973.

Unidade e luta. Lisbon: Publicações Nova Aurora, 1974. Pp. 243.
Identified in IICT reference catalogue. A 1976 edition cited by Lopes (1983).

1975

Resistência cultural: textos de apoio ao 1 Encontro Nacional de Educação. [Lisbon?]: Edições AEUL, October, 1975. Pp. 36.
Cabral's writing on cultural resistance.

L'Unité et lutte. Vol. 1: L'arme de la théorie. Paris: François Maspero.
French edition of collected works. Identified in the IICT reference catalogue.

L'Unité et lutte. Vol. 2: La pratique revolutionnarie. Paris: François Maspero.
French edition of collected works. Identified in IICT reference catalogue.

1976

Obras escolhidas de Amílcar Cabral. Vol. 1: A arma da teoria: unidade e luta I. Lisbon: Seara Nova, 1976. Pp. 248.
First volume of collected works of Cabral, organized by Mário de Andrade. Includes an introduction by the Comité Executivo da Luta do PAIGC.

1977

A arma da teoria. Praia: Edição UL, March 1977. Pp. 42.
Reprinting of important texts of Cabral because they offer militants "a profound understanding of his thought and of his practical and theoretical work." Included are excerpts from his presentation to the Franz Fanon Center, Milan, May 1–3, 1964; an analysis of Cape Verde, Dakar, July 20, 1963; responses to questions at the Seminário de Quadros, November 19–24, 1969; speech, Cairo, March 25–31, 1961; and the "A arma da teoria" speech, Havana, January 6, 1966.

Obras escolhidas de Amílcar Cabral. Vol. 2: A prática revolucionária: unidade e luta II. Lisbon: Seara Nova, 1977. Pp. 224.
Second volume of collected works of Cabral, organized by Mário de Andrade.

1979

Análise de alguns tipos de resistência. Bolama: Edição do PAIGC, Imprensa Nacional, 1979. Pp. 137.

Transcription and translation of conversations in Creole by Cabral to the Seminário de Quadros, November 19–24, 1969. Organized into four topics: political, economic, cultural, and armed resistance.

Unity and Struggle: Speeches and Writings. Translated by Michael Wolfers. New York: Monthly Review Press and London: Heinemann, 1979. Pp. 298.

Thirty-six texts, selected by the PAIGC, from Cabral's writings and speeches. Organized into two parts, "The Weapon of Theory" and "Revolutionary Practice," with an introduction by Basil Davidson, pp. ix–xvii, and biographical notes, drawn from "an unpublished work," by Mário de Andrade, "Amílcar Cabral: essai de biographie politique", pp. xviii–xxxv (published in an expanded version—see Andrade, 1980). The French edition, *Unité et lutte* (Paris: Maspero, 1980; 330 pp.), was reviewed by Gérard Chaliand, "L'oeuvre exceptionnelle d'Amílcar Cabral," *Livres Partisans* (April–June 1980), 1–2. The original French edition was dated 1975. See Cabral (1974, 1976, and 1977) for the Portuguese version.

1980

"A arma da teoria" and "A cultura nacional," pp. 21–92 in Carlos Comitini, *Amílcar Cabral, a arma da teoria.* Rio de Janeiro: Codecri, 1980.

1981

Cultura y liberación nacional. Mexico City: Escuela Nacional de Antropología e Historia, Instituto Nacional de Antropología e Historia. Pp. 181.

1983

Princípios do partido e a prática política. Lisbon: Colecção "Cabral Ka Muri," Edição do Departamento de Informação, Propaganda e Cultura do CC do PAIGC, 1983.

Series of six pamphlets: (1) "Unidade e luta," pp. 24; (2) "Partir da realidade de nossa terra. Ser realista," pp. 31; (3) "O nosso partido deve ser dirigido pelos melhores filhos do nosso povo," pp. 24; (4) "A independência de pensamento e de acção . . . ," pp. 23; (5) "A democracia revolucionária . . . ," pp. 32; (6) "As lições positivas e negativas da revolução africana," pp. 16. Reprints of important texts by Cabral.

1984

Assembleia Nacional Popular, orgão supremo de soberania do povo guineense. [Bissau]: Edição do Departamento de Informação, Propaganda e Cultura do Secretariado do Comité Central do PAIGC (1), [1984?] Pp. 16.

Includes excerpts from Cabral's "Mensagem do ano novo," January 1973, pp. 2–4; and "O estado da Guiné-Bissau," December 3, 1971, pp. 5–16.

1987

"A língua portuguesa e o crioulo," p. 15 in Ministério de Educação, Direcção Nacional de Educação de Adultos, *Antologia de textos*. Maputo, 1987.
Brief text by Cabral in a seventh- to ninth-year class of adult education classes.

1988

Estudos agrários de Amílcar Cabral. Lisbon and Bissau: Instituto de Investigação Científica Tropical and Instituto Nacional de Estudos e Pesquisa. Pp. 781.
A compilation of texts written by Cabral on his agrarian research together with interpretative essays by others. Divided into three sections: interpretative essays by others; the technical-scientific bibliography of Cabral (fifty-nine texts); and scientific studies by Cabral.

── 2 ──
Amílcar Cabral's Articles in Periodicals

The following articles from journals and newspapers are listed in alphabetical order within the year published.

1946

"A Ilha," *A Ilha* (Ponta Delgada), (July 22, 1946).
　　Published in Vol. 1, p. 23 in Cabral, *Obras escolhidas* (1976). Also in Moser (1981: 16) and in *Seara Nova* No. 1550 (December 1974), 36–37; see Osório (1988: 29) for additional sources where published and p. 69 for reprinting of the poem. Poem written in Praia during 1945.

1948

["Soneto do nosso amor."] *O Metalúrgico* (July 15, 1948) and (August 23, 1948).
　　Cited in Osório (1988: 30–31) as a poem written for his first wife.

1949

"Algumas considerações acerca das chuvas," *Cabo Verde: Boletim de Propaganda e Informação* 1 (1949), 5–7.
　　Dated September 8, 1949, in Praia. Reprinted in Cabral (1988: 59–61).

"Em defesa da terra," *Cabo Verde: Boletim de Propaganda e Informação* 1 (November 1, 1949), 2–5; continued (see 1950).
　　Reprinted in Cabral (1988: 63–66). Written in Praia on September 27, 1949. Essays on the problems of soil.

"Hoje e amanhã," *Mensagem* No. 11 (May–December 1949). Reprinted in *Nô Pintcha* 511 (September 12, 1978), 4–5.
　　Written originally in October 26, 1944, under the pseudonym of Arlindo António. Originally published by the *Boletim* of the Casa dos Estudantes do Império 2, No. 11 (May–December 1949). Cited by Andrade in Cabral, *Unity and Struggle* (1979).

"Poema," *Mensagem* No. 11 (May–December), 15.
　　Reprinted in Moser (1981: 18) and in Osório (1988: 71). Poem written in Lisbon in 1946. Marrocu (1985) cites this as "Quem é que não se lembra . . . ," the words of the first verse.

"Regresso . . . ," *Cabo Verde: Boletim de Propaganda e Informação* 1 (November 1, 1949), 11.

Poem reprinted in Vol. 1, p. 24, in Cabral, *Obras escolhidas* (1976); in Moser (1981: 16–17); and in Osório (1988: 74).

"Rosa negra," *Mensagem* No. 6 (January 1949), 12.
Reprinted in *Nô Pintcha* 511 (September 12, 1978), 4; in Moser (1981: 19); and in Osório (1988: 73). Poem written in Lisbon.

1950

"Em defesa da terra," *Cabo Verde: Boletim de Propaganda e Informação* 1 (November 1, 1949), 2–5; continued in 1 (March 1, 1950), 15–18; 2 (November 1950), 19–22; 2 (December 1, 1950), 6–8.
Reprinted in Cabral (1988: 63–79). Focus on problems of agriculture in drought-prone Cape Verde; at the time Cabral was a fifth-year student at the Instituto Superior de Agronomia de Lisboa.

1951

"Apontamentos sobre poesia caboverdiana," *Cabo Verde: Boletim de Propaganda e Informação* 3 (December 1, 1951), 5–8.
Notes on poetry of Cape Verde; argues that only with the appearance of *Claridade* was there a true literature for Cape Verde.

1952

"Em defesa da terra," *Cabo Verde: Boletim de Propaganda e Informação* 3 (February 1, 1952), 24–25.
Reprinted in Cabral (1988: 177–179). Continued focus on the problems of Cape Verde.

1953

"Posto Agrícola Experimental dos Serviços Agrícolas e Florestias," *Ecos da Guiné* (Bolama) 3, 30 (1953), 25–28; continued in 3, 31 (1953), 17–20; 3, 34–35 (1953), 40–43; 3, 36–37 (1953), 17–20.
Published as a series under "Boletim Informativo" Nos. 1–5. Reprinted in Cabral (1988: 181–206). Reports prepared at Pessubé from November 1952 to March 1953.

"Le rôle de l'étudiant africain," *Présence Africaine* No. 14 (Special Issue, 1953).
Reprinted in Cabral, *Unité et Lutte* (1975: Vol. 2, 32–38). Cited in Marrocu (1985).

1954

"Acerca da contribuição dos 'povos' guineenes para a produção agrícola da Guiné. I—Area cultivada," *Boletim Cultural da Guiné Portuguesa* 9 (October 1954), 771–777.

212   *An Annotated Bibliography*

Reprinted in Cabral (1988: 263–267). An essay, written in Bissau during 1954, on the contributions of Africans to agricultural production in Guinea.

"Acerca da utilização da terra na Africa negra," *Boletim Cultural da Guiné Portuguesa* 9 (April 1954), 401–416.
Reprinted in Cabral (1988: 241–249). Argues that the use of land in Africa should not lead to exploitation of man, that the African must be assisted in the fight against climate, and that African culture and cultivation systems must be supported.

"Para o conhecimento do problema da erosão do solo na Guiné. I—Sobre o conceito de erosão," *Boletim Cultural da Guiné Portuguesa* 9 (January 1954), 163–194.
Reprinted in Cabral (1988: 207–225). A detailed paper on soil erosion in Guinea.

"A propósito de mecanização da agricultura na Guiné Portuguesa," *Boletim Cultural da Guiné Portuguesa* 9 (April 1954), 389–400.
Reprinted in Cabral (1988: 233–239). A paper, written in Bissau during 1953, that argues mechanization of agriculture must take into account the needs of people, their traditional ways of living and cultivating, and so on.

"Queimadas e pousios na circunscrição de Fulacunda em 1954," *Boletim Cultural da Guiné Portuguesa* 9 (July 1954), 627–646.
Reprinted in Cabral (1988: 251–262). Based on a text written in Bissau in July 1954. An essay on burned and uncultivated land in Fulacunda. Acknowledges the assistance of Abílio Duarte and Maria Helena Cabral.

(with Maria Helena Cabral). "Breves notas acerca da razão de ser, objectivos e processo de execução do recenseamento agrícola da Guiné," *Boletim Cultural da Guiné Portuguesa* 9 (January 1954), 195–201.
Reprinted in Cabral (1988: 227–231). Written in Bissau, January 1954. Notes on the agricultural census in Guinea, coauthored with his first wife.

1956

"O estudo do micro-clima de um armazém em Malange (Angola)," *Anais da Junta de Investigação do Ultramar* 11, No. 2 (1956), 199–225.
Reprinted in Cabral (1988: 275–290). Climatic study in Malange, Angola.

"O problema do estudo macro- e micro-climático dos ambientes relacionados com os produtos armazenados," *Anais da Junta de Investigação do Ultramar* 11, No. 2 (1956), 187–195.
Reprinted in Cabral (1988: 269–273). Study of climatic conditions and of agricultural products stored in warehouses.

"Recenseamento agrícola da Guiné. Estimativa em 1953," *Boletim Cultural da Guiné Portuguesa* 11 (July 1956), 7–243.
Reprinted in full in Cabral (1988: 291–443). Reprinted in part in Cabral, *Obras escolhides* (1976: Vol. 1, 33–43). Analysis and results of an agricultural census. Important foundation of information, based on a study of December 1954.

1958

"A propos du cycle cultural arachide-mils en Guinée Portugaise," *Boletim Cultural da Guiné Portuguesa* 13 (April 1958), 149–156.

Reprinted in Cabral (1988: 455–459). Text of paper to a conference in Banbey, Senegal, during September 1954.

"Feux de brousse et jachères dans le cycle cultural; arachide-mils," *Boletim Cultural da Guiné Portuguesa* 13 (July 1958), 257–268.
Reprinted in Cabral (1988: 461–467). Technical paper originally presented to a September 1954 conference in Senegal.

1959

"A agricultura da Guiné. Algumas notas sobre as suas características e problemas fundamentais," *Agros* 43, No. 4 (1959), 335–350.
Reprinted in Cabral, *Obras escolhidas* (1976: I, 44–56) and in Cabral (1988: 523–536).

1960

(with Maria Irene Moreira). "Da ocorrência de algumas pragas de produtos ultramarinos em porões de navios mercantes (carreira da Guiné)," *Garcia de Orta* 8, No. 1 (1960), 47–57.
Reprinted in Cabral (1988: 767–778). Specialized study on infestations of colonial products transported on merchant ships.

1961

(under pseudonym of Abel Djassi). "As realidades nas colónias portuguesas da Africa," *Portugal Democrática* (January 1961), 7.
Cited in Marrocu (1985) and identified in the IICT reference catalogue.

1962

"Guinée, Cap Vert, face au colonialisme portugaise," *Partisans* 7 (November–December 1962), 80–91.
On the problem of Portuguese colonialism.

"La Guinée Portugaise et les Iles du Cap Vert," *Voice of Africa* 2 (May 1962), 37–39.
Condemnation of Portuguese colonial practices.

Letter to Sekou Touré, *Foreign Radio Broadcasts* (October 11, 1962), 17–18.
Radio broadcast from Conakry in celebration of the fourth anniversary of independence in Guinea.

"Liberation Movement in Portuguese Guinea," *Voice of Africa* 2 (March 1962), 32.
Decries the colonial oppression and lauds the PAIGC successes since August 3, 1961.

1963

"Le crime de colonialisme," *Révolution Africaine* No. 17 (May 25, 1963), 12–13.
Exposé of the crimes of Portuguese colonialism.

"A guerra na Guiné," *Portugal Democrático* 8 (October 1963), 3.
On the colonial war in Guinea-Bissau.

"800.000 hommes en guerre," *Révolution Africaine* No. 7 (March 16, 1963), 8–9.
Press conference of March 8, 1963.

"Notre lutte en Guiné," *Révolution Africaine* No. 29 (August 17, 1963), 4–5.
Interview.

"O PAIGC pede à ONU auxílio concreto," *Portugal Democrático* 8 (December 1963), 4.

"Solução pacífica para Guiné e Cabo Verde," *Portugal Democrático* 7 (February–March 1963), 6.
Statement before the Fourth Committee of the United Nations.

"The War in 'Portuguese Guinea,'" *African Revolution* 1 (June 1963), 103–108.
Analysis of the armed struggle and an optimistic appraisal.

1964

"The Struggle in Guinea," *International Socialist Journal* 1 (August 1964), 428–446.
In French as "La lutte en Guinée," *Revue International du Socialisme* No. 4 (1964), 439–453. Also in *Translations on Africa* (1964: 29–40), identified in the IICT reference catalogue. Reprinted by Africa Research Group, Cambridge, Massachusetts, [1970].

1965

"Contra a guerra colonial: mensagem de Amílcar Cabral ao povo da Guiné e de Cabo Verde," *FPLN Boletim* (August 1965), 14–15.
Message on the liberation struggle.

"Contre la guerre coloniale," *FPLN Portugal* (August 1965), 14–15.
On the colonial struggle.

"Liberating Portuguese Guinea from Within," *New African* 4 (June 1965), 85.
Interview with Frene Ginwala. Cabral affirms that the liberated areas have "all the instruments of the state."

"La lutte du PAIGC," *Remarques Africaines* 7 (May 26, 1965), 19–22.
Text of speech in Algiers.

1966

"L'arme de la théorie," *Partisans* 26–27 (1966), 109–119.
Reprint of speech in Havana, Cuba, during January 1966.

"Portuguese Colonial Policy," *Africa Quarterly* 5, No. 4 (1966), 287–299.
Cited in McCarthy (1977: item 1639).

"The Social Structure of Portuguese Guinea and Its Meaning for the Struggle for National Liberation," *Translations on Africa* No. 420 (August 24, 1966), 37–48.
Cited in McCarthy (1977: item 1652).

"Structure sociale de la Guinée 'Portugaise,'" *Révolution Africaine* No. 178 (June 24–July 1), 18–19.
On the social structure and its significance in Guinea.

1967

"Amílcar Cabral fala ao povo português," *Luso-Canadiano* 7 (August 18, 1967), 1, 3.
Interview.

"Breve análise de la estructura social de la Guinea 'Portuguesa,'" *Pensamiento Crítico* Nos. 2–3 (March–April 1967), 24–48.
Analysis of social structure in Guinea-Bissau.

"Fundamentos y objetivos de la liberación nacional en relación con la estructura social," *Pensamiento Crítico* Nos. 2–3 (March–April 1967), 3–22.
On the goals of the national liberation struggle.

"Mankind's Path to Progress," *World Marxist Review* 10 (November 1967), 88–89.
Message of solidarity on the fiftieth anniversary of the Russian Revolution.

1968

"Determined to Resist," *Tricontinental* No. 8 (September–October 1968), 114–126.
Interview on the resistance struggle in Guinea-Bissau.

"Independence Struggle in Guinea and Cape Verde," *Guardian* 21 (December 7, 1968), 19.
Interview, reprinted from *Tricontinental* No. 8 (September–October 1968), 114–126.

"Lutter jusqu'à l'indépendance complète," *Revue de la Politique Internationale* No. 434 (May 1968), 3–6.
Interview.

1969

"Afrique: les peuples opprimés des colonies," *Voix Ouvrière* (September 1969), 5–6.
Jointly with Agostinho Neto and Marcelino dos Santos.

"Fight for Life in Guinea-Bissau," *Translations on Africa* No. 860 (1969), 84–90.
Interview from *France Nouvelle* (November 19, 1969). Cited in Pyhälä and Rylander (No Date).

"Guinea (B): Political and Military Situation," *Tricontinental* No. 37 (April 1969), 25–34.
A report on the liberation struggle.

"Guinea: The Power of Arms," *Tricontinental* No. 12 (May–June 1969), 5–12.
Elaborates on the use of the peasantry in the early phases of the liberation struggle.

1970

"Amílcar Cabral fala da luta do seu povo," *Portugal Democrático* 14 (March 1970), 4.
Excerpts from speech.

"Declarações de Cabral e de M. Santos," *Portugal Democrático* 15 (September 1970), 2–7.
An interview in Rome, jointly with Marcelino dos Santos.

"Frente al ultra colonialismo portugues," *Pensamiento Crítico* No. 36 (January 1970), 186–197.
On the struggle against Portuguese colonialism.

"'Our Army Is Our Whole People,'" *Newsweek* (March 9, 1970), 38–39.
Interview with Richard Levine.

"PAIGC: Optimistic and Fighter," *Tricontinental* Nos. 19–20 (July–October 1970), 164–174.
Includes an extract of his speech and the "General Declaration" of June 22–29, 1970, from the Rome Conference in Support of the Portuguese Colonies.

"Report on Portuguese Guinea and the Liberation Movement," *Ufahamu* 1 (Fall 1970), 69–103.
Full report of February 26, 1970, before the U.S. House of Representatives, Subcommittee on African Affairs.

1971

"PAIGC Attacks," *Tricontinental* No. 68 (November 1971), 38–39.
Brief report on the success of the PAIGC.

1972

"Amílcar Cabral: demain l'état indépendant de la Guinée-Bissau," *Afrique-Asie* 18 (November 27, 1972), 24–26.
Cited in Marrocu (1985).

"Amílcar Cabral, Leader of the PAIGC," *IFCO News* 3 (November–December 1972), 4–8.
Text of speech given on October 15, 1972, at Lincoln University, where Cabral received an honorary doctorate.

"A Brief Report on the Situation of the Struggle (January–August 1971)," *Ufahamu* 2 (Winter 1972), 5–29.

Reprinted from 1971 document published in Conakry by the PAIGC.

"Entrevista com Amílcar Cabral para as revistas anticolonialismo e polémica," *Anticolonialismo* No. 2 (February 1972), 4–5.
Interview.

"Frutos de una lucha," *Tricontinental* 31 (July–August 1972), 61–77.
Published in the English edition of this journal.

"Guinea (B) on Verge of Victory," *Guardian* (November 1, 1972).
Interview with Barry Rubin.

"Identity and Dignity in Struggle," *Southern Africa* 5 (November 1972), 4–8.
Text of address at Lincoln University, October 15, 1972.

"Identity and Dignity in the National Liberation Struggle," *Africa Today* 19 (Fall 1972), 39–47. Address at Lincoln University, October 15, 1972.

"Nkrumah: un combattant de la liberté," *Afrique-Asie* 11–12 (August 21, 1972), 87.
Portrait of Nkrumah. Cited by Marrocu (1985) and the IICT reference catalogue.

"Le Portugal est-il impérialiste?" *Afrique-Asie* No. 3 (May 2, 1972), 34–35.
Affirms that Portugal acts in imperialist interests.

"Why Portugal Cannot Win in Guinea (B)," *Guardian* (January 12, 1972).
Cited in Lopes (1983).

1973

"Amílcar Cabral," *Tricontinental* 7, No. 87 (1973), 25–32.
Excerpts from past speeches.

"Cinquante ans de lutte pour la libération nationale," *Questions Actuelles du Socialisme/Socialist Thought and Practice* (March–April 1973), 98–110.
An overview of fifty years of liberation struggle. Cited in McCarthy (1977: item 1588) and the IICT reference catalogue.

"Dieci anni di lotta armata," *L'Unitá* (January 23, 1973).
Speech of October 16, 1963, before the UN Fourth Committee.

"Fifty Years of the Struggle for National Liberation," *Socialist Thought and Practice* No. 51 (March–April 1973), 87–98.
Statement to associates of the Institute for the International Workers' Movement in Belgrade.

"An Informal Talk by Amílcar Cabral," *Southern Africa* 6 (February 1973), 6–9.
Talk to small gathering in New York during October 1972.

"Liberación nacional y estructura social," *La Cultura en México* No. 575, Supplement to *Siempre* No. 1025 (February 14, 1973), I–VI.
Analysis of the ongoing revolution in Guinea-Bissau.

"Original Writings," *Ufahamu* 3 (Winter 1973), 31–41.
Reprint of two articles written during the early 1950s. Includes "The Contribution of the Guinean Peoples to the Agricultural Production of Guinea," pp. 32–35, and "On the Utilization of Land in Africa," pp. 35–41.

"Realidades," *Tricontinental* No. 33 (1973), 97–109.

Interview on the armed struggle in Guinea-Bissau.

"The Struggle Has Taken Root," *Black Scholar* 4 (July–August 1973), 28–33.
Also in *Tricontinental* No. 84 (1973), 41–49. Press conference in Conakry, September 1972.

"Support for the People's Legitimate Aspirations to Freedom, Independence and Progress," *Objective: Justice* 5 (January–March 1973), 4–7.
Excerpts from a statement to the UN Fourth Committee, October 16, 1972. Includes a prefatory statement identifying Cabral and some of his past statements.

"We Want Our People to Take the Authority for Their Own Lives in Their Own Hands," *Liberation News Service* No. 497 (January 27, 1973), 5–7.
Interview.

1974

"A cultura e o combate pela independência," *Seara Nova* No. 1544 (June 1974), 5–8, 48.
From a document presented to UNESCO in July 1972. Extract of a study on culture presented to UNESCO in Paris, July 1972. (See CIDAC: GB Cult I-9.)

"Culture et libération," *Jeune Afrique* No. 683 (February 1974), 32–34.
Extracts of a text presented to UNESCO in Paris, July 3–7, 1972. Distinguishes between culture and cultural manifestations to show how culture can be fundamental to a liberation movement and its mobilization of people in the struggle for independence.

"A evolução do PAIGC analisada por Amílcar Cabral," *Revista Expresso* No. 72 (May 18, 1974), 17–18.
On the rise of the PAIGC.

"Extirper l'imaginaire," *Afrique-Asie* No. 66 (September 28–October 6), Special Supplement, XLVI–XLVII.
Excerpt from Cabral's writing on culture.

"National Liberation and Culture," *Transition* 9, No. 45 (1974), 12–17.
Text of lecture to Syracuse University on February 20, 1970.

"Um poema de Amílcar Cabral," *Seara Nova* No. 1550 (December 1974), 36–37.
Poem "Ilha," originally published in *A Ilha* (July 22, 1946). Poem written in Praia during 1945.

"The Role of Culture in the Battle for Independence," *Notes from the Belly of the Beast* (April 17, 1974), 1, 4.
Speech to a CONCP conference in Tanzania in 1965. Text from paper presented to UNESCO, Paris, July 1972.

"Who Is General Spínola?" *Tricontinental News Service* 2 (May 8, 1974), 3–4.

1975

"'Acabar com todos os abusos,'" *Nô Pintcha* No. 104 (November 27, 1975), 3.
Argues the need to eliminate abuses in Guinea and Cape Verde.

"'Agricultura hoje e amanhã,'" *Nô Pintcha* No. 115 (December 23, 1975), 3.
On the role of cooperatives in agriculture.

"Amílcar Cabral e o não alinhamento," *Nô Pintcha* No. 69 (September 2, 1975), 8.
Reprint of a text on nonalignment.

"Angola: 'sua luta é nossa própria luta,'" *Nô Pintcha* No. 87 (October 18, 1975), 3.
Excerpt from an intervention in the Seminário de Quadros in 1969.

"'Aquele que hoje confia é rico,'" *Nô Pintcha* No. 110 (December 11, 1975), 3.
Argues in favoring of destroying the economic colonial system.

"Construir uma vida nova," *Nô Pintcha* No. 100 (November 20, 1975), 3.
Excerpt from an unidentifiable speech.

"'Dar mais, cada dia mais em todos os planos da nossa vida,'" *Nô Pintcha* (October 2, 1975), 3; continued in No. 81 (October 4, 1975), 3; No. 82 (October 7, 1975), 3; No. 83 (October 9, 1975), 3; No. 84 (October 11, 1975), 3; No. 85 (October 14, 1975), 3.
Text from November 1969 on the tasks of the party.

"Democracia revolucionária," *Nô Pintcha* No. 96 (November 8, 1975), 3.
A note on revolutionary democracy.

"Devemos desenvolver a economia para continuar a luta," *Nô Pintcha* No. 111 (December 13, 1975), 3.
Sets forth the need to develop the economy.

"É a consciência do homem que guia a arma," *Nô Pintcha* No.102 (November 22, 1975), 3.
Excerpt from an unidentifiable speech on human conscience in guiding the struggle.

"Evolução e perspectivas da luta," *Voz di Povo* 1, No. 12 (October 18, 1975).
Cited in Marrocu (1985). The IICT reference catalogue cites the issue as No. 11.

"Fazer avançar o nosso povo," *Nô Pintcha* No. 116 (December 27, 1975), 3.
An appeal to work and advance.

"'Fazer o máximo para depender cada vez menos das importações,'" *Nô Pintcha* No. 112 (December 16, 1975), 3.
Focuses on the need to become self-sufficient.

"Guiné-Cabo Verde, unidade e luta," *Nô Pintcha* No. 44 (June 5, 1975), 5, 7.
Brief text on need for unity between Guinea-Bissau and Cape Verde.

"Homenagem a Eduardo Mondlane," *Nô Pintcha* No. 39 (June 24, 1975), 4.
Brief homage to Eduardo Mondlane, leader of FRELIMO; excerpt from his 1970 speech at Syracuse University.

"Independência de pensamento e acção," *Nô Pintcha* No. 86 (October 16, 1975), 3.
Reprint of text from Seminário de Quadros in 1969.

"'Lavrar a terra é o trabalho mais digno do nosso povo,'" *Nô Pintcha* No. 114 (December 20, 1975), 3.
Advocates working the land.

"A luta é vitória permanente contra as dificuldades," *Nô Pintcha* No. 97 (November 11, 1975), 3.
Excerpt from an unidentified speech on overcoming obstacles.

"'Lutamos para libertar o povo de toda a espécie de exploração,'" *Nô Pintcha* No. 90 (October 25, 1975), 3.
Excerpt from his writings on exploration and liberation.

"Marchar com os próprios pés, guiados pela nossa cabeça," *Nô Pintcha* No. 117 (December 31, 1975), 3.
New Year's message of January 3, 1973.

"'Não lutamos contra o povo português,'" *Nô Pintcha* No. 105 (November 29, 1975), 3.
Argues that the objective is to win allies, including the Portuguese people.

"Nós e o nosso continente," *Nô Pintcha* No. 58 (August 7, 1975), 5.
Praise for the establishment of the Organization of African Unity.

"'Nós queremos que a maioria tenha o poder nas mãos,'" *Nô Pintcha* No. 94 (November 4, 1975), 3.
Excerpt from an unidentified speech on majority power.

"'A nossa luta é uma luta política,'" *Nô Pintcha* No. 109 (December 9, 1975), 3.
While the struggle for independence is political, colonialism is an economic phenomenon.

"'O nosso partido está aberto aos melhores filhos da nossa terra,'" *Nô Pintcha* No. 91 (October 28, 1975), 3.
Brief excerpt from a speech on the party.

"'Nunca dizer mentiras, não enganar ninguém,'" *Nô Pintcha* No. 103 (November 25, 1975), 3.
Excerpt from an unidentifiable speech.

"O que é a luta?" *Nô Pintcha* No. 88 (October 21, 1975), 3.
Excerpt from an interview in the Seminário de Quadros in 1969.

"'O que é o povo?'" *Nô Pintcha* No. 93 (November 1, 1975), 3.
Excerpt from an unidentified speech on the role of the people in the revolution.

"Orgulho do nosso partido," *Nô Pintcha* No. 59 (August 9, 1975), 8.
Text of one of his talks at the Seminário de Quadros in 1969.

"Um poema de Amílcar Cabral," *Nô Pintcha* No. 11 (April 19, 1975), 6.
Includes the poem "Ilha," dated 1945 in Praia and published in *Ilha* (Ponta Delgada) (June 22, 1946); and a poem in homage to Amílcar Cabral by Nagig Said.

"'Porque é que nós criamos um partido?'" *Nô Pintcha* No. 89 (October 23, 1975), 3.
Excerpt from his thinking on establishing the party.

"'. . . Que o nosso povo mande no seu destino,'" *Nô Pintcha* No. 100 (November 18, 1975), 3.
Support for participation in the struggle.

"Realidade económica," *Nô Pintcha* No. 63 (August 19, 1975), 8.
Text on the economic reality, to the Seminário de Quadros do Partido, in 1969.

"Revolução: o homem novo," *Nô Pintcha* No. 53 (July 26, 1975), 4.
Excerpt from speech in Havana, January 1966, with reference to the new man and the Cuban Revolution.

"'Saber escolher com quem devemos ter amizade,'" *Nô Pintcha* No. 108 (December 6, 1975), 3.

Speech excerpt on finding friendship among other nations.

"'Ser capaz de servir em qualquer terra combatendo o mesmo inimigo,'" *Nô Pintcha* No. 107 (December 4, 1975), 3.
Compares the struggle in Guinea to that in Mozambique.

"Ser fiel aos princípios do partido," *Nô Pintcha* No. 99 (November 15, 1975), 3.
Note on party loyalty.

"Sobre a criação da Assembleia Nacional Popular da Guiné," *Nô Pintcha* No. 77 (September 24, 1975), 6–8, 12.
Text on the creation of the Assembleia Nacional Popular.

"Texto de Amílcar Cabral," *Voz di Povo* 1, No. 11 (September 18, 1975).
Cited in Marrocu (1985) and in the IICT reference catalogue.

"'Todo o homem pode viver e trabalhar na nossa terra,'" *Nô Pintcha* No. 106 (December 2, 1975), 3.
Argues that all people should be able to live in a liberated Guinea-Bissau.

"'Todos somos necessários. Ninguém é indispensável,'" *Nô Pintcha* No. 98 (November 13, 1975), 3.
Appeal to participate in the struggle.

"'Transformar o partido cada dia numa organização melhor,'" *Nô Pintcha* No. 92 (October 30, 1975), 3.
Excerpt from a speech on the party.

"Unidade e luta," *Nô Pintcha* No. 41 (June 28, 1975), 5.
Brief text on the meaning of unity and struggle.

"Voices of Revolution," *Guardian* 27 (January 22, 1975), 11.
Excerpt from an informal talk with 120 Black Americans in New York City on October 20, 1972.

1976

"O absurdo da nossa situação," *Nô Pintcha* No. 214 [sic] (August 19, 1976), 3.
Continued in ensuing issues to No. 241 (October 23, 1976). Excerpts from his *Relatório geral . . .* (1961).

"A acção directa nos centros urbanos," *Nô Pintcha* No. 175 (May 15, 1976), 3.
On urban armed struggle.

"O acordar do desejo de liberdade," *Nô Pintcha* No. 209 [sic] (August 5, 1976), 3.
Reflections on awareness among African intellectuals about the need to seek independence.

"'Acumular experiência e criar,'" *Nô Pintcha* No. 141 (February 26, 1976), 3.
On experience and armed resistance.

"Adaptar a luta à realidade," *Nô Pintcha* No. 173 (May 11, 1976), 3.
On relating the struggle to national reality.

"Amílcar Cabral," *Nô Pintcha* No. 163 (April 15, 1976), 3.
Suggests need to improve organization.

"O aparecimento do capitalismo," *Nô Pintcha* No. 199 (July 13, 1976), 3.
On the emergence of capitalism, primitive accumulation, and monopolies.

"'Aqueles que tentam explorar o nosso povo são criminosos,'" *Nô Pintcha* No. 121 (January 10, 1976), 3.
Condemnation of exploitation.

"Armas só nas mãos dos camaradas," *Nô Pintcha* No. 171 (May 4, 1976), 3.
Arm only the comrades.

"O capitalismo monopolista," *Nô Pintcha* No. 200 (July 15, 1976), 3.
On the rise of monopoly capitalism.

"'Combater a corrupção,'" *Nô Pintcha* No. 123 (January 15, 1976), 3.
Opposed to corruption.

"'Combater as nossas fraquezas para levantarmos as nossas forças,'" *Nô Pintcha* No. 124 (January 17, 1976), 3.
On overcoming weaknesses.

"'Combater o oportunismo na cultura,'" *Nô Pintcha* No. 139 (February 21, 1976), 3.
Opportunism in culture must be overcome.

"Como caímos nas mãos dos 'tugas,'" *Nô Pintcha* No. 148 (March 11, 1976), 3.
Historical perspective on African resistance.

"Como é que Portugal colonizou os nossos países?" *Nô Pintcha* No. 186 (June 12, 1976), 3.
On Portuguese colonialism.

"'Como os colonialistas garantiam a sua dominação,'" *Nô Pintcha* No. 208 (July 31, 1976), 3.
Despite resistance, Portuguese colonial policy ensured domination.

"Como os 'tugas'nos dividiram," *Nô Pintcha* No. 146 (March 6, 1976), 3.
An historical overview. Fragment from unidentifiable speech.

"A conquista das matérias-primas," *Nô Pintcha* No. 183 (June 8, 1976), 3.
On exploiting raw materials.

"Cooperação com as forças em Portugal que são contra o colonialismo," *Nô Pintcha* No. 187 (June 15, 1976), 3.
Anticolonial forces within Portugal are helpful in the struggle.

"As crianças devemos dar o melhor que temos," *Nô Pintcha* No. 126 (January 22, 1976), 3.
On cultural resistance and providing for children.

"De novo sobre os nossos bolseiros," *Nô Pintcha* No. 182 (June 5, 1976), 3.
Anticipating problems among students studying abroad.

"'Defender as conquistas da luta,'" *Nô Pintcha* No. 152 (March 20, 1976), 3.
On defense of victories won in struggle.

"O desenvolvimento das sociedades," *Nô Pintcha* No. 195 (July 3, 1976), 3.
Imperialism and capitalism are the consequences of the development of societies.

"'Devemos evitar a bebida ao máximo,'" *Nô Pintcha* No. 160 (April 8, 1976), 3.
Plea to avoid drinking alcohol.

"'Devemos incutir, meter no espírito de cada um, a certeza da nossa vitória,'" *Nô Pintcha* No. 131 (February 3, 1976), 3.
Speech excerpt on the certainty of victory.

"A dominação colonial na Guiné," *Nô Pintcha* No. 205 (July 27, 1976), 3.
On colonial domination and its impact on Guinea.

"É dentro da caldeira que o arroz se cose," *Nô Pintcha* No. 203 (July 22, 1976), 3.
Analysis of how a weak Portugal is bolstered by other countries and the struggle in Cape Verde is building.

"A Escola-Piloto tem que ser cada dia mais exigente," *Nô Pintcha* No. 166 (April 22, 1976), 3.
On the importance of the teacher training school.

"Eu jurei a mim mesmo dar a minha vida ao serviço do meu povo na Guiné e Cabo Verde," *Nô Pintcha* No. 125 (January 20, 1976), 3.
Excerpt from the final meeting of the Seminário de Quadros in 1969.

"'Fizemos o Congresso de Cassacá para pormos o Partido no caminho certo,'" *Nô Pintcha* No. 137 (February 17, 1976), 4.
Excerpt from intervention at the Seminário de Quadros in 1969. Also in same edition, "Esclarecemento para a reorganização do Partido, da população e das forças armadas de acordo com as decisões do nosso 1 Congresso."

"A força das armas," *Nô Pintcha* No. 174 (May 13, 1976), 3.
On the use of arms in struggle.

"A história da escravatura," *Nô Pintcha* No. 145 (March 4, 1976), 3.
Brief explanation of slavery.

"Levantar as mulheres da nossa terra," *Nô Pintcha* No. 179 (May 29, 1976), 3.
On the importance of women.

"Levantar bem alto o nome daqueles que cumprem o trabalho do partido," *Nô Pintcha* No. 159 (April 6, 1976), 3.
Capable and conscientious, hardworking people must serve the party.

"Libação íntima com o povo," *Nô Pintcha* No. 172 (May 8, 1976), 3.
On the ties between the revolutionary forces and the people.

"Uma lição da história," *Nô Pintcha* No. 209 (August 3, 1976), 4ff.
Message of August 3, 1965, on the massacre of Pidjiguiti.

"'Lutar no interesse do povo,'" *Nô Pintcha* No. 153 (March 23, 1976), 3.
Speech excerpt on the nature of the people's struggle.

"'O maior milagre da nossa terra,'" *Nô Pintcha* No. 138 (February 19, 1976), 3.
Affirms a miracle in the mobilization of men and women in the struggle to end suffering and oppression.

"Manter a nossa unidade contra tudo e contra todos." *Nô Pintcha* No. 204 (July 24, 1976), 3.
A plea for unity in the liberation struggle.

"O massacre de Pidjiguiti e o novo caminho da luta," *Nô Pintcha* No. 210 (August 7, 1976), 3.
On the Pidjiguiti massacre.

"Melhorar cada dia mais a assistência sanitária," *Nô Pintcha* No. 167 (April 24, 1976), 3.
From a speech, urging improvement in medical services in the liberated zones.

"Melhorar cada dia mais o nosso ensino," *Nô Pintcha* No. 165 (April 20, 1976), 3.

On improving education.

"Melhorar o trabalho político no seio das Forças Armadas," *Nô Pintcha* No. 157 (April 1, 1976), 3.
Ties military activities to political questions.

"Melhorar o trabalho político no seio do nosso povo," *Nô Pintcha* No. 156 (March 30, 1976), 3.
A plea for improving political work.

"Melhorar os próprios responsáveis," *Nô Pintcha* No. 170 (May 1, 1976), 3.
On strengthening defense.

"A mobilização no campo," *Nô Pintcha* No. 211 (August 10, 1976), 3.
On popular mobilization in the countryside.

"No fundo de mim mesmo," *Nô Pintcha* No. 225 (September 12, 1976), 9.
Reprinted in Moser (1981: 17) and Osório (1988: 70). Poem written in Lisbon in 1946.

"'A nossa luta é na nossa terra,'" *Nô Pintcha* No. 189 (June 19, 1976), 3.
Argues that the struggle is for liberation of Guinea and not of Portugal.

"A nossa luta insere-se na luta geral dos povos contra o imperialismo," *Nô Pintcha* No. 185 (June 10, 1976), 3.
On imperialism.

"A nossa resistência cultural," *Nô Pintcha* No. 128 (January 27, 1976), 3.
On cultural resistance.

"As nossas Forças Armadas merecem todos os elogios," *Nô Pintcha* No. 169 (April 29, 1976), 3.
Praise for the armed forces.

"OAU: uma grande esperança para os povos da Africa," *Nô Pintcha* No. 193 (June 2, 29, 1976), 3.
The OAU represents a great hope for African peoples.

"O papel de Honório Barreto na conquista da Guiné pelos 'tugas,'" *Nô Pintcha* No. 147 (March 9, 1976), 3.
Historical perspective.

"'Para ser militante do partido é preciso dar provas concretas,'" *Nô Pintcha* No. 158 (April 3, 1976), 3.
Argues that authority must be based on serious work.

"Para uma melhoria das nossas Forças Armadas," *Nô Pintcha* No. 168 (April 27, 1976), 3.
For improving the armed forces.

"'O partido de Amílcar Cabral temperado na dureza do combate libertador está hoje mais forte do que nunca," *Nô Pintcha* No. 242 (October 26, 1976), 4–6.
Speech in Havana, Cuba.

"A política de 'assimilação,'" *Nô Pintcha* No. 206 (July 29, 1976), 3.
Explanation of slavery, miscegenation, and Portuguese policy that gave citizenship to inhabitants of Cape Verde.

"Por uma Africa nova e melhor," *Nô Pintcha* No. 149 (March 13, 1976), 3.
On the armed struggle and Cape Verde.

"'A posição do partido em relação à traição do Rafael Barbosa,'" *Nô Pintcha* No. 242 (October 26, 1976), 3ff.

On the question of Rafael Barbosa; an excerpt from his intervention at the Seminário de Quadros during November 19–24, 1969. This issue and No. 243 (October 28, 1976) contain other reports on the activities of Barbosa.

"O povo em armas," *Nô Pintcha* No. 150 (March 16, 1976), 3.
On the armed struggle.

"A preparação da luta armada," *Nô Pintcha* No. 212 (August 12, 1976), 3.
On armed struggle in the colonies.

"'Preparamo-nos hoje para fazer melhor na etapa seguinte,'" *Nô Pintcha* No. 151 (March 18, 1976), 3.
Explains the current struggle of violence as the means toward a better stage in life.

"Primeiro a sociedade depois a família," *Nô Pintcha* No. 196 (July 6, 1976), 3.
On family and society.

"A propósito da mecanização da agricultura na Guiné," *Nô Pintcha* No. 225 (September 12, 1976), 10–13.
Reprint of article on the mechanization of agriculture, published in 1954.

"Quem é membro do nosso partido?" *Nô Pintcha* No. 176 (May 18, 1976), 3.
On party membership.

"'Quem para de trabalhar hoje porque trabalhou ontem muito não vale nada, nunca valeu nada,'" *Nô Pintcha* No. 122 (January 13, 1976), 3.
Appeal to work.

"A questão da língua portuguesa," *Nô Pintcha* No. 140 (February 24, 1976), 3.
Believes that the Portuguese language will serve as a means of unifying disparate peoples.

"A razão dos descobrimentos europeus," *Nô Pintcha* No. 144 (March 2, 1976), 3.
Speech excerpt on work.

"Realizar cada obra até ao fim," *Nô Pintcha* No. 136 (February 14, 1976), 3.
An appeal for disciplined work.

"'Reforçar a nossa aprendizagem,'" *Nô Pintcha* No. 137 (February 17, 1976), 3.
On education and eliminating illiteracy.

"Saber para onde é que vamos," *Nô Pintcha* No. 154 (March 25, 1976), 3.
On the liberation struggle.

"O sistema de escravatura," *Nô Pintcha* No. 197 (July 8, 1976), 3.
On slavery.

"O sistema feudal," *Nô Pintcha* No. 198 (July 10, 1976), 3.
Brief treatment of the meaning of feudalism in history.

"A situação dos quadros no começo," *Nô Pintcha* No. 180 (June 1, 1976), 3.
On militants and their privileges.

"Só é filho do nosso povo aquele que é patriota," *Nô Pintcha* No. 130 (January 31, 1976), 3.
Speech excerpt on people and patriotism.

"Sobre a criação da Assembleia Nacional Popular da Guiné," *Nô Pintcha* No. 258 (December 7, 1976), 3.
Report to the CSL on January 8, 1973.

"Solidariedade com os movimentos de libertação nacional no munudo," *Nô Pintcha* No. 214 (August 17, 1976), 3.
A plea for solidarity among all national liberation movements.

"'Somos uma parte do povo africano,'" *Nô Pintcha* No. 142 (February 28, 1976), 3.
Shows how Guineans are African people.

"As superstições são o reflexo do nível de desenvolvimento," *Nô Pintcha* No. 129 (January 29, 1976), 3.
Argues that supersititions interfere with progress.

"Tem uma grande importância a maneira como nos comportamos," *Nô Pintcha* No. 134 (February 10, 1976), 3.
Appeal to pay attention to time, culture, and action.

"Temos de combater a mentalidade dos colonialistas," *Nô Pintcha* No. 127 (January 24, 1976), 3.
Appeal to struggle against the colonialists.

"'Temos de reforçar a nossa segurança,'" *Nô Pintcha* No. 161 (April 10, 1976), 3.
A plea to improve security.

"'Temos que saber bem o que é o imperialismo,'" *Nô Pintcha* No. 194 (July 1, 1976), 3.
On imperialism.

"'Temos que trabalhar muito mais,'" *Nô Pintcha* No. 162 (April 13, 1976), 3.
Calls for more dedication.

"'Temos que trabalhar muito para aproveitarmos o tempo,'" *Nô Pintcha* No. 135 (February 12, 1976), 1.
On the need to intensify work.

"'Temos que trabalhar para fazer progredir o nosso campo, tanto no plano cultural, como noutros planos,'" *Nô Pintcha* No. 133 (February 7, 1976), 3.
Appeal to work hard in the revolutionary struggle.

"'Ter consciência do que estamos a fazer,'" *Nô Pintcha* No. 181 (June 3, 1976), 3.
Plea to be conscious of all activity.

"Tirar da nossa terra o máximo que ela pode dar," *Nô Pintcha* No. 118 (January 3, 1976), 3.
An appeal to produce from the land to the maximum.

"'Todos os filhos da nossa terra têm que ter direito a avançar a manifestar e a criar cultura,'" *Nô Pintcha* No. 132 (February 5, 1976), 3.
On the need for culture.

"Trabalhar para aumentar a produção," *Nô Pintcha* No. 164 (April 17, 1976), 3.
Harder work will lead to greater production.

"O trabalho político é fundamental na luta," *Nô Pintcha* No. 155 (March 27, 1976), 3.
On the nature of political work in the liberation struggle.

"O trabalho político no seio dos bolseiros," *Nô Pintcha* No. 178 (May 25, 1976), 3.
Continued in No. 179 (May 27, 1976), 3. On the importance of students studying abroad.

"Transformar o pensamento em acção para servir melhor o nosso partido," *Nô Pintcha* No. 120 (January 8, 1976), 3.
On the need to apply thought to action to serve the party.

"As três grandes forças anti-imperialistas," *Nô Pintcha* No. 201 (July 17, 1976), 3.
Continued in No. 202 (July 20, 1976), 3. Three forces must come together to oppose imperialism: the socialist state, the workers' movement, and the national liberation movement.

"Uma das exigências fundamentais da nossa luta: evitar os erros que ja cometemos evitar cometer novos erros," *Nô Pintcha* No. 213 (August 14, 1976), 3.
Urges awareness of errors.

"Uma terra só pode avançar com um bom sistem de transportes," *Nô Pintcha* No. 119 (January 6, 1976), 3.
On the need for a good system of transportation.

"Vamos reforçar a nossa vigilância para desmascarar e eliminar os agentes do inimigo," *Nô Pintcha* No. 243 (October 28, 1976), 3.
Message of March 1972.

"Voices of Revolution," *Guardian* 28 (March 3, 1976), 11.
Excerpt from speech.

1977

"A arma da teoria," *Nô Pintcha* No. 409 (December 10, 1977), 3, to No. 437 (February 23, 1978).
Selections from his major writing on theory and practice.

"Baseamos a nossa luta nas realidades concretas do nosso país," *O Militante* No. 2 (August 1977), 55–62, and No. 3 (September–October 1977), 55–60.
Text of the informal meeting with Afro-Americans, New York, October 20, 1972. In same issue, supplement, pp. 5–8, is an excerpt from Cabral speaking to the Seminário de Quadros, November 19–24, 1969.

"A condição para a ajuda que nós recebemos é que não deve haver nehumas condições," *O Militante* No. 5 (December 1977–January 1978), 49–59.
Excerpts of hearings in Washington, D.C., before the House Subcommittee on African Affairs, February 1970.

"Criar e desenvolver na nossa situação específica uma solução própria," *O Militante* No. 1 (July 1977), 44–46.
Speech in London, October 27, 1971.

"Esperamos após a libertação ter boas relações com Portugal e trabalhar lado a lado pela democracia, paz e progresso," *O Militante* No. 4 (November 1977), 29–34.
Calls for cooperation with Portugal after independence.

"Eu sou tudo e sou nada," *O Militante* No. 2 (August 1977), 44.
Also in Moser (1981: 20). Poem originally written in 1944, probably in Mindelo.

"Fidelidade aos princípios do partido," *Nô Pintcha* No. 372 (September 20, 1977), 3, to No. 385 (October 22, 1977).
Selection from writings on adhering to party principles.

"Identidade e dignidade no contexto da luta de libertação nacional," *Raizes* No. 4 (October–December 1977), 3–14.
Text of speech to Lincoln University, October 15, 1972.

"Independência de pensamento de acção," *Nô Pintcha* No. 348 (July 26, 1977), 3, to No. 349 (July 28, 1977), 3.
Argues for struggle for "our land" and not for that of others, although solidarity with the struggles of others must be maintained.

"As lições positivas e negativas da revolução africana," *Nô Pintcha* No. 391 (November 5, 1977), 3, to No. 407 (December 8, 1977).
On the negative and positive lessons of revolution in Africa.

"A maior festa da história de toda a humanidade," *O Militante* 4 (November 1977), 35–36.

"'A mais bela obra de Lenine,'" *Nô Pintcha* No. 247 (November 6, 1976), 3.
Text of speech in Moscow.

"Nem toda a gente é do partido," *Nô Pintcha* No. 356 (August 13, 1977), 3 to No. 368 (September 10, 1977).
Selection from writings that emphasizes that party cadres must respect each other, be humane, and work together.

"O nosso partido e a luta devem ser dirigidos pelos melhores filhos do nosso povo," *Nô Pintcha* No. 327 (May 21, 1977), 3, to No. 334 (June 16, 1977), 3.
Selections from writings on the party, its responsibilities and organization.

"Para melhoria do nosso trabalho político," *Nô Pintcha* No. 386 (October 25, 1977), 3, to No. 390 (November 3, 1977).
Selection from writings on how to improve political work.

"Partir da realidade da nossa terra," *Nô Pintcha* No. 301 (March 22, 1977), 3, to No. 326 (May 19, 1977).
Selections from writings on the liberation struggle.

"Os princípios do partido," *Nô Pintcha* No. 291 (February 26, 1977), 3, continued in No. 292 to No. 300 (March 19, 1977).
On fortifying the party.

"The Role of Culture in the Struggle for Independence," *International Journal of Politics* 7 (Winter 1977–1978), 18–43.
Speech originally delivered to UNESCO, Paris, July 3–7, 1972.

"Ter ideologia é saber o que se quer em determinadas condições próprias," *O Militante* No. 3 (September–October 1977), 55–59.
Excerpt of conversation with Afro-Americans in New York, October 20, 1972.

"Uma luz fecunda ilumina o caminho da luta: Lenine e a luta de libertação national," *O Militante* No. 1 (July 1977), 47–49.
Speech in Alma Ata, 1970, in commemoration of Lenin on the eightieth anniversary of his birth.

1978

"Amílcar Cabral e a informação," *Nô Pintcha* No. 447 Supplement (March 27, 1978), 1ff.
Excerpt from the Seminário de Quadros, November 1969.

"Cultura nacional: o carácter de classe da cultura," *Nô Pintcha* No. 439 (March 4, 1978), 3, to No. 476 (June 15, 1978), 3.
On national culture. Series of excerpts from his Syracuse paper.

"Identidade e dinidade no contexto da luta de libertação nacional," *O Militante* No. 6 (February 1978), 39–45.
Extract from speech at Syracuse University, October 15, 1972.

"Libertação nacional—um problema essencialmente político," *Nô Pintcha* No. 423 (January 19, 1978), 5.
Excerpt from his New Year's message of January 1973.

"A prática revolucionária," *Nô Pintcha* No. 477 (June 17, 1978), 3, to No. 574 (April 5, 1979).
On revolutionary practice.

"O primeiro texto filosófico de Amílcar Cabral," *Nô Pintcha* No. 511 (September 12, 1978), 4–5.
Written originally in October 26, 1944, under the pseudonym of Arlindo António, when Cabral was twenty years old. Originally published as "Hoje e amanhã" by the *Boletim* of the Casa dos Estudantes do Império 2, No. 11 (May–December 1949); published also in *Mensagem* No. 11 (May–December 1949). Cited by Andrade in Cabral, *Unity and Struggle* (1979).

"Temos que melhorar o nosso comportamento," *O Militante* No. 7 (March–April 1978), 35–42.
Extract of a speech, originally in Creole, to the meeting of the Conselho Superior da Luta do PAIGC, in 1971. Emphasis on discipline and honest behavior.

"Voices of Revolution," *Guardian* (New York) 30 (January 18, 1978), 22.
Excerpt from speech, "The Weapon of Theory," given at the First Tricontinental Conference of the Peoples of Asia, Africa, and Latin America in Havana, Cuba, in January 1966.

1979

"A liberdade com um reconquistada," *Nô Pintcha* No. 564 (February 22, 1979), 4–5.
On freedom.

"Libertação nacional e cultura," *Nô Pintcha* No. 580 (April 28, 1979), 3.
Excerpts from a speech at Syracuse University on February 20, 1970.

"As lições de Pidjiguiti," *Nô Pintcha* No. 581 (April 28, 1979), 3, continued in No. 591 (May 26, 1979).
From *Libertação* No. 21 (August 3, 1962).

"Manifesto do Movimento Anti-Colonialista (MAC)," *O Militante* No. 11 (January–February 1979), unpaged.
Reprinting of the founding document of the MAC, originally conceived in Paris in 1957 and redrafted and released on January 1, 1960, and which Cabral considered to be an important and historical document in the struggle against Portuguese colonialism.

"Realidade cultural," *Nô Pintcha* No. 575 (April 10, 1979), 3, to No. 579 (April 24, 1979).
Excerpts from Cabral's intervention at the Seminário de Quadros, November 19–24, 1969.

1980

"Como é que se diz quadrada, em Balanta?" *Nô Pintcha* No. 667 (January 17, 1960), 3, to No. 684 (March 13, 1980).

This and ensuing very brief excerpts from writings and speeches appear on the bottom quarter of the third page of each edition of this newspaper. The title of each excerpt varies from issue to issue and the original source of each is usually identified: from Seminário de Quadros, November 1969, and other speeches.

"As manobras do inimigo," *O Militante* No. 15 (January 1980), 19–21.

Excerpt of a message dated March 1972.

"Se existe um herói no meu país esse é o meu povo," *Nô Pintcha* No. 666 (January 22, 1980), 4–5.

Cabral's last interview, on Voice of Ghana in January 1973.

"A última entrevista de Amílcar Cabral: cada povo deve criar a usa própria luta," *O Militante* No. 16 (February 1980), 24–28.

Last interview of Cabral, Accra, January 8–13, 1973, to Radio Voice of Ghana. Review of successes in the liberation struggle.

1982

"A diferença entre cultura e manifestações," *Nô Pintcha* No. 878 (May 22, 1982), 5.

Brief excerpt from writings on culture.

"O direito à história," *Nô Pintcha* No. 866 Supplement (April 10, 1982), 1.

Excerpt from writings.

1983

"Cabral fala de Cassacá," *Nô Pintcha* No. 1040 (February 18, 1984), 4–5.

Excerpt from speech at the Seminário de Quadros in 1969.

"Original Writings," *Ufahamu* 11, No. 1 (1983), 7–62.

Reprinting of several writings.

"O pensamento de Amílcar Cabral vive e triunfa," *O Militante* No. 21 (January–February 1983), 11–24.

In memory of Cabral and the tenth anniversary of his death, this dossier includes a document on ideology and another on agriculture.

1986

"L'arme de la théorie: fondements et objectifs de la libération nationale et structure nationale et structure sociale," *Revue Sciences Sociales* (July–September 1986), 75–100.

On conceptualizing the armed struggle in the thought of Cabral.

1987

"25 de Maio: pensar com Cabral," *Libertação* 1 (Second Series), No. 8 (May 29, 1987), 1, 12.

Excerpt from unidentified text in which Cabral emphasizes human liberation from exploitation, national sovereignty, and African unity.

—— 3 ——

Interpretations and Review of Cabral, His Thought, and His Work

The following listing includes general works on Guinea-Bissau and Cape Verde, with reference to Cabral as described in the annotations. Books and monographs, chapters in books, pamphlets, periodical articles, and ephemera are included in a single list. The list includes relevant documents and articles from offical publications: *Alerta* (Praia), 1974; *BISE (Boletim de Informação Sócio-Económica)* (Bissau), 1985–1988; *Blufo: Orgão Mensal dos Pioneiros Abel Djassi*, 1977; *Boletim Cultural da Guiné Portuguesa* (Lisbon), 1946–1974; *Boletim Oficial* (Bissau), Nos. 1–34, 1975; *Cabo Verde: Boletim de Propaganda e Informação* (Lisbon), 1949–1952; *Chibinho* (Prais), 1979; *Estudos e Documentos ICS* (Bissau); *Libertação* (Conakry), First Series, 1960–1965, and *Libertação: Unidade e Luta* (Bissau), Second Series, 1986–1987; *O Militante* (Bissau), 1977–1983; *Nô Pintcha* (Bissau), 1975–1987; *PAIGC Actualités*, 1969–1972; *Ponto & Virgula*, 1983–1985; *Raizes* (Praia), 1977–1984; *Soronda: Revista de Estudos Guineenses* (Bissau), 1986–1987; *Unidade e Luta* (Praia), 1980. Articles and documents from *Portuguese and Colonial Bulletin* (London) and *People's Power* (London) have been included.

I have also identified important newspaper articles focused on Cabral, drawn from a systematic review of the Lisbon daily and weekly press and foreign newspaper reports based on journalists' visits to Cape Verde and Guinea-Bissau before and after the death of Cabral and independence. Most of these materials can be found in the clipping files of the Centro de Informação e Documentação Amílcar Cabral (CIDAC). Some articles can be found in *Facts and Reports* (Amsterdam), a systematic reprinting of newspaper and journal articles on liberation struggles in Africa.

I have included the more useful and relevant of some one thousand references on Cabral and Guinea-Bissau and Cape Verde that I have identified, photocopied, and placed into my personal archive over the past thirty years. Important materials published after Cabral's death in 1973 and after independence of Guinea-Bissau and Cape Verde are also included to allow for analysis of ensuing developments. I have excluded well-known works by James Duffy, R. J. Hammond, William Minter, and many others who focused on Portuguese colonialism in southern Africa but did not concentrate on Guinea-Bissau and Cape Verde.

The references below serve as a guide to the life and thought of Cabral as well as to historical developments in Guinea-Bissau and Cape Verde. The reader may wish to seek additional references in the following bibliographical sources: Blackey (1976); Bowman (1984); Chabal (1983: 241–269); Chilcote (1974 and 1987); CIDAC (1977); Lopes (1983); Marrocu (1985); McCarthy (1977); Pyhälä and Rylander (No Date). Where I indicate that the reference is cited in one of these sources, I have not personally consulted the reference and cannot verify the accuracy of the entry, but I have entered the information together with the original source.

A., B. 1973 "Amílcar Cabral—a Commentary," *Intelligence Report* (March), 1–2.

Alleges that Cabral was assassinated by alienated elements within the PAIGC and that the Portuguese PIDE should not be implicated. This report has "limited distribution" in Lisbon.

Aaby, Peter 1977 "Guinea-Bissau-en landsby i revolutionen," *Jordens Folk Etnografisk Revy* 12, No. 3, 323–331.

Cited in Chabal (1983: 258)

―――. 1978 "The State of Guinea-Bissau: African Socialism or Socialism in Africa?" Uppsala: Research Report (45), Institute of African Studies. Pp. 35.

Analyzes whether Guinea-Bissau will become another example of elitist rule termed as "African socialism" or a genuine socialist society and concludes that there is a possibility for socialism, based on ideas and practices initiated by Cabral and continued by the revolutionary leadership.

―――. 1980 "Guinea-Bissau's udviklingsstrategi mellem skylla og karybdis: verdensmarkedet og storfamilien," *Marxistisk Anthropologi* 4, 33–65.

Cited in Bowman (1984: 234).

AEISCSP [1973] *Homenagem a Amílcar Cabral*. Porto: Edição da AEISCSP. Pp. 14.

Texts and summary of Cabral's thought, organized by student activists at the University of Porto. (See CIDAC: GB Partido IV-9.)

Afrika-Komitee 1974 *Ein Volk in bewegung kann niemand aufhalten. Die Unabhängigkeit Guinea-Bissaos*. Berlin: Verlag für Politik und Ökonomie, Oberbaum Verlag. Pp. 208.

Detailed description and analysis of the liberation struggle, with attention to the PAIGC and Amílcar Cabral.

Afrique-Asie 1974 "Guerre et paix en Guiné-Bissau: naissance d'une nation," *Afrique-Asie* Spécial Guiné Bissau No. 66 (September 23–October 6), I-XLVIII.

Supplement on Guinea-Bissau and Cabral. Articles by Bruna Amico, Mário de Andrade, Aquino de Bragança, Basil Davidson, Simon Malley, Stephanie Urdang, and others.

―――. 1983 "Sur les traces d'Amílcar Cabral," *Afrique-Asie* Spécial Cap-Vert No. 286 (January 3), 37–68.

Entire issue on Cape Verde, including a piece on Cabral by Simon Malley and reports by Aristides Pereira and Pedro Pires. Also a report by Mário de Andrade on the 1983 symposium on Cabral, "A la lumière de la pensée de Cabral."

Agarychev, Anatoly 1970 *Guiledj Must Fall. Reports from the Liberated Regions of Guinea Bissau*. Budapest: World Federation of Democratic Youth. Pp. 47.

Based on firsthand observations of Cabral and the PAIGC inside liberated areas. Cited in Chabal (1983: 258) and Pyhälä and Rylander (No Date).

Agüero, Celma 1983 "Ideología y autopercepción: la idea de Cabral sobre el estado," *Estudios Asia Africa* 18 (No. 3), 452–472.

On Cabral's conception of the state.

Ahlsen, Bengt 1972 *Portugisiska Afrika. Beskrivning av ett kolonial imperium och dess sönderfall*. Stockholm: Utbildningsförlaget. Pp. 140.

On Portuguese colonialism and imperialism in Africa, including Guinea-Bissau and Cape Verde. Cited in Pyhälä and Rylander (No Date).

Ahmadi, M. 1965 "'Portuguese' Guinea in Flames," *World Marxist Review* 8 (June), 51–52.

Brief report on the liberation struggle.

Ahmed, Feroz 1973 "Amílcar Cabral: An Editorial," *Pakistan Forum* 3 (January), 3–4, plus an interview.

Alegre, Manuel 1983 "O duplo sentido cultural da obra de Amílcar Cabral." Praia. Paper presented to the Simpósio Internacional Amílcar Cabral, January 17–20. Pp. 9.
Published in Simpósio Internacional Amílcar Cabral (1984: 225–234). Emphasis on cultural themes in the thought of Cabral.

Almada, Fidélis Cabral de 1981 "Vamos reestruturar e revitalizar o nosso partido—o PAIGC," *Nô Pintcha* No. 827 (November 4), 4–5. Continued as "O assassinato de Cabral," No. 828 (November 8), 3; other parts in No. 829 (November 10, 1981), 3; No. 830 (November 12), 3.
Ties the history of the PAIGC and the changes necessary for the future to Cabral and his ideas of the past; the second part focuses on the details of the assassination of Cabral.

Almada, Maria Dulce de *See under* Duarte.

Almeyra, Guillermo M. 1978 "Le développement. Acte culturel," *CERES* 11 (January–February), 23–28.
The author, an Argentine journalist, views development as a cultural act; his essay begins with reference to Cabral's conception of culture as a transforming element. (See CIDAC: GB Cult I–5.)

Amadè, Emilio Sarzi 1964 "Guinea Portoghese: guerra di liberazione in pieno sviluppo," *L'Unitá* (May 20).
Interview with Cabral.

Amadou, Fodé 1973 "Le complot des assassins," *Afrique-Asie* (February 5).
Reprinted in *Facts and Reports* 3 (1973), document 298. Details on the assassination of Cabral.

Ameillon, B. 1964 *La Guinée, bilan d'une indépendance.* Paris: François Maspero.
Cited in Chabal (1983A: 258).

American Committee on Africa 1973 "Statement on the Assassination of Amílcar Cabral." New York, January 22. Pp. 2, mimeographed.
Extols his feats and proclaims that the armed struggle has been won.

Amílcar Cabral 1973A *Amílcar Cabral.* No Place. Pp. 26.
Texts on and by Cabral.

———. 1973B *Cuaderno Amílcar Cabral.* Madrid. Pp. 26.
Cited in Lopes (1983: 52).

———. 1973C *Paz para os povos: o assassinato de Amílcar Cabral.* Lisbon: Cadernos Textuais. Pp. 111.
On the assassination of Cabral.

———. 1981 "Amílcar Cabral," p. 384 in *Guia do terceiro mundo.* Lisbon: Tricontinental Editora.
Cited in Lopes (1983: 52).

———. 1983 "Amílcar Cabral," pp. 158–167 in *Fighters for National Liberation.* Moscow: Progress Publishers.
Biographical sketch of Cabral and his thought.

Amílcar Cabral Foundation 1984 "Statutes." [Praia, 1985]. Pp. 8, mimeo.
Contains the statutes of the foundation, formally established September 12, 1984, and a list of elected committees, led by Ana Maria Cabral, the second wife of Amílcar, who was the inspiration behind the institution. The idea for the foundation whose purposes are to collect, preserve, and study the work of Amílcar, was endorsed by the Simpósio Internacional Amílcar Cabral, Praia, January 17–20, 1983.

Andelman, David A. 1970 "Profile: Amílcar Cabral. Pragmatic Revolutionary Shows How an African Guerrilla War Can Be Successful," *Africa Report* 15 (May), 18–19.
Brief biographical note. Argues that the history, character, and success of the revolution in Guinea-Bissau were due to Cabral.

Andersson, Sven 1974 *Anförande i riksdagen den 20 mars 1974*. Stockholm: Riksdagens Protokoll.
Pamphlet on Sweden's recognition of Guinea-Bissau.

Andrade, Mário de 1973A "Amílcar Cabral: profil d'un révolutionnaire africain," *Présence Africaine* No. 86, 3–19.
A profile of Cabral.

————. 1973B *A geração de Cabral. Palestra feita na Escola-Piloto em 8 de Fevereiro de 1973*. [Conakry]: Instituto Amizade, PAIGC. Pp. 31.
Speech on Rádio Libertação commemorating Cabral. Focused on his life, thought, and action and, specifically, on their experiences as students in Lisbon before 1960. (See CIDAC: GB Biog I-7 and Partido II-8.)

————. 1974A "Amílcar Cabral et la guerre du peuple," *Afrique-Asie* No. 66 (September 28–October 6), Special Supplement, VIff.
An appreciation of Cabral.

————. 1974B *A guerra do povo na Guiné-Bissau*. Lisbon: Cadernos Livres (1), Sá da Costa Editora. Pp. 33.
"Texto de uma comunicação feita no 24 Congresso Internacional de Sociologia realizado em Argel, em Março de 1974, em nome da Delegação da República da Guiné-Bissau, sob o título 'Aspectos da sociologia da guerra do povo na Guiné-Bissau: alguns conceitos da estratégia revolucionária de Amílcar Cabral.'" Chapter 3, pp. 19–33, focuses on Cabral and his role in the struggle.

————. 1975A "A geração de Cabral." Conakry: Instituto de Amizade, 1975. Pp. 32, mimeo.
Cited in Lopes (1983: 52).

————. 1975B "Guiné-Bissau (o pensamento de Amílcar Cabral)," *O Século Ilustrado* (August 16).
Interview with Guerra Carneiro. Cited in Lopes (1983: 55).

————. 1975C "L'oeuvre de Cabral," *Afrique-Asie* No. 75 (January 27), 14–15.
Cited in Chabal (1983A: 259).

————. 1976 "Amílcar Cabral e a reafricanização dos espíritos," *Nô Pintcha* No. 225 (September 12), 8–9.
Praise for Cabral and his thought.

————. 1977A "A evolução do pensamento político de Amílcar Cabral e a proclamação do Estado de Guiné-Bissau," *O Militante* No. 3 (September–October), 45–49.
Conclusion of below (1977B). Relates Cabral's thought to the proclamation of the state of Guinea-Bissau.

————. 1977B "Três datas gloriosas," *O Militante* No. 2 (August), 42–50.
Focus on three important dates: September 12, 1924 (birth of Cabral); September 19, 1956 (founding of the PAIGC); and September 24, 1973 (proclamation of the State of Guinea-Bissau).

————. 1978A "O carácter universal do pensamento e da acção do PAIGC," *O Militante* No. 10 (September–December), 11–16.
Paper presented on the twenty-second anniversary of the founding of the PAIGC. Traces the role of Cabral and the evolution of the party.

————. 1978B "Enraizado nas massas populares o PAIGC clarificou ideias e formulou princípios válidos para a libertação de todos os povos," *Nô Pintcha* No. 514 (September 19), 2–3.
A review of Cabral and his generation, the liberation struggle, and the PAIGC on its twenty-second anniversary.

————. 1979 "Reflexões sobre a política nacional de informação," *Nô Pintcha* No. 579 Supplement (April 24), 1–14.
Speech of March 28 to the Second Seminar of Information. At the time Andrade was Comissário de Estado de Informação.

————. 1980 *Amílcar Cabral: essai de biographie politique*. Paris: Maspero. Pp. 170.
Sympathetic portrayal of Cabral and his life and struggle. Partially appears in English in Cabral (1979: xviii–xxxv).

————. 1983A "La dimension culturelle dans la stratégie de la libération nationale: identité, pouvoir culturel et démocratie." Praia: Simpósio Internacional Amílcar Cabral, January 17–20. Pp. 32, mimeo.
Published as "A dimensão cultural . . ." in Simpósio Internacional Amílcar Cabral (1984: 271–292). Examines the cultural aspects of the thought of Cabral in the national liberation struggle.

————. 1983B "A la lumière de la pensée de Cabral," *Afrique-Asie* No. 286 (January 3), 66–68.
A tribute to Cabral on the tenth anniversary of his death.

————. 1983C "Uma das leituras de Cabral é a de renovação," *O Jornal* (January 28).
Interview with António Duarte in Cape Verde, emphasizing the "humanism" and "renewal" in the political thought of Cabral.

————. 1985 "Amílcar Cabral et l'idéologie de la libération nationale," in Fondation Internationale Lelio Basso (1985).
Examines Cabral's thinking on national liberation, in particular his notion of a people's war, resistance, and the role of culture in the struggle.

————. 1986 "Uma leitura africana da *Claridade*." Mindelo: Paper sponsored by the Fundação Amílcar Cabral in commemoration of the fiftieth anniversary of the Movimento Claridoso, São Vicente, November 23, 1986. Pp. 9, mimeo.
Focusing on the importance of the cultural magazine *Claridade*, founded half a century earlier, he introduces Cabral's role in the literary movment of Cape Verde. (Located in CIDAC: CV-Lit I-8.)

Andrade, Mário de, and Maria da Luz Boal 1974 "Aspects de la sociologie de la guerre du peuple de la Guinée-Bissau: quelques concepts de la stratégie révolutionnaire d'Amílcar Cabral." Algiers: Délégation de la République de Guinée-Bissau au XXIVème Congrès International de Sociologie, PAIGC, March 25. Pp. 30.
A look at concepts of revolutionary strategy in the thought of Cabral. (See CIDAC: GB Estado I-26.)

Andrade, Mário de, and Arnaldo França 1977 "A cultura na problemática da libertação nacional e do desenvolvimento, à luz do pensamento político de Amílcar Cabral," *Raizes* No. 1 (January–April), 3–19.
Speech on Cabral's life and thought, presented to the colloquium "Cultura e Desenvolvimento" in Dakar, October 2–9, 1976.

Andreassen, Knut, and Birgitta Dahl 1971 *Guinea-Bissau. Rapport om ett land och en befrielserörelse*. Stockholm: Prisma. Pp. 216.

Report on the liberation struggle in Guinea-Bissau. Cited in Pyhälä and Rylander (No Date).

Andreini, Jean Claude, and Marie-Laure Lambert 1978 *La Guinée-Bissau, d'Amílcar Cabral à la reconstruction nationale.* Paris: L. Harmattan. Pp. 215.
Analysis of the task of nation-building in the wake of independence and the legacy left by Cabral.

Angola Comité 1971 *Guinée-Bissau en de kaap verdische eilanden.* Amsterdam. Pp. 52.
Brief review of conditions and the liberation struggle in Guinea-Bissau, including reference to Amílcar Cabral.

Antunes, José Freire 1977 "Cabo Verde na rota de Cabral," *Diário de Notícias* (July 9 and 11).
Two articles review conditions in Cape Verde since independence in 1975, with brief reference to the contributions of Cabral.

Araújo, Adriano 1962 "A situação na Guiné," *Portugal Democrático* 7 (December), 1.
A brief report on the liberation struggle under the leadership of Cabral.

Araújo, José 1978 "Vigilância e coesão para defesa das conquistas da luta," *O Militante* No. 10 (September–October), 17–19.
Evokes reference to Amílcar Cabral in a speech calling for vigilance and cohesion in common struggle.

Arruda, Marcos No Date "Pode a Europa aprender alguma coisa da Guiné-Bissau?" Bissau. Pp. 11, mimeo.
Argues that education is the key to change and evokes "the rich heritage of Amílcar Cabral" to demonstrate his point. (See CIDAC: GB Cult I-6.)

————. 1978 "Uma educação criadora para as sociedades africanas independentes," *Economia e Socialismo* No. 30 (September), 18–29.
Argues that culture, important in the liberation struggle according to Cabral, now assumes a new dimension in national reconstruction after independence.

Assembleia Nacional Popular 1973 "Proclamação do Estado da Guiné-Bissau." Boé Region, September 24, 1973. Pp. 5, mimeo.
Proclamation of the independence of Guinea-Bissau.

Azevedo, Ario Lobo de 1983 "Amílcar Cabral agrónomo." Praia: Paper presented to the Simpósio Internacional Amílcar Cabral, January 17–20. Pp. 6.
Published in *Simpósio Internacional Amílcar Cabral* (1984: 127–132) and in Cabral (1988: 11–13) as "A propósito da dimensão humana de Amílcar Cabral." A memoir by one of Cabral's teachers of agronomy.

Banazol, Luís Ataíde 1974 *Guiné-Bissau, três vezes vinte cinco.* Lisbon: Prelo Editora. Pp. 94.
One of many examples of memoirs by Portuguese military officials whose experience in Guinea-Bissau, especially the impact of Cabral and the liberation struggle, led to the coup of April 25, 1974, within Portugal.

Barbosa, Teobaldo 1984 "Uma acção que ultrapassou fronteiras," *Nô Pintcha* No. 1114 (December 6), 5.
The actions of Cabral transcend his national borders.

Barreto, Luís Soares 1988 "As preocupações ecológicas," pp. 43–44 in Cabral (1988).
A brief assessment of Cabral's interest in ecological problems and the impact of soil erosion and technology on people.

Belchior, Manuel [1973] *Os congressos do povo da Guiné.* [Lisbon]. Pp. 118.

Review of the people's congresses in liberated zones of Guinea-Bissau.

Benot, Yves 1981 *Ideologias das independências africanas*. Lisbon: Sá da Costa Editora. 2 vols.

Vol. 1, pp. 425–429, includes Cabral's "Proposta de Cabral ao problema da 'Alavanca.' O papel dos intelectuais revolucionários." Vol. 2, pp. 143–149, includes his "Proposta da CONCP e de Cabral" as well as "Análise da sociedade africana por Cabral."

———. 1983 "Amílcar Cabral et le mouvement ouvrier international." Praia: Paper presented to the Simpósio Internacional Amílcar Cabral, January 17–20.

Published as "Amílcar Cabral e o movimento operário internacional" in Simpósio Internacional Amílcar Cabral (1984: 471–492). Also as "Amílcar Cabral and the International Working Class Movement," *Latin American Perspectives* 11 (Spring 1984), 81–96. Shows that Cabral's thought related directly to the international workers' movement.

Bernardi, Paola Belpassi 1983 *Pedagogia adattata e scuola. Istituzione formative e trasmissione culturale in Guinea-Bissau*. Milan: Franco Angeli Editore, 1983. Pp. 309.

Detailed study of education and cultural change in Guinea-Bissau, with historical content dating from the liberation struggle into the independence period.

Bienen, Henry 1977 "State and Revolution: The Work of Amílcar Cabral," *Journal of Modern African Studies* 15, No. 4, 555–568.

Argues that Cabral, more than any other African leader, focused on the development of the state and the building of a revolutionary movement in a very underdeveloped society, but that he was "not a comprehensive thinker about revolutionary processes."

Biggs-Davison, John Alex 1970 *Portuguese Guinea: Nailing a Lie*. London: Congo Africa Publications. Pp. 44.

Report by a conservative member of Parliament, based on four visits to the Portuguese colony during the 1960s. Extensive reference to Cabral and insurgent forces but sympathetic to the Portuguese administration in Guinea-Bissau.

———. 1971 "The Current Situation in Portuguese Guinea," *African Affairs* 70, No. 281 (October), 385–394.

A review of the liberation struggle in an attempt to expose its weaknesses and leftist influences while supporting continued Portuguese presence in Guinea-Bissau.

Blackey, Robert 1974 "Fanon and Cabral: A Contrast in Theories of Revolution for Africa," *Journal of Modern African Studies* 12, No. 2 (June), 191–209.

Comparison of the thought of Fanon and Cabral.

———. 1976 *Modern Revolutionists: A Bibliography*. Santa Barbara, California: CLIO Books.

A general section on Africa, pp. 201–216, is followed by a section on Guinea-Bissau and Cabral.

Bockel, Alain 1976 "Amílcar Cabral: marxiste africain," *Ethiopiques* 5 (January), 35–59.

Biographical sketch of Cabral as an African Marxist.

Borisov, S. 1975 "Cape Verde Islands," *International Affairs* (Moscow) No. 8 (August), 140–142.

Brief review of developments leading to independence.

Bosgra, S. J., and A. Dijk 1969 *Angola, Mozambique, Guinée. De strijd tegen het Portugese kolonialisme*. Amsterdam: Angola Comité. Pp. 167.

An indictment of Portuguese colonialism in Africa and optimism for the liberation struggle, especially under Cabral. Cited in Pyhälä and Rylander (No Date).

Bowman, Joye L. 1984 "Guiné-Bissau ensaio historiográfico sobre as obras

publicadas desde 1960," *Revista Internacional de Estudos Africanos* 1 (January–June), 217–241.
A bibliography of sources since 1960, including many references by and about Cabral.

Bozev, Nikolai 1969 *Sto dini a partizanite na Gvineia.* Sofia: Voynizd.
Cited in McCarthy (1977: item 1577).

Bragança, Aquino de 1972 "Amílcar Cabral. Demain l'état indépendant de la Guinée-Bissau," *Afrique-Asie* No. 18 (November 27), 24–26.
Optimism on Cabral and prospects for independence.

———. 1973A "Elogie d'une bourgeoisie africaine (l'expérience révolutionnaire de Guinée-Bissau)," pp. 512–524, in *Problèmes actuels de l'unité africaine.* Algiers: SNED.
Cited in Chabal (1983: 260).

———. 1973B "La longue marche d'un révolutionnaire africain," *Afrique-Asie* No. 23 (February 5–18), 12–20.
Also as "Guiné: a longa marcha de um revolucionário africano," *Revista Expresso* No. 87 (August 31), 20–21. Details of Cabral's revolutionary experience.

———. 1973C "The Plot Against Cabral," *Southern Africa* 6 (May), 4–8.
Translated from "Le complot contre Cabral," *Afrique-Asie* No. 24 (February 19–March 4), 8–15, reprinted in *Facts and Reports* 3 (1973), Document 370. Review of events leading to the assassination of Cabral. A useful, detailed analysis.

———. 1976 *Amílcar Cabral.* Lisbon: Iniciativas Editoriais. Pp. 34.
A sympathetic portrait and appreciation of Cabral and his accomplishments.

———. 1983 "Cabral e Machel são os verdadeiros herdeiros de Marx," *O Jornal* (January 28).
Interview asserts that Cabral used Marxism "as a means of analysis." Also that "Cabral and Machel are the kind of Marxists who appeared after Lenin, in the tradition of Mao and Ho Chi-Min" and that they were not orthodox but followed in the tradition of Marx.

Bragança, Aquino de, and Immanuel Wallerstein (eds.) 1978 *Quem é o inimigo?* Lisbon: Iniciativas Editoriais. 3 vols.
Collection of documents of the liberation movements and their leaders in the struggle to free the African colonies.

Buijtenhuijs, R. 1975 "La Guinée-Bissau indépendante et l'héritage de Cabral," *Kroniek van Afrika* 2, 153–166.
Cited in Chabal (1983: 260).

Bull, Benjamin Pinto 1989 *O crioulo da Guiné-Bissau: filosofia e sabedoria.* Lisbon and Bissau: Instituto de Cultural e Lingua Portuguesa and Instituto Nacional de Estudos e Pesquisa. Pp. 352.
A study of the Creole language, its decline during the colonial period, and its importance after independence. Includes reference to Cabral and his activities in Portugal in the 1950s and in Guinea. The author is professor of Portuguese literature at the University of Dakar.

Bulletin of the Africa Institute of South Africa 1973 "Amílcar Cabral Falls to Terrorism," *Bulletin of the Africa Institute of South Africa* 9, No. 2, 76–77.
On Cabral's assassination.

Burness, Donald 1977 *Fire: Six Writers from Angola, Mozambique, and Cape Verde.* Washington, D.C.: Three Continents Press. Pp. 148.
Most of the authors herein wrote about the struggle under colonialism. The focus on Baltasar Lopes in Cape Verde examines his literary contribution and recalls his founding of *Claridade*, which emphasized themes of Cape Verde and economic conditions.

C., R. 1984 "Regresso de Amílcar," *Ponto & Virgula* No. 8 Supplement (March–April), xiii.
Brief story based on Cabral's poem, "Regresso."

Cabral, Fidelis 1964A "Guiné e Cabo Verde a caminho da libertação," *Classe Operária* No. 461 (February 16–29), 8.
Interview on the liberation struggle, published in the newspaper of the Maoist Partido Comunista do Brasil (PC do B).

————. 1964B "O PAIGC vai passar à acção armada em C. Verde," *Portugal Democrático* 9 (March), 3.
Review of the liberation struggle by a representative of the PAIGC.

Cabral, Jorge 1984 " A questão nacional o desenvolvimento e a democracia," *Nô Pintcha* No. 1070 (June 20), 4–5.
Draws upon Cabral and his conception of democracy with focus on the national question and development.

Cabral, Juvenal 1947 *Memórias e reflexões*. Praia.
Memoirs written by Amílcar's father. States that the name Amílcar was drawn from the memory of the African (Hamilcar) who challenged Rome. Cited by Andrade, in Cabral (1979), and in his biography of Cabral (Andrade, 1980).

Cabral, Luís 1969 "'Portuguese' Guinea: United Front Against Imperialism," *Tricontinental* No. 15 (November–December), 141–146.
Sees the liberation struggle in Guinea-Bissau as a link in a united front of movements.

————. 1975A "Interview with Luís Cabral," *Southern Africa* 8 (October), 12–14.
Interview with Richard Lobban on July 8, 1975.

————. 1975B "Let us Create a Life of Work and Progress," *Southern Africa* 8 (July–August), 27–29.
Excerpts from New Year's speech and optimism for Guinea-Bissau in the period of nation-building.

————. 1975C "'A nossa prioridade das prioridades e a que Amílcar definia: o homem,'" *Nô Pintcha* No. 41 (June 28), 3.
Interview in *Afrique-Asie*.

————. 1975D "'Vigilancia, camaradas! em toda a parte, vigilancia'—Luís Cabral, no 12 de setembro," *Nô Pintcha* No. 74 (September 16), 1, 5–6.
Speech in memory of Amílcar Cabral.

————. 1976A "Da formação do partido à proclamação do estado," *Nô Pintcha* No. 226 (Special Issue, September), 4–5 ff.
Memoir on the founding of the PAIGC with reference to Amílcar.

————. 1976B "'Our Line Depends on Us, on the PAIGC, on Our Militancy, and on Our Ever Deepening Identification with the Interests of Our People,'" *People's Power* No. 4 (September–October), 12–33.
Translation of a speech to the opening session of the National Assembly in Bissau, April 22, 1976. Review of problems and progress after independence.

————. 1976C "Speech Given by Luís Cabral, President of the Council of State of Guinea-Bissau and Joint General Secretary of the PAIGC, at the Amílcar Cabral Polytechnic Institute in San Nicolás de Bari, Havana Province, on October 20, 1976," *Granma Weekly Review* (October 31), 2.

————. 1976D "Voices of Revolution," *Guardian* 28 (June 23), 22.
Interview of May 16, reprinted from *Afrique-Asie*.

————. 1977 "Os elementos fracos e oportunistas serão afastados pouco a pouco das fileiras dos militantes do PAIGC," *O Militante* No. 4 (November), 7–10.
Speech prior to the Third Congress of the PAIGC.

———. 1978A *Guiné-Bissau: o estado da nação*. Bissau: Imprensa Nacional da Guiné-Bissau. Pp. 50. Also Edições Nô Pintcha, 1978. Pp. 28.
State-of-the-nation address of May 9, 1978. Reviews progress in the era of reconstruction.

———. 1978B "PAIGC cada dia mais forte," *O Militante* No. 10 (September–December), 8–10.
Speech in celebration of the twenty-second anniversary of the founding of the PAIGC, with brief reference to Amílcar Cabral.

———. 1979 *Strategy in Guinea-Bissau*. London: State Papers and Party Proceedings (Series 3, No. 3), Mozambique, Angola, and Guiné Information Centre. Pp. 30.
Text of his speech to the People's National Assembly in May 1979. A review of accomplishments in the postindependence period.

———. 1980 "Ser mais exigentes, mais rigorosos," *O Militante* No. 15 (January), 8–11.
Speech to the opening of the Fourth Ordinary Meeting of the Conselho Nacional da Guiné.

———. 1984 *Crónica da libertação*. Lisbon: O Jornal. Pp. 464.
Memoirs of the liberation struggle by the brother of Amílcar Cabral and president of Guinea-Bissau until the coup of November 1980. Dedicated to the memory of Amílcar on the tenth anniversary of his death. Written in Praia and dated October 1983.

Cabral, Luís, António Zola, and Toumara Sangare 1971 "Ways of the Anti-imperialist Struggle in Tropical Africa," *World Marxist Review* 14 (August), 83–93.
Focus on armed struggle and liberation.

Cabral, Vasco 1965 "Discours de M. Vasco Cabral . . . ," No Place: DOC/045/A, Séminaire Economique de Solidarité Afro-Asiatique, February 22–27. Pp. 9, mimeo.
Report on the PAIGC liberation struggle under the leadership of Amílcar Cabral.

———. 1967 "We Build as We Fight," *World Marxist Review* 10 (February), 30–31.
Focus on the liberation struggle in Guinea-Bissau.

———. 1973A "Guinea-Bissau: Free Territory of Africa," *Tricontinental News Service* 1 (January 1), 20–23.
Interview with Marc Cooper and Gary Cristall in which the success of the liberation struggle is emphasized.

———. 1973B "Intervention du camarade V. Cabral, membre du CEL du PAIGC, au symposium en mémoire d'Amílcar Cabral." Conakry, January, mimeo.
Cited in Chabal (1983: 261).

———. 1973C "Successful Development of the Liberation Struggle: The Foundations of Independence and Statehood Have Been Laid," *Review of International Affairs* (September 20).
Reprinted in *Facts and Reports* 3 (1973), Document 1388. Identifies Cabral as responsible for party unity and leadership.

———. 1976 "Continuar a obra do Cabral," *Nô Pintcha* No. 125 (January 20), 7.
Speech in memory of Amílcar Cabral.

———. 1977A "Amílcar Cabral: revolucionário do nosso tempo," *O Militante* No. 4 (November), 23–26.
A brief remembrance of Cabral.

———. 1977B "A nova via de desenvolvimento da Guiné-Bissau," *Economia e Socialismo* 21 (December), 49–58.
Interview with Marcos Arruda.

———. 1977C "O pensamento e a acção de Amílcar Cabral," *O Militante* No. 1 (July), 40–43.
Paper presented in Bissau in January 1977 comprising a brief review of Amílcar Cabral's ideas and writing.

———. 1980A "Cada dia mais partido," *Nô Pintcha* No. 737 (September 23), 3–6.
An overview of the PAIGC and Cabral's role on the twenty-fourth anniversary of the founding of the party.

———. 1980B *1956–1980. PAIGC. 24 anos de luta.* Bissau: Editado pela SIPC do Secretariado do CNG do PAIGC, September. Pp. 20.
Speech of September 19, 1980, on the twenty-fourth anniversay of the founding of the PAIGC. Evokes the memory and accomplishments of Cabral.

———. 1981 "Amílcar Cabral, património da humanidade progressista," *Nô Pintcha* No. 849 (January 23), 4–5.
An overview of the accomplishments of Amílcar Cabral, on the anniversary of his death.

———. 1982 "Amílcar Cabral, património da humanidade progressista," *Economia e Socialismo* Nos. 57–58 (April–July), 46–50.
Text of speech on the commemoration of the ninth anniversary of the death of Cabral.

———. 1983A "Amílcar Cabral pensador das auroras libertadores dos povos e das amanhãs que cantam!" Bissau: Secretariado do Comité Central do PAIGC. Pp. 8, mimeo.
Speech of January 20, 1983, in memory of Cabral on the tenth anniversary of his death. (See CIDAC: GB Partido II-55.)

———. 1983B *A luta é a minha primavra. Poemas.* Oeiras: Africa Editora. Pp. 109.
Poems reflecting personal and historical impressions of Guinea-Bissau. Review of ceremony presenting the book in *Nô Pintcha* No. 939 (February 2), 3.

———. 1984A "Acção do líder do Congresso de Cassacá," *Nô Pintcha* No. 1115 (December 8), 4, 7.
Paper to the Conferência Internacional sobre a Personalidade Política de Amílcar Cabral.

———. 1984B "Amílcar Cabral—património da humanidade progressista," *Nô Pintcha* No. 1113 (December 4), 4ff.
Personal portrait of Cabral.

———. 1984C "Contribuição ao estudo do pensamento de Amílcar Cabral: o Congresso de Cassacá." Bissau: Conferência Internacional sobre a Personalidade Política de Amílcar Cabral, December 3–7. Pp. 7, mimeo.
Analysis of the Congress of Cassacá, which resulted in changes in party organization and strategy.

———. 1984D "Uma teoria revolucionária para forjar o futuro," *Nô Pintcha* No. 1116 (December 16), 4.7.
Closing comments to the Conferência Internacional sobre a Personalidade de Política Amílcar Cabral.

———. 1987A "Cultura e libertação," *Diário* (September 19).
Focus on culture as an element in the liberation struggle. Message to the International Literary Symposium Against Apartheid, Brazzaville.

———. 1987B "PAIGC: 30 anos de luta," *Diário* (February 1).
A sketch of the founding of the PAIGC and Cabral's role.

Cabral, Vasco, and Mário de Andrade 1978 "Cabral estudante," *Nô Pintcha* No. 423 (January 19), 4–5.
Interview focused on student contacts with Cabral.

Cadernos Textuais [1973] *Paz para os povos. Por uma paz justa e democrática pela segurança dos povos e pela cooperação internacional o assassinato de Amílcar Cabral.* [Lisbon]: Cadernos Textuais. Pp. 111.
Documents by the MPLA, FRELIMO, and Samora Machel on the assassination of Cabral. The last part consists of a speech by Leonid Breshnev, October 26, 1973, which focuses on questions of peace.

Caio, Horácio 1970 *Portuguese Guinea, 9 Days in March: The Visit of the Minister for Overseas Provinces Tore the Veil from an International Lie.* Lisbon: Secretariado Nacional da Informacão. Pp. 43.
Propagandistic depiction of Portuguese success in its colonial war to discredit international recognition of the effort of Cabral and the PAIGC.

Camara, Sylvain 1961 "La première conférence des organisations nationalistes de la Guinée Portuguaise et des Iles du Cap-Vert," *Afrique Nouvelle* (July 19), 4.
An early report of the activities of the PAIGC. See also Congrès des Nationalistes de la Guinée Portuguaise et des Iles du Cap-Vert, "Résolution," *Afrique Nouvelle* (July 26, 1961), 4.

Campbell, Bonnie K. 1977 *Libération nationale et construction du socialisme en Afrique: Angola/Guiné-Bissau/Mozambique.* Montreal: Nouvelle Optique. Pp. 341.
An overview of progress in establishing socialism in the former Portuguese colonies, including Guinea-Bissau.

Cardoso, Bernardino 1982 "I Congresso Extraordinário do PAIGC e nova ordem económica internacional," *O Militante* (November–December), 38–43.
Speech on Guinea-Bissau and the new international economic order.

Cardoso, Carlos 1984 "Os fundamentos do conteúdo e dos objectivos da libertação nacional no pensamento de Amílcar Cabral." Bissau: Conferéncia Internacional sobre a Personalidade Política de Amílcar Cabral, December 3–7, 1984. Pp. 12, mimeo.
A look at the concept of national liberation in the thought of Cabral. (See CIDAC: GB Personalidade Político I-5.)

Cardoso, Renato 1986 *Cabo Verde: opção por uma política de paz.* Praia: Instituto Caboverdiano do Livro. Pp. 109.
Includes a section on Cabral, "A herança de Cabral: um movimento de libertação em busca da paz," pp. 19–22.

Cardoso Arias, Santiago, and Fernando G. Dávalos 1973 "Abren en la Embajada de Guinea libro de condolencia por el asesinato del líder africano Amílcar Cabral," *Granma Revista Semanal* 8, No. 6 (February 11), 7.
On the assassination of Cabral.

Carneiro, Eduardo Guerra 1975 "De como o revôlver do repôrter são palavras frágil rastilho," *Vida Mundial* No. 1882 (October 9), 25–27, and "Com os camponeses de Tombali," No. 1883 (October 16), 25–27.
Two-part report on impressions of Guinea-Bissau after the death of Cabral and independence.

————. 1982 *Estudos de economia caboverdiana.* Fila da Maia: Imprensa Nacional, Casa da Moeda. Pp. 342.
Essays on the Cape Verde economy with historical perspective prior to and after independence.

————. 1984 *Cabo Verde (aspectos sociais. Secas e fomes do século XX)*. Lisbon: Ulmeiro. Pp. 207.
Study of drought and hunger in Cape Verde and the problems faced in national reconstruction.

Carreira, António 1977 *Cabo Verde. Classes sociais, estrutura familiar, migrações*. Lisbon: Ulmeiro. Pp. 81.
Brief overview of recent information on Cape Verde, with a look at geographical information, demographic data, family structure, and migration data. Complements the sparse analysis of Cape Verde by Cabral.

Carvalho, Augusto de 1973A "Guiné: laboratório sócio-político no mundo português," *Revista Expresso* No. 6 (February 10), 13–14.

————. 1973B "A quem aproveita a morte de Amílcar Cabral?" *Expresso* No. 4 (January 27), 3ff.
Speculation on who benefits from the death of Cabral.

————. 1978 "De Amílcar Cabral a cooperação, algo foi feito e muito há a fazer," *Revista Expresso* No. 271 (January 7), 4–5R.
Cabral urged cooperation that the current regime must achieve.

————. 1980A "Um golpe com armas como resposta a um 'golpe constitucional' com nacionalismo como vaga de fundo," *Revista Expresso* No. 421 (November 22), 1–4R.
Analysis of the coup of November 14.

————. 1980B "O 14 de Novembro na Guiné-Bissau," *Expresso* No. 422 (November 29), I–IX.
On the coup of November 14, 1980.

————. 1981 "Na cena da Guiné-Bissau Rafael Barbosa pode aparecer de repente," *Revista Expresso* No. 437 (March 14), 9.
Speculates that Rafael Barbosa, one of the early leaders of the PAIGC but accused of collaboration with the Portuguese, could emerge in the political scene after the coup of November 14.

————. 1983 "Amílcar Cabral hoje," *Expresso* (January 22).
Review of the symposium in Praia in commemoration of the tenth anniversary of the death of Cabral.

————. 1984 "Nino Vieira: socialismo na Guiné-Bissau?" *Expresso* (January 7), 20–22R.
A portrayal of and interview with João Bernardino Vieira, who places Cabral into historical context. See also article in *Expresso* No. 605 (June 2, 1984), 14.

Casals, Rodolfo 1973 "El asesinato de Amílcar Cabral no extinguirá la llama liberadora que flamea en Guinea (Bissau)," *Granma Revista Semanal* 8, No. 4 (January 28), 2–3.
Argues that the liberation struggle will continue in the wake of Cabral's assassination.

Centro de Estudios de Africa y Medio Oriente (Habana) 1983 "Algunas consideraciones sobre la figura de Amílcar Cabral y su concepciónes sobre la cultura en la lucha de liberación nacional." Praia: Paper presented to the Simpósio Internacional Amílcar Cabral, January 17–20. Pp. 8.
Published in Portuguese in Simpósio Internacional Amílcar Cabral (1984: 293–302). Focus on the cultural aspects in the thought of Cabral.

Centro di Documentazione "Franz Fanon" 1964 "La guerra di liberazione nella Guinea 'portoghese,'" *Bollettino* 2 (September), 1–13.
Report on the liberation struggle, with reference to the role of Cabral.

César, Amândio 1965 *Guiné 1965: contra-ataque*. Braga: Editora Pax. Pp. 234D.

A conservative, neo-official account of the liberation struggle, with exaggeration of Portuguese success.

Chabal, Patrick 1978 "The Life and Thought of Amílcar Cabral." No Place: Social and Political Sciences Committee, May 1. Pp. 78, typescript.
A preliminary study of Cabral later superceded by his monograph (1983). (See CIDAC: GB Biog I-6.)

————. 1980 "Amílcar Cabral as Revolutionary Leader." Ph.D. Thesis, Trinity College, Cambridge University, August.
The basis for his published monograph on Cabral (1983).

————. 1981A "Guiné-Bissau, Cap-Vert: histoire et politique," *Le Mois en Afrique* Nos. 190–191 (October–November), 119–139.
Historical overview of Guinea-Bissau and Cape Verde with brief reference to Cabral's role.

————. 1981B "'Lala quêma di sucundi Ka têm.' National Liberation in Portuguese Guinea, 1956–1974," *African Affairs* 80, No. 318 (January), 75–99.
Cited in Chabal (1983: 261).

————. 1981C "The Social and Political Thought of Amílcar Cabral: A Reassessment," *Journal of Modern African Studies* 19, No. 1 (March), 31–56.
Argues that Cabral was independent in his thinking, linked ideas to reality, and maintained internal coherence and consistency over time.

————. 1983A *Amílcar Cabral: Revolutionary Leadership and People's War.* Cambridge: African Studies Series (37), Cambridge University Press. Pp. 272.
See the critical reviews of Mário de Andrade, Rob Buijtenhuijs, and Jean Copans, "A livre ouvert," *Politique Africaine* No. 19 (September 1985), 95–117; and for a generally supportive review, see Ronald H. Chilcote in *Africana Journal* 14, No. 1 (1986), 50–51.

————. 1983B "Party, State, and Socialism in Guinea-Bissau," *Canadian Journal of African Studies* 17, No. 2 (1983), 189–210.
An overview.

————. 1983C "People's War, State Formation and Revolution in Africa: A Comparative Analysis of Mozambique, Guinea-Bissau and Angola," *Journal of Commonwealth and Comparative Politics* (November), 104–125.
A comparative examination of the liberation movements and the aftermath of independence.

————. 1984 "Socialismo na Guiné-Bissau: problemas e contradições no PAIGC desde a independência," *Revista Internacional de Estudos Africanos* No. 1 (January–June), 139–165.
Argues that the present problems are largely political and based on the conflict between party and state, that the Luís Cabral regime failed to implement the party economic program and bypassed democratically elected institutions by using the party to control the state, thereby provoking a new form of class struggle. All this after Cabral and the party had provided the basis for a powerful postcolonial state.

Chaliand, Gérard 1964 *Guinée "Portugaise" et Cap Vert en lutte pour leur indépendance.* Paris: François Maspero. Pp. 50.
Journalistic and historical account of the early period of Cabral in the liberation struggle.

————. 1967A *Lutte armée en Afrique.* Paris: François Maspero. Pp. 166.
A survey and optimistic assessment of armed struggle in Africa, with particular attention to Cabral and the PAIGC. See also *Bewaffneter Kampf in Afrika.* Munich: Trikont Verlag, No Date. Pp. 177.

———. 1967B "Les maquis de Guinée 'portugaise,'" *Les Temps Modernes* No. 22, 1874–1884.
Report on the liberation struggle.

———. 1969 *Armed Struggle in Africa: With the Guerrillas in "Portuguese" Guinea.* Introduction by Basil Davidson. Translated by David Rattray and Robert Leonhardt. New York: Monthly Review Press. Pp. 142.
One of the early important journalistic accounts of Cabral and the liberation struggle. English edition of his work originally published in French (1967). For a review, see Gerald Bender in *Africa Report* 15 (May 1970), 34–36.

———. 1973A "The Legacy of Amílcar Cabral," *Ramparts* 9 (April), 17–20.
A sympathetic review of Cabral's accomplishments, written in memoriam after his assassination.

———. 1973B "The PAIGC Without Cabral: An Assessment," *Ufahamu* 3 (Winter), 87–95.
Interview, February 8, 1973, in which the accomplishments of Cabral are weighed against the future of PAIGC struggle without him.

———. 1975 "Téorico, prático, organizador, diplomata: a obra exceptional de Amílcar Cabral," *Voz di Povo* 1, No. 10 (September 12).
Cited in Chabal (1983A: 261).

———. 1976 *Mythes révolutionnaires du tiers monde.* Paris: Editions du Seuil. Pp. 266.
Book dedicated to Cabral focused on the Third World, with a section on Cabral's contributions to a theory of armed struggle, pp. 101–113. The English edition, *Revolution in the Third World: Myth and Prospects*, Hassocks, Sussex: Harvester Press, includes a chapter on "The Independence of Guinea-Bissau and the Heritage of Cabral."

———. 1977 "Amílcar Cabral (1924–1973): de la guerre de libération à la théorie de la révolution," pp. 69–99, vol. 4, in Charles-André Julien, *Les africains.* Paris: Editions Jeune Afrique.
Cited in Lopes (1983:52) as published in 1978.

———. 1977–1978 "Amílcar Cabral," *International Journal of Politics* 7 (Winter), 3–17.
A sympathetic and appreciative portrayal of Cabral and his thinking.

———. 1980 "L'Oeuvre exceptionnelle d'Amílcar Cabral," *Livres-Partisans* (April–June), 1–2.
Cited in Lopes (1983: 54).

———. 1983 "Amílcar Cabral e a contribuição do PAIGC aos movimentos de libertação nacional," in Simpósio Internacional Amílcar Cabral (1984: 463–467.
On Cabral's contribution to liberation movements.

Chaves, António Rego 1975 "Guiné-Bissau: a luta continua," *Seara Nova* No. 1555 (May), 30–32.
Despite independence the struggle will carry on.

Chilcote, Ronald H. 1967 *Portuguese Africa.* Englewood Cliffs, New Jersey: Prentice-Hall. Pp. 149.
Chapter 5, pp. 83–104, traces African resistance up to the liberation struggle of Cabral and the PAIGC.

———. 1968 "The Political Thought of Amílcar Cabral," *Journal of Modern African Studies* 6, No. 3, 373–388.
An early assessment of the thought of Cabral.

———. 1972 "Portuguese Guiné, Cape Verde, São Tomé and Príncipe," pp. 64–80

in *Emerging Nationalism in Portuguese Africa: A Bibliography of Documentary Ephemera Through 1965*. Stanford: Hoover Institution, Stanford University, 1969.
See list of documents under Amílcar Cabral, pp. 64–69; documents of the Chilcote Collection on Portuguese Africa, on microfilm at Stanford University and University of California, Riverside. See related documents published by the United Nations, pp. 93–110.

————. 1974 "Amílcar Cabral: A Bio-Bibliography of His Life and Thought, 1925–1973," *Africana Journal* 5, No. 4, 289–307.
Comprehensive bibliography and discussion of Cabral and his contributions.

————. 1983 "Cabral in the Historical Context of His Epoch: The Implications of His Theory of Class and Class Struggle." Praia: Paper presented to the Simpósio Internacional Amílcar Cabral, January 17–20.
Translated as "Cabral no contexto histórico da sua época: as implicações da sua teoria de classe e luta de classes," in *Simpósio Internacional Amílcar Cabral* (1984: 153–183). For a review of the symposium, see Chilcote, "Debating Cabral's Contributions," *Guardian* (New York) 35 (March 2, 1983), 19.

————. 1984 "The Theory and Practice of Amílcar Cabral: Revolutionary Implications for the Third World," *Latin American Perspectives* 11 (Spring), 3–14.
Introduction to a special issue on the thought of Cabral.

————. 1987 *The Portuguese Revolution of 25 April 1974: Annotated Bibliography on the Antecedents and Aftermath*. Coimbra: Centro de Documentação 25 de Abril, Universidade de Coimbra. Pp. 327.
Covers 1,116 books, monographs, and pamphlets and 1,047 periodical references to the revolutionary events of 1974 and 1975. While not focused on Cabral and the PAIGC, many of these references reflect his role and influence on the Portuguese Left and the impact of his struggle upon the Portuguese break from dictatorship and colonialism.

CIDAC 1973 "Documentos sobre o assassinato de Amílcar Cabral." Lisbon.
Dossier of documents on the assassination of Cabral in January 1973. (See CIDAC: GB Partido I-10.) Some thirty-seven periodical articles and documents on the assassination of Cabral.

————. 1977 "Contribuição para uma bibliografia sobre a Guiné-Bissau." Lisbon: Centro de Documentação e Informação.
A bibliography of materials in CIDAC and in the Junta de Investigações Científicas do Ultramar, organized into fifty-eight topics.

————. 1980A "Guiné-Bissau: golpe de estado 14 Novembro 1980. Impresna portuguesa." Lisbon.
Collection of clippings on the coup of November 14, 1980, from the Portuguese press, organized by CIDAC. (See CIDAC: GB Estado I-44.) Also available in the archives of CIDAC, "A técnica da imprensa portuguesa sobre o golpe de estado da Guiné-Bissau," [Lisbon, 1980]. Pp. 9, mimeo, which examines the political line and coverage of the Lisbon press.

————. 1980B "Relatório sobre a situação actual na Guiné-Bissau." Lisbon: CIDAC, December 1980. Pp. 18, mimeo.
Report on the coup of November 14, 1980, based on observations of a delegation from CIDAC during a visit to Guinea-Bisau and Cape Verde.

————. 1983 "Homenagem a Amílcar Cabral." Lisbon: Centro de Informação e Documentação Amílcar Cabral. Unnumbered pages, mimeo.
Collection of documents by Cabral, a list of historical details, and a sketch of his life.

————. 1983 "A relação cidade-campo desde a luta de libertação até à

independência." Praia: Paper presented by Luís Moita to the Simpósio Internacional Amílcar Cabral, January 17–20. Pp. 15.
Focus on the theme of strategy in urban and rural areas during the liberation struggle, with attention to Cabral's thinking.

CLACS 1973 "Há um mes foi assassinado Amílcar Cabral," *Vencerão* No. 6, 1–8.
Cited in Lopes (1983: 53). See also "Um ano sobre o assassinato de Amílcar Cabral," *Vencerão* No. 8, 1–12.

Claxton, S. L. 1972 "Twentieth Century Warrior Battles for Freedom," *Core Magazine* (Winter), 48–50.
Cited in McCarthy (1977: item 1692).

Coimbra, J. Henriques 1986 "Guiné-Bissau: uma oposição a abater," *Revista Expresso* (May 17), 38R.
Reviews the series of deaths under mysterious circumstances since the November 14, 1980, coup in Guinea-Bissau.

Colonialismo 1978 *Colonialismo e lutas de libertação: 7 cadernos sobre a guerra colonial.* Porto: Afrontamento. Pp. 329.
Dossier of documents on the colonial struggles in Portuguese Africa, including the role of Cabral.

Comissariado de Estado da Coordenação Económica e Plano 1980 *Introdução a geografia económica da Guiné-Bissau.* Bissau. Pp. 149.
Preface by Vasco Cabral and a note by Ladislau Dowbor. Intended to be a background text, including data of the economy and a concluding part on objectives and strategy in planning the economy. (See CIDAC: GB Ec I-5.)

Comitato Cabral No Date "Amílcar vive!" Torino. Unpaged, mimeo.
Various tributes and poems to Cabral.

Comité de Soutien à l'Angola et aux Peuples des Colonies Portugaises 1963 "Communiqué Guinée 'Portugaise': bilan des derniers six mois de lutte." Paris, July 13. Pp. 4, mimeo.
Review of the liberation struggle the first half of 1963.

———. [1964] "Bilan d'une année de lutte; janvier–décembre, 1963." Paris. Pp. 13, mimeo.
Assessment of the liberation struggle in Guinea-Bissau.

———. [1965] "Guinée 'Portugaise' et Iles du Cap-Vert, l'an deux de la guerre de Guinée, janvier–décembre, 1964." Paris. Pp. 15, mimeo.
Assessment of the armed struggle during 1964.

Comitini, Carlos. 1980 Amílcar Cabral, *a arma da teoria.* Rio de Janeiro: Codecri. Pp. 93.
A brief biography of Cabral, pp. 7–12; a testimonial, pp. 13–16; details on the assassination, pp. 17–20; and reprinting of two texts, "A arma da teoria" and "A cultura national."

Committee for Freedom in Mozambique, Angola, and Guiné [197?] *Revolution in Guinea: An African People's Struggle.* London. Pp. 45.
A positive review of the liberation struggle.

Conchiglia, Augusta 1985 "Il colpo di stato del 14 Novembre," in Fondation Internationale Lelio Basso (1985).
Shows how after the coup of 1980 the Guinean regime under Nino Vieira attempted to return to the political thought of Cabral and delves into the differences between Vieira and Aristides Pereira over the coup.

Conferência da Organizações Nacionalistas das Colónias Portuguesas 1970

Libération des Colonies Portugaises: Guinée et Cap-Vert. Algiers: Information CONCP. Pp. 159.
An overview of the history of the liberation struggle and the accomplishments of the PAIGC and Cabral.

Conferência Internacional sobre a Personalidade Política de Amílcar Cabral 1984A "Conferência International sobre a Personalidade Política de Amílcar Cabral." Bissau, December 3–7. Pp. 141, mimeo.
Proceedings of the International Conference on the Political Personality of Amílcar Cabral. Papers by Carlos Cardoso, Lúcio Lara, Lars Rudebeck, and V. G. Solodóvnikov and messages and statements by representatives of the ANC and other organizations.

————. 1984B "Declaração final," *Nô Pintcha* No. 1115 (December 8), 10.
Resolution in praise of Cabral.

Connelly, Ed 1974 "What Tasks Ahead for Guinea-B?" *Guardian* 26 (October 16), 15.
Interview with PAIGC leader Gil Fernandes on problems after the death of Cabral.

Continuar Cabral (See *Simpósio Internacional Amílcar Cabral.*)

Copans, Jean 1985 "Amílcar Cabral ou le mythe du bon passeur," *Politique Afrique* (September), 104–112.

Cornwall, Barbara 1972 *The Bush Rebels: A Personal Account of Black Revolt in Africa.* New York: Holt, Rinehart and Winston. Pp. 252.
Includes firsthand impressions of Cabral and a description of activities with the PAIGC inside liberated areas of Guinea-Bissau, pp. 118–249.

Correa Wilson, Roberto 1973 "Guinea Bissau: nación independiente," *Bohema* 65 (October 5), 78ff.
A review of the liberation struggle from its inception to independence, with reference to Amílcar Cabral.

Crespo, Vítor 1977 "Conferência de debate." Lisbon: Paper in Commemoration of the Fourth Anniversary of the Death of Amílcar Cabral, January 20, 1977. Pp. 9, typescript.
Praise for Cabral by a Portuguese naval officer and one of the leaders of the coup of April 25, 1974, which overturned the dictatorship in Portugal and led to independence of the colonies. Crespo stresses a passage in Cabral's writings on how the the liberation struggle will eliminate both Portuguese colonialism and fascism.

Crimi, Bruno 1972 "Amílcar Cabral prêt pour l'indépendance," *Jeune Afrique* No. 619 (November 18), 12–16.
Enthusiasm for the accomplishments of Cabral.

————. 1975 "La vérité sur l'assassinat d'Amílcar Cabral," *Jeune Afrique* No. 734 (January 31), 18–21.
Details on Cabral's assassination, with attention to the role of the Portuguese secret police, the PIDE. See "Les assassins de Cabral," *Jeune Afrique* No. 630 (February 3, 1973), 8–12, cited by McCarthy (1977: item 1699).

Crimi, Bruno, and Uliano Lucas 1970 *Guinea Bissau. Una rivoluzione africana.* Milan: Vangelista Editore. Pp. 207.
Firsthand report on the revolution under Cabral and the PAIGC.

Cruz, David Francisco Vera 1988 "O trabalho como pedologista. II," pp. 41–42 in Cabral (1988).
Shows Cabral's concern for conserving the fragile soils in the face of human misuse and mechanization.

Cruz, Luís Fernando Diaz Correia da 1968 "Alguns aspectos da subverção na província portuguesa da Guiné," *Ultramar* 8 (April–June), 125–147.

A Portuguese perspective on "subversion" and the resistance in Guinea. Cited in McCarthy (1977: item 1700).

Curto, José C. 1981 "Amílcar Cabral and History," *History Journal* (Concordia University) (April), 79–98.
Cited in Revista Internacional de Estudos Africanos 1 (January–June 1984), 254.

Dadoo, Yusuf M. 1973 "Amílcar Cabral—Outstanding Leader of African Liberation Movement," *African Communist* No. 53 (Second Quarter), 38–43.
Praise and review of the accomplishments of the slain Cabral by the chairman of the South African Communist party.

David, Paulo 1986 "In memoriam: Amílcar Cabral," *Diário Popular* (September 19).
A brief remembrance of Cabral and his accomplishments.

Davidson, Basil 1964 "Profile of Amílcar Cabral," *West Africa* 28 (April 18), 427; also "In 'Portuguese' Guinea," *West Africa* 28 (September), 996.
Early journalistic accounts of Cabral and the liberation struggle.

————. 1969 *The Liberation of Guiné: Aspects of an African Revolution.* Baltimore: Penguin Books. Pp. 169.
See also A libertação da Guiné: aspectos de uma revolução africana (Lisbon: Sá da Costa, 1975. Pp. 209); Révolution en Afrique: La liberation de la Guinée Portugaise (Paris: Editions du Seuil, 1969. Pp. 185); and Frihetskampen i Guinea-Bissau. Aspekter på en afrikansk revolution (Stockholm: Natur och Kultur, 1969. Pp. 190). Revised and expanded edition published as *No Fist Is Big Enough to Hide the Sky* (see 1981D). An early and important account of Cabral, the PAIGC, and the liberation struggle. Foreword by Cabral, pp. 9–15.

————. 1970 "The Liberation Struggle in Angola and 'Portuguese' Guinea," *Africa Quarterly* 10, No. 1, 25–31.
Update and review of progress in the liberation struggles.

————. 1973A "Cabral's Monument," *New Statesman* (January 26), 117–118; also in *Southern Africa* 6 (February), 9–11.
Disputes Portuguese interpretations of Cabral's assassination and reviews the accomplishments of the liberation struggle.

————. 1973B "Dans les maquis de Guinée-Bissau," *Le Monde Diplomatique* (February), 7.
A Review of Cabral's accomplishments, an assessment after his assassination.

————. 1973C "Guinea-Bissau: Building for Independence," *New World Review* 41 (Second Quarter), 36–43.
Detailed report based on a visit to liberated areas. Includes a portrayal of Cabral.

————. 1974A "Com o PAIGC na Guiné-Bissau," *O Século Ilustrado* No. 1909 (August 10), 4ff.
See similar reports in *West Africa* (April 29 and September 9, 1974) and in *Le Monde Diplomatique* (October 1974). Also *Transition* 9, No. 45 (1974), 10–21. Report on visit with the PAIGC.

————. 1974B *Growing from Grass Roots: The State of Guinea-Bissau.* London: Committee for Freedom in Mozambique, Angola, and Guiné, [1974]. Pp. 20.
Brief note on the establishment of the state in Guinea-Bissau together with documents. (See CIDAC: GB Estado I-24.)

————. 1974C "'No Fist Is Big Enough to Hide the Sky': A Report on the Further Liberation of Guiné," pp. 283–301 in Ralph Miliband and John Saville (eds.), *The Socialist Register* 1973, London: Merlin Press.

————. 1975 *Os camponeses africanos e a revolução*. Lisbon: Cadernos Livres (4), Sá da Costa. Pp. 51.

————. 1976 "The PAIGC Republics: Guinea-Bissau and Cape Verdes," *West Africa*, Five-Part Series (March 29 to April 26), 448ff.
An overview and positive assessment in the aftermath of Cabral's passing and independence.

————. 1977A "PAIGC: The Congress of Unity," *People's Power* No. 10 (October–December), 5–9.
Report on the PAIGC Third Congress of November 15–20, 1977.

————. 1977B "People's Elections in Guinea-Bissau: On the Recent Elections for Regional Councils," *People's Power* No. 6 (January–February), 27–31.
Analysis of local elections in liberated zones during 1972.

————. 1978A "Claim No Easy Victories," *People's Power* No. 12 (Autumn–Winter), 27–33.
A report on the People's National Assembly, Second Legislative Session from May 10–20, 1978, with reference to the conception of popular participation in the thought of Cabral.

————. 1978B "PAIGC Looks to Economic Independence," *Southern Africa* 9 (January–February), 6–8.
Optimism for Guinea-Bissau's economic planning and projects. Argues that the PAIGC continues to follow the principles and practices of Amílcar Cabral.

————. 1979 "Cabral on the African Revolution," *Monthly Review* 31 (July–August), 33–44.
Reprint of the introduction to Cabral's collection of speeches (1979), including personal impressions and a brief sketch of Cabral's accomplishments.

————. 1981A "Cape Verde Republic: Liberation and Progress," *People's Power* No. 17 (Spring), 5–15.
Review of progress in Cape Verde in the aftermath of independence and nation-building, with reference to the principles of Cabral.

————. 1981B *Crossroads in Africa*. London: Spokesman Press. Pp. 99.
Reviewed by Redseaman in *Guardian* (New York) 34 (February 3, 1982). Based on a lengthy interview with Antonio Bronda, the London correspondent for *L'Unita*, Davidson bases his overview on his experience with Cabral in Guinea-Bissau and argues that "democracy of mass participation" is the only means toward revolution.

————. 1981C "No Fist Is Big Enough to Hide the Sky: Building Guinea-Bissau and Cape Verde," *Race and Class* 23 (Summer), 43–64.
From his book with the same title (see 1981D).

————. 1981D *No Fist Is Big Enough to Hide the Sky: The Liberation of Guinea-Bissau and Cape Verde*. London: Zed Press. Pp. 187.
Revision and updating of his classic study (1969). Examines the period of reconstruction up to 1979.

————. 1981E *The People's Cause: A History of Guerrillas in Africa*. Harlow: Longman's. Pp. 198.
Reviewed by Cedric J. Robinson, *Race and Class* 32 (Spring), 333–337. A history of African liberation and resistance movements, including that of Cabral.

————. 1983 "On Revolutionary Nationalism: The Legacy of Cabral." Praia: Paper presented to the Simpósio Internacional Amílcar Cabral, January 17–20. Pp. 38.
Published in *Latin American Perspectives* 11 (Spring 1984), 15–42. Published as "Sobre o nacionalismo revolucionário: o legado de Cabral" in Simpósio Internacional

Amílcar Cabral (1984: 83–126). A serious look at the concept of revolution and nationalism in the thought of Cabral.

————. 1984 "On Revolutionary Nationalism: The Legacy of Amílcar Cabral," *Latin American Perspectives* 11 (Spring). (See 1983.)

————. 1986 "On Revolutionary Nationalism: The Legacy of Amílcar Cabral," *Race and Class* 27, No. 3, 21–45.

————. 1987 "A experiência de Cabo Verde tem valor para toda a Africa," *O Diário* (March 5), 12–13.
Interview with Miguel Urbano Rodrigues in which attention is given to memories of Cabral and his accomplishments in Cape Verde.

————. 1988 *As ilhas afortunadas: um estudo sobre a Africa em transformação.* No Place: Instituto Caboverdiano do Livro e do Disco. Pp. 247.
Published in English as *The Fortunate Isles: A Study in African Transformation.* Trenton: Africa World Press, 1989. Pp. 221. The recent history of Cape Verde, including the role of Cabral and his comrades (especially in chapters 4 to 6, pp. 63–126).

Dávila, Julio D. 1987 "Guinea-Bissau's Socialism: The Politics of Shelter in a Small Economy," *Third World Planning Review* 9, No. 3, 255–273.
After brief reference to Cabral, the author examines housing and urban and regional policies and the difficulty of resolving economic problems in Guinea-Bissau in the post-1974 governments.

Davis, Jennifer [1974] *The Republic of Guinea-Bissau: Triumph over Colonialism.* New York: Africa Fund. Pp. 15.
Portrayal of Guinea-Bissau, with reference to Cabral, after its proclamation of independence on September 24, 1973.

Delgado, Manuel 1977 "A herança ideológica de Cabral," *Seara Nova* No. 1576 (February), 33–37.
A critique of an article by Rob Buijtenhuijs, "A Guiné Bissau e a herança de Cabral," *Seara Nova* (November 1975), and a defense of Amílcar Cabral.

Dellah, Ahmed 1973 "L'opération Amílcar Cabral," *Révolution Afrique* (June 14).
Reprinted in *Facts and Reports* 3 (1973), Document 733. Brief report on the plot to assassinate Cabral.

Demetrescu, Jeffrey 1968 "Revolution in Southern Africa and Guinea-Bissau," *Journal of Contemporary Revolutions* No. 1, 71–79.

Dessarre, Eve 1961 "'Vous savez ce que c'est la chicotte,'" *Afrique Action* (September 20–October 6), 19–21.
A look at the early resistance in Guinea-Bissau.

Dias, H. 1966 "'Portuguese' Guinea," *Portuguese and Colonial Bulletin* 5 (December 1965–January 1966), 300.
Report on the armed struggle.

Diawara, Mohamed T. 1983 "L'Idéologie de l'unité africaine." Praia: Paper presented to the Simpósio Internacional Amílcar Cabral, January 17–20.
Published as "A ideologia de unidade africana" in Simpósio Internacional Amílcar Cabral (1984: 409–416).

Dickinson, Margaret (ed.) 1980 *When Bullets Begin to Flower: Poems of Resistance from Angola, Mozambique and Guiné.* Nairobi: East African Publishing House. Pp. 131.
Poems of resistance, including those of five poets from Guinea-Bissau and Cape Verde.

DIDILD 1979 *Os continuadores da revolução e a recordação do passado recente.* Bissau: DIDILD, 1979. Pp. 93.
Past and present in the continuing revolution of Guinea-Bissau.

Diggs, Charles C., Jr. 1973 "Statement on the Proclamation of Independence of the Republic of Guinea-Bissau," *Issues* 3 (Fall), 30–33.

Dowbor, Ladislau 1983 *Guiné-Bissau: a busca da independência económica.* São Paulo: Coleção Tudo é História (77), Editora Brasiliense. Pp. 122.
Impressions and recommendations of a Brazilian economist and consultant to the government of Guinea-Bissau. Considers Cabral a very important figure but makes clear that his stature and contributions have not made Guinea-Bissau an oasis of development and that many problems remain to be solved.

Duarte, Abílio 1963 "Aiding the Struggle in 'Portuguese' Guinea," *Revolution* 1 (August–September), 44–47.
Brief report.

————. 1965 "'Portuguese' Guinea," *Information Bulletin* (Supplement to *World Marxist Review*) No. 42 (May 13), 53–54.
Views reprinted from *L'Alger Republicain* (March 10, 1965).

————. 1974 *Sobre a situação em Cabo Verde.* Lisbon: Cadernos Livres (3), Sá da Costa Editora. Pp. 52.
Report by a PAIGC leader and Cape Verdean on the situation in Cape Verde just prior to independence.

Duarte, António 1983 "Amílcar Cabral visto pela viúva," *História* No. 61 (November), 13–23.
Brief biographical sketch based on an interview with Cabral's first wife, Maria Helena Vilhena Rodrigues.

Duarte, Manuel 1977 "Cabral e a legalidade internacional," *Raizes* No. 3 (July–September), 3–24.
Focus on Cabral's strategy in awakening international opinion to an understanding of the liberation struggle.

Duarte, Maria Dulce Almada 1978 "A problemática da utilização das línguas nacionais: lingua, nação, identidade cultural," *Raizes* Nos. 5–6 (January–June), 35–80.
An analysis of language, nation, and cultural identity as drawn from the historical experience of Cape Verde.

————. 1983 "A dimensão cultural na estrategia de libertação nacional: os fundamentos culturais da unidade Guiné-Cabo Verde." Praia: Paper presented to the Simpósio Internacional Amílcar Cabral, January 17–20. Pp. 13.
Published in Simpósio Internacional Amílcar Cabral (1984: 205–223). Also as "The Cultural Dimension in the Strategy for National Liberation: The Cultural Bases of the Unification Between Cape Verde and Guinea-Bissau," *Latin American Perspectives* 11 (Spring 1984), 55–66. Published as *Os fundamentos culturais da unidade.* Praia: Edição do DIP do PAIGV, 1983. Pp. 16. A very interesting paper on the role of culture in the liberation struggle, with direct reference to Cabral.

Duarte, Maria Dulce Almada (ed.) 1962 "Sobre a situação do povo de Cabo Verde." Conakry: Partido Africano da Independência da Guiné e Cabo Verde. June. Pp. 26, mimeo.
A detailed assessement of the situation in Cape Verde written while the armed struggle within Guinea-Bissau under Cabral was under way.

Dumont, René, and Marie-France Mottin 1980 *L'Afrique étranglée: Zambie, Tanzanie, Sénégal, Côte d'Ivoire, Guiné-Bissau, Cap-Vert.* Paris: Editions du Seuil. Pp. 264.
Comparative study, with emphasis on the problems that have impeded development in six African countries, including Guinea-Bissau and Cape Verde.

Duncan, Richard L., Rosemary Galli, and Robert Comfort 1981 "Human Resources

and Development in Guinea-Bissau and Cape Verde." [Bissau]. Pp. 153, typescript.
A report on human resources and potential training programs in rural areas; attributes "the seeds of Guiné-Bissau's development policy to Amílcar Cabral" (41).

Economist 1973 "Without Cabral," *Economist* 146 (January), 29ff.
Assessment after the assassination of Cabral.

Ehnmark, Anders, and Jean Hermasson 1973 *Exemplet Guinea-Bissau.* Stockholm: Pan/Norstedts. Pp. 99.
Journalistic report on the liberation struggle and Cabral's feats. Cited in Pyhälä and Rylander (No Date).

Emília, Georgette 1975 *Na Guiné com o PAIGC.* [Lisbon]: Edition of the Author. Pp. 93.
Narrative of travels in Guinea-Bissau after independence, with occasional reference to Cabral.

Engellan, Patrik 1974 *Guinea Bissau. En landanalys.* Stockholm: SIDA. Pp. 74.
Cited in Chabal (1983: 263) and Pyhälä and Rylander (No Date).

Eriksen, Tore Linné 1973 "Amílcar Cabral og Guinea-Bissau. En frigioringsleder og en utvikingsmodell," *Kirke og Kultur* (Oslo) 78, No. 2, 13.
Cited in Chabal (1983: 263) and Pyhälä and Rylander (No Date).

Escobar, Miguel António, Arturo Ornelas, and Hilda Varela 1976 *Quelques aspects de la réflexion sur la lutte de libération en Guinée-Bissau.* Geneva: Séminaire de M. Fawzi Mellah, IUED.

Especial Guiné-Bissau 1974 "Da Conferência de Berlim à revolução de 25 de Abril: a luta corajosa dum povo pela sua liberdade," *Diário de Notícias* (August 27).
A review of the liberation struggles, the PAIGC, and the role of Cabral. Includes a biography, "Amílcar Cabral: uma profunda fé nos destinos de Africa."

Faber, Dan André, and Jean Mettas 1962 "Guinée 'Portugaise', 1962," *Les Temps Modernes* No. 198 (November), 956–960.
A review of the armed struggle in Guinea during 1962, with a brief reference to Cabral.

Faculté de Sciences Sociales 1974 "Hommage à Amílcar Cabral," Conakry: IPGAN, Université de Conakry. Pp. 70.
Cited in Lopes (1983: 54).

Falola, Toyin 1983 "Amílcar Cabral on African Economic Development: Tentative Analysis," *Lusophone Areas Studies Journal* (July), 64–72.
Focus on Cabral's writings on economic development through quotes and brief discussion.

Federação dos Estudantes Marxistas-Leninistas, Comité Estrela Vermelha Ribeiro Santos [1973] "Honra a Amílcar Cabral. O povo da Guiné vencerá!" Pp. 2, mimeo.
Marxist-Leninist student defense of Cabral following his assassination.

Feio, Jorge 1974 "Amílcar Cabral: o preço foi a vida," *O Século* (September 10), 2ff.
Biography of Cabral and report of the author's travels in Guinea-Bissau after independence.

Felgas, Hélio 1966 *Os movimentos terroristas de Angola, Guiné, Moçambique.* Lisbon.
An exposé of "terrorist" movements, including the PAIGC under Cabral.

Felkai, Istvan 1983 "Guinée-Bissau: tenir la promesse faite aux paysans . . ." *Le Monde Diplomatique* (April).

Translated as "Guiné-Bissau quer cumprir promessa feita aos camponeses," *Diário de Notícias* (May 14, 1983). A look at conditions in Guinea-Bissau, with brief reference to the historical place of Cabral.

Fernandes, Gil 1970 "Talk with a Guinean Revolutionary," *Ufahamu* 1 (Spring), 6–21.
Impressions of the struggle by a former Guinean student in the United States and at the time the PAIGC representative in Cairo.

Ferrão, José Eduardo Mendes 1988 "A actividade no domínio da agricultura. I," pp. 17–21 in Cabral (1988).
An appraisal of Cabral's research and writing on agricultural problems in Guinea-Bissau. Emphasizes two aspects: his preoccupation with the condition of the black African and his meticulous approach to technical work.

Ferreira, Eduardo de Sousa 1973 "Amílcar Cabral: Theory of Revolution and Background to his Assassination," *Ufahamu* 3 (Winter), 49–68.
A look at theory in the thinking of Cabral and details on his death.

Ferreira, Luís Alberto 1979 "Guiné-Bissau: para onde corre a 'temperatura' de PAIGC?" *Revista Expresso* No. 324 (January 13), 8R.
Analysis of the PAIGC.

Ferreira, Manuel 1975 *No reino de Caliban. Antologia panorâmica da poesia africana de expressão portuguesa.* Lisbon: Seara Nova. 2 vols.
The first volume includes biographical sketches and poems of major writers in Cape Verde and one writer from Guinea-Bissau. While there is no direct reference to Cabral, the selections reflect life under colonial rule and the use of culture to focus on cultural roots.

Fighters for National Liberation 1983 *Fighters for National Liberation.* Moscow: Progress Publishers.
Political profiles, including one on Cabral, pp. 158–167.

Figueiredo, António de 1973 "Amílcar Cabral," *Race Today* (February), 40.
Portrait of the fallen Cabral. Cited by McCarthy (1977: item 1732).

Figueiredo, Xavier de 1982 "Guiné-Bissau: o amargo destino de Luís Cabral," *Revista Expresso* No. 480 (January 9), 23–25R.
A review of the deposition, imprisonment, and liberty of Luís Cabral, attributing some of his difficulties to his having lived "in the shadow" of Amílcar.

Fisas Armengol, Vicenç 1974 *Amílcar Cabral y la independencia de Guinea Bissau.* Barcelona: Editorial Nova Terra. Pp. 130.
On Cabral and the independence of Guinea-Bissau. Cited in Lopes (1983:54).

Fondation Internationale Lelio Basso pour le Droit et la Libération des Peuples 1985 *Luttes de libération nouveaux. Acteurs et nouveaux objectifs?* Rome: Cahier (3). Pp. 84.
Essays on Guinea-Bissau and Cabral, including a bibliography of his writings.

Forrest, Joshua B. 1987A "Guinea-Bissau Since Independence: A Decade of Domestic Power Struggles," *Journal of Modern African Studies* 25, No. 1, 95–116.
Analysis drawn from his dissertation research, with attention to the proposition that the "evolution of national-level conflicts since independence makes it clear that politics in Guinea-Bissau cannot be comprehended within the analytic frameworks of class and ideology as had been suggested by Cabral, but must instead focus on the more politically salient factors of institutional, ethnic, and leadership competition" (96).

———. 1987B "State, Peasantry, and National Power Struggles in Post-Independence Guinea-Bissau." Ph.D. Dissertation, University of Wisconsin, Madison. Pp. 792.

Argues that Cabral's emphasis on class and ideology was misplaced in the light of the postindependence period.

Fortes, Fernando 1975 "O acontecemento mais importante da história do nosso povo," *Nô Pintcha* No. 75 (September 18), 1, 6.
Interview on his participation in founding of the PAIGC, September 19, 1956. The entire issue also filled with information on this event.

Foy, Colm 1979 "Unidade e Luta: The Struggle for Unity Between Guinea-Bissau and Cape Verde," *People's Power* No. 15 (Winter), 10–27.
An examination of the notion of unity and struggle, so important to Cabral's thought, and its implications.

————. 1982 "Cape Verde: Land and Labor," *People's Power* No. 20 (Summer), 28–32.
A look at agriculture in Cape Verde. Affirms the new agrarian reform law "represents the most significant articulation to date of . . . the agrarian theories of Amílcar Cabral."

————. 1983 "Amílcar Cabral," *People's Power* No. 20 (Summer), 19–28.
A brief, sympathetic biography of Cabral and his struggle and influence up to the coup of November 14, 1980.

Freire, Paulo 1978 *Cartas à Guiné-Bissau de uma experiência em processo.* Lisbon: Temas e Problemas-Serie Documentos, Moraes, December. Pp. 193.
See *Pedagogy in Process: The Letters to Guinea-Bissau.* Translated by Carmen St. John Hunter (New York: Seabury Press and London: Writers and Readers Publishing Cooperative. Pp. 178); and *Lettres à la Guinée-Bissau sur l'alphabétisation* (Paris: François Maspero, 1978). Report and analysis of a consulting team, led by Freire, which focused attention on integrating and renovating the educational system in the early years after independence. Draws upon the thinking of Cabral on culture and the re-Africanization of people.

Frente de Libertação de Moçambique 1973 "Falar de Amílcar Cabral é falar da luta do povo." Conakry, January 31. Pp. 6, mimeo.
Praise for the assassinated Cabral.

————. 1983 "Saudação do Comité Central do Partido FRELIMO ao Simpósio Amílcar Cabral." Praia: Simpósio Internacional Amílcar Cabral, January 17–20. Pp. 4.
Message from Mozambique presented by Pascoal Macomí.

————. 1984 "Soube assumir o internacionalismo," *Nô Pintcha* No. 1115 (December 8), 8. Paper to the Conferência Internacional sobre a Personalidade Política de Amílcar Cabral, in Bissau.

Galli, Rosemary E. 1986 "Amílcar Cabral and Rural Transformation in Guinea-Bissau: Preliminary Critique," *Rural Africana* 25–26 (Spring-Fall), 55–73.
Examines the failure of the state to mobilize the peasantry as part of its rural development policy. Argues that the leadership has confused politics with control and this stems from a misunderstanding of the role of the state in economic development and from a paternalistic conception of the relationship of the state to the peasantry. Looks at writings of Cabral and concludes that he formulated an idealistic conception of the state's role and ignored the crucial power relationship of the state to the Guinean peasantry.

————. 1987 "On Peasant Productivity: The Case of Guinea-Bissau," *Development and Change* 18 (January), 69–98.
Argues that despite the support of peasants as fighters and producers during the liberation struggle, the new state has ignored the needs of peasants and has tried to appropriate as much surplus as possible from them for purposes other than rural development. Reveals contradictions in Cabral's thinking and in the policies and actions of the PAIGC.

Galli, Rosemary E., and Jocelyn Jones 1987 *Guinea-Bissau: Politics, Economics and Society*. London: Frances Pinter. Pp. 217.
A critical study, emphasizing how centralization of power in Guinea-Bissau led to political and economic problems before and after independence.

Galtung, Ingegerd 1974 "Reports from So-called Liberated Portuguese Guinea Bissau." Lisbon. Pp. 32.
Cited in Chaliand (1983: 264) and Pyhälä and Rylander (No Date).

Gamacchio, Piero 1985 "Il pensiero politico di Amílcar Cabral e i problemi della transizione in Guinea," in Fondation Internationale Lelio Basso (1985).
Examines Cabral's thinking on the question of transition in Guinea-Bissau. Argues that while Cabral developed a theory of political participation resting on four fundamental principles (criticism and self-criticism, collective action, democratic centralism, and revolutionary democracy), his directives have not been fully applied in the model of party and society that evolved after his death.

Garrison, Lloyd 1963 Series of articles on Guinea-Bissau, *New York Times* (September 8, 10, 15).

Gebauer, H. 1978 *Zu dan wirtschaftlichen und gesellschaftlichen Problemen in Guinea-Bissau*. Bochum: Amílcar Cabral Gesellschaft. Pp. 72.

Gerweck, Uta 1974 *Guinea-Bissao. Nationaler Befreiungskampf und kollektiver Fortschritt*. Nuremberg: Laetare. Pp. 138.
Cited in Chabal (1983: 264) and Pyhälä and Rylander (No Date).

Gibson, Richard 1972 "Guiné and the Cape Verde Islands," pp. 243–263 in his *African Liberation Movements: Contemporary Struggles Against White Minority Rule*. New York: Oxford University Press.
An analysis of the liberation struggle.

Gjerstad, Ole, and Chantal Sarrazin 1975 "Guinea-Bissau: Aspects of a Difficult Transition," *LSM News* 2 (Summer) 16–20.
Analysis of problems in the first year of independence.

Glisenti, Marcela 1973 "Cabral il cavour africano: una testimonianza sul leader assassinato," *Paese Sera* (January 23).
Testimonial to Cabral.

———. 1983 "Sur la dimension culturelle de Amílcar Cabral, révolutionnaire et leader politique. . . ." Praia: Paper presented to the Simpósio Internacional Amílcar Cabral, January 17–20. Pp. 8, mimeo.
Published as "Sobre a dimensão cultural . . ." in Simpósio Internacional Amílcar Cabral (1984: 261–269). A look at the cultural dimension in the thought of Cabral.

Goldfield, Steve 1973 "Amílcar Cabral and the Liberation Struggle in Portuguese Guinea," *Socialist Revolution* Nos. 13–14 (January–April), 127–130.
A review of Cabral's role in the liberation struggle.

Goulet, Denis 1977 "Political Will: The Key to Guinea-Bissau's 'Alternative Development Strategy,'" *International Development Review* 19, No. 4, 2–8.
Optimistic that political will and a dedicated leadership, imbued with the principles of Cabral, will prevail in a strategy of alternative development.

———. 1978B "Progress in Guinea-Bissau: An Assessment," *Southern Africa* 9 (January–February), 6–8.
Brief review of progress.

———. 1978A *Looking at Guinea-Bissau: A New Nation's Development Strategy*. Washington, D.C.: Occasional Paper No. 9, Overseas Development Council.

Analysis of developmental strategy and prospects.

Gouveia, Artur Soares 1988 "A intervenção no âmbito da fitossanidade do armazenamento," pp. 29–32 in Cabral (1988).
A brief review of Cabral's writings on agricultural storage.

"La guerra de Guinée 'Portugaise' 1964" 1964 *Fiches d'Information* 10 (January), 1–10.
Details on Cabral and his liberation struggle in Guinea-Bissau.

"La guerra di liberazione nella Guinea Portoghese" 1964 *Bollettino* 2 (September), 1–13.
Detailed analysis of the liberation struggle and Cabral's activities.

"Guinea-Bissau: On the Ground. Agricultural Problems in Four Regions" 1976 *People's Power* No. 1 (March–April), 5–11.
Review of agricultural problems in four regions, based on reports in the official newspaper *Nô Pintcha.*

"Guiné-Bissau, ontem, hoje e amanhã" 1981 *Tempo* (Special Issue, November 19), 1–39.
Various articles on politics, economy, planning, and education, with a special piece "O papel e o pensamento de Amílcar Cabral," pp. 4–5ff., that deals with his life and thought and the founding of the PAIGC.

Hadjor, Kofi Buenor 1974 "The Revolution in Guinea-Bissau," *Africa* No. 32 (April), 12–14.
Brief assessment of the PAIGC and its successes, including a review of Cabral's role and thinking in the liberation struggle.

Hamilton, Russell G. 1975 *Voices from an Empire: A History of Afro-Portuguese Literature.* Minneapolis: Minnesota Monographs in the Humanities (9), University of Minnesota Press.
Includes attention to African protest in the literature of the colonial period. Chapters 11–14, pp. 233–362, focus on literature in Cape Verde, with emphasis on themes expressing tensions between Africa and Europe; and chapter 15, pp. 358–362, deals with the sparse literature in Guinea-Bissau. Reference to Cabral, who wrote that the Cape Verdean literary generation in 1952 needed to seek a poetry in search of "another land within our land" (152), a step toward cultural autonomy.

Handem, Diana Lima 1986 *Nature et fonctionnement du pouvoir chez les Balanta Brassa.* Bissau: Instituto Nacional de Estudos e Pesquisa. Pp. 271.
An important monograph on the functioning of power and political structure among the Balanta Brassa peoples, with reference to their integration into the national liberation struggle and the thinking of Cabral.

Henriksen, Thomas H. 1976 "People's War in Angola, Mozambique and Guinea-Bissau," *Journal of Modern African Studies* 14, No. 3, 377–399.
An overview of the African liberation struggle.

Hill, Sylvia 1983 "Connecting the Struggles: Solidarity Work in the African-American Community." Praia: Paper presented to the Simpósio Internacional Amílcar Cabral, January 17–20. Pp. 24.
Published in *Latin American Perspective* 11 (Spring 1984), 67–80. Also as "Unindo as lutas: trabalho de solidariedade na comunidade afro-americana" in Simpósio Internacional Amílcar Cabral (1984: 547–571). Draws upon Cabral's efforts to link his African struggle to that of blacks in the United States and extends the analysis into the 1980s.

Hochet, Anne-Marie 1983 *Paysanneries en attente: Guiné-Bissau.* Dakar: Série Etudes et Recherches (79), ENDA. Pp. 174.
A focus on the peasantry in Guinea-Bissau from the revolutionary struggle into the

period of reconstruction. Shows that government spending in agriculture was inadequate to meet needs in the rural sector and the PAIGC has not followed Cabral's emphasis. Argues that peasants are capable of substantial production even without state support and contradicts Cabral's view that peasants are "culture-bound subsistence producers of relatively low productivity" (87).

Hodges, Tony 1977 "Cape Verde Under the PAIGC," *Africa Report* 22 (May–June), 43–47.
Report on progress in Cape Verde since independence.

Houser, George M. 1973 "The Birth of Guinea Bissau," *Christian Century* (October 31). Reprinted by the American Committee on Africa, New York, 1973. Pp. 2.
Optimism for the independence of Guinea-Bissau.

———. 1975 "A Report on Guinea-Bissau, Cape Verde and Angola." New York: American Committee on Africa. Part I: "Guinea Bissau," May 21, 1975, 12 pp.,mimeographed; Part II: "Cape Verde," May 23, 1975, 10 pp., mimeographed.

———. 1989 *No One Can Stop the Rain: Glimpses of Africa's Liberation Struggle*. New York: Pilgrim Press.
Includes a chapter on Cabral and his accomplishments, "Guinea-Bissau: 'Our People Are Our Mountains,'" pp. 199–218.

Houtart, François, and Geneviève Lemercinier 1983 "La culture dans une perspective marxiste. Réflexions au départ de la pensée d'Amílcar Cabral." Praia: Paper presented to the Simpósio Internacional Amílcar Cabral, January 17–20. Pp. 19, mimeo.
Published as "A cultura numa perspectiva marxista . . ." in Simpósio Internacional Amílcar Cabral (1984: 235–259). Examination of the theme of culture in the Marxist perspective of Cabral.

Hubbard, Maryinez L. 1973 "Culture and History in a Revolutionary Context: Approaches to Amílcar Cabral," *Ufahamu* 3 (Winter), 69–86.
Reprinted in *Facts and Reports* 3 (1973), Document 627. Also as "Cabrals syn på kulturen och historien," *Södra Afrika* (Lund) Nos. 21–22 (1974), 46–57. Focus on history, culture, and revolution in the thought of Cabral.

Humbaraci, Arslan, and Nicole Muchnik 1974 *Portugal's African Wars: Angola, Guinea Bissao, Mozambique*. New York: Third Press, Joseph Okpaku Publishing Company.
Scattered reference to Cabral, with general discussion of Guinea-Bissau on pp. 133–144.

Hunt, Geoffrey 1985 "Two African Aesthetics: Soyinka vs. Cabral," pp. 64–93 in Georg M. Gugelberger (ed.), *Marxism and African Literature*. London: James Curry.
Focuses on Cabral's conception of culture to expose the neocolonial view of the Nigerian novelist Wole Soyinka: "It is because Soyinka does not appreciate this essential identity that his view of culture and tradition and the 'return to the source' can diverge so widely from Cabral's" (89).

IDAC [1976] *Guinea-Bissau: Reinventing Education*. Geneva: IDAC Document (11–12). Pp. 83.
Examines education in Guinea-Bissau, with close reference to Cabral's conception of culture and education.

Ignatiev, Oleg 1966 *Pepel i plamia kafina*. Moscow: Molodia Gvardiia.
Cited in McCarthy (1977: item 1752).

———. 1970 *Goriachie tochki. Reportazhi, ocherki, issledovaniia o tom, kak s*

oruzhiem v rukakh boriutsia narody za sviou svobodu i nezavisimost.
Moscow: Molodia Gvardiia.
Cited in McCarthy (1977: item 1751).

————. 1972 *Po tropam voiny: dnevniki s trekh frontov Gvinei (Bissau).*
Moscow: Politizdat.
Cited in McCarthy (1977: item 1753). Cited in Pyhälä and Rylander (No Date) as *Along the Paths of War: Diaries from Three Fronts of Guinea (Bissau),* Moscow: Political Literature Publisher, 1972. Pp. 176.

————. 1973 "Living Up to Cabral's Revolutionary Ideal," *Daily News* (Dar es Salaam), (May 15).
A review of developments in Guinea-Bissau, following the assassination of Cabral.

————. 1975A *Amílcar Cabral, filho de Africa: narração biográfica.* Lisbon: Prelo Editora. Pp. 197.
Biography of Cabral by a Soviet journalist, based on several visits with Cabral and the PAIGC inside liberated areas.

————. 1975B *Três tiros da PIDE: quem, porquê e como, mataram Amílcar Cabral?* Lisbon: Prelo Editora. Pp. 185.
Analyzes the circumstances of the assassination of Cabral. Recounts personal impressions and experiences with Cabral.

————. 1984 "Um lutador revolucionário internacionalista," *Nô Pintcha* No. 1113 (December 4), 6.
Brief memoir of Cabral.

Information Bulletin 1972 ["USSR-Guinea and Cape Verde Islands,"] (Supplement to *World Marxist Review*) Nos. 221–222 (September 5), 80–81.
A Soviet perspective on the liberation struggle.

Intercontinental Press 1973 "Amílcar Cabral Assassinated in Conakry," *Intercontinental Press* 11 (February 5), 119.
Brief report on the assassination of Cabral.

International Journal of Politics 1977–1978 "Amílcar Cabral," *International Journal of Politics* 7, No. 4, 3–17.
Brief biographical sketch.

International Union of Students 1971 *Report of a Visit to the Liberated Areas of Guinea-Bissau.* Helsinki: International Union of Students and National Union of Finnish Students. Pp. 48.
Report based on visits in December 1970 and January 1971, including a brief interview with Cabral.

Jégou, Jacques 1983 "L'Afrique lusophone dix ans après la mort d'Amílcar Cabral," *Afrique Contemporaine* (July-September), 28–33.
With the symposium and memory of Cabral in Praia during January, the author assesses conditions in Lusophone Africa and concludes that not all goes as Cabral envisaged.

Jinadu, L. Adele 1978 "Some African Theorists of Culture and Modernization: Fanon, Cabral and Some Others," *African Studies Review* 21 (April), 121–138.
An analysis of views on culture and modernization in the colonial and postcolonial state, with emphasis on Cabral and Fanon.

Joint Publications Research Service Documents (International Development Series) 1963 "Guerrillas of Portuguese Guinea," *Translations on Africa,* 24, 314, Film D3, Reel No. 7, 20–23.

————. 1964A "Liberation Movement in Portuguese Guinea (PAIGC) Totes up

1964 Achievements," *Translations on Africa* 30, 946, No. 220, ID/28, 5–10.

———. 1964B "Portuguese Guinea's War of Liberation," *Translations on Africa*, 24, 923, Film D3, Reel No. 7, 15–19.

———. 1964C "The Struggle of 'Portuguese Guinea,'" *Translations on Africa*, 25, 775, No. 77, Film D3, Reel No. 11, 29–40.

———. 1964D "Ultimate Victory Foreseen for PAIGC," *Translations on Africa* 31, 337, No. 229, ID/28, 19–22.

Jones, Jocelyn 1979 "Agricultural Development in Guinea-Bissau," *People's Power* 14 (Summer), 39–42 and 16 (Summer 1980), 44–50. Two-part article assessing progress in agricultural development in the period following independence.

Jong, Joop de, and Rob Buijtenhuijs 1979 *Guiné-Bissau: een bevrijdingsbeweging aan de macht*. Wageningen: De Uitbuyt. Pp. 191.
Includes attention to Cabral's life and thought.

Joswiakowski, Gerhard 1962 "'Portugiesisch'—Guinea im Kampf gegen Salazar und NATO," *Deutsche Aussenpolitik* No. 8, 703–705.

Julião, Francisco 1973 "Gloria eterna al gran lutador," *Siempre* No. 1024 (February 7), 46–47.
An exiled Brazilian socialist praises Cabral and his accomplishments.

Junta de Investigações do Ultramar 1972 *Prospectiva do desenvolvimento económico e social da Guiné*. Lisbon. Pp. 239.
Officially sanctioned Portuguese study of prospects for economic and social development on the eve of independence of Guinea-Bissau; contains useful data and maps.

Kelani, Haissam 1975 "Conditions in the Cape Verde Islands on the Eve of Independence," *Objective: Justice* 7 (April–June), 3–10.
Identifies problems ahead for the new government.

Kennedy, James H. 1986 "José Carlos Schwartz: Bard of Popular Mobilization in Guinea-Bissau," *Présence Africaine* 7, Nos 1–2, 91–101.
A review of the poetry of diplomat and popular poet José Carlos, whose expression denounced officials who embraced foreign trappings rather than held firmly to the principles of Amílcar Cabral.

Kihm, Alain 1980 "La situation linguistique en Casamance et Guinée Bissau," *Cahiers d'Etudes Africaines* 20, No. 3, 369–386.
An analysis of language in the Casamance region affected by the liberation struggle.

Kofi, Tetteh A. 1981 "Prospects and Problems of the Transition from Agrarianism to Socialism: The Case of Angola, Guinea-Bissau, and Mozambique," *World Development* 9, Nos. 9–10, 851–870.
Argues that Cabral, more than any other leader, concretized African realities into the framework of Marxism-Leninism.

Kondratowicz, Andrzej 1975 *Amilkar Kabral: Syn Afriki*. Moscow: Idzdatel'stvo Politiceskoj Literatury. Pp. 158.
Cited in Revista Internacional de Estudos Africanos 1 (1984), 260.

Korneev, L. 1961 "Portuguese Guinea Will Be African," *Aziia i Afrika Segodnia (Asia and Africa Today)* No. 12 (December), 30–31ff.
Description of the growing liberation movement and its activity in Guinea-Bissau.

Kornegay, Francis A., Jr. 1973 "A Bibliographic Memorial to Amílcar Cabral," *Ufahamu* 3 (Winter), 152–160.

Bibliography of sources by and about Cabral.

Krautsova, T. I. 1973 "Amilkar Kabral (1924–1973)," *Narody Azii i Africa* 2, 76–87.
McCarthy (1977: item 1760) dates this reference to 3 (1974); also Chabal (1983: 265).

Lacina, Karel 1979 "The Role of the PAIGC in the Struggle of the African Progressive Forces for a Socialist Orientation," pp. 291–305 in *The Most Recent Tendencies in the Socialist Orientation of Various African and Arab Countries.* Prague: Academy of Social Sciences.

Lanutti, Giancarlo 1973 "Amílcar Cabral, un capo della nuova Africa: il dirigente e l'educatore," *L'Unitá* (January 1).
An appreciation of Cabral and his contributions.

Lara, Lúcio 1983 "Mensagem do camarada Lúcio Lara." Praia: Message presented to the Simpósio Internacional Amílcar Cabral, January 17–20. Pp. 5.
Message of praise for Cabral from a representative of the MPLA of Angola.

———. 1984A "Discurso do . . ." Bissau: Conferência Internacional sobre a Personalidade Política de Amílcar Cabral, December 3–7. Pp. 8, mimeo.
Personal impressions of Cabral's past activities.

———. 1984B "Era respeitado pelos próprios inimigos," *Nô Pintcha* No. 1115 (December 8), 4, 7. Paper to the Conferência Internacional sobre a Personalidade Política de Amílcar Cabral.

———. 1984C "Teve grande influência no arranque do movimento libertador," *Nô Pintcha* No. 1114 (December 6), 8.
Praise for Cabral by the Angolan leader.

Ledda, Romano 1967 Series of reports, *L'Unitá* (April 16, 17, 18, and 23).
Impressions of the liberation struggle based on travels with Cabral in liberated areas of Guinea-Bissau.

———. 1970 *Una rivoluzione africana.* Bari: De Donato Editore. Pp. 135.
A favorable report on Cabral and the liberation struggle in Guinea-Bissau.

Legum, Colin 1973 "Portugal's Ché Guevara," *Observer* (January 14).
Reprinted in *Facts and Reports* 3 (1973), Document 163.

Leitão, José 1983 "Amílcar Cabral e Honório Barreto," *Diário de Lisboa* (June 28).
Examines Cabral's historical role in contrast to the experience of Portuguese colonialism in Cape Verde and Guinea-Bissau.

Lemos, Mário Matos e 1984 "Quem assassinou Amílcar Cabral?" *Diário de Notícias* (December 12).
Details on alleged contacts between Amílcar Cabral and Spínola in 1970 and thereafter, part of a Portuguese plan to resolve their problem in Guinea-Bissau. In a recently published memoir, Luís Cabral (1984) denies that such contacts took place.

Lima, Mesquitela 1980 "Amílcar Cabral e a cultura," *Raizes* Nos. 7–16 (July 1978–December 1980), 3–7.
Brief talk in Luanda, in memory of Cabral in 1975. Emphasis on Cabral's conception of culture in the liberation struggle.

Lino, Roque 1985 "O PS e Mário Soares homenageiam Amílcar Cabral," *Nô Pintcha* No. 1123 (January 12), 5.
Interview with the Portuguese socialist and praise for Cabral.

Lipsinka, Suzanne 1970 "Deux semaines dans le maquis de la Guinée Bissau," *Africasia* 16 (May 25–June), 10–14; continued in No. 17, 28–32, and No. 18, 14–20.

Report of visit to liberated areas of Guinea-Bissau. Cited in Chabal (1983: 265).

Lobban, Richard 1973 "The Progress of the War in Guinea-Bissau," *Southern Africa* 6 (August–September), 4–6.
A firsthand look at the liberation struggle, based on a month's visit to liberated areas. See a related report in *Africa* (August 24, 1973).

———. 1974 "Guinea-Bissau: 24 September 1973 and Beyond," *Africa Today* 21 (Winter), 15–24.
An assessment of Guinea-Bissau, the PAIGC declaration of independence, and prospects for the future.

———. 1975A "The Cape Verde Islands: Colonialism on the Wane," *Southern Africa* 7 (January), 4–7.
Review of conditions on the eve of independence.

———. 1975B "The Struggle Continues: Guinea-Bissau in Perspective," *Southern Africa* 7 (September), 24–25.
A review of conditions and progress after independence.

———. 1979 *Historical Dictionary of the Republics of Guinea-Bissau and Cape Verde.* Metuchen, New Jersey: Scarecrow Press. Pp. 193.
A useful reference work of terms and events relevant to the two countries, drawn together by an observer of the liberation struggle and independence movements. Includes a biographical note on Cabral, pp. 29–30.

Lohikoski, Mikko, and Börje J. Mattsson 1971 *Report of a Visit to the Liberated Areas of Guinea-Bissau.* Helsinki: International Union of Students and National Union of Finnish Students. Pp. 48.
Optimistic report of the liberation struggle, attached as a separate leaflet, pp. 49–61.

Lopes, Carios 1977 "O intelectual e a revolução," *O Militante* No. 5 (December 1977–January 1978), 45–48.
Unsigned by "a young Guinean intellectual" (Carlos Lopes, 1987B: 288) who turns to Fanon and Cabral to set forth a conception of intellectual in the context of the liberation struggle. Suggests that the party is "the collective intellectual."

———. 1981 "L'arme de la théorie dans la pensée d'Amílcar Cabral." Geneva: Séminaire de Guy Kouassigan, IUED. Pp. 40.
Cited by Lopes (1983: 55).

———. 1982 *Etnia, estado e relações de poder na Guiné-Bissau.* Lisbon: Edições 70. Pp. 142. Also *Etnie, état et rapports de pouvoir en Guinée-Bissau,* Geneva: Institut Universitaire d'Etudes du Développement, 1982. Pp. 117.
A useful general study by a Guinean social scientist with focus on the background of the liberation struggle, ethnicity and state, and national unity, with particular attention in the third part, "Amílcar Cabral e a unidade national," pp. 101–109, to the thought and influence of Cabral.

———. 1983 "Cabral e a unidade nacional," *Nô Pintcha* No. 942 (February 12), 5.
On national unity and the notion of class-nation in the thought of Cabral.

———. 1984 "As dominantes teóricas no pensamento de Cabral," *Revista Internacional de Estudos Africanos* No. 2 (June–December), 63–92.
On the major theories in the thought of Cabral.

———. 1986 "A Guiné-Bissau a procura de um modelo social," *Soronda: Revista de Estudos Guineenses* No. 1 (January), 5–38.
Originally presented to the Seminário "Portugal, os EUCA e os Paises Africanos da Lingua Oficial Portuguesa," Lisbon, May 14–16, 1985. A sketch of historical details and moments of African resistance is related to the unity of the independence struggle under the direction of Cabral. Argues that the concept of social class is useful in

understanding relations of production and exploitation, but it must be applied to conditions in which classes develop; these conditions necessitate a national project and a model of accumulation.

————. 1987A "A articulação classe-espaço-nação na Guiné-Bissau," *Terra Solidária* No. 6 (March–April), 1–4.
Thoughts on class and nation in the search for a model for analysis of Guinea-Bissau. Searches for a historical context but makes no direct reference to Cabral.

————. 1987B *A transição histórica na Guiné-Bissau: do movimento de libertação nacional ao estado.* Bissau: Colecção "Kacu Martel" (2), Instituto Nacional de Estudos e Pesquisa. Pp. 296.
An important work that examines the transition from the liberation movement to the building of the state in Guinea-Bissau; the second part specifically looks at the "mobilizing power of Amílcar Cabral." Originally a research project, proposed as "La transformation d'un mouvement de libération nationale en état: le cas de la Guinée-Bissau," Geneva: Projet de Mémoire de Diplôme de Recherche en Etudes du Développement, Institut Universitaire d'Etudes du Développement, June 1981, 16 pp., mimeo; completed as "A transição histórica na Guinée-Bissau: do movimento de libertação nacional ao estado," Geneva: Institute Universitair d'Etudes du Développement, November 1982, 395 pp., typescript. See also the English edition, *Guinea Bissau: From Liberation Struggle to Independent Statehood,* London: Zed Press and Boulder: Westview Press, 1987. Pp. 194.

————. 1988 *Para uma leitura sociológica da Guiné-Bissau.* Bissau: Instituto Nacional de Estudos e Pesquisa. Pp. 394.
A collection of previously published articles, including part 2, chapters 4 and 5, pp. 161–195, "As dominantes teóricas no pensamento de Cabral."

Lopes, Carlos (ed.) No Date *Guinea Bissau. Alfabeto.* [Rome:] Terra & Terra Immagini. Pp. 93.
Photographs and text organized alphabetically around themes related to Guinea-Bissau. The letter "C" entitled "Cabral ka muri" (in Creole) or "Cabral is not dead."

————. 1983 "Guiné-Bissau: referências bibliográficas para a pesquisa em ciências sociais (1960–1980)," *Estudos e Documentos ICS* No. 4 (May), 1–101.
Includes some 1,100 bibliographical references topically organized, including listing of Cabral's writings and commentaries on him, pp. 48–56. An earlier version appeared in Geneva, April 1982. Pp. 103, mimeo.

Lopes, Carlos, and Olívia Mendes 1982 *Ku mininos di nô terra (ideias para a educação pré-escolar).* Bissau: Departamento de Edição/Difusão do Livro e do Disco. Pp. 140.
Documents and analysis of preschool education in Guinea-Bissau, with no particular reference to Cabral.

Lopes, Carlos, and Lars Rudebeck 1988 *The Socialist Ideal in Africa: A Debate.* Uppsala: Scandinavian Institute of African Studies. Pp. 25.
Lopes draws on the thinking of Cabral and provides observations on socialism and the transition from national liberation movements to socialist construction, which provoke a response from Rudebeck, who argues there is a link between the two and disputes the need for capitalism to solve problems in Africa and who believes that democratic goals are advanced through people's power rather than through liberal democracy.

Luke, Timothy W. 1981 "Cabral's Marxism: An African Strategy for Socialist Development," *Studies in Comparative Communism* 14 (Winter), 307–330.
Argues that Cabral gave equal emphasis to many elements of socialism and that he was preeminent as a theorist of socialist development: "the most comprehensive and serious effort to constitute an organically rooted, historically grounded and nonstatist form of Marxism yet conceived" in Africa.

Luzzato, Luicio 1983 "Communication: les mouvements de libération nationale dans le droit international et l'oeuvre de Amílcar Cabral à ce propos." Praia: Paper presented to the Simpósio Internacional Amílcar Cabral, January 17–20. Pp. 8.
Published as "Os movimentos de liberatação nacional no direito internacional . . ." in Simpósio Internacional Amílcar Cabaral (1984: 529–538). Examines Cabral's thought in the context of international law.

Lyon, Judson M. 1980 "Marxism and Ethno-Nationalism in Guinea-Bissau, 1956–1976," *Ethnic and Racial Studies* 3 (April), 156–168.
Argues that "Cabral's own 'detribalized' ethnic background, and his predilection for Marxian analysis, tended to blind him to the potentialities of ethno-nationalism in Guinea-Bissau" (157).

Machado, Pedro 1971 "Guinea: por los caminos del pueblo y la guerrilla," *OCLAE* No. 57 (September), 44–48.
Progress report on the liberation struggle in Guinea-Bissau.

Machel, Samora [1973] "Discurso de Samora Machel aguando do assassinato de A. Cabral." Conakry: Edições CEC. Pp. 7, mimeo.
In memoriam for Amílcar Cabral. (See CIDAC: GB Partido IV-8.)

————. 1973 "Falar de Amílcar Cabral e falar da luta do povo," *A Voz da Revolução* (Special Issue), 4–7.
Cited in Chabal (1983: 265).

Magubane, Bernard 1971 "Amílcar Cabral: Evolution of Revolutionary Thought," *Ufahamu* 1 (Fall), 71–87.
A sympathetic portrayal of Cabral and his thought. 1983 "Toward a Sociology of National Liberation from Colonialism: Cabral's Legacy," Praia: Paper presented to the Simpósio Internacional Amílcar Cabral, January 17–20. Published as "A sociologia da guerra popular . . ." in Simpósio Internacional Amílcar Cabral (1984: 327–361).

Malley, Simon 1983 "Sur les traces d'Amílcar Cabral," *Afrique-Asie* (January 3, 38.
A brief tribute to Cabral on the tenth anniversary of his death.

Marable, Manning 1984 "The Road Toward Effective African Liberation: The Cases of Ghana and Guinea-Bissau," pp. 190–209 in J. W. Forje (ed.), *Third World Development and the Myth of International Cooperation. London.*

Marcum, John 1973 "Guinea-Bissau: Amílcar Cabral. The Meaning of an Assassination," *Africa Report* 18 (March), 21–23.
Sympathetic overview of Cabral and his contributions in the aftermath of his assassination.

Margarido, Alfredo 1966 "Les partis politiques en Guinée portugaise, en Angola, et aux Iles du Cap Vert," *Le Mois en Afrique* No. 7 (July), 43–71.
Includes analysis of Cabral and the PAIGC, pp. 59–68.

————. 1986 "A *Claridade* e o discurso nacionalista. Com algumas considerações a respeito do seu parentesco com o nativismo." Mindelo: Paper sponsored by the Fundação Amílcar Cabral in commemoration of the fiftieth anniversary of the Movimento Claridade, São Vicente, November. Pp. 15, mimeo.
Provides a political context for the rise of the Claridade movement and the thought of Cabral. (Located in CIDAC: CV-Lit I-8.)

Maria, Victor 1962 "La Guinée 'Portugaise,'" *Voice of Africa* 2 (March), 34–35.
Brief review of the liberation struggle.

Maria, Victor Saude 1980 "Recuperar a linha de Cabral," *Nô Pintcha* No. 753 (November 24), 7.

The vice-president explains the rationale for the November 14, 1980, coup and calls for a return to the line of Amílcar Cabral.

Mário, Gérard 1967 "Guinée-Bissao, défaite du colonialisme portugais," *Voix Ouvrière* (February), 4.
Criticism of Portuguese colonial policy in Guinea-Bissau.

Marrocu, Franco 1985A "Materiali per un'analisi della questione agraria in Guinea: il censimento e altri scritti agrari di Amílcar Cabral," in Fondation Internationale Lelio Basso (1985).
Examines the agrarian question in Guinea-Bissau, based on the writings of Cabral.

──────. 1985B "Ricerca bibliografica sugli scritti, editi e inediti, di Amílcar Cabral," in Fondation Internationale Lelio Basso (1985).
A useful bibliography of Cabral's published and unpublished writings.

Martelli, George 1965 "The Portuguese in Guinea," *World Today* 21 (August), 345–351.
Claiming to be "the first foreign journalist to travel about the country without restriction," the author alleges that Cabral turned against the Portuguese when he realized he could not head a colonial government department in Bissau.

Martíchine, O.V. 1981 *Afrikanskaya revolyutsionnaya demotraktija.* Moscow: Izdatel'stvo Politicheskoy Literatury. Pp. 264.
A survey of revolution in Africa, including a focus on the experience of Cabral.

──────. 1983 "Amílcar Cabral no contexto da época contemporânea." Praia: Paper presented to the Simpósio Internacional Amílcar Cabral, January 17–20. Pp. 17, mimeo.
Published in Simpósio Internacional Amílcar Cabral (1984: 65–81). A Soviet retrospective of Cabral and his thought.

Marton, Imre 1980 "Amílcar Cabral: culture, prolétariat et processus révolutionnaire," *Aujourd' hui Afrique* 21, 34–45.
A look at Cabral's conception of culture as an arm in the resistance struggle.

──────. 1982 "Amílcar Cabral: cultura, proletariado e processo revolucionário," *Unidade e Luta* 11 (May), 25–29.
Drawn from his earlier piece (1980).

──────. 1983 "L'apport d'Amílcar Cabral à une universalisation concrète de la pensée revolutionnaire, marxiste." Praia: Paper presented to the Simpósio Internacional Amílcar Cabral, January 17–20. Pp. 34.
Published as "A contribuição de Amílcar Cabral para uma universalização concreta do pensamento revolucionário, marxista" in Simpósio Internacional Amílcar Cabral (1984: 539–546). An overview and appreciation of Cabral's thought by a Hungarian sympathizer and friend.

──────. 1984 "On the Tenth Anniversary of Amílcar Cabral's Death," *Africana Budapest* No. 1, 98–102.
An appreciation of Cabral's contributions.

Marx, Andy 1973 "Learn from Life, Learn from Our People, Learn from Books, Learn from the Experience of Others . . . ," *Liberation News Service* No. 496 (January 24), 1–2.
Optimism for the liberation of Guinea-Bissau on the eve of Cabral's assassination.

Masilela, Ntongela 1973 "Amil Cabral," *Ufahamu* 3 (Winter), 42.
A poem in memory of Cabral, by a South African living in exile.

Matatu, Godwin 1974 "Portugal, Africa and the Future," *Africa* No. 35 (July), 12–17.

Analysis of Portugal's liberation from dictatorship as a consequence of the African struggle for independence in Africa, including that of Cabral and the PAIGC.

Mateus, Alvaro 1983 "Saudação do Partido Comunista Português." Praia: Message presented to the Simpósio Internacional Amílcar Cabral, January 17–20. Pp. 5, mimeo.
Message of the PCP in commemoration of Cabral.

Mathews, Richard 1961 "Portuguese Guinea to Erupt?" *Africa Report* 6 (August), 2ff.
Sees trouble for Portuguese colonialism due to the stirrings of the liberation struggle.

Matteos, Salahudin Omawale 1973 "The Cape Verdeans and the PAIGC Struggle for National Liberation," *Ufahamu* 3 (Winter), 43–48.
A close look at the struggle for independence in Cape Verde.

McCarthy, Joseph M. 1977 *Guinea-Bissau and Cape Verde Islands: A Comprehensive Bibliography*. New York: Garland Publishing. Pp. 196.
A general bibliography, especially useful for historical, social, and cultural background, although the bibliographical citations are sometimes erroneous in detail.

McCollester, Charles 1973 "The African Revolution: Theory and Practice: The Political Thought of Amílcar Cabral," *Monthly Review* 24 (March), 10–21.
A useful analysis of theoretical directions in the thought of Cabral. Argues that "the thought of Cabral is a combination of careful, painstaking, theoretical analysis and reflection with a patient step-by-step application of theory to the practical questions of winning a war and constructing a new society" (10).

McCulloch, Jock 1981 "Amílcar Cabral: A Theory of Imperialism," *Journal of Modern African Studies* 19 (September), 503–510.
Examines Cabral's thinking on the question of imperialism.

————. 1983 *In the Twilight of Revolution*. Boston: Routledge and Kegan Paul. Pp. 159.
An essential study of Cabral and the independence movement. Critical, perceptive, and provocative.

Medeiros Ferreira, José 1983 "Aspectos do pensamento político de Amílcar Cabral (à luz duma entrevista concedida, em Londres em Outubro de 1971, à revista *Polêmica*)." Praia: Paper presented to the Simpósio Internacional Amílcar Cabral, January 17–20. Pp. 13, mimeo.
Published in Continuar Cabral (1984: 171–183). Delves into a London interview with Cabral in 1971.

Meintel, Deirdre 1984 *Race, Culture, and Portuguese Colonialism in Cabo Verde*. Syracuse: Maxwell School of Citizenship and Public Affairs, Syracuse University. Pp. 201.
A useful study of the colonial background, with a few references to Cabral that place his liberating role into context.

Melo, António, et al. 1974 *Colonialismo e lutas de libertação: 7 cadernos sobre a guerra colonial*. Porto: Afrontamento.
Reprint of seven texts on the liberation struggle in Portuguese Africa, including an analysis of Guinea-Bissau (160–205) and several excerpts from Cabral's writings.

Mendes, Francisco 1977 "Devemos caminhar com os próprios pés," *O Militante* No. 4 (November), 17–18.
Appeal to militants to carry on with the task of nation-building.

Mendes, Mário 1984 "Defensor da libertade do pensar e agir," *Nô Pintcha* No. 1114 (December 6), 6.
Warm words for Cabral and his accomplishments.

Mendonça, Luís 1982 "Direito e luta de libertação nacional," *Economia e Socialismo* No. 56 (January), 23–34.
Associates the reconstruction of Cape Verde closely with the thought of Cabral.

Mendy, Justin 1967 "Une lutte que finit et que commence. I. L'arme à la main. II. La seconde guerre. III. Réflexions sur la lutte," *Afrique Nouvelle*, Nos. 1025, 1026, 1027 (March 30–April 19), 8–9ff.; 12–13; 8–9.
Series of reports on the armed struggle in Guinea-Bissau.

Mettas, Jean, and Dan Sperber 1973 "Assassinat d'un combattant," *Le Nouvel Observateur* 89 (February 4), 47.
Commemoration of Cabral as assassinated hero.

MLSTP 1983 "Mensagem do representante do MLSTP no Simpósio Internacional Amílcar Cabral." Praia: Simpósio Internacional Amílcar Cabral, January 17–20. Pp. 5.
Message from the MLSTP in São Tomé and Príncipe in commemoration of Cabral.

Moita, Luís 1976 "A Guiné-Bissau em fase de reconstrução nacional," *Economia e Socialismo* 3 (June), 4–23.
A close look at reconstruction in Guinea-Bissau after Cabral.

————. 1978 "Notas sobre os congressos do PAIGC e do MPLA," *Economia e Socialismo* 23 (February), 41–49.
Impressions of party congresses during 1977 and the search for a developmental model in the aftermath of Cabral and independence.

————. 1979 *Os congressos da FRELIMO, do PAIGC e do MPLA: uma análise comparativa.* Lisbon: Colecção Africa em Luta, Nova Serie (1), Ulmeiro. Pp. 80.
Comparative analysis of the party congresses of the FRELIMO, PAIGÇ, and the MPLA.

————. 1983 "A relação cidade-campo desde a luta de libertação até à independência." Praia: Paper presented to the Simpósio Internacional Amílcar Cabral, January 17–20. Pp. 14, mimeo.
Published in Simpósio Internacional Amílcar Cabral (1984: 305–325). Focuses on the distinctions between city and countryside in Cabral and in the postindependence period.

Molina, Gabriel 1967 "Guinea Bissau Guerrilla Jungle," *Tricontinental* No. 3 (November–December), 54–64.
A report on the liberation struggle.

————. 1973 "Memories of Amílcar,' *Granma Weekly Review* (January 28).
Sympathetic portrait of Cabral by a Havana journalist.

Moolman, J.H. 1974 "Portuguese Africa: The Untenable War," *Africa Institute Bulletin* 12, No. 6, 243–260.
Includes analysis of the struggle under Cabral.

Mondlane Stichting, Eduardo 1981 *Staatsgreep in Guiné-Bissau.* Amsterdam: Edition of the Author. Pp. 79.
Focus on the coup of November 1980 that deposed Luís Cabral.

Monteiro Júnior, Júlio 1974 *Os rebelados da Ilha Santiago de Cabo Verde.* [Praia?:]Centro de Estudos de Cabo Verde.
Cited by Davidson as a study of "dissident peasants who defied authority in the 1960s and were persecuted for doing so"; they were a Christian sect who referred to Cabral as "Amílcar Cristo" (Davidson, 1988: 209).

Moran, Emílio F. 1982 "The Evolution of Cape Verde's Agriculture," *African Economic History* No. 11, 65–86.
Examines agriculture in its historical context and concludes that Cape Verde is "a classic

case of a social system adjusted less to its physical environment than to its political environment." Useful background piece with no direct reference to Cabral.

Morgado, Michael S. 1974 "Amílcar Cabral's Theory of Cultural Revolution," *Black Images* 3 (Summer), 3–16.
Focus on Cabral's concept of culture in the liberation struggle.

Moser, Gerald 1978 "The Poet Amílcar Cabral," *Research in African Literatures* 9 (Fall), 176–197.
Review of the work of Cabral as poet.

————. 1981 "O poeta Amílcar Cabral," *Raizes* Nos. 17–20 (January–December), 3–20.
Focus on the poetry of Cabral. Includes eleven of his poems.

Mota, A. Teixeira da 1954 *Guiné Portuguesa*. Lisbon: Agência Geral do Ultramar. 2 vols.
Detailed account of the geography, peoples, and history of Guinea during the colonial period.

Mozambique Revolution 1973 "Homage to Amílcar Cabral," *Mozambique Revolution* No. 54 (January–March), 1–10.
Five documents in memory of Cabral: an editorial comment, "A Loss and a Lesson"; a statement from the FRELIMO Central Committee, "This Murder Will Be Avenged"; a message from Samora Machel; a message at a symposium on January 31, 1973, Conakry; and "The Conspiracy" from FRELIMO's internal bulletin.

M'Pangulula, Malandila B. [1973] "The Rise of Cabral. PAIGC and the Struggle for a Free Guinea," No Place. Pp. 5, mimeo.
Assessment of Cabral in the wake of his assassination. Argues that his philosophy was Cabralism and that "while he was the man to lead Guinea-Bissau to independence, he was not at all the man to govern it, once independence was won" because the question of Cape Verde had to be solved.

Mujer 1983 "Simpósio Amílcar Cabral," *Mujer* No. 10 (December), 1–20.
Entire issue in celebration of the tenth anniversary of Cabral's death. Includes brief note "Amílcar Cabral: o homem e a sua obra" and an interview with four women from Cape Verde, "Como conhecemos e vimos Cabral."

Murteira, Mário 1978 "O desenvolvimento dos menos desenvolvidos: reflexões sobre as economias da Guiné e Cabo Verde," *Economia e Socialismo* No. 30 (September), 3–17.
Begins with the difficult proposition before Cabral in the 1950s of how to win independence and suggests that the task of economic development facing the leaders of the PAIGC will be equally difficult, given the backwardness of the independent Guinea-Bissau and Cape Verde.

Neves, Carlos Manuel Beata 1979 "Uma inteligência e uma capacidade de direcção invulgares," *Nô Pintcha* No. 551 (January 20), 4–5.
Memoir by one of the instructors at the Instituto Superior da Agronomia where Cabral studied twenty-five years earlier.

Niedergang, Marcel 1973 "Un diplomate combattant," *Le Monde* (January 24).
Cited in Lopes (1983: 52).

Nikanorov, Anatoli 1975 *Amílcar Cabral*. Lisbon: (Combatentes do Povo), Edições Sociais. Pp. 45.
Originally published as *Amílcar Cabral*, Moscow, 1973. Pp. 39. Discussion of the assassination of Cabral and some biographical data. Includes four of Cabral's speeches in Moscow, from 1967 to 1972.

Nô Pintcha 1975A "12 de Setembro de 1924–12 de Setembro de 1975: Gloria

eterna a Amílcar Cabral," *Nô Pintcha* No. 73 (September 12), 1–16.
Entire issue dedicated to commemoration of the fifty-first anniversary of the birth of Amílcar Cabral. Includes messages in his memory and two texts about Cabral, written in 1974 by Aristides Pereira.

————. 1975B "O 2 aniversário da proclamação do Estado da Guiné-Bissau," *Nô Pintcha* No. 77 (September 24), 1–12.
Entire issue on second anniversary of independence. Includes proclamation of September 23, 1973, the constitution, and a text by Amílcar Cabral, "Sobre a criação da Assembleia Nacional Popular da Guiné."

————. 1976 "Lembranças de Iva Evora, mãe de Amílcar Cabral," *Nô Pintcha* 2, No. 225 (September 12).
Reminiscences of the mother of Amílcar.

————. 1977A "12 de setembro: dia da nacionalidade: o perfil de um guerrilheiro, cada bala um acto político," *Nô Pintcha* No. 369 Supplement (September 12), 1–4.
Details on Cabral and his life in memory of his birth, including excerpts from his speech in Havana during January 1966.

————. 1977B "Morreu a mão de Amílcar Cabral," *Nô Pintcha* No. 356 (August 13), 1.
Note on the death of Iva Pinhel Evora, born December 31, 1893, in Praia, daughter of António Pinhel Evora and Maximiana Monteiro.

————. 1981 "Os ensinamentos da história," *Nô Pintcha* No. 762 (January 17), 4–5.
Frequent reference to the thought of Cabral.

————. 1982 "Amílcar Cabral combatente da causa humana," *Nô Pintcha* No. 899 (September 11), 8.
Note in commemoration of Cabral's fifty-eight birthday.

————. 1983 "10 aniversário do assassinato de Cabral: homenagem aos nossos heróis nacionais," *Nô Pintcha* No. 935 (January 20), 8.
Homage to Cabral on the tenth anniversary of his assassination.

————. 1984 "Estratega e político de envergadura," *Nô Pintcha* No. 1089 (September 12), 6–7.
Also a profile of Cabral, "Perfil do combatente," in commemoration of the anniversary of his birth.

————. 1985A "Contribuição de Amílcar Cabral," *Nô Pintcha* No. 1195 (December 14), 8–9.
Report on the contributions of Cabral at the Seminário Estudantil Internacional sobre Cultura e Luta de Libertação Nacional.

————. 1985B "Uma vida ao serviço da humanidade," *Nô Pintcha* No. 1181 (September 12), 4–5.
In memory of the birth of Cabral.

Notícias de Portugal "Assassinado Amílcar Cabral, dirigente do PAIGC," *Notícias de Portugal* 26 (January 27), 7, 14.
Report by the official Portuguese news service on the assassination of Cabral. The report emphasizes ethnic differences with the PAIGC.

Nyang, Sulayman Sheih 1976 "The Political Thought of Amílcar Cabral: A Synthesis," *Odu* (Ile-Ife) 13 (January), 3–20. Also in Africana Research Bulletin (Freetown) 5 (January 1979), 48–77.
A sympathetic appraisal of Cabral's thinking, with emphasis on his theory of colonialism, armed struggle, and national liberation.

Nyangoma, Nadine 1983 *Morrer de pé*. Dakar: Novas Edições Africanas. Pp. 117.
Fiction in French based on the "Epopeia da revolta camponesa dirigida por Amílcar Cabral." The Belgian author resides in Bissau, where she teaches French in the Liceu Nacional. See details in "Romance sobre a luta do PAIGC," *Diário Popular* (June 15, 1983), which has freely translated the title, publisher and description above from French to Portuguese.

Nwagor, Azinna 1975 "Imperialism and Revolution in Africa," *Monthly Review* 26 (April), 18–30.
Analysis of an essay on imperialism by Amílcar Cabral.

Nzongola-Ntalaja 1983 "Amílcar Cabral and the Theory of the National Liberation Struggle." Praia: Paper presented to the Simpósio Internacional Amílcar Cabral, January 17–20. Pp. 19.
Published in *Latin American Perspectives* 41 (Spring 1984), 43–54. Published as "Amílcar Cabral e a teoria da luta de liberatação nacional" in Simpósio Internacional Amílcar Cabral (1984: 185–201). Focus on theoretical aspects of armed struggle in the thought of Cabral.

Obichere, Boniface I. 1973 "Nationalism in Guinea-Bissau." New York: Paper presented to the Fourteenth Annual Meeting of the International Studies Association, March.
Includes discussion of Cabral and the liberation struggle with a focus on nationalism and struggle for independence.

————. 1975 "Reconstruction in Guinea-Bissau: From Revolutionaries and Guerrillas to Bureaucrats and Politicians," *Current Bibliography on African Affairs* 8, No. 3, 204–219.
A brief general overview of developments, with some attention to the influence of Cabral.

Objective: Justice 1973 "Amílcar Cabral," *Objective: Justice* 5 (January–March), 2–3.
Editorial in praise of Cabral.

O'Brien, Jay 1977 "Tribe, Class and Nation: Revolution and the Weapon of Theory in Guinea-Bissau," *Race and Class* No. 19 (Summer), 1–18.
In-depth examination of class and ethnicity focused on the problem confronting Cabral of how to provide the revolutionary struggle with proletarian leadership in the absence of a proletariat.

Ochetto, Valerio 1973 "Cabral: Il meccanismo dell'assassinio," *Il Giorno* (January 24).
Insights into Cabral and his thought and an effort to understand his assassination.

Ogawa, Dadahiro 1974 *Nô Pintcha*. Tokyo: Taimatsu-Sha. Pages unnumbered.
Focus on the PAIGC under the leadership of Cabral.

Okafor, F. O. E. 1988 "The PAIGC and the Economic Development of Guinea-Bissau: Ideology and Reality," *Developing Economies* 26 (June), 125–140.
A useful discussion of policy and practice in the independence period, the legacy of Cabral's thinking, and the importance of economic and political considerations in the tendency toward "the bureaucratization of the party and adoption of a development path inimical to the interests of the rural majority" (138).

Oliveira, Miguel Darcy de 1978 "Guiné-Bissau: èducation et processus révolutionnaire," *L'Homme et la Societé* Nos. 47–50, 197–217.
Cited in Chabal (1983: 266). On establishing an educational system within a revolutionary context.

————. 1981 "Cultura, luta e poder: a experiência da Guiné-Bissau," *Revista da Cultura e Política* No. 516, 131–141.

Culture and the struggle for power in Guinea-Bissau.

Omowale Matteos, Salahudin 1973 "The Cape Verdeans and the PAIGC Struggle for National Liberation," *Ufahamu* 3 (Winter), 43–48.

Opoku, K. 1978 "Cabral and the African Revolution," *Présence Africaine* Nos. 105–106 (First and Second Quarters), 45–60.
Examines themes in the thought of Cabral: social structure and revolution, party leadership and membership, culture and national liberation, and African unity in the revolution.

Oramas, Oscar 1978 "Amílcar's Thoughts and Concepts," *Tricontinental* No. 56, 95–102.
Brief review of ideas and concepts in the writings of Cabral.

Organisation des Etudiants Finlandais 1972 *M. Amílcar Cabral, secrétaire général de PAIGC . . . a visité la Finlande les 19–22 octubre 1971.* Finland: Kirjapainc Sanan Tie Tampere. Pp. 24.
English text in Committee for Amílcar Cabral's Visit to Finland, "Memorandum on Amílcar Cabral's Visit to Finland, October 19–22, 1971." No Place. Pp. 7, mimeo. Finnish student report on the visit of Cabral.

Ortega N., Osvaldo 1973 "Amílcar Cabral, maestro y revolucionario," *Punto Final* No. 177 (February 13), 16–17.
A brief appreciative note on Cabral after his death.

Osório, Oswaldo [1988] *Emergência da poesia em Amílcar Cabral: 30 poemas.* Praia: Colecção Dragoeiro, Grafedito. Pp. 80.
Includes a chronology of Cabral's poetry (fifty-six poems) and a brief analysis.

OSPAAL 1966 *La lucha de liberación nacional en Guinea (Bissau) y Cabo Verde.* Havana: OSPAAL, December. Pp. 35.
A review of the liberation struggle.

Oudes, Bruce 1972 "The Not so Much Fable of Bissau Desh," *Africa Today* 19 (Fall), 48–53.

Partido Africano da Independência da Guiné e Cabo Verde No Date *Statuts et programme.* Conakry. Pp. 27.
Statutes and program of the party while under Cabral's leadership.

————. 1960 "Memorandum enviado ao governo português pelo Partido Africano da Independência (Guiné e Cabo Verde)," *Portugal Democrático* 6 (January), 6–7.
Appeal to the Portuguese government to negotiate independence. See also "Propositions du Parti de l'Indépendance," *Afrique Nouvelle* No. 699 (December 28), 7.

————. 1961 "Programa mínimo," *Portugal Democrático* 5 (June), 6.
Minimum program.

————. 1962 "Le peuple de la Guinée 'Portuguesa' devant l'Organisation des Nations Unies." [New York]. Pp. 85 mimeo.
Presented to the UN Special Committee in June 1962 as a major effort in Cabral's campaign to win international support to the cause of the PAIGC.

————. 1963A "Declaração," *Portugal Democrático* 8 (October), 3.

————. 1963B "Développement de la lutte de libération nationale: l'action du PAIGC." [Algiers]. Pp. 8, mimeo.
Analysis of the liberation struggle under the leadership of Cabral.

————. 1963C "Extraits de quelques articles de l'organe du Partido Africano da Independência de la Guinée 'Portugaise' et des Iles du Cap-Vert." [Conakry]. April. Pp. 17, mimeo.

Extracts from *Libertação*, organ of the PAIGC, presented to the Conférence des Journalistes Afro-Asiatiques in Djakarta, Indonesia. Reflects the role of Cabral in the liberation struggle.

————. 1964 "Le PAIGC à la Conférences des Chefs d'Etat et de gouvernement des pays non-alignés—le Caire, octobre 1964." [Cairo]. Pp. 11, mimeo.
Report on developments in Guinea-Bissau.

————. 1966 "Guinée 'Portugaise' et Cap Vert: la situation actuelle de la lutte de libération nationale." Conakry, February. Pp. 16, mimeo.
Analysis of the armed struggle with optimistic assessment of prospects for independence.

————. 1969 "Guinea (B): Wreaking Havoc on the Colonialist Troops," *Tricontinental* No. 36 (March), 39–40.
On the successes of Cabral and the PAIGC.

————. 1970 *O nosso livro*. Bissau: Ediçao da Comissão Social e Cultural do PAIGC (Sub-Comissão do Ensino). Pp. 104.
Printed in Uppsala in 1974. A first-grade primer that includes a brief story about Cabral and his words "As crianças são da nossa luta."

————. 1971A "Amílcar Cabral, juge le Portugal," *Africasia* No. 53 (November 15), 13–16.
On Cabral's challenge to Portugal.

————. 1971B "M. Amílcar Cabral, secrétaire général de PAIGC . . . a visité la Finlande les 19–22 Octobre 1971." [Helsinki]: PAIGC, 1971. Pp. 24, mimeo.
Details on Cabral's visit to Finland.

————. 1972 *Manual político do PAIGC*. Lisbon: Cadernos Maria da Fonte, Livraria Ler. Pp. 112. 2d ed. [Lisbon]: Colecção 'Libertação Nacional,' Edições Maria da Fonte. Pp. 126.
Translated as Politisches Handbuch der PAIGC (Afrikanische Partei für die Unabhängigkeit von Guinea-Bissau und Kapverde), übersetzt und herausgegeben im Einvernehmen mit der PAIGC vom Komitei Südliches Afrika Heidelberg. Heidelberg: Verlag Jürgen Sendler, 1974. Pp. 70. The PAIGC political manual, comprising twenty-four themes, each of which draws upon principles and direction in the thought of Cabral.

————. 1973A *Amílcar Cabral: vida e obra.* No Place: PAIGC/Comité de Acção de Angola, June 14. Pp. 8.
A brief biographical sketch of Cabral, his life and distinction. (See in CIDAC: GB Biog I-1.) Also published as PAIGC/Servir Culturais do Conselho Superior da Luta, "Amílcar Cabral: o homem e a sua obra." No Place: Edição dos Serviços Culturais do Conselho Superior da Luta, July 1973. Pp. 10, mimeo. (See CIDAC: GB Biog I-2.) Translated into French as "Amílcar Cabral: l'homme et son oeuvre." Brussels: Association des Etudiants Portugais de Bruxelles, July 1983, mimeo. (See CIDAC: GB Biog I-5.)

————. 1973B "A conspiração contra Cabral." No Place: Edição do GADCG, October. Pp. 9, mimeo.
Party analysis of the assassination of Cabral.

————. 1973C "Sur le lâche assassin et du fondateur et premier dirigeant de notre parti, Amílcar Cabral. Message du Comité Executif de la lutte à notre peuple et à nos combattants." [Conakry] and Oslo: Conférence Internationale d'Experts pour le Soutien des Victimes du Colonialisme et de l'Apartheid en Afrique Australe, April 9–14, 1973. Pp. 10 (unnumbered), mimeo.
On the assassination of Cabral and the position of the party.

————. 1974A *Guinea-Bissau: Toward Final Victory*. Richmond, British Columbia: LSM Press. Pp. 98.
Historical overview of the independence struggle.

————. 1974B *História da Guiné e ilhas de Cabo Verde.* Lisbon: Edições Afrontamento. Pp. 182.
An official PAIGC history of colonialism and the liberation struggle.

————. 1974C "Program of the PAIGC," *Intercontinental Press* 12 (July 22), 1006–1008.

————. 1974D *Sobre a situação em Cabo Verde.* Lisbon: Cadernos Livres (3), Sá da Costa. Pp. 52.
Analysis of the conditions in Cape Verde presented to the UN Committee on Decolonization in New York, March 29, 1974.

————. 1974E "Sur la situation aux Iles du Cap Vert. Rapport présenté au Comité de Décolonisation de l'ONU lors de la neuf cent soixante-dixième séance tenue au siège, à New York, le 29–3–1974." Conakry: Services d'Information du PAIGC, April. Pp. 46, mimeo.
Analysis of the situation in Cape Verde prior to independence.

————. 1975 "Cape Verde: Agreement between Portugal and PAIGC," *Objective: Justice* 7 (April–June), 14–15.
Accord on independence for Cape Verde.

————. 1976A *Guiné Bissau: 3 anos de independência.* Lisbon: Colecção Africa em Luta (2), CIDAC. Pp. 193.
Analysis of the first three years of independence.

————. 1976B *Relatório geral do CEL e resolução geral do CSL. Reunião Ordinária de 27 à 31/8/76.* Bolama, October. Pp. 80.
Documents of the meeting of August 27–31, 1976.

————. 1977A "A quatro meses do III Congresso: pensar com Amílcar Cabral," *O Militante* No. 1 (July), 52–60.
Quotes from Cabral and direct appeal to his thinking in an effort to stimulate party militants to address ten important themes of the forthcoming Third Congress.

————. 1977B *Report of the Supreme Council of the Struggle to the Third Congress of the PAIGC.* London: Mozambique, Angola, and Guiné Information Centre. Pp. 63.
Report dated November 15–20, 1977.

————. 1977C *Teses para o Congresso da Independência para a unidade e o desenvolvimento.* Praia: Comissão Preparatória do III Congresso de PAIGC. Pp. 37.
Party theses for the Third Congress. See also the six theses in *O Militante* No. 4 (November 1977).

————. 1979 *Decisões sobre alguns problemas actuais da nossa vida nas regiões libertadas: 30 Agosto 70 e 7 de Janeiro de 1972.* Bolama. Pp. 22.
Analysis of party decisions in liberated areas August 1970 and January 7, 1972. (See CIDAC: GB Partido I-19.)

————. 1983 A "Estatutos e programa do PAIGC. Aprovado no 1o Congresso Extraordinário do PAIGC," *O Militante* No. 21 (January–February), 39–55.
Approved after the November 14, 1980, coup and the split between Guinea-Bissau and Cape Verde. Set forth in the name and memory of Amílcar Cabral.

————. 1983B *Princípios do partido e a prática política.* Bissau: Departamento de Informação, Propaganda e Cultura do Secretariado do Comité Central do PAIGC, Colecção Cabral ka Muri (Nos. 1–6).
Series of six pamphlets. (See CIDAC: GB Partido II-39 to 44.)

Partido Africano da Independência de Cabo Verde (PAIGC) 1981A *Do PAIGC ao PAICV. Documentos.* [Praia]. Pp. 132.

The Cape Verde militants form the PAICV and restructure the party in protest over the November 14, 1980, coup that deposed Luís Cabral. These documents evoke the memory and example of Amílcar Cabral.

―――. 1981B *PAICV First Congress*. Praia: PAICV. Pp. 35.

Resolutions and proceedings of the First Congress of the PAICV of Cape Verde, in Praia during January 16–20, 1981, including a remembrance of Cabral. See also *I Congresso do PAICV (16–20/1/81)* [Praia, 1981]. Pp. 48.

―――. 1988 *O PAICV e o exercício do poder político num mundo em transformação, um partido para o futuro*. Praia: PAICV 3 Congresso, November 25–30. Pp. 105.

Refers on pp. 30–31 to culture and Cabral's conception of it and goes on to relate cultural values of Cape Verdean society to modernization.

Partido Comunista de Portugal (Marxista-Leninista) 1973 "Amílcar Cabral assassinado pela PIDE!" [Lisbon], January 22. P. 1, mimeo.

PCP (M-L) solidarity statement in the aftermath of Cabral's assassination.

Partido Comunista Português, Comité Central 1973A "Amílcar Cabral foi assassinado mas o PAIGC vencerá!" [Lisbon]: Direcção da Organização Regional do Sul, January. Pp. 2, mimeo.

Despite Cabral's assassination, the PAIGC will win its liberation struggle.

―――. 1973B "Assassinaram Amílcar Cabral! Reforcemos a luta anticolonialista!" Lisbon: Comité Local de Lisboa, January. P. 1, mimeo.

Call for strengthening of the anticolonial struggle in the wake of Cabral's assassination.

―――. 1973C "Declaração do Partido Comunista Português sobre o assassinato de Amílcar Cabral." January 21. P. 1. Also in *Avante!* No. 450 (February), 1, 4.

PCP statement on Cabral after his assassination.

―――. 1984 "Rejeitava o oportunismo e o dogmatismo," *Nô Pintcha* No. 1115 (December 8), 3ff.

On Cabral and his principled positions. Paper to the Conferência Internacional sobre a Personalidade de Política Amílcar Cabral.

Paulini, Thomas 1984 *Guinea-Bissau: Nachkoloniale Entwicklung eines Agrarstaates*. Göttingen: Herodot Verlag. Pp. 174.

Pélissier, René 1989 *Naissance de la Guiné: Portugais et Africains en Sénégambie (1841-1936)*. Orgeval, France: Edition of the Author. Pp. 486.

An account of Portuguese activity in Guinea-Bissau from 1841 to 1936, with attention to African resistance. According to its promotion literature: "The recurrent fighting (more than 80 campaigns and operations) also reveals that the war by Amílcar Cabral in the '60s and '70s had stronger historical roots than was generally thought to be the case."

People's National Assembly (Guinea-Bissau) 1973 "Text of the Proclamation of the State of Guinea-Bissau by the People's National Assembly," *Issues* 3 (Fall), 28–29.

―――. 1976 "Second Ordinary Session," *People's Power* No. 4 (September–October), 5–11.

Report on the meeting of the People's National Assembly in the aftermath of independence.

Pereira, Aristides 1975 "Dimensão africana da obra de Amílcar Cabral," *Voz di Povo*, 1, No. 10 (September 12).

Cited in Chabal (1983: 267).

――――. 1976A *Balanço de 20 anos de luta pela libertação nacional da Guiné e de Cabo Verde (1956–1976).* São Vicente. Pp. 46; Bissau. Pp. 13; Bolama: Imprensa Nacional da Guiné-Bissau. Pp. 42.
Analysis of PAIGC party history over a twenty-year period by breaking it into seven periods. Cabral identified as the initiator of these developments. (See CIDAC: GB Partido I-13, 14, and 15.)

――――. 1976B "Como se conheceram, a primeira conversa, as suas relações," *Nô Pintcha* No. 225 (September 12), 2.
Recollections of Cabral on his fifty-second birthday. This issue also includes comments by Cabral's mother, Iva Pinhal Évora; Nino; Chico Té; José Araújo; Carmen Pereira, and Mário de Andrade.

――――. 1976C "'Construiremos a unidade da Guiné e Cabo Verde e o progresso social das nossas pátrias,'" *Nô Pintcha* No. 228 (Special Issue, September), 10–16.
A memoir on founding the PAIGC, with many references to Cabral.

――――. 1976D "'A nossa linha ideológica foi sempre inspirada pelo pensamento de Amílcar Cabral,'" *Nô Pintcha* No. 197 (July 8), 3.
Reprint of an interview in *Afrique-Asie.*

――――. 1976E "Relatório do secretariado-geral do PAIGC ao Conselho Superior da Luta," *Nô Pintcha* No. 220 Supplement (August 31), 1–4; continued in No. 221 (September 2), No. 222 (September 4), No. 223 (September 7).
Report to the CSL at a time when Cabral is officially buried in Bissau.

――――. 1977A "A luta continua pela independência económica," *O Militante* No. 4 (November), 5–6.
Speech prior to the Third Congress of the PAIGC.

――――. 1977B "'A luta que travamos é a continuação da luta de libertação nacional,'" *Nô Pintcha* No. 359 (August 20), 3.
Interview with the Portuguese daily *Diário,* including comments on the role of Cabral in the liberation struggle.

――――. 1978 *Reforçar a organização do partido.* Bissau: PAIGC, 1978. Pp. 15.
Appeal to strengthen the party organization following the wisdom of Cabral. Speech to the CSL in March 1978 in Bissau.

――――. 1979 *Melhorar os nossos métodos de trabalho.* Bissau: PAIGC. Pp. 23.
Assessment of progress. Speech to the CSL in Mindelo during March 1979.

――――. 1980A "Alerta para os desvios à linha de Cabral," *Nô Pintcha* No. 708 (June 21), 4–5.
Speech to the Conselho Superior da Luta warning of the deviations from the thinking of Cabral.

――――. 1980B "Mensagem a nação do camarada Aristides Pereira, Secretário Geral do PAIGC e Presidente da República de Cabo Verde." Praia, December 5, 1980. Pp. 8, mimeo.
Includes review of developments since the coup of November 14, 1980, a reconciliation meeting in Luanda, and appeal for release of the imprisoned Luís Cabral.

――――. 1980C *Vencer a batalha da ideologia.* Bissau: II Reunião Ordinária do Conselho Superior da Luta do PAIGC, June. Pp. 34.
A major address to the PAIGC. (See CIDAC: GB Partido I-16.)

――――. 1982 "A esperança está a converter-se em certeza," *Unidade e Luta* No. 13 (July–August), 4–10.
Optimism for Cape Verde, evoking the memory of Cabral.

――――. 1983A "Allocution de son Excellence Aristides Pereira, Secrétaire

Général du PAICV et Président de la République du Cap Vert." Praia: Speech to the Simpósio Internacional Amílcar Cabral, January 17–20. Pp. 20, memo.
A memoir and appreciation of Cabral by a close associate and now president of Cape Verde. Published as "O perfil de Cabral e a actualidade do seu pensamento" in Simpósio Internacional Amílcar Cabral (1984: 33–54). Also published as *Continuar Amílcar Cabral-Simpósio A. Cabral, Cabo Verde. Janeiro 1983*. Praia: Edição do DIP do PAICV, February, 1983. Pp. 20. (See CIDAC: Pensamento Político I-10.)

————. 1983B "Relatório do Conselho Nacional ao II Congresso do PAICV," Praia, June 21–26. Pp. 198, mimeo.
Report to the PAICV Second Congress that draws upon the legacy of Cabral.

Pereira, Carmen 1976 "Em 1976 descobrí que Abel Djassi era Cabral," *Nô Pintcha* 2, No. 225 (September 12), 6.
Cited in Chabal (1983: 267).

————. 1984 "Defensor intransigente da mulher," *Nô Pintcha* No. 1113 (December 4), 7.
Cabral viewed as a defender of women and their rights.

Pereira, Francisca 1984 "Fez despertar nas mulheres o espírito de luta e trabalho," *Nô Pintcha* No. 1114 (December 6), 5.
The emerging place of women in Guinea-Bissau is due in part to Cabral.

Pereira, Luísa Teotônio, and Luís Moita [1976] *Guiné-Bissau: 3 anos de independéncia*. Lisbon: Edição CIDAC. Pp. 198.
Analysis of the party and the state; social, political, and economic options; agricultural projects; small industries; public health; and foreign policy. Includes documents in an appendix.

Pereira, Miguel Serras 1975 "A independência é só a primeira etapa," *Vida Mundial* No. 1869 (July), 10–12.
A report on Cape Verde at independence and after the death of Cabral.

Pierson-Mathy, Paulette 1980 *La naissance de l'Etat par la guerre de libération nationale: le cas de la Guinée-Bissau*. Paris: UNESCO. Pp. 155.
Translated as *El nacimiento del estado por la guerra de liberación nacional: el caso de Guinea-Bissau*. Barcelona: UNESCO and Ediciones del Zerbal, 1982. Pp. 178. A study of the liberation struggle and the formation of the revolutionary state, with frequent reference to Cabral.

————. 1983 "La contribution d'Amílcar Cabral au droit de la libération des peuples." Praia: Paper presented to the Simpósio Internacional Amílcar Cabral, January 17–20. Pp. 18.
Published as "A contributo do Amílcar Cabral . . ." in Simpósio Internacional Amílcar Cabral (1984: 503–527). Focus on Cabral's contribution to peoples' liberation rights.

Pimenta, José Moura 1963 "Soldats portugais DESERTEZ!" *Révolution Africaine* (July 13).
Appeal of a Portuguese officer and deserter who supported the PAIGC and supports his position with reference to a conversation with Cabral.

Pinto, Cruz 1972 "Guinea-Bissau's Liberation Struggle Against Portuguese Colonialism," *Freedomways* 12, No. 3, 189–195.
Brief attention to the role of Cabral in the liberation struggle both in Guinea-Bissau and Cape Verde by a PAIGC representative.

Pires, Olivio 1980 "A democracia nacional revolucionária na Guiné-Bissau e Cabo Verde," *O Militante* No. 18 (April–May), 6–14.
A theoretical piece on revolutionary democracy with roots in the thought of Cabral.

————. 1983 "Libertação nacional moral, partido e democracia." Praia: Paper presented to the Simpósio Internacional Amílcar Cabral, January 17–20. Pp. 20.

Published in Simpósio Internacional Amílcar Cabral (1984: 445–461); also published as *Liberatação nacional de democracia revolucionária. Simpósio A. Cabral, Cabo Verde, Janeiro 1983.* Praia: Edição do DIP do PAICV, May. Pp. 16. Focus on party and democracy in the armed struggle and thought of Cabral. (See CIDAC: GB Pensamento Político I-11.)

Pires, Pedro 1975 "O exemplo de um pensamento revolucionário," *Voz di Povo* 1, No. 10 (September 12).

Cited in Chabal (1983: 267).

———. 1976 "The Cape Verde Islands: 'No Miracles in Politics,'" *People's Power* No. 2 (May–June), 12–21.

Translation of an interview originally in *Nô Pintcha* Nos. 156 and 157 (March 27 and 30). Realistic but also optimistic about the prospects for resolving the difficult problems of Cape Verde in the aftermath of independence.

———. 1983 "O discurso de encerramento proferido pelo Camarada Pedro Pires . . ." Praia: Paper presented to the Simpósio Internacional Amílcar Cabral, January 17–20. Pp. 6, mimeo.

Pyhälä, Mikko, and Kristina Rylander No Date *Guinea Bissau: en selektiv litteratur förteckning: A Selected Bibliography.* Uppsala: Scandinavian Institute of African Studies. Pp. 37.

Bibliography of relevant articles and monographs published during the 1960–1975 period. (See in CIDAC: GB Bibl I-2.) Chabal (1983: 267) lists a date of publication as 1975.

R., D 1977 "Cabo Verde: o porquê da conspiração: a luta de classes existe em Africa," *Diário de Lisboa* (June 29).

Interesting analysis of class struggle in Cape Verde two years after independence, which the author attributes to tolerance by the revolutionary government of merchants and landowners, whose property has not been expropriated. Examines this problem in Mindelo, in particular, and relates to Cape Verdeans in the United States.

Reed, Rick 1973 "A Song of World Revolution: In Tribute to Amílcar Cabral," *Institute of the Black World Monthly Report* (February).

Reis, Daniel 1976A "Dois anos de paz na Guiné-Bissau," *Diário de Lisboa* (May 3, 4, 6, 7, 10, and 17).

Series of six articles on progress and life in Guinea-Bissau after the death of Cabral; the role of Cabral is related to current developments.

———. 1976B "Guiné-Bissau, revolução a 40 graus: a formação da consciência nacional enraíza-se na história africana," *Diário de Lisboa* (February 5), 10–11ff.

Focus on political education in Guinea-Bissau.

———. 1977 "A Guiné-Bissau avança," *Diário de Lisboa* (July 23).

Historical and current assessment of developments in Guinea-Bissau.

———. 1980 "Os portugueses da Guiné," *Diário de Lisboa* (May 16, 17, 20, 21, and 27).

Series of reports on Portuguese who have remained in Guinea-Bissau after independence.

Renaudeau, Michel, et al. No Date *Guiné-Bissau: reconstrução nacional.* Paris: Editions Delroisse. Pp. 196.

A survey of the struggle for reconstruction.

Republic of Cape Verde 1976 *Livro de história. Ensino primário.* Praia: Gabinete de Estudos e Orientação, Ministério da Educação, Cultura, Juventude e Desportos. Pp. 205.

Elementary history text, including in chapter 5 a description of the PAIGC and biography of Amílcar Cabral, pp. 176–179.

————. 1980 *República de Cabo Verde: 5 anos de independência, 1975–1980.* Lisbon: Comissão do V Aniversário da Independência Nacional. Pp. 94.
Review of progress of first five years since independence. Discussion on the party includes biographical data on Cabral, pp. 25–27.

Republic of Guinea-Bissau No Date *Os continuadores da revolução e a recordação do passado recente.* Bolama: Imprensa Nacional Emprasa Pública. Pp. 93.
Poems by students of the Escola Piloto de Bolama (moved from Conakry after independence). Many poems evoke the memory of Cabral and his accomplishments.

————. 1974 "La République de Guinée-Bissau en chiffres." Bissau: Comissariat d'Etat à l'Economie et aux Finances, February. Pp. 37, mimeo.
Initial statistics of the new government.

————. 1977 *Mantenhas para quem luta! A nova poesia da Guiné-Bissau.* Bissau: Conselho Nacional de Cultura. Pp. 103.
Poetry on the revolution and independence, including an initial poem, "Camarada Amílcar" by Agnelo Augusto Regatta.

Resistência Popular Anti-Colonial, O Comité Amílcar Cabral (Comité Directivo da RPAC) [1973] "Os colonialistas assassinaram o patriota Guineense Amílcar Cabral!" No Place. Pp. 2, mimeo.
Blames the Portuguese colonial regime for the assassination of Cabral.

Ribeiro, Sérgio 1983 *A questão da unidade no pensamento de Amílcar Cabral.* Lisbon: Tricontinental Editora. Pp. 55.
Focuses on the theme of unity and elaborates on various aspects of unity in the thought of Cabral. Prepared October–November 1982. Prefaces by Vasco Cabral and Alfredo Moura. Served as basis for a presentation at the Simpósio Internacional Amílcar Cabral in Praia, January 17–20, 1983, same title, 32 pp. Also published in Simpósio Internacional Amílcar Cabral (1984: 363–408).

Ricardo, Rui Pinto 1988A "Amílcar Cabral, o engenheiro agrónomo. As carreiras escolas e profissional," pp. 15–16 in Cabral (1988).
A brief review of Cabral's years as student and professional.

————. 1988B "O trabalho como pedologista. I," pp. 37–39 in Cabral (1988).
Shows how Cabral was able to balance his professional and scientific concerns with a concern for the human condition.

Rodrigues, Avelino 1972 "Guiné: a guerra camulfada," *Diário de Lisboa* (August 28, 29, 30, 31, and September 1 and 2).
Series of six articles on the war in Guinea based on two weeks with Spínola and Portuguese armed forces. While the author did not interview Cabral or travel with the PAIGC in liberated zones, he makes frequent reference to their impact.

Rodrigues, Miguel Urbano 1973 "Homenagem a um herói," *Portugal Democrático* 17 (March), 2.
Praise for Cabral after his death.

————. 1984A "Amílcar e as paredes do tempo," *Diário* (January 23).
An appreciation of Cabral, his contributions and work.

————. 1984B "Homenagem a um herói," *Seara Nova* No. 1548 (October), 47–48.
A memoir of the author's impressions of Cabral, dating to his first contact with him in Conakry in 1961.

Romano, Luís 1975 *Famintos (Romance do povo caboverdiano sob o domínio colonialista).* Lisbon: Publicações Nova Aurora. Pp. 341.

Originally written in the 1940s, circulated clandestinely, and eventually published in Brazil in 1962. Poetry and short stories on life under colonialism in Cape Verde.

Routeau, Luc, and Olivier Noyer 1971 "Je reviens de Guinée-Bissau," *Jeune Afrique* No. 532 (March 16), 5–9.
Cited in Chabal (1983: 268). Report based on a visit to liberated areas of Guinea-Bissau.

Rudebeck, Lars 1972 "Political Mobilization for Development in Guinea-Bissau," *Journal of Modern African Studies* 10 (May), 1–18.
Analysis of political mobilization and the political education program of the PAIGC in the liberated zones of Guinea-Bissau.

————. [1973] "Political Mobilization for National Liberation and Development in Guinea-Bissau: A study of the Conditions and Mechanisms of Mobilization." Uppsala. Pp. 33.
Manuscript, consisting of the table of contents and the concluding chapter of a book written for publication by the Scandinavian Institute of African Studies. Examines the process of mobilization in liberated zones prior to independence.

————. 1974 *Guinea-Bissau: A Study of Political Mobilization.* Uppsala: Scandinavian Institute of African Studies. Pp. 277.
An important study of PAIGC mobilization in the liberated zones prior to 1974, with detailed reference to the role and contributions of Cabral. For a review, see Stanley Yoder in *Ufahamu* 5, No. 3, 171–175.

————. 1977 *Problem des demokratischen Neuausbaus in Guinea-Bissau und den Kapverden.* Heidelberg.

————. 1978 *Guinea-Bissau: Difficulties and Possibilities of Socialist Orientation.* Uppsala: AKUT.
Cited in Chabal (1983: 268).

————. 1979A "Development and Class Struggle in Guinea-Bissau," *Monthly Review* 30 (January), 14–32.
Argues that the application of Cabral's theory has been general in the postliberation period and that while socialism remains distant in a material sense, Guinea-Bissau can be socialist "in the sense of using Marxist points of departure."

————. 1979B "Socialist-oriented Development in Guinea-Bissau," pp. 322–344 in Carl G. Rosberg and T. M. Callaghy (eds.), *Socialism in Sub-Saharan Africa.* Berkeley: Institute of International Studies.

————. 1981A "Consequences of Decolonization even Through Political Mobilization for Armed Struggle," contribution to the seminar "Liberation and Development," Turku: Institute of Political History, University of Turku, Finland, July 16–19, 1981. Pp. 9, typescript.
A serious look at the problems affecting the PAIGC.

————. 1981B "State and Class in Guinea-Bissau in View of the November 1980 Coup," [Uppsala], [1980]. Pp. 11, typescript.
A brief look at class and ideological forces as they affect state-building after the November 14, 1980, coup. (Located in CIDAC: GB-E I-40.)

————. 1982 *Problèmes de pouvoir populaire et de développement: transition difficile en Guinée-Bissau.* Uppsala: Research Report (6), Scandinavian Institute of African Studies. Pp. 73.
A critical assessment of the difficult transition to popular power and development in Guinea-Bissau; focus on the legacy left by Cabral and the problem of development up to and beyond the coup of November 14, 1980.

————. 1983 "On the Class Basis of the National Liberation Movement of Guinea-Bissau." Paper presented to Department of Afro-American and

African Studies, University of Wisconsin Madison, May 25–27. Pp. 22, typescript.
A serious look at class relations and contradictions of class in Guinea-Bissau. Argues that mobilization was class-based and guided by the thinking of Cabral.

———. 1984A "On the Transition from National Liberation Movement to State Power in Guinea-Bissau." Paper presented at Münster, March 30. Pp. 8, typescript.
Discusses structural obstacles to development in the postindependence period as the regime substituted international support for popular support and mobilization in rural areas. Sets forth twelve provocative theses on the transition from national liberation to state power. (Located in CIDAC: GB-E I-40.)

———. 1984B "Sur la transition de mouvement de libération national au pouvoir d'état." Bissau: Conférence Internationale sur la Personalité Politique d'Amílcar Cabral, December 3–7, 1984. Pp. 11, mimeo.
Analysis of Cabral's writing on coming to power. (See CIDAC: GB Pensamento Político I-2.)

———. 1988 "Kandjadja, Guinea-Bissau, 1976–1986: Observations on the Political Economy of an African Village," *Review of African Political Economy* No. 41 (September), 17–29.
Critical observations on institutional changes in the northern Guinea-Bissau village of Kandjadja shortly after independence, 1976 to 1986, based on field research.

Ruiz García, Enrique 1973 "El asesinato de Amílcar Cabral y el imperialismo en Africa," *La Cultura en México* No. 575, Supplement to *Siempre* No. 1025 (February 14), III.
On the assassination of Cabral.

Santiago de Base, A. 1979 *Beginn einer Gesundheitsversorgung für Alle um Kapverde und Guinea-Bissau*. Bochum: A. Cabral Gesellschaft. Pp. 60.

Santo, Alda Espírito 1983 "Mensagem da camarada Alda Espírito Santo, membro du Bureau Político do MLSTP, ao Simpósio Internacional Amílcar Cabral." Praia: Paper presented to the Simpósio Internacional Amílcar Cabral, January 17–20. Pp. 4.
Praise for Cabral in retrospect.

———. 1984 "Uma figura imortal," *Nô Pintcha* No. 1115 (December 8), 9.
Paper to the Conferência Internacional sobre a Personalidade Política de Amílcar Cabral.

Santos, Fernando Piteiro 1984 "Amílcar Cabral, a guerra e a paz," *Diário de Lisboa* (December 14).
Draws from writings by and about Cabral; references to his inclination toward peace.

Sarrazin, Chantal 1975–1976 "Women of Guinea-Bissau," *LSM News* 2 (Winter), 25–30.
Analysis of the role of women in the revolutionary struggle before and after independence.

Sarrazin, Chantal, and Ole Gjerstad 1978 *Sowing the First Harvest: National Reconstruction in Guinea-Bissau*. Oakland: LSM Information Center. Pp. 103.
A collection of articles and interviews gathered during a three-month visit to Guinea-Bissau. Reflects upon past and present in the liberation struggle and reconstruction after independence and relates to the important role of Cabral during this period. Reviewed favorably by Barbara Chasin, "Guinea-Bissau: Post-Liberation," *Guardian* 31 (January 10, 1979), 16.

Saul, John 1973 "Neo-colonialism vs. Liberation Struggle: Some Lessons from Portugal's African Colonies," pp. 303–318 in Ralph Miliband (ed.), *The Socialist Registe 1973*. London: Merlin Press, 1973.

Emphasis on the thought of Cabral in realization of a genuine liberation struggle. National productive forces must be freed from every kind of foreign domination in order to avoid the mere Africanization of the existing colonial structure.

Schiefer, Ulrich 1984 "Guiné-Bissau zwischen Weltwirtschaft und Subsistenz. Transatlantisch orientierte Strukturen an der oberen Guinéküste." Ph.D. Dissertation, University of Münster.
The author, a German sociologist, worked for the government of Guinea-Bissau in 1978–1980 and questions an independence movement like the PAIGC that reaches power after a long struggle then pursues a development project that contradicts all its ideological pledges. He asks, Why pursue an industrialization project doomed to failure? Schiefer argues that the badly planned and overly ambitious industrialization policies of the PAIGC led to economic ruin as most projects were taken over by the new regime from the colonial administration. In a critical review, Lars Rudebeck argues that it was not peasant resistance to a market economy but lack of state support for peasants that led to the collapse, and he refers to Cabral's unresolved conflict between conventional modernization thinking and revolutionary democratic thinking. See Rudebeck, "Notas de leitura: Lars Rudebeck sobre Ulrich Schiefer," *Soronda: Revista de Estudos Guineenses* No. 4 (July 1987), 174–184.

Schiefer, Ulrich, et al. 1982 "Dokumentation zum Staatsstreich in Guiné-Bissau im November 1980. Documentação sobre o golpe de estado na Guiné-Bissau." Munster, January 1982. Pp. 4, mimeo.
Brief list of sources on the November 1980 coup.

Schilling, Barbara, and Karl Unger 1971 *Angola, Guinea, Moçambique. Dokumente und Materialen des Befreiungskampfes der Völker Angolas, Guineas und Moçambiques.* Frankfurt: Verlag Marxistische Blätter. Pp. 156.
Cited in Chabal (1983: 268) and Lopes (1983: 39).

Schwarz, Carlos Silva 1988 "Monografias de produtos agrícolas," pp. 33–35 in Cabral (1988).
Emphasis on Cabral's concern to deal with the impact of mechanization on farming.

Segal, Aaron 1973 "Amílcar Cabral: In Memoriam," *Third World* 2, No. 4 (April), 7–8.
Sympathetic note in memory of Cabral.

Senghor, Léopold Sédar 1975 "Amílcar Cabral foi para mim mais que um irmão," *Revista Expresso* No 113 (March 1), 1.
Remembrance of Cabral.

————. 1980 "Amílcar Cabral foi um homem de cultura," *Nô Pintcha* No. 673 (February 9), 4.
Brief praise for Cabral by the former president of Senegal.

————. 1983 "Allocution du Président Léopold Sédar Senghor." Praia: Speech to the Simpósio Internacional Amílcar Cabral, January 17–20. Pp. 9, mimeo.
Published in Simpósio Internacional Amílcar Cabral (1984: 59–63). The former president of Senegal offers praise and memoirs of Cabral.

Sesana, Renato 1974 *Liberate el mio populo. Diario di viaggio di un prete fra i guerriglieri della Guinea-Bissau.* Bologna: EMI, 1974.
Cited in Chabal (1983: 268).

Shauro, E. A. 1983 "The Level of Political Consciousness of the Younger Generation in Guinea-Bissau," pp. 104–118 in *Africa in Soviet Studies,* Moscow.

Sidenko, V. 1963 "The War in Portuguese Guinea," *New Times* No. 40 (October 9), 18–19.
Report on the liberation struggle and the leadership of Cabral.

Sigrist, Christian 1979 "The Case of Guinea-Bissau and the Cape Verde Islands." No Place: Paper presented to the Symposium "Three Worlds or One?" [Berlin], June 22–23. Pp. 25, typescript.
A look at traditional society, tribal structure, and the potential for rebellion in the anticolonial struggle, with reference to Cabral's thinking on the subject. (Located in CIDAC: GB-Hist, I-1.)

———. 1980 "Sistemas políticos acéfalos e libertação nacional," *Economia e Socialismo* 50 (May), 43–58.
Also as "Guinea-Bissau: Akephale politische Systeme und nationale Befreiung," pp. 66–81 in J. H. von Grevemeyer (ed.), *Traditionale Gesellschaften und Europäischer Kolonialismus*, 1981. Rudebeck (1983) cites an English version, "Traditional Societies and Western Colonialism: The Case of Guinea Bissau and the Cape Verde Islands," Berlin: Institute of Comparative Social Research, 1979. Examines tribal structure, especially among the Balantas during the colonial resistance and revolutionary mobilization in Guinea-Bissau, and provides detailed referencing to the thought of Cabral.

Silva, Carlos da 1974 "Conhecí Amílcar Cabral. Contribuição tendo a vista o traçado do seu perfil," *Diário de Notícias* (September 10).
Cited in Chabal (1983: 268).

Silva, José Avito da 1988 "A actividade no domínio da agricultura. II," pp. 23–27 in Cabral (1988).
An appreciative appraisal of Cabral's research and writing on agriculture.

Silveira, Onésimo da 1974 "PAIGC og mordet pa Cabral," *Arbeiderblat* (April 6).
Cited in Lopes (1983: 53).

Simpósio Internacional Amílcar Cabral 1984 *Continuar Cabral*. Odivelas: Grafedito/Prelo-Estampa. Pp. 705.
Essays on Cabral by scholars, journalists, and associates of Cabral, in commemoration of the tenth anniversary of his death in 1973. Conference in Praia during January 1983 sponsored by the Republic of Cape Verde.

Sine, Babakar 1983 "Etude comparative de l'évolution de deux parties: le PAIGC et le PAI Senegal." Praia: Paper presented to the Simpósio Internacional Amílcar Cabral, January 17–20. Pp. 6.
Published as "Estudo comparativo da evolução de dois partidos . . ." in Simpósio Internacional Amílcar Cabral (1984: 437–443). A comparison of parties formed in Senegal and Guinea-Bissau, with attention to Cabral's contribution.

Solodóvnikov, Vassili. G. 1983 "Amílcar Cabral—Theoretician of the African Revolution." Praia: Paper presented to the Simpósio Internacional Amílcar Cabral, January 17–20. Pp. 22, mimeo.
Published as "Amílcar Cabral como teórico da revolução africana" in Simpósio Internacional Amílcar Cabral (1984: 417–436). A Soviet appraisal of Cabral's theoretical contributions.

———. 1984A "Amílcar Cabral e o seu contributo para a teoria e prática do movimento de libertação nacional na época moderna." Bissau: Conferência Internacional sobre a Personalidade Política de Amílcar Cabral, December 3–7. Pp. 33, mimeo.
Examines Cabral's contributions to the theory and practice of contemporary national liberation movements.

———. 1984B "Destacada personalidade do Movimento de Libertação," *Nô Pintcha* No. 1113 (December 4), 5.
Sympathetic portrayal of Cabral.

Southern Africa 1973 "Long Live the Spirit of Amílcar Cabral," *Southern Africa* 6 (February), 4–5.

Editorial in praise of Cabral in the wake of his assassination.

Spínola, António de 1970 *Por um Guiné melhor*. Lisbon: Agência Geral do Ultramar. Pp. 396.
Memoirs and proposals for containing revolution in Guinea-Bissau by the Portuguese commander in the colony and an adversary of Cabral.

SUCO 1977 *La pensée politique d'Amílcar Cabral*. Montreal, Dossier (1), Secteur Education, SUCO, March. Pp. 76.
Texts on and by Cabral (See CIDAC: GB Pensamento Político I-6.)

Suret-Canale, Jean 1983 "Amílcar Cabral et l'analyse sociale." Praia: Paper presented to the Simpósio Internacional Amílcar Cabral, January 17–20. Pp. 12, mimeo.
Published as "Amílcar Cabral e a análise social" in Continuar Cabral (1984: 135–151). A French historian of Africa offers a positive assessment of the contributions of Cabral.

Teixeira Pinto, João 1936 *A ocupação militar da Guiné*. Lisbon: Divisão de Publicações e Biblioteca, Agência Geral das Colónias. Pp. 217.
An account of the Portuguese military campaigns in Guinea-Bissau. Written from a Portuguese perspective but useful for identifying historical points of African resistance to Portuguese colonial rule and for placing in context the national liberation movement of Cabral and the PAIGC.

Tempo Cadernos Especial 1981 "Guiné-Bissau: ontem, hoje e amanhã . . ." *O Tempo* (November 19), 1–14.
Historical details on Cabral and the PAIGC; this collection of articles includes one on Cabral, "O papel e o pensamento de Amílcar Cabral," pp. 4–5.

Terrani, Graziano, and Renato Kizito Sesana 1974 *Guinea Bissau. L'ora della libertà*. Bologna: Ed. Missionaria Italiana. Pp. 173.
On the liberation struggle, Cabral's accomplishments, and the tasks ahead. Cited in Pyhälä and Rylander (No Date).

Thorud, Johan 1972 *Gerilja-samfunnet. Guinea Bissau frihetskamp mot Portugal*. Oslo: Tiden. Pp. 145.
On the guerrilla struggle in Guinea-Bissau. Cited in Pyhälä and Rylander (No Date).

Time 1973 "The Gentle Rebel," *Time* (February 5), 40.
Report on the assassination of Cabral, described as "Africa's most responsible leader."

Ulyanovsky, Rostislav A. 1980 "Amílcar Cabral," pp. 221–231 in his *Present-day Problems in Asia and Africa*, Moscow: Progress Books.
Also in R. A. Ulianovski et al., *Retratos políticos dos lutadores pela independência nacional*. Moscow: Edições da Literatura Política, 1983. Pp. 18, typescript of text with all material and references translated into Portuguese from the Russian. (See CIDAC: GB Biog I-3.)

―――. 1984 "Scientific Socialism and Amílcar Cabral," *Africa Communist* No. 99 (Fourth Quarter), 49–60.
Attempts to show relationship of Cabral's thinking to scientific socialism.

União Democrática das Mulheres da Guiné e Cabo Verde [1962] "Statuts." Conakry. Pp. 5, mimeo.
Statutes of the women's movement, arm of the PAIGC under Cabral's leadership.

União Nacional dos Trabalhadores da Guiné [1962] *Estatutos*. August. Pp. 20.
Statutes of the labor organization, affiliated with the PAIGC under Cabral's leadership.

Unidade e Luta 1980 "Que futuro para o PAIGC?" *Unidade e Luta* Second Series No. 3 (October–December), 1–39.
Includes analysis of the repercussions of the coup of November 14, 1980, in Guinea-

Bissau, including a section "Mais grave que o assassinato de Cabral," p. 8. Also suggests that the alleged racist (antimestizo Cape Verdeans) and nationalist (pro-Guinea-Bissau) motives of the coup were not dominant and that the PAIGC has been assaulted by an ascendant petty bourgeoisie with ties to old opposition forces like the FLING and UPANG. This source includes an article by Manuel Delgado, "Assalto da pequena burguesia," pp. 29–31.

United Nations, General Assembly. 1962 Background Paper on Portuguese Guiné, A/AC.108/L 9; Background Paper on Cabo Verde, A/AC 108/L10, November 28. Pp. 39 plus Annex, 3 pp.
Papers reflect conditions through 1960.

————. 1974 *Pelas regiões libertadas da Guiné-Bissau*. Lisbon: Cadernos Maria da Fonte (8), Livraria Ler. Pp. 88.
Partially published in *Boletim Anti-Colonial* Nos. 8–9 (August–September 1973) and in *Boletim Anti-Colonial*, Porto: Afrontamento, 1975, pp. 151–172. The first part comprises the report of correspondents of the Hsinghua Agency; the second part consists of the report of the April 2–8, 1972, visit to liberated zones of Guinea-Bissau by the UN special mission, which expresses concern for the devastation caused by the Portuguese and praises the progress of Africans in liberated areas.

United States, Department of State 1967 *Background Notes: Portuguese Guinea*. Washington, D.C. Pp. 4.
Brief review of the country that does not acknowledge the presence of Cabral and the PAIGC in the ongoing liberation struggle.

Urdang, Stephanie No Date *A Revolution Within a Revolution: Women in Guinea-Bissau*. Somerville, Massachusetts: New England Free Press. Pp. 20.
Overview of the positive role of women in the liberation of Guinea-Bissau.

————. 1974A "Fighting the Other Colonialism: The Women's Struggle in Guinea-Bissau," *Southern Africa* 7 (September), 4–8.
On the liberation of women in Guinea-Bissau.

————. 1974B "Translating the Spirit of the People: A New System of Justice in Guinea-Bissau," *Southern Africa* 7 (October), 4–7.
On the judicial system.

————. 1975A "Fighting Two Colonialisms: The Women's Struggle in Guinea-Bissau," *African Studies Review* 18 (December), 29–34.
Draws upon Cabral's thinking to emphasize that women must be liberated from the colonialist legacy.

————. 1975B "Towards a Successful Revolution: The Women's Struggle in Guinea-Bissau," *Objective: Justice* 5 (January–March), 11–17.

————. 1976 "Return to Guinea-Bissau," *Southern Africa* 9 (September), 4–8; 9 (October), 21–23; and 9 (November), 24–26.
Reports based on eight weeks inside the country. Emphasis on the emerging role of women.

————. 1977 "Revolution Opens New Doors," *Guardian* 29 (March), S-2.
Brief, optimistic report on progress after independence in Guinea-Bissau.

————. 1979 *Fighting Two Colonialisms: Women in Guinea-Bissau*. New York: Monthly Review Press. Pp. 320.
An important study of women and their role in the revolutionary process prior to and after independence.

Van Lierop, Robert 1974 "'Those Who Mend the Sky . . .' Visit to Guinea-Bissau," *Southern Africa* 7 (February), 4–7.
Report on the liberation struggle, based on a visit to Guinea-Bissau during November 1973.

Venter, Al 1973A *Portugal's Guerrilla War: The Campaign for Africa.* Cape Town: John Malherbe. Pp. 220.

A South African journalist visits Portuguese-controlled areas of Guinea-Bissau and offers an analysis of the ten-year liberation struggle.

————. 1973B *Portugal's War in Guiné-Bissau.* Pasadena: Munger Africana Library Notes (19). Pp. 202.

For an extensive review of this work, see Ronald H. Chilcote, "The Struggle for Guinea-Bissau," *Africa Today* 21 (Winter 1974), 57–62.

Vida Mundial 1974 "Amílcar Cabral, guerra do povo da Guiné," *Vida Mundial* No. 1739, 25–27.

Vieira, João Bernardo (Nino) 1972 "Guinea-Bissau: Along the People's Paths," *Tricontinental* No. 70 (January), 43–47.

Comments on armed struggle in Guinea-Bissau.

————. 1980 "A herança do homem e do chefe," *Nô Pintcha* No. 733 (September 11), 8.

Interview in which his association with Cabral is recalled.

————. 1983A "Materializar o pensamento de Cabral," *Nô Pintcha* No. 994 (September 10), 4–5.

Inaugural address to the first Congresso da Juventude Africana Amílcar Cabral, with attention to the thought of Cabral.

————. 1983B "Nino fala de Cabral," *Nô Pintcha* No. 954 (March 30), 4–5.

Opening speech to the Simpósio Internacional Amílcar Cabral e a Luta de Libertação Nacional e Social. On same pages is a "Declaração final do Simpósio."

————. 1984A *Aprofundar o legado teórico de Amílcar Cabral. Intervenção do Camarada General da Divisão João Bernardo Vieira, Secretário Geral do PAIGC na Conferência Internacional sobre a Personalidade Política de Amílcar Cabral.* Bissau: Edição do DIPC CC do PAIGC (4). Pp. 8.

Speech on Cabral. (See CIDAC: GB Partido II-47.)

————. 1984B "Aprofundar o pensamento revolucionário de Cabral," *Nô Pintcha* No. 1114 (December 6), 4, 7.

Opening speech to the Conferência Internacional sobre a Personalidade Política de Amílcar Cabral.

————. 1984C "Cabral—um estratega militar ímpar," *Nô Pintcha* No. 1113 (December 4), 3.

On Cabral's military strategy.

Vieyra, Justin 1965 "Amílcar Cabral: liberté pour 350.000 Guinéens," *Jeune Afrique* No. 230 (May 2), 23.

Praise for Cabral and his struggle in Guinea-Bissau.

————. 1966 "Com os guerrilheiros de Amílcar Cabral," *Portugal Democrático* 10 (August), 4ff.; 10 (September), 4; 10 (October), 4.

Reports on a visit with Cabral in liberated areas of Guinea-Bissau.

Voice of Africa "The War in Guinea-Bissau," *Voice of Africa* 4 (September–October), 26–29ff.

Includes a brief portrayal of Cabral.

Voz di Povo 1983 "Simpósio Amílcar Cabral," *Voz di Povo* No. 328 Supplement (January 19).

Includes texts: "A luz do pensamento de Cabral," "As memórias cruzadas na memória de Amílcar Cabral," "Cabral visto por antigos companheiros," and a speech by Aristides Pereira.

Wallerstein, Immanuel 1971 "The Lessons of the PAIGC," *Africa Today* 18 (July), 62–68.
Review of books by Cabral and Gérard Chaliand.

————. 1983 "A integração do movimento de libertação nacional no quadro da libertação internacional." Praia: Paper presented to the Simpósio Internacional Amílcar Cabral, January 17–20. Pp. 7, mimeo.
Published in Simpósio Internacional Amílcar Cabral (1984: 493–501). Short paper that criticizes Cabral's notion of the possible "suicide" of the petty bourgeoisie.

Wallerstein, Immanuel, and Aquino de Bragança (eds.) 1982 *The African Liberation Reader: Documents of the National Liberation Movements.* London: Zed Press. 3 vols.
Includes many documents on Cabral and the PAIGC in Guiné-Bissau. Vol. 1, "The Anatomy of Colonialism," contains an excerpt from Djassi (1960) (6–7) and portions of three speeches by Cabral (67–70 and 157–166). Vol. 2, "The National Liberation Movements," includes excerpts from two of Cabral's speeches (23–25 and 178–179). Vol. 3, "The Strategy of Liberation," includes parts of five speeches and writings (23–27; 163–165; 189–190; 197–203).

Washington, Shirley 1976 "Some Aspects of Post-War Reconstruction in Guinea-Bissau." Ph.D. Dissertation, Howard University. Pp. 585.

————. 1980 "New Institutions for Development in Guinea-Bissau," *Black Scholar* 7. A look at Cabral's thinking on institution-building based on practice in the liberated zones of Guinea-Bissau.

Wästberg, Per 1973 "Arret efter Cabral," *Dagens Nyheter* (January 25).
Cited in Lopes (1983: 53).

Wengler, Jürgen 1980 "Gesellschaftliche Entwicklungs- und Lernprozesse in Guinea-Bissau und auf den Kapverden." Ph.D. Dissertation, University of Munster.
Cited in Bowman (1984: 241).

Wessing, Koen 1974 *Imagens da Guiné-Bissau. Djarama PAIGC. OBRIGADO PAIGC.* Lisbon: Edição CIDAC, September. Unnumbered pages (48).
A photographic essay on Guinea-Bissau.

Whitaker, Paul M. 1970 "The Revolutions of 'Portuguese' Africa," *Journal of Modern African Studies* 8, No. 1, 15–35.
A review of the liberation struggles, including that of Cabral and the PAIGC.

Woollacott, John 1983 "A luta pela libertação nacional na Guiné-Bissau e a revolução em Portugal," *Análise Social* 19, Nos. 77–79, 1131–1155.
Examines the national liberation struggle in Guinea-Bissau and its impact upon revolution in Portugal in 1974.

World Council of Churches 1970 Profile of the PAIGC. Geneva. Pp. 10.
A sympathetic appraisal of the PAIGC and Cabral in the era of liberation struggle in justification of a $20,000 grant for economic, educational, social welfare, and health programs in liberated areas.

Zartman, I. William 1964 "Africa's Quiet War: Portuguese Guinea" *Africa Report* 9 (February), 8–12.
An early report on the armed struggle in Guinea-Bissau. Emphasizes the PAIGC but identifies rival nationalist groups as well.

————. 1967 "Guinea: The Quiet War Goes On," *Africa Report* 12 (November), 67–72.
Positive assessment of the liberation struggle in Guinea-Bissau.

————. 1968 "The Content of Nationalism in Guinea-Bissau." Riverside and Los Angeles: Paper presented to University of California Project "Brazil–Portuguese Africa," February 13 and 14. Pp. 28, iv, mimeo.
Quantitative analysis of themes of nationalism in *Libertação: Unidade e Luta*. Includes reference to Cabral and the PAIGC.

Ziegler, Jean 1974 "Avec les maquisards de Guinée-Bissau," *Nouvel Observateur* (March 24).
Reprinted in *Facts and Reports* 4 (1974), Document 585. Based on a visit to liberated Guinea-Bissau, with frequent reference to Cabral's contributions.

————. 1983A *Contre l'ordre du monde. Les rebelles. Mouvements armés de libération nationale du tiers monde*. Paris: Editions du Seuil. Pp. 603.
Focus on rebellions in the Third World; includes a chapter on Cabral, "La longue marche d'Amílcar Cabral," pp. 259–297, followed by another chapter on the transformation of anticolonial struggles to wars of national liberation. Examines theory and practice of Cabral.

————. 1983B "Les mouvements armés de libération nationale du Tiers-Monde— Etat de la question dix ans après la mort d'Amílcar Cabral." Praia: Paper presented to the Simpósio Internacional Amílcar Cabral, January 17–20. Pp. 23.
Published as "Problemática da análise dos movimentos de libertação nacional" in Simpósio Internacional Amílcar Cabral (1984: 583–608). A Swiss scholar of Africa positively assesses the influence of Cabral upon national liberation movements in the Third World ten years after Cabral's death.

Index

References are to the main text only, not the appendix or bibliography. This index was prepared by Jennifer Dugan-Abassi, a doctoral candidate in political science at the University of California, Riverside.

About the Book
and the Author

A guide to the revolutionary thought and practice of Amílcar Cabral, this study introduces Cabral's writings on colonialism and imperialism, nationalism and national liberation, class and class struggle, and the state. Professor Chilcote also includes the verbatim text of his interviews with leaders of Guinea-Bissau and Cape Verde, assessing the impact of Cabral's thinking on those who followed in his path. A comprehensive bibliography of works by and about Cabral completes the text.

Ronald H. Chilcote is professor of political science at the University of California, Riverside. Among his publications are *Theories of Comparative Politics and Dependency and Marxism*.